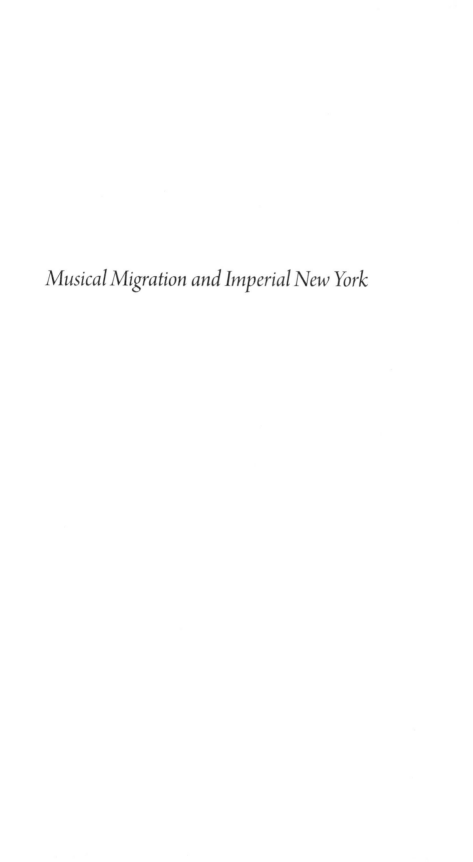

Musical Migration and Imperial New York

NEW
MATERIAL
HISTORIES
of
MUSIC

---

a series edited by
James Q. Davies *and*
Nicholas Mathew

Musical Migration and Imperial New York

EARLY COLD WAR SCENES

Brigid Cohen

The University of Chicago Press CHICAGO AND LONDON

The University of Chicago Press, Chicago 60637
The University of Chicago Press, Ltd., London
© 2022 by The University of Chicago
Published 2022
Printed in the United States of America

31 30 29 28 27 26 25 24 23 22   1 2 3 4 5

ISBN-13: 978-0-226-81801-6 (cloth)
ISBN-13: 978-0-226-81802-3 (e-book)
DOI: https://doi.org/10.7208/chicago/9780226818023.001.0001

This book has been supported by the General Fund of
the American Musicological Society, funded in part by
the National Endowment for the Humanities and the
Andrew W. Mellon Foundation.

Library of Congress Cataloging-in-Publication Data

Names: Cohen, Brigid Maureen, author.
Title: Musical migration and imperial New York : early Cold War scenes / Brigid Cohen.
Other titles: New material histories of music.
Description: Chicago : University of Chicago Press, 2022. | Series: New material histories
of music | Includes bibliographical references and index.
Identifiers: LCCN 2021042869 | ISBN 9780226818016 (cloth) | ISBN 9780226818023 (ebook)
Subjects: LCSH: Music—New York (State)—New York—20th century—History and criticism. |
Avant-garde (Music)—New York (State)—New York—History—20th century.
Classification: LCC ML200.8.N4 C65 2022 | DDC 780.9747/1—dc23
LC record available at https://lccn.loc.gov/2021042869

♾ This paper meets the requirements of ANSI/NISO Z39.48-1992
(Permanence of Paper).

For Mary Burns, Martin Cohen, and Julian Steege, keepers of history.

In memory of Peter-Lawrence Pope and Richard Colburn Steege,
sentinels of community.

Contents

Figures

Introduction

A RECENT HISTORY OF MUSIC,
CITIZENSHIP, AND AMERICAN EMPIRE

This book is a study of music, migration, and citizenship in the early Cold War, with an emphasis on New York as a capital of empire. Although the city has long held sway internationally as a cultural and economic powerhouse, its standing in the world increased dramatically after World War II. During this period, New York emerged as an archetypal global city under the pressure of the Cold War—when the United States asserted heightened economic and geopolitical dominance—absorbing a growing wave of immigration in the wake of the world war, the Holocaust, decolonization movements, and the internal Great Migration.[1] The city throbbed as the heart of a new kind of American empire that thrived not only on cultural diplomacy and financial aid abroad, but also on covert operations and proxy wars. As such, it revived strategies and legacies of empires past. This study traces a history of New York avant-gardes in critical engagement with these conditions, proposing a fresh reading of mid-century concert composition, electronic music, jazz, conceptual and performance art, and Fluxus. Figures at the center of this study include Edgard Varèse, Charles Mingus, Vladimir Ussachevsky, Halim El-Dabh, Michiko Toyama, Yoko Ono, and George Maciunas. Some of these creators, like Ono, are well known but little understood as composer/artists. Others, like Toyama, barely figure in existing historical accounts. Each of these artists drew from their experiences of uprooting to navigate urgent questions of empire that oriented global art movements for years to come.

My history reads against the grain of a US imperialism that, as many scholars have observed, usually refused to say its name.[2] In the 1950s, artists and critics celebrated New York City as the capital of the "American Century," in a bid for global prominence with missionary ambitions to spread "American principles" throughout the world.[3] New York stood to inherit the "great traditions" of art from the war-ravaged cities of Europe and to salvage or redeem them through their transplantation into American democracy. Such a vision held tremendous appeal for audiences both at home and abroad, winning sympathy for an enhanced US political, economic, military, and cultural presence in global affairs. New York composers and critics sought to historicize their own participation in this rise to global stature by espousing labels that continue to define narratives of US art music. For example, the 1950s and early 1960s saw the solidification of the "uptown scene," the "downtown scene," and the "American experimental tradition" as largely white-coded camps, canons, and identities to be embraced or rejected by musicians and musical commentators. Jazz, in turn, underwent a separate canonization as a Black-coded music with interracial participation in the same period of ferment. These overlapping communities laid claim, in different ways, to ideas and institutions of high art within economies of prestige dependent upon elite critical reception, grant-giving, and other noncommercial funding sources that had become augmented in the postwar culture boom. The communities also embodied the infamous paradox ingrained in US institutions more generally: they trumpeted ideas of freedom and democracy, yet remained entrenched within discriminatory structures that operated along the lines of race, gender, class, native/nonnative status, and other parameters. These segregated frameworks and genealogies, while amply challenged, still haunt musicological accounts of late twentieth-century North American art music, and shape the contours of its historiography.

In response to this haunting, my study makes a shift of perspective to frame postwar American art musics as practices of empire. More specifically, I accentuate questions of *citizenship in empire* by focusing on displaced and minoritarian creators who cut across New York's music and art scenes. These artists dramatize a dual dynamic: they served as essential mediators of transnational community—helping to exert US influence abroad—while remaining subject to the vicissitudes of unequal citizenship status at home (an inequality even more extreme for Black musicians, whether native-born or immigrant).[4] They benefited from the Cold War's burgeoning arts patronage and infrastructure, and they wielded power through their transnational connections. Yet they could not easily assimilate on a symbolic level as "American" during the Cold War—a setting in which restrictive notions of American identity served as a bulwark against threats from abroad and within. To study these scenes of displacement, this book draws on scholarship of the last decade that works to decenter and diversify terms such as "musical experimentalism."[5] It also builds upon a powerful foundation of literature about music, cultural diplomacy, and the Cold War.[6] Yet my goals remain distinctive, as I train my focus on musical migration within US imperial power formations—with impulses of global expansionism *and* internal hierarchy intertwined with the management of displaced peoples. It is my contention that this musical migration, born of empire, gave life to powerful musical concepts and movements in mid-century New York.

My narrative intervenes in the historiography of the recent past and in current debates about sound, governance, mobility, and worldhood. The process of apprehending recent history can resemble those nebulous states between dreaming and waking that are infused with a mixture of confusion and insight. In such a liminal moment, the sober light of one reality begins to radiate in tandem with the intuitions and affective charge of another—the cold dawn intensifying and mingling with dream feelings and images.[7] As a white, native-born U.S. citizen and child of the Cold War, I grew up in some version of the dream ideologies at the heart of this narrative. Yet I am finishing this book from a particular historical vantage point—during the COVID-19 crisis in the fourth year of Donald Trump's presidency—that makes some elements in my account vibrate with magnified intensity while others appear like ruins from a distant past. My chapters touch on what Saidiya Hartman calls "scenes of subjection" that entangled pleasure and terror in displays of mastery that were essentially musical.[8] These everyday cruelties—manifestations of race hierarchy and other degradations of citizenship—feel like portents of comparable or worse situations to come. My narrative also describes a force field of US global prestige and power—understood in relation to a newly accelerated postwar phase of US-led globalization, related international treaty negotiations, and public investments that would radiate outward as exemplary models abroad—that now seems old and wrecked, or like some barely animate remains of life. To apprehend these contemporaneous elements (the self-repeating scenes of debased democracy) and the anachronistic ones (the swagger of US global hegemony) as interlinked—*that* is what defines the study of US empire, and the task of understanding an American present with extensive terrestrial consequences.

As a history of music, my narrative theorizes linkages between human actors, institutions, state authority, temporality, and a world of objects of common concern in the years around 1960. In this pursuit I am drawn to Walter Benjamin's proposition "To write history means giving dates their physiognomy."[9] With these words, he wrested physignomy from the Nazi racial science of his day to change the term's function. The study of physiognomy, in Benjamin's sense, concerns itself with tone, comportment, habitual behaviors, inclinations, and ways of thinking and feeling that shine through exteriors. It concerns personae and character types—not simply individuals, but rather individuals who are molded by technologies, institutions, and infrastructures, just as the individuals themselves mold those things. To highlight such types, behaviors, and relationships is to historicize them and to refute their inevitablilty. To give dates their physiognomy is also to set those dates apart, to refuse their uncritical naturalization within a larger continuity (such as "Cold War consensus period," "American experimental tradition," or "postwar avant-garde"). At its best, such an approach encourages a confrontation with the past in the present—"face-to-face," so to speak—in a process of interpretation and judgment.

I make prominent mention of *worldhood* as a key term in this study of music and empire because *globality* and *globalization*, while important, are not enough. Worldhood suggests dimensions of power, rough materiality, uneven temporality, and malleability that globalization lacks in its projection of hard, smooth curvature. Worldhood implies the emergence of worlds, or processes of "worlding," in which things, perceptions, and realities come into assemblage.[10] The Cold War scenes of my study unfolded in the midst of emergent conditions we now associate with globalization—through rapid postwar developments in information and communication technology, in transportation, in the proliferation of international trade and security agreements, and in a continuous increase in trade and the number of transnational corporations.[11] By many accounts, these processes in themselves represented the "worlding" of a new world order. Under the conditions of the Cold War, New York came into view as a global city in the classic sense—as a primary node in global economic networks. Yet my range of inquiry is far from limited to a descriptive account of the relationship between musical activities and globalization, which created an apparent shrinkage of cultural and geographical distances (for some) alongside long-term transformations in the global economy. Nor does my historiography subscribe to the linear temporal model that undergirds many theorizations of globalization, which posit a succession of superceding historical phases and risks homogenizing their scenes of inquiry. The term *world* brings greater temporal complexity and texture to the table. From its earliest uses, *world* referred to the temporal world, its materiality, and its duration in connection with the Latin concept of *mundus*. Etymologically, its Old High German cognate *weralt* combines *wer* ("who/man") with *alt* ("old").[12] In some English usages, *world* denotes a long space of time: "It'll be a world before she's back."[13] *World* describes long-lasting US imperial formations that remain a focus of this study, structures of governance that were always ghosted by the legacies of other empires including European high imperialist ones. It concerns state ambitions on a planetary scale. Yet it also evokes the imaginative realm that music and the sonic arts instantiate when they invite alternatives to the present through their own "worlding."[14] This study tracks relationships between such imaginative practices and structures of empire without seeing the former as a mere reflection or product of the latter. The multiple registers of *world* allow for precisely such a concept that exceeds the flattening confines of globality.[15]

This thematics also raises the question of scholarship's place in the world, and of my own worldly situation as a scholar and citizen. A self-reflexive turn in writing does not come naturally to me; this is because of my introversion and my disciplinary training in a field that often projects authority in erudite displays of exnomination. But I know I need to lay my cards on the table even when that gesture feels elusive. My perspective as a thinker and scholar emerges from estranging experiences of "home" during the Cold War, experiences I associate with mundane scenes of charged remembrance and forgetting. I think, for example, of my elementary school in Celle, Germany, where we received telling history lessons such as a 1986 tour of our suburb, constructed as a silk manufacturing colony for parachutes in the mid-1930s, which our sexagenarian teacher treated as a monument to the economic revival from that earlier period she had lived through. We searched out the neighborhood's surviving mulberry bushes, took in their aroma, felt their leaves in our fingers, and sketched out their morphology on paper. I would later discover that W. G. Sebald concluded *The Rings of Saturn* with images of the ravenous caterpillars, boiled coccoons, and billowing white silk sheets of Celle—as vivid a statement on the materiality of "worlding" as ever there was. I spent much of my childhood in the 1980s living as a US expatriate in this town, a West German *Kleinstadt* with a British NATO military base, less than fifty miles from the East German border and fifteen miles from Bergen-Belsen. An American transnational oil corporation had transferred my father from Texas to a German afffiliate, where the company partnered with the West German government in the development of natural gas fields. (My father was an engineer and first-generation college graduate—a beneficiary of the Cold War education boom.) My family's ethnic background is Irish, English, and Ashkenazi; my surname is Hebrew, my first name Irish. I mention these facts because they resonated strangely (and sometimes provoked embarassment or hostility) in the German town fragmented by British military facilities.[16] It would be an understatement to say that traumatic legacies of state power visibly infused everyday life in this balkanized setting. I remember frequent war games, tanks in the streets, the threat of IRA bombs, and most especially the hierarchies of citizenship in my classrooms and social spaces, which were usually German but often British. In my elementary school, our teacher consistently administered discipline to Turkish and Kurdish students most harshly, and other students with foreign parentage counted somewhere in the middle. I associate this experience of hierarchy with gaping silences in historical memory. If my own memory serves, our school field trip to Bergen-Belsen resulted in just such a silence. We walked along the oblong mounds of mass graves, and we spent time in a small, musty visitor's center that displayed snapshots of Anne and Margot Frank alongside unfathomable images taken by British troops to document the atrocities of the camp they had liberated. I expected a follow-up discussion about the trip, but our class routine proceeded as normal. Throughout this period, I longed for the United States—or at least the American zone—which I associated with vague ideas of freedom, equality, and belonging, but I hardly knew what those places or that longing meant.

Remigration to the United States only complicated the picture. My estranging experiences of heirarchy, militarization, and obfuscation in West Germany shadowed classroom experiences in North Dallas and Richardson, Texas—a site of enormous immigration and refugee resettlement during the culture wars of the late 1980s and 1990s, with a public school system that quickly moved toward minority-white demographics. Together with my friends, I observed a different set of race-, language-, and gender-based hierarchies and history lessons—with, for example, a focus in seventh-grade Texas history on cattle trails rather than enslavement and the Civil War. At a high school football game in 1995, talking over the sounds of the band, I asked a fellow white student from our rival school why he called our school a "ghetto." "Look," he said with a tone of self-evidence, "you have a Black homecoming queen." Racism and misogyny were integral to this declaration: the boy's words directed my eyes and mind to join him in fixing my popular classmate into an object of shame. Implicit was also a statement about US citizenship: our school (a "ghetto") was somehow illegitimate—not a "normal" (i.e., white) place to come of age as an American through higher learning, football attendance, and homecoming elections. Such racist policing was commonplace. But, as I developed a stronger sense of belonging in my school and nation, I also came to believe that "we" were somehow on a path of progress and rectitude at the Cold War's end, with the increasing racial and ethnic diversification of our high school (where more than eighty languages and dialects were spoken), and with music and the arts reigning supreme. This feeling was grounded in specific friendships. At the time, my standing as a native-born white citizen likely rendered my belief in our community as "the future," as a harbinger of more equitable social realities to come, as more optimistic than it should have been. The tumult of subsequent decades would disabuse me of the simpler aspects of this vision. My original "home"—in a space between Celle and Richardson—infuses my thoughts and feelings about New York City, my current home and object of study. It motivates my commitment to the study of historical trauma, hierarchies of citizenship, and migration, and this rooting informed my conversations with interlocutors for this project, even though they did most of the talking. This "home" has also oriented me toward a concern with internal heirarchies of citizenship and how they articulate with state power in world affairs—or what constitutes the logic of empires and their sustained hauntings.

Gradated Citizenship, Nomadic Music

Within the world of my study, "empire" and "imperialism" always suggest migrating streams of peoples, fluctuating borders, and ambiguities of sovereignty in the distribution and management of state power.[17] In scholarship on the Cold War, scholars and critics have often leveraged the terms "imperialism" and "neo-imperialism" as a shorthand for US-led capitalism. While such usage captures a vital dimension of the relevant power formations, these terms concern more than just economic control. They evoke dilemmas of citizenship and border-crossing that cut across histories of empire predating the coinage of "imperialism" as a keyword in the nineteenth century.[18] Empire is "a political unit that is large and expansionist (or with memories of an expansionist past), reproducing differentiation and inequality among people it incorporates."[19] It entails internal diversity and attendant hierarchies of citizenship that in modern times have usually been racialized, but can also be determined by gender, migration status, class, language, and so on. It depends upon internal modes of subjugation, regulating the diversity within, that interact with external exercises of power at and beyond the empire's borders.[20] A productive vagueness characterizes these borders: "Colonial empires were always dependent on social imaginaries, blueprints unrealized, borders never drawn, administrative categories of people and territories to which no one was sure who or what should belong."[21] The very elusiveness of the national border forms the "quintessential concept" in US discourses of belonging, as the border shifts "from area of contention to separating line to welcoming portal to cultural buffer."[22] In navigating this ambiguity, empire continuously extends its authority in order to manage internal conflicts that threaten the status quo. In modern forms of empire, the preservation of that social and economic status quo tends to justify further extensions of authority that beget still further extensions. "Imperialism is . . . subject to a paranoia of a world that is perpetually slipping from its grasp."[23] In its capitalist manifestations, the never-ending accumulation of power appears to protect the never-ending accumulation of capital that justifies itself through ideologies of progress (even in situations that are actually inefficient and unprofitable).[24]

These imperial forms replicate themselves in patterns of durability. By the 1950s, the United States had long practiced the so-called "formal empire" of direct territorial rule in such colonies as Guam, the Philippines, and Puerto Rico—a process that grew from the nation's roots in settler colonialism and slavery to enact new projects of territorial expansion, resource extraction, market control, race ideology, and the administration of peoples. Following these developments, however, US Cold War foreign and economic policies focused on the consolidation of "informal empire" over nominally independent states. Soft power strategies famously bolstered coercive military and economic policies to draw foreign peoples and governments toward US policy objectives. The government launched a "crusade of ideas": public agencies and private foundations working in partnership to develop ambitious new programs to enhance the reputation of the United States internationally and to spread values, ideas, vocabularies, institutions, and norms perceived as beneficial to national interests.[25] As W. E. B. Du Bois argued, "the essentials of colonialism" returned "under the name of Free Enterprise and Western Democracy" within a US-led Cold War setting—an imperialism on the world stage that mirrored racialized internal colonialism at home.[26] This postwar American approach to empire building replicated European imperial precedents (which also made powerful use of client states and soft power), despite official US statements to the contrary.[27] Under these conditions, distinctions between "formal" and "informal" empire—between prewar Euroamerican high imperialism and postwar US expansionism— become confounded. In its political and social dimensions, Cold War American music history is best studied within an imperial framework that tracks linkages between external power plays and internal hierarchy.

Music plays a powerful role in this setting, since it has long worked as a medium of collective gathering and as a carrier of extraordinary aspiration in the imagination of social realities. As many have argued, music serves as a mutable, fluid medium for building or breaking down community boundaries: it contributes to processes of subject formation and knowledge production that sustain migrating streams of peoples, states, and empires.[28] In the words of Edward Said, "music remains situated within the social context as a special variety of aesthetic and cultural experience that contributes to what . . . we might call the elaboration or production of civil society."[29] To elaborate civil society through musical activity is to refine ways of knowing, feeling, being, and acting in concert with others. Music possesses, in Said's terms, the "nomadic ability to attach itself to, and become part of social formations, to vary its articulations and rhetoric depending on the occasion as well as the audience, plus the power and the gender [and here we might also add the racial] situations in which it takes place."[30] The work of the Egyptian-born composer Halim El-Dabh, who also happens to have been an acquaintance of Said's, makes this idea concrete.[31] El-Dabh's tape composition *Leiyla and the Poet* (1959) initially served as an experiment in the representation and translation of Arab traditions for US audiences, in keeping with his background as an amateur ethnographer and his mission as an Egyptian cultural diplomat in New York supported by the US State Department. In this capacity, he sought to enhance mutual positive feelings between members of Egyptian, Arab, and US civil societies through involvement in cross-cultural traditions of music. Yet by the end of the 1960s, *Leiyla* suggested lines of Afrodiasporic solidarity in a setting where El-Dabh actively identified as an African-descended US citizen and a contributor to the Black Arts movement in connection with civil rights agendas. Later, El-Dabh's tape music would be reclaimed as a forerunner of African electronic music at the inaugural 2005 UNYAZI Electronic Music Symposium and Festival in Johannesburg, the first such event on the African content, dedicated to "fostering community" in South Africa while embracing ideas of African unity.[32] *Leiyla*'s history points to nomadic qualities of music on multiple levels. It evokes nomadic circumstances of musical creation (with El-Dabh figuring as a migrating subject with a changing and complex minoritarian citizenship status) and nomadic qualities of the music itself in its ability to slip into or out of different community affiliations that it nurtured powerfully. If, as Said wrote, our current era is "the age of the refugee, the displaced person," then it is no wonder that Said dedicated himself to the study of these nomadic qualities of music, which disrupt and fragment homogenizing accounts of civil society.[33] My study keeps faith with this legacy of thought, which restores "cultural matters of musical creativity" to the study of empire.[34]

Such a study requires examining how musical experiences, knowledge, and institutions shape citizenship across a highly differentiated spectrum. Citizenship signals "the complete and unmarked enjoyment of the full range of economic and material opportunities and resources, political and legal rights, and broader civil and social recognition and moral esteem that individuals in society have available to them," as Lawrence Bobo puts it.[35] Music informs questions of moral esteem alongside civil and social recognition; it generates economic and material opportunities; and it energizes movements for political and legal rights. Music shapes the "cultural citizenship" of immigrants and minoritarians—the "self-making and being made in relation to nation states and transnational processes" that institutions of education, media, discipline, and surveillance enable.[36] Cultural citizenship pertains to mundane distinctions of accent, demeanor, dress, expression, leisure, etc., through which individuals draw citizenly boundaries. Music molds cultural citizenship, because listening and aural imagination routinely map race, culture, ethnicity, nationality, and belonging onto sound.[37]

Similarly, music is a realm where individuals constantly contest the *symbols* of a nation and its citizenship. "Symbolic citizenship" is that which allows an individual to share in a society's symbolic wealth and not feel ignored or demeaned by its official, state-supported symbols and culture.[38] The "official" patronage networks of government and foundation-sponsored music institutions play a substantial role in shaping such ideas of "symbolic wealth" for a nation. What kind of musics and individuals do these institutions support? Sindhumathi Revuluri argues that the insitutions of Western art music (often promoted as "official culture" by state institutions) themselves show "parallels to the inclusive and exclusive institutions of citizenship," with complex gatekeeping mechanisms that sort individuals by class, race, gender, ethnicity, and so on.[39] For musicians and composers to have access to this economy of prestige and patronage affects their citizenship in its economic, cultural, and symbolic dimensions. My narrative turns again and again to the question of who could gain a foothold in the musical institutions under consideration and under what terms—questions that, in turn, bore for musical migrants upon the larger question of whether they could stay in the United States, make a living there, and possibly, if they were foreign-born, embark on a path to naturalization.

In the scenes of my narrative, foreign-born white privilege consistently trumps native-born Black identity on questions of US citizenship in all of its dimensions; yet my study also foregrounds a spectrum of differentiated citizenships that operated along multiple axes that buttressed and complicated the Black-white binary. This approach resonates with Bobo's argument that there have existed "multiple or contending racial orders" in US history to create "blockages and detours that have stood in the way of fulfilling [the] goal" of full and equal citizenship for Black citizens, whose humanity had been systemically denied in connection with the institutions of slavery and the aftermath of state-sanctioned violence and inequality.[40]

The central events of my study transpired in the decade leading up to the 1964 Civil Rights Act, the 1965 Civil Rights Act, and the 1965 Immigration Act. Between 1945 and 1965, New York received the second wave of the African American Great Migration; the Puerto Rican Great Migration; a large influx of immigrants from Northern, Western, and Central Europe; and a growing stream of elite migrants and expatriates connected with transnational corporations, diplomatic services, NGOs, and educational exchange programs. This period saw enormous contestation over questions of citizenship in its legal, political, and cultural dimensions. The protagonists in my chapters still contended with the nativist code of the 1924 Immigration Act, which almost completely excluded immigration from Asia, the Middle East, and Africa while severely limiting those from Southern and Eastern Europe. Because of this code, approximately 80 percent of the city's population was native-born in 1960, the highest it had been that century.[41] The ongoing Red Scare, moreover, intensified the effects of an array of xenophobias and racisms including but not limited to anti-Blackness. White male immigrants, such as Ussachevsky and Varèse, who likely felt threatened by these conditions sought musical association with—and exercized insitutional power over—those further down on the race and gender hierarchies, such as Toyama and Mingus respectively. These power dynamics created situations conducive to unequal professional opportunity, at best, and exploitation and denigration, at worst. Meanwhile, political contestations over citizenship promised alternatives to the status quo and stimulated enormous music-sonic-artistic creativity in connection with this struggle.

For those deprived of full citizenly belonging, the increasingly globalized world at mid-century fostered diasporic citizenly identifications that held great political and cultural appeal. Every protagonist in this study embraced some version of such diasporic affiliation, though its manner of expression varied wildly from case to case. For example, Toyama and Ono's connection with Japan remained painfully fraught by their experiences of female second-class citizenship there, which motivated their gendered exile in Europe and the United States. Yet for Mingus and El-Dabh, notions of Afrodiasporic solidarity formed a positive image, in contrast to the racist status quo in the United States. In following such threads, this study resonates with literatures on music, cosmopolitanism, and diaspora while locating itself firmly within the study of migration and unequal citizenship in empire.[42]

To this end, the uprooted protagonists and histories of this study lie at an oblique angle to dominant histories of New York avant-garde musics without necessarily being subaltern. The dominant art music canons associated with Cold War New York overwhelmingly privilege native-born creators—with John Cage standing at the center. Indeed, the very idea of the "American experimental tradition," coined by Cage and the critic John Yates in the late 1950s, built upon more or less explicitly nativist genealogies (from Ives to Varèse, Cowell, Ruggles, and finally Cage) that began to congeal in the 1920s. By underscoring nonnative and minoritarian creators involved in the Cold War scene of that canon's formation, however, we denaturalize the genealogy while accentuating charged questions of citizenship in empire that prefigure dilemmas of our own time.

Let me emphasize here that the displaced stories of this book are not simply ones of resistance, defiance, or erasure; I do not frame the subjects of my narrative as one-dimensional heroes or sufferers whom we should emulate or pity. Rather, these creators were agents who helped to build cultural infrastructures while remaining subject to complex mechanisms of inclusion and exclusion. Their settings and modes of uprooting were multifarious, ranging across a spectrum from forced to voluntary, and characterized by unruly mixtures of privilege and dispossession that confound the very linearity of that spectrum. Some arrived in the United States as cultural diplomats, some as refugees, some as elites connected with transnational corporations; and some grappled with histories of internal or external migration triggered by state-sanctioned violence and economic dispossession. In most cases, as we will see, their diasporic connections held a strong potential use value for US imperial projects of soft power. Yet as minoritarian or displaced individuals, few would receive top billing in the national histories and canons that were so vital to soft-power projects. (Varèse, who received star recognition in the late 1950s, is perhaps the one exception.) Within music institutions these creators were, to varying degrees, *close* to power, but they were never fully *in* power in terms of cultural prestige or administrative leverage. As such, their narratives provide a glimpse behind the curtain of the mythologies of uptown/downtown and American experimentalism.

Schooling the Mind, Body, and Soul

I have chosen to focus my narrative on the years around 1960 because I am interested in the fat years of empire—the times of self-historicization, hubris, grant-giving, and technological advancement following postwar recovery. Here, dates assume their physiognomy. Let the world's fairs resume. Convert wartime technologies to civilian use. Remake city neighborhoods in the image of a world-class modernity. Build arts complexes, establish exchange programs. Renovate and expand university campuses, create state-of-the-art laboratories and academic programs. The city's changing infrastructure and technologies are partly what enabled new trajectories of musical creation, life narrative, and persona. The physiognomy of the city became transfigured, just like the physiognomy of the composer's studio and related tools of music making.

Under these conditions, what it meant to *be* a composer or musician changed. Established personae came into flux in connection with the transforming infrastructures, demographics, and contestations over citizenly recognition in the city. I use the term "persona" here in a specific sense. As Lorraine Daston and H. Otto Sibum write,

> Intermediate between the individual biography and the social institution lies the persona: a cultural identity that simultaneously shapes the individual in body and mind and creates a collective with a shared and recognizable physiognomy. The bases for personae are diverse: a social role (e.g. the mother), a profession (the physician), an anti-profession (the flâneur), a calling (the priest). . . . Personae are creatures of historical circumstance; they emerge and disappear within specific contexts. . . . Personae are as real or more real than biological individuals, in that they create the possibilities of being in the human world, schooling the mind, body, and soul in distinctive and indelible ways.[43]

In the scenes of my study, New York's changing physiognomy brought forth precisely such "new possibilities of being in the human world"—possibilities toward which musical creators needed to feel their way in tentative acts of trial and error. A number of figures in my study assembled personae as composer-diplomats who focused on notions of cultural exchange, supported by state- and foundation-based patronage. Another set (overlapping with the previous) emerged as composer-technicians who adapted new sound technologies in close collaboration with others, taking advantage of the resources of an expanded military-industrial-educational complex.[44] Still others became artist-provocateurs, reviving a radical avant-garde persona, à la Duchamp, once associated with the imperial metropoles of Europe. Most of my protagonists blended elements of creative personae from various cultural traditions. This circumstance reminds us both of the interculturality of these urban scenes and of the city's slowly changing norms concerning who could become a "composer"—heretofore conceived overwhelmingly as a masculine, white category—and under what terms. Such questions of persona are far from superficial. Rather they get to the heart of how individuals feel, act, and know. They help us to draw connections between localized behaviors, stances, knowledge formation, and acts of imagination—including worlds of musical poetics—and larger social processes without necessarily drawing a determinist line between them. This perspective links up with new directions in the study of music, biography, citizenship, and power.[45] It also provides conceptual tools for addressing questions of ideology—the *in between* of subjects and institutions—with nuance.

In this study I understand ideology to describe habitual ways of knowing, feeling, and being that often go unmarked or unsaid. Rather than being rigid or fixed, ideology is tractable, variegated, and sticky. It smooths over contradictions between pluralism and hierarchy, between capitalist opportunity and entrenched inequalities, between imperialism and democracy.[46] Ann Laura Stoler equates ideology with a sort of changeable "common sense" that makes up the substance of imperial governance: "those habits of heart, mind, and comportment that derive from unstated understandings of how things work in the world, the categories to which people belong, and the kind of knowledge one needs to hold[,] unarticulated but well-rehearsed convictions and credulities."[47] Musical activities are ideological insofar as they participate in the constitution of these habits and beliefs. Yet the "coordinates" of what constitutes common sense remain "pliable" in an "imperial order in which social reform, questions of rights and representation, and liberal impulses and more explicit racisms" play a significant role.[48] Musical personae, including that of the "composer," produce certain ways of feeling, doing, and knowing that may yield to alteration in a flux of citizenly contestations. The nomadic qualities of music, in Said's sense—the way music can always slip away from given affiliations or meanings—sometimes even push against "commonsense" identifications and thought patterns, or spin out in multiple directions to trace out ideology's contradictions. For all of these reasons, my study seeks never to lose touch with the worlds of musical poetics and sonic creation that animated its protagonists' imaginations, despite a larger focus on national and geopolitical history.

The structure and methods of this book are designed to address the challenge of enormously different *scales* in the study of creative practice, power, and ideology. From chapter to chapter, my narrative tends to move outward from small to progressively larger scales of analysis—from that of the scene of interaction (chapter 1) to the institution (chapters 2 and 3), to the discourse (chapter 4), and to the genocidal succession of empires (chapter 5). More concretely, these chapters deal with the Greenwich House improvisation sessions (chapter 1), the Columbia-Princeton

Electronic Music Center (chapters 2 and 3), Cold War Orientalism (chapter 4), and US power in relation to the "bloodlands" of occupied Central and Eastern Europe (chapter 5). My approach to these scenes brings extensive archival research and engagement with archival theory into dialogue with interview-based ethnography and the close interpretation of aesthetic practices. I dwell particularly on nonnotated or unconventionally notated musical and sonic practices—improvisation, electronic music, conceptual art, performance art, and Fluxus—because the flexibility of such practices is especially amenable for intercultural poetics, or those poetics that show the intermingling of different cultural traditions. It is my conviction that these distinctive practices merit sustained attention in the study of migration.

In my approach, I tend to rework classic postcolonial concepts—such as third space and Orientalism—that continue to call out for more extensive adaptation within North American settings. I also draw from media studies and history of science in order to deal with the technologies, institutions, and infrastructures from which relevant aesthetic practices emerged. (The importance of magnetic tape and related sound technologies runs like a thread through most of the chapters.) In many cases, the largely white historical scenes of my study generated certain ways of asserting American power and leadership in a perceived contest of Western technological and cultural advancement. This pervasive mentality tended to disparage women and artists of color as incapable of mastering—let alone developing—the relevant technologies. Yet sound laboratories also afforded energetic experiments in self-making that subverted the very terms of that Eurocentric and masculinist worldview.[49] My protagonists' creative output and histories refute that way of thinking which persists today.

My narrative begins by exploring a certain historiographical silence that emerged following the 1957 Greenwich House sessions—a series of tape-recorded, informal improvisation sessions that brought together an interracial group of jazz musicians with white concert avant-gardists in the space of a historic settlement house music school (chapter 1). The French-American composer Edgard Varèse organized the sessions in order to record sound samples for incorporation into a new commissioned tape composition that would premiere at the 1958 Brussels World's Fair, an event that heralded the resumption of such celebrations of capital and empire after the hiatus imposed by World War II. It is my argument that Varèse anxiously sought to appropriate "Black" sounds to strengthen his white American bona fides (to compensate for his immigrant status) while preparing to represent the United States on the world stage. Indeed, Varèse's involvement with jazz provided fodder for his inclusion in the canon of "American experimentalism" as it took hold during this period—as is evident in State Department–distributed materials on the subject—even though he finally decided not to include the Greenwich House recordings as sound samples in his *Poème électronique* (1958), which premiered in Brussels.

Charles Mingus, too, showed up for the Greenwich House sessions in connection with a series of classical-jazz crossover (or "third stream") events during the late 1950s, about which he expressed intense ambivalence. During this period, Mingus increasingly came to treat musical composition and performance as a space for civil rights protest and articulation of African diasporic solidarity. In connection with this agenda, Mingus showed sustained interest in classical-jazz crossover events, because they complicated the racial codes through which music genres operated. Yet third stream events tended to reproduce racial inequalities in reception, pay, and leadership that belied any symbolic stance of racial equality through integration. As I show, Mingus's ambivalence about this dynamic plays out in the earliest drafts of his memoir from 1957 and in his program work about slavery and rebellion, *Pithecanthropus Erectus* (1956). It also inflected his interactions with Varèse, who displayed demeaning primitivist attitudes toward the musicians at Greenwich House. As an expression of defiance at the sessions, Mingus called out, "And look, look. . . . this is not *natural* for me!" while Varèse conducted and recorded the improvisation. With these words, Mingus interrupted the émigré's process of recording clean sound samples, and renegotiated the terms of the entire improvisation. This complex scene of dueling authority and ambivalence—which eludes simple narratives of exchange or appropriation—finds resonance with the idea of third space, which Homi Bhabha defines as an "intercultural site of enunciation, at the intersection of different languages jousting for authority, a translational space of negotiation [that] opens up through the process of dialogue" across an uneven field of power.[50] The Greenwich House sessions also stand out as a scene of subjection (in Hartman's sense)—an intimate encounter seemingly guided by notions of enjoyment, humanity, and consent that brings forth dehumanizing cruelties rooted in systemic anti-Blackness.[51] The sessions' status in these terms—as a third space and as a scene of subjection—amply accounts for the silences in oral history and historiography that later muted the scene's memory.

My subsequent narrative considers third space as it played out within a major institution of electronic music and cultural diplomacy (chapters 2 and 3). In 1958 a massive grant from the the Rockefeller Foundation

(RF) made possible the establishment of the Columbia-Princeton Electronic Music Center (CPEMC), the first large-scale studio of its kind in North America. Existing narratives of the CPEMC identify it as the anchor of the "uptown scene"—a site for the transplantation of European traditions on American soil, and a bastion for "Western music" rooted in pitch-oriented, fully notated composition. This historiography, however, ignores the CPEMC's Rockefeller-supported mission in global cultural diplomacy alongside the extensive roster of visiting composers at the CPEMC who arrived from many parts of the world, especially the Middle East, East Asia, and Latin America. The CPEMC thus assumed a contradictory character: on the one hand, it was a bastion for Western culture; on the other, it was a global center for pluralist exchange. "Acropolis," a long-standing nickname for Columbia's campus, emerges here as a metaphor for the studio's contradictory character as a site of both defensive gatekeeping and cross-cultural interface. The CPEMC's own status as an Acropolis shines through in its founding documents, which were authored by Vladimir Ussachevsky, a composer and Russian-Manchurian immigrant who had formerly worked as an intelligence analyst for the Office of Strategic Services (OSS) and the State Department. In the 1950s, Uss5achevsky consulted with his former OSS colleague Charles Burton Fahs—then the director of the Humanities Division of the RF—in order to craft a mission statement for the CPEMC that would dovetail with the foundation's postwar agenda. In their terms, the studio would contribute to their goal of creating a US-based internationalist space for creativity and advanced research that would also enhance strategic cultural-diplomatic relationships. Electronic music spoke to the dream of an intercultural approach to composition and knowledge production, because it could bypass practices of Western notation and treat pitch, timbral, and temporal values of music with singular flexibility.

The cases of Ussachevsky, Michiko Toyama, and Halim El-Dabh demonstrate how the sound laboratory worked at the heart of imperial circulations of labor, expertise, and subjectivity. The US management of migrating peoples interacted with cultural diplomacy in vexed ways. I show that from 1945 until 1965 the FBI and the Immigration and Naturalization Service (INS) targeted Ussachevsky in spurious counterintelligence investigations that were ultimately premised on his Manchurian-Russian ancestry. Columbia University and the Rockefeller Foundation, however, served as Ussachevsky's armor: his cultural diplomacy efforts in connection with these institutions provided cover to fend off surveillance-driven investigations of him and his family. Meanwhile, the poetics of electronic music served as a realm for working through experiences of sound-based technopower, as exemplified in *Wireless Fantasy* (1960), a work that plays with the history of Morse code and other technologies.

Under the auspices of an "East-West exchange," Ussachevsky also built upon European imperialist legacies of ethnographic sound recording, sponsoring Toyama and El-Dabh as the first foreign-born visitors to the studio. Magnetic tape enhanced the promise of earlier recording technologies, such as gramophones and wire recordings, to capture transient musical performances of cultural "others" and to render those practices useful for the production of knowledge. For El-Dabh and Toyama, however, such activities became fraught with dilemmas of racialized self-representation when they sought to translate their "own" traditions in electronic music. Toyama cultivated a tape aesthetic, exemplified in *Waka* (1960), that highlighted classical Japanese lineages of female authorship while tapping into the downtown spoken word, jazz, and global gagaku scenes. A lone woman composer in an overwhelmingly masculine profession, and without funding to extend her stay in the United States, she launched an ambitious but unsuccessful plan to found her own studio at Kyoto University in 1960. El-Dabh, who fared better in grant applications, pursued a path to US citizenship while developing a mystical, liberatory poetics variously adaptable to the purposes of Egyptian revolutionary nationalism, Arab or African diasporic solidarity, anticolonialism, and US civil rights. After their residencies at the CPEMC, Toyama and El-Dabh both found themselves subject to a racialized critical backlash and fewer professional opportunities as composers. Their trajectories responded to the gatekeeping mechanisms of the Acropolis at every juncture, prefiguring dilemmas faced by a later wave of Latin American composers who worked at the CPEMC from the mid-1960s onward.

Yoko Ono's debut takes center stage in chapter 4 together with the Cold War Orientalist discourses she confronted, like El-Dabh and (especially) Toyama. A mediator of art communities across North America, East Asia, and Europe, Ono eventually helped to secure alternatives to the "official" foundation- and government-supported arts networks of Cold War cultural diplomacy and soft power. Like the work of Mingus, Ono's early career is a touchstone for understanding how New York avant-gardes became politicized in the 1960s, and how they mediated larger networks transnationally. While seldom explored in existing scholarship, her early career rooted itself in the catastrophe of state-sponsored violence. In her written manifesto, "The Word of a Fabricator" (1962), Ono took her friend and mentor John Cage to task for his Zen-inspired poetics of indeterminacy, which she deemed politically debilitating. Rather than "blowing in the gentle wind," as she put it, she wanted her own work to participate in acts of "rescue" in the midst of atrocities.[52] Ono's critique of Cage's indeterminacy also intimates a larger challenge to Cold War Orientalism, which Christina Klein identifies as a mid-century US discourse of fascination with Pacific Rim cultures (like Zen) attending expanded US geopolitical power abroad. In Klein's terms, Cold War Orientalism produced "narratives of anti-conquest" (not unlike Cage's turn away from ego) in a manner that ultimately legitimated "U.S. expansion while denying its coercive or imperial nature."[53] Having experienced the violence of the Showa-period Japanese militarized society and the US bombings in Japan, Ono could not easily ignore the violent and imperial nature of either nation in which she had been raised, nor could she let go of "consciousness" and "intentionality" in her practice, which aspired to respond to those political realities. Chapter 4 stresses the importance of *AOS—To David Tudor* (1961) alongside other works premiered at Carnegie Recital Hall in New York in 1961 and at the Sōgetsu Art Center in Tokyo in 1962. Ono designated *AOS* as an "opera" about "the blue chaos of war" inspired by personal memory. Eschewing the Zen-inspired placidity then in vogue downtown, this piece worked *operatically* in a heightened affective register: its performances in New York and Tokyo variously included primal screaming, amplified recordings of Hitler and Hirohito, graphic simulations of violence, and so on. Tellingly, Ono used the term "opera" etymologically, to mean something intended to work in a spirit of public engagement. With this series of moves, she developed a strategy for countering the gendered and racialized discourses of Orientalism that pervaded the scenes of her debut in the United States and Japan.

My narrative closes by attending to the genocidal hauntings of empire, a theme that manifests prominently in early Fluxus and yet meets with general silence in critical and scholarly literature on the community (chapter 5). When George Maciunas founded Fluxus in 1962, he launched a transnational sponsoring organization for artists, musicians, and writers dedicated to questioning boundaries between art and life. This initiative helped to coalesce disparate strands of artistic experimentation that had developed across East Asia, Western Europe, and the United States. In 1962, Maciunas had just moved from New York City to Wiesbaden, Germany, to work as a graphic designer in the US Air Force. This move marked his first return to Germany after having previously lived there as a stateless refugee between his family's 1944 flight from Lithuania and their 1948 resettlement in the United States. As Said has observed, to live in exile is to apprehend multiple environments in contrapuntal relationship with one another.[54] Said's idea pertains strongly to Maciunas's own successive "homes." In Nazi Germany, he had felt simultaneous persecution and protection as a Lithuanian refugee who worked side-by-side with his engineer father in the armaments industry at the Siemens Corporation. This childhood experience had come after living through the Nazi and Soviet occupations of his homeland, including the Lithuanian-assisted genocidal killing of Jews on the streets of Kaunas, his hometown. Upon his 1962 return to Germany, Maciunas was working for a neo-imperial superpower at the height of the Cold War, and he showed a contrapuntal apprehension of remembered environments. Drawing on archival documents and interviews, I show how he compared notes on empires past and present in the still denazifying Wiesbaden. The Russian empire, the Soviet Union, the Third Reich, and US imperialism all drew his attention in a study of comparisons. This activity, in turn, informed Maciunas's new work as a self-styled saboteur, appropriating US military resources for the staging of Fluxus festivals that, in his view, furthered "a-national," "anti-imperialist," and "anticapitalist" goals. This ethos infused his signature composition *In Memoriam to Adriano Olivetti* (1962), which honors a Jewish-Italian saboteur at the heart of Mussolini's economic elite while pointing toward the violence of bureaucratic workings in empire. Maciunas "played" at empire, jokingly mimicking its processes, personae, technologies, and symbols in Fluxus administration and performance. Such a poetics worked through tangled questions of victimhood and complicity that evoke his Lithuanian family story. While the mythology of the downtown New York scene has often cast its subject as a new beginning apart from Europe, Maciunas's story evokes the hauntings that bind scenes of empire across divergent times and places, thus inviting a rich reappraisal of politicized art and music practices of the 1960s. This reappraisal of Fluxus opens the door for new interpretations of the work of its practitioners—from Benjamin Patterson to Yoko Ono to Philip Corner and beyond—whose work contravenes any easy celebration of American experimentalism as a culmination of the "American century." It also links up with relational work on genocide and empire, following Hannah Arendt and Timothy Snyder, which proposes that "what happened to one group is intelligible only in light of what happened to another."[55] And the community entanglements of Fluxus open up further pathways— following Hartman and Alexander Weheliye—to explore questions of slavery denialism as genocide denialism.[56]

The Said and the Unsaid

My storytelling has not been compelled by the dream of relaying a complete or representative narrative, but rather by webs of silence that have surrounded fragmentary scenes of memory. My focus on institutions of composition and high art precludes any pretense of comprehensive representation, because these institutions themselves are definitionally exclusionary. The silences perpetuated by communities around these institutions are always telling of *something*, although that something remains far from uniform. There is that which does not need to be said because it is common knowledge, there is that which should not be said because it is taboo or shameful, and there is that which goes unsaid because it cannot yet be put into words.[57] Some forms of unspoken memory hover at the interstices between these discursive systems of exclusion, which blur in relation to one another. This idea reminds us that the most shameful conduct is also sometimes thoroughly conventional—unsayable both as taboo and as common knowledge. Yet these intersecting systems of unsayability cannot completely obliterate all traces of what they obscure. We hear Mingus's bass playing and voice resonating on recordings from tape reels in the Edgard Varèse Collection that fail to credit him for his contributions. Freedom of Information Act requests bring forth FBI and INS investigation files on Ussachevsky, revealing a world of trouble he assiduously kept secret from colleagues and students. Letters from Toyama surface in various archival research collections despite a general amnesia concerning her presence at the CPEMC. A newspaper account of Ono's first public screams in *AOS* provides perspective on a painful, liberating utterance that remains inaccessible by audio recording. Attending to systems of silence and unsayability is essential to studying the nexus of ideology, power, music, and the sonic arts.

This idea guides my work of archival research and my task of building relationships with an older generation of research associates who share their oral history. I take seriously Hartman's exhortation to write "with and against the archive" in order to "imagine what cannot be verified" and yet needs to be reckoned with.[58] Genocide looms as an extreme but persistent possibility on modern empire's horizon. Its effects infuse the historical situations of my study, producing unspeakable wounds and truths unverifiable by standard documentary methods. (I think, for example, of the Siemens Corporation archives, which contain a "remarkably poor" collection from the years of World War II that blocks the verification of facts concerning the technocorporate side of war and genocide.)[59] Archival collections themselves construct power. In music and the arts, institutional archives skew toward canons, and they tend to organize themselves around the Euroamerican persona of the genius and his—usually "his"—works. These practices necessitate engagement with informal archives and "activist archives" assembled by those—like El-Dabh and Ono—who surely knew they would need to develop systems for preserving their own work for posterity.[60] (Other "activist archives"—such as those of Charles Mingus and Benjamin Patterson—have since been institutionalized in a number of research centers such as the Library of Congress and the Getty Foundation.) Working in archives requires examining patterns of collection, organization, erasure, and neglect, alongside critical appraisal of the archives' privileges of access. I value long-term relationships with archives cultivated by habits of return, which enable such a detailed metastudy. Yet the long labor of combing through files also requires a compensatory resistance to losing oneself in the past and its paper trails. The study of recent history promises guidance here, because of the relative plenitude of people and infrastructures that remain from recent times. In many cases I have been able to exit the archives and enter into the physical spaces where events transpired, or to meet face-to-face with interlocutors who share their own, at times conflicting, memories of those historical scenes. Responding to the facial expressions, humor, questions, and silences of these interlocutors is one way "to give dates their physiognomy." Such relationships intimate history's stakes in the present, and the historian's responsibility to the other and to remembrance.

To this end, each relationship unfolded as its own world in a mixed exchange of posted letters, emails, phone calls, in-person visits, and co-teaching in the classroom. I tended to follow the other's lead about the format and topics of our dialogue, although I sometimes shared archival material as conversation starters. Too many of our dialogues were cut short. Halim El-Dabh, Jonas Mekas (the filmmaker and close friend of Maciunas), and Mario Davidovsky (the composer associated with the CPEMC) passed away well before my study reached completion. The tone of our encounters—as much as the content of the conversations themselves—often pointed to the material conditions of the historical scenes. Yoko Ono replied once and only once: to an inquiring letter I mailed in 2008, she responded with an overnight Fedex package containing photocopies of her own archival materials. Follow-up inquiries, which focused more extensively on herself and her work, went unanswered, in a gesture I connect with the justifiable need of celebrity for protective silence, especially given Ono's own experiences of gendered and racialized exploitation in the media. Similarly, I will never forget the intense concern Deborah El-Dabh expressed in negotiating the terms of the contract concerning my interviews with her husband—which contrasted with Halim's own eagerness to turn on the voice recorder and start talking.[61] To be sure, I associate her worry with the hardships of economic and symbolic citizenship her husband had faced as a brown-skinned immigrant carving out a path in composition and academia. Likewise, I will not forget Pril Smiley's avid questions about current conditions for women students, staff, and faculty in the Columbia University Department of Music, the workplace she occupied with joy and difficulty in the 1960s and 1970s. Or the intelligence and painful emotion with which Philip Corner spoke about the relatively taboo nature of race as an open topic for conversation in the Fluxus community. Or Mario Davidovsky's vehement tone of apology and careful diction when referring to factionalist conflicts at the CPEMC. Or the gentleness of the composer Alice Shields, the engineer Peter Mauzey, and the jazz bassist Bill Crow teaching my graduate and undergraduate students the value of attentive listening to words and sounds. Or the composer alcides lanza conscientiously typing up thorough responses to my questions after our phone conversation about the CPEMC. Following up with interlocutors is of paramount importance in order to make sure that what one takes from a meeting is what that person actually wants to give. Following up is also necessary to discover what particular forms of reciprocity may be called for in the evolving professional relationship, a process that is never predictable or formulaic.

My work on the German-Jewish-American composer Stefan Wolpe also provided an entrée to my community of interlocutors and relevant archives: it figures as an antecedent and companion to this book. Some of my interlocutors had known Wolpe, and this connection often served as a starting point for conversation, just as my research on Wolpe served as a starting point for this book project. Although hardly well known, Wolpe is a creator who continues to summon the imagination of alternative music historiographies and futures. Wolpe mediated disparate communities across three continents—from Dada, the Bauhaus, and agitprop theater in Weimar Germany to pacifist movements in Mandatory Palestine to bebop, Abstract Expressionism, and post-tonal composition scenes in Cold War New York. My book *Stefan Wolpe and the Avant-Garde Diaspora* is both a study of the refugee composer and an intervention in music history's long-standing investment in national models of history. What often become lost in such nation-based frameworks are the chancy spaces of cultural translation that make the arts possible, in addition to the uprooted lives of individuals deprived of citizenly belonging. (The ongoing need for such critique manifests itself in the contemporary scholarly reference to Wolpe as "a German composer," which effaces his one-time statelessness and its genocidal origin.)[62] Recognizing New York as an imperial capital is one way to acknowledge and study the unpredictable connections that define lives in uprooting, and which bring newness into a world riven by inequalities. Although I devote scarce attention to Wolpe in the pages to come, the physiognomy of this book is connected with his own, its structure intimating his presence. He abides as a member of the Eighth Street Artists' Club and a student and teacher of bebop performers (chapter 1); as a denizen of Morningside Heights and habitué of concerts at Columbia University (chapters 2 and 3); as a friendly mentor, together with his wife the poet Hilda Morley, to Yoko Ono (chapter 4); and as a refugee from the bloodlands that are silently fundamental to Fluxus history (chapter 5). It was Ono's early poems about violence, hunger, and dislocation—which she gave to Wolpe as a token of friendship in 1950s New York, which he preserved in his archive, and which she described in a letter to me—that launched the beginnings of this book.

If the very substance of empire lies in its dreams, dispositions, attentions, and forebodings, then music and the sonic arts should contribute prominently to the study of that substance.[63] A new generation of scholarship about music, sound, and power promises to transform this field of inquiry. In connection with my own project, I think especially of a growing wave of literatures that address US imperialism in relation to sound technologies, cultural institutions, philanthropy, and music education in East Asia, Oceania, Latin America, and Africa, with more projects yet to come.[64] I also think of emerging studies of music and sound that work from the perspective of multiple empires in interaction, an approach that provincializes Euroamerican forms of empire.[65] And I think of critical histories of "man" and "humanity" in relation to such fields of contestation.[66] The turn of empire studies toward conceptualizing affect, sensory regimes, and the circulation of subjectivity—the treatment of these things as more than mere "reflection" or superstructure—brings them into the neighborhood of music and sound studies, where these questions have long predominated. A focus on individual creators, alongside the poetics of musical and sonic creation, is far from antithetical to the analysis of structural inequalities. Rather, for students of empire and imperialism, they provide "sensorial insights . . . crucial to the critical impulses that lie unarticulated on . . . tongues."[67] And these critical impulses participate in the speculative project to imagine the world otherwise, a task all the more urgent in the midst of epochal changes that are impossible to foretell.

✳ 1 ✳

Third Space, Scene of Subjection

MINGUS AND VARÈSE AT GREENWICH HOUSE

"Only time you drop the blues is when you drop saying 'nigger' or saying 'black.' If you call us Americans, the blues might be gone. . . . When they start calling us *first-class* citizens—which will never be, I gotta figure— then there maybe won't be no reason for the blues."

CHARLES MINGUS, interviewed by John F. Goodman, 1972[1]

"And look, look, uhh . . . this is not *natural* for me!"

CHARLES MINGUS, the Greenwich House sessions, 1957[2]

A rudimentary outline of the story is clear.[3] In the spring and summer of 1957, Edgard Varèse led a series of improvisation sessions in downtown New York with jazz musicians including Eddie Bert, Don Butterfield, Bill Crow, Art Farmer, Teo Macero, Hal McKusick, Charles Mingus, Hall Overton, Frank Rehak, and Ed Shaughnessy. (The full roster cannot be known with certainty.) The sessions took place at the Music School of Greenwich House—one of the city's oldest settlement houses—which by mid-century had become a venerable classical music venue where Varèse held an informal teaching affiliation. Most of the jazz musicians present, as recalled in oral accounts,[4] had been participants in the Jazz Composers Workshop (JCW), a loose, racially integrated group of musicians invested in crossover between classical concert and jazz traditions (table 1.1), and whose name became the title of a Mingus album featuring Macero. The musicians' interactions with Varèse at the Greenwich House sessions created something of a sensation, attracting John Cage, Merce Cunningham, and others who observed the music making from the sidelines on at least one occasion.[5] Like Varèse, these informal audience members were associated with the newly crystallizing canons of the New York School and American experimentalism. Composer, producer,

TABLE 1.1. Musicians participating in the 1957 Greenwich House
sessions, as recalled in oral accounts

REMEMBERED BY EARLE BROWN	REMEMBERED BY TEO MACERO	REMEMBERED BY BILL CROW
Art Farmer (tpt)	Art Farmer	Art Farmer
Teo Macero (ts)	Teo Macero	Teo Macero
Ed Shaughnessy (d)	Ed Shaughnessy	Don Butterfield
Hal McKusick (cl and as)	Don Butterfield (tu)	Eddie Bert
Hall Overton (p)	Eddie Bert (tb)	Teddy Charles (vib)
Frank Rehak (tb)	Charles Mingus (b)	

and saxophonist Macero and composer Earle Brown organized the sessions, using their contacts as tape editors and commercial recording engineers at Columbia and Capitol Records respectively to assemble the
sessions' personnel.

Their existence long a subject of rumor, recordings from the Greenwich House sessions finally made their way onto Internet sites in the last
several years.[6] Yet few scholars have addressed the sessions as a historical
episode, a fact that is remarkable given the iconic status of the musicians
involved. In 1958, Cage brought some slender remembrance to the events
by writing of Varèse's jazz experiment in passing, expressing a dissatisfaction characteristic of his well known dismissal of jazz.[7] The music critic
Peter Yates referred equally briefly, though approvingly, to Varèse's jazz
interests in an important 1959 essay that first coined the term "American experimental tradition."[8] More recently, Olivia Mattis has written a
valuable article documenting the sessions in relation to Varèse's creative
projects, specifically his composition of the *Poème électronique* (1958).[9]
Virtually no scholarship, however, has questioned in any detail what the
sessions may have meant to the jazz musicians who participated. This lacuna speaks to a wider, racialized rift in the historiography of postwar
American music as described by George Lewis—a historiography that
tends to narrate jazz history on a separate track from stories of the downtown New York concert avant-garde, despite evidence of mutual awareness and interaction between creators working in the two scenes.[10] Though
more recent scholarship has taken important steps toward counteracting
this pattern, the scarcity of literature on the Greenwich House sessions
nonetheless perpetuates the long-standing gap identified by Lewis.[11]

This chapter addresses dilemmas of race, citizenship, and the arts in
downtown New York during the postwar period of national-imperialist
canon formation and self-proclaimed American cultural ascendancy. It

locates these dilemmas at the Greenwich House sessions—a scene of extreme power imbalances, ambivalent emotions, and ambiguous creative outcomes, documented within a scattering of archival artifacts and oral history. At the center of my study is a series of recordings preserved in the Edgard Varèse Collection at the Paul Sacher Foundation in Basel: the master tapes from which the Internet copies derive.[12] These recordings speak to a kind of after-hours experimentation and sociability not usually archived or remembered within official history.[13] They open up novel perspectives on a liminal encounter between downtown concert vanguardists and jazz experimenters, testifying to a long and largely unspoken history of mutual fascination, crossed signals, and fraught negotiations of authority. The traces of such an unstable encounter often lie at the periphery of archives, in the silent margins. They do not lend themselves to the formation of an easy or stable historical narrative. This story therefore maintains "enigma" at its heart in a triple sense: as a set of problems unsolved, as a narrative partially obscured, and as a parable with a moral and political charge for sustained interpretation. It foregrounds dilemmas central to the study of racialized hierarchies of citizenship that play out in scenes of intercultural encounter that define New York as an imperial metropolis.

Although the Greenwich House session tapes provide evidence of a tacit history of connection between jazz musicians and concert vanguardists, the sessions were strikingly short in duration and their creative legacy remains elusive. We will see that Varèse appears to have approached the encounter as a source of sound samples for electronic composition to be showcased internationally at the Brussels World's Fair, yet he ultimately refrained from using any of the material toward that end. The jazz musicians did not incorporate innovations from the sessions into their subsequent work in any obvious or specific way, with the arguable exceptions of Teo Macero, who used graphic notation in one of his subsequent jazz compositions, and Frank Rehak and Don Butterfield, who collaborated in later years with Cage.[14] Remarkably, none of the participants claimed ownership of the sessions' innovations publicly. As Earle Brown put it, the sessions did not have "much to do with history or anything because it was just to do . . . sort of a fun thing and Varèse never did any serious scores [related to the sessions]."[15] The jazz bassist Bill Crow, who participated in one of the unrecorded rehearsals, remembered it as a highly unusual gig with experimental yet aesthetically questionable musical results. After receiving word of the event by phone on short notice, he joined it because "jazz musicians respond when someone says something's happening."[16] (We will return to Brown's and Crow's words later.)

If the Greenwich House sessions may be considered "experimental" in the sense that they were a "try" at something without an anticipated outcome, then this experiment would seem to have been defined by a spirit of boundary crossing by virtue of its personnel. Yet a term like "boundary crossing" hardly captures the strange and muted history of what happened in the sessions' wake.

Indeed, it is difficult to seize upon a single term or concept to evoke the acute asymmetries of power and knowledge that shaped the musicians' interactions and the persistent silences that followed. Contrary to the mythology of his marginalization, Varèse embarked on these sessions at the height of his newly revitalized career. In popular media and avant-garde communities alike, he was received as a genius and icon of a modernist high art tradition that commanded profound cultural capital.[17] (Brown's linking of "history" with Varèse's "serious scores" intimates this capital.) Varèse held a remarkably secure socioeconomic position in comparison with the sessions' gigging musicians—a differential all the more acute for Black musicians such as Art Farmer and Charles Mingus, who struggled to make a living within the racist structures of the music industry. Seen through the lens of such inequality, the sessions figure as yet another episode in a history of exploitative appropriations of jazz and other African diasporic traditions—especially given that we have no evidence that the musicians received any remuneration.[18] Indeed, Brown and Macero organized the sessions explicitly for Varèse's benefit, on his home turf, at the educational institution where he taught. Yet the dynamics of appropriation at Greenwich House are disarmingly murky. Varèse's cultural capital, already strong, appears to have benefited more from the sessions' low-key legend (furthered in print by Cage and Yates) than from any direct incorporation of the sound recordings in his own composition. Moreover, the agency of the jazz musicians themselves should not be understated: they made the sessions possible. We will see that some of them, including Macero and Mingus, had decidedly more knowledge of Varèse's music than he did of theirs. Simple notions of "exchange" and "appropriation" hardly do justice to the multilayered complexities of the encounter.

In the face of this inadequacy, I attempt to carve out a space between two concepts—"third space" and the "scene of subjection"—in order to theorize entanglements of encounter such as those at Greenwich House. Let us consider each concept before conceptualizing the interval between them. Far from a mere label, third space is an concept that has sparked disparate interpretations across the arts, humanities, and social sciences.[19] As noted in the introduction to this book, Homi Bhabha defines "third space" as an "intercultural site of enunciation, at the intersection of different languages jousting for authority, a translational space of negotiation [that] opens up through the process of dialogue" across power differentials.[20] For our purposes, the concept is valuable because it foregrounds acts of cultural translation in which actors' initial terms of interaction become renegotiated in real time. Third-space encounters play out within an uneven field of power, dramatizing and potentially destabilizing those imbalances. Third space exceeds the mastery of its participants: in the transitional flux of translation, actors become caught in ambivalence and uncertainty, their intentions internally divided and disjunct from their contingent aftereffects. Third space poses a challenge for historiography not only because of its transitory, transitional qualities—which often evade standard documentary and archival practices—but also because its disparate "languages" and translational dynamics remain partially opaque to the historical actors themselves.

Like "third space," Saidiya Hartman's "scene of subjection" describes situations of extreme power imbalance and opacity that trouble notions of individuality and free will. The scene of subjection is an intimate encounter, guided by notions of enjoyment, humanity, and consent, that brings forth dehumanizing cruelties rooted in systemic anti-Blackness. In her discussion of slavery and its aftermath, Hartman focuses on the "forms of subjectivity and circumscribed humanity imputed to the enslaved" that everyday institutions such as minstrelsy and the expressive arts propagate and police.[21] These insidiously create "scenes in which terror can hardly be discerned."[22] The "expressive and affective capacities of the subject, sentiment, enjoyment, affinity, will, and desire facilitated subjugation, domination, and terror precisely by preying on the flesh, the heart, and the soul."[23] Under these terms, ostensible notions of formal equality—rooted in notions of consent and humanity—become unified with racial subjugation, and the experience of such subjugation finds expression in forms that elude the historical record.[24]

It is my conviction that the Greenwich House sessions are a scene of subjection that is *also* a third space, opening up new possibilities to theorize the "in-between" of these concepts. Brown's blithe reference to the sessions as not "much to do with history," but rather "sort of a fun thing," intimates precisely Hartman's scene of enjoyment and choice which would both license and mask racial subjugation. The sessions' apparent lack of remuneration reinforced the pretexts of casual fun and free consent while reinforcing racialized pay inequality. The presence of a small, white audience, on at least one occasion, confirmed the spectatorial element of the proceedings: it showcased Varèse managing a mixed assemblage of Black and white bodies while dabbling in the consumption of

"Black sounds" for his own pleasure and professional benefit. At the same time, however, the Greenwich House recordings show how the initial terms of the encounter became remade in real time, revealing its qualities as a third space. We will see that the musicians—and Charles Mingus in particular—talked back to Varèse, altering the musical and social character of the proceedings. In the cramped quarters of the townhouse space, a contest of authority unfolded in words, language, and gesture as Varèse and the musicians questioned one another, spoke over one another, changed the physical setup of music making, and labored in a palpable effort to "translate" between different musical idioms and conventions associated with post-bebop improvisation and composition on the one hand, and Varèse's brand of concert experimentalism on the other. Varèse projection of mastery hardly remained intact, even though he still held the ultimate upper hand of complete citizenship by virtue of his white privilege.

For all of these reasons, this chapter understands both Bhabha's and Hartman's concepts as the most promising signs under which to construe the Greenwich House sessions, while cautioning against placing too positive a valence on the sessions as a site for any long-term dismantling of power. This approach navigates between the Scylla and Charybdis of "exchange" and "appropriation," avoiding both the naive egalitarian promise of the former and the implication of unidirectional agency in the latter. By interrogating the Greenwich House sessions as a transitory third space, this chapter finds relevance for a postcolonial concept—often associated with scenes of European colonialism—within Cold War New York as an imperial metropole. At the same time, Hartman's concept keeps this chapter grounded in the US-based histories of slavery that are fundamental to the nation's race-based heirarchies of citizenship. Both concepts keep faith with the project to produce alternative histories of experimentalism in music, or, in Lewis's words, "to grow up and recognize a multicultural, multiethnic base for experimentalism in music, with a variety of perspectives, histories, traditions or methods."[25] They link up with a growing secondary literature on jazz-classical crossover practices as well as scholarship on creative process and cross-cultural encounter in music more generally. Finally, they encourage us to attend precisely to the ambivalent nature of cultural choices as they play out within conflicting webs of freedom and constraint.[26] As Bhabha and Hartman remind us, choice is never a punctual or impermeable thing.[27] Rather, musicians might enter a "translational" creative encounter—shifting toward a new cultural affiliation—but then vacillate, reaffirm their choice, or step back. Imbalances of power set the stage for such wavering movements of approach and withdrawal and for unruly mixtures of joy, fear, hope, and despondency.

Within the larger ensemble of participants, this chapter focuses on Edgard Varèse and Charles Mingus in particular, in order to appreciate just how wildly divergent the terms of such an ambivalent encounter could be. To be sure, each musician participating in the sessions calls out for his own narrative at Greenwich House, bringing many unexplored possibilities to the fore. At the same time, the full personnel and full racial makeup of the sessions remains in question, because of Varèse's pointed negligence in not crediting the musicians involved—a circumstance that may have rendered additional Black musicians invisible to the historical record. I have deliberately chosen to juxtapose Varèse and Mingus, even though the latter was not an organizer of the sessions, because both composers distinguished themselves from the rest by speaking out publicly— though in opposite ways—on questions of music, race, nation, and citizenship within their respective fields.

Given their radically disparate experiences of citizenship in the United States, the two composers had very different reasons to speak out on questions of music, race, and national belonging. As an African American of mixed European, African, and Asian descent, Mingus could not experience the benefits of full national citizenship to which Varèse had access in the United States via naturalization. As a white male, Varèse the naturalized citizen enjoyed radically greater protection and rights under the law than did the native-born Mingus, who occupied the precarious status known in the terminology of human rights scholarship as "second-class citizenship," "semicitizenship," or "incomplete citizenship."[28] As already noted, following Lawrence Bobo, full citizenship designates complete access to opportunities, political and legal rights, civil and social recognition, and moral esteem that other members of society have available to them.[29] Mingus devoted much of his musical activity and speech to protesting the manifold elements of second-class citizenship: the systematic undermining of economic opportunities, the debasement of political and legal rights, police brutality, mass incarceration, housing inequality, and the policing of Black citizens' opportunities to express themselves with freedom and to be heard.[30]

Varèse the immigrant, on the other hand, enjoyed full legal, political, and economic benefits, but had reason to feel anxious about questions of cultural or symbolic citizenship (which also affected Mingus even more strongly). I refer here to national community-based bonds—often premised on particularities of speech, language, appearance, demeanor, habit, and other less tangible qualities—that define mutual citizenly recognition within the nation and extend beyond the technicalities of state citizenship.[31] The arts are a prime realm for enacting such citizenly distinctions and enforcing symbolic boundaries of belonging. Varèse and Mingus both had a stake in redefining their own symbolic citizenships, each of which could be called into question as insufficiently American, especially within restrictive Cold War national discourses that tended to define qualities of "Americanness" in narrow terms. The Red Scare had intensified effects of xenophobia connected with the nativist currents that had permeated arts institutions thoroughly by the 1950s. Yet Varèse's white privilege and full citizenly enfranchisement afforded him far greater leverage toward this end. And, as we will see, he had long worked aggressively to situate himself on the upper end of nativist race hierarchies.

By 1957, Varèse was a veteran of debates about "Americanism" in music, his earliest pronouncements on this theme having even predated his arrival in the United States in 1917.[32] His efforts to define modern "American" culture shaped both his early pursuit of electronic music technologies and his enduring primitivist fascination with Native American cultures. In the 1920s in New York he had established himself as an ardent promoter of new musics, garnering breathless reviews as a composer and conductor while spearheading new music organizations in the city.[33] He also acted as a transatlantic emissary of American musics during multiple trips abroad, before spending the years of World War II in relative seclusion in his Greenwich Village apartment, temporarily abandoning composition and curtailing his musical activities.

Varèse began to pursue an interest in jazz only in the 1950s, during the genre's heyday in the Village, after a history of dismissing it in racially denigrating terms—a history to which we will return at length. Charlie Parker had famously expressed an unfulfilled intention to study with the composer, which may have piqued his interest.[34] Varèse's turn toward jazz also followed his mid-century membership in the racially exclusionary, largely masculine space of the Eighth Street Artists' Club—the nexus of the New York School and the birthplace of Abstract Expressionism— where jazz found sensationalist reception in efforts to create "an American artistic identity within the parameters of modernism."[35] Such assertions of Americanness assumed special importance in an art community that had been denounced on the floor of Congress in 1949 for being "un-American."[36] Yet Varèse's experience in French art communities was equally significant; we will see that his newfound enthusiasm for jazz tended to assume the characteristics of an exoticist negrophilia akin to that of his Parisian friends Fernand Léger and Le Corbusier. The racially appropriative work of this French avant-garde also became refracted within the discourses of the Eighth Street Artists' Club, which turned to it as a source of legitimation even while straining to define itself in maverick defiance of it.[37]

In a downtown scene teeming with ambivalence toward its European heritage, Varèse's new interactions with jazz musicians could implicitly strengthen his white American bona fides through proximity to an "indigenous" Black tradition. In 1957, Varèse was busy preparing to compose sounds for the multimedia spectacle that would become the *Poème électronique* at the Philips Pavilion designed by Le Corbusier for the 1958 Brussels World's Fair—an exemplary occasion for Cold War competition in the arts. The Greenwich House sessions thus took place in the run-up to this collaborative project, which held major implications for Varèse's career and legacy. The Brussels World's Fair presented a new opportunity for the immigrant to present himself as a national emissary on a highly publicized international stage—a high-stakes setting that makes the prelude of his foray into jazz all the more suggestive. Indeed, Varèse brought at least one of the Greenwich House tape reels (along with Mingus's album *Pithecanthropus Erectus*) to Eindhoven, where he composed the *Poème électronique* at the Philips Corporation headquarters.[38]

In contrast to Varèse's comparatively great cultural mobility, Mingus had long oriented his avant-garde musical activities as a conscious and public response to his civic disenfranchisement in the country of his birth. Throughout his adult life he spoke out against the binary construction of race that determined his second-class citizenship. As a lighter-skinned person of multiethnic background, he felt a lack of belonging and acceptance on both sides of the binary paradigm—an estrangement he painstakingly probed in his 1971 memoir *Beneath the Underdog*. He identified instead with the multiethnic and racially integrated community in which he grew up, in Watts, South Los Angeles, where he had devoted himself to a culturally eclectic range of musical passions, from the music of his local Holiness Church to radio broadcasts of Duke Ellington's band, and from recordings of Richard Strauss's tone poems to film music. In Los Angeles he had studied composition with Lloyd Reese and classical bass with Herman Reinshagen of the New York Philharmonic, while learning from many of the great jazz masters of the West Coast. Before settling in New York in 1951, he had established his national reputation as a bass virtuoso, touring with Kid Ory and Barney Bigard, Louis Armstrong, Lionel Hampton, and Red Norvo. By the late 1950s, Mingus's accomplishments as a bracingly innovative composer and bandleader began to take precedence over his renown as a bassist. At the same time, he increasingly treated musical composition and performance as a space for civil rights protest and for articulation of African diasporic solidarity, exemplified in "Haitian Fight Song" (1957) and "Fables of Faubus" (1959).[39] Varèse did not participate in such public protest. His friend and student Chou Wen-chung "worked with Varèse several times a week during that time and never heard any talk about civil rights," though "Varèse worked with many different musicians and favored racial equality."[40] Given that Varèse refrained from going on the record as a civil rights proponent, he and Mingus were surely worlds apart in their politics of musical practice.

In the midst of civil rights activism, Mingus engaged in an intensive and sustained way with European traditions of high modernism while searching for alternatives to Eurocentric musical practice. These experiments lay at the center of his Jazz Workshop, the midsize group he founded as a successor to the JCW to explore alternatives to existing methods and business models of jazz composition, rehearsal, marketing, and performance. His activities resonated with the work of other activist musicians in his milieu, notably his frequent collaborator and business partner Max Roach. Mingus was attracted to the anticommercial ideologies of aesthetic modernism in what became a lifelong effort to defy the racist structures of the music industry: "Please, please don't ever try to put or bring anyone's real music onto that selling level. So Beethoven was poor, Bartok, and you go on from there. . . . Love of beauty of life of all her artistic wonders is enough merit for one soul to consume in each life span."[41] Mingus also welcomed crossovers between diverse traditions as a means to destabilize racially coded genres. In 1957, Gunther Schuller commissioned Mingus's *Revelations* for the Brandeis Festival, the same year that Schuller famously coined the term "third stream" to designate a style that fuses "basic elements of jazz and Western art music."[42] All of these conditions form the backdrop to Mingus's agonistic participation in the Greenwich House sessions.

Neither Varèse nor Mingus so much as mentions their 1957 interaction in preserved autobiographical statements, interviews, or writings. Mingus's voice surfaces in the session recordings, Macero (an authoritative witness, as Mingus's decades-long collaborator) remembered Mingus as a participant,[43] and Varèse's address appears in Mingus's address book (figure 1.1).[44] Yet without this scattered evidence, one would hardly know of their encounter. Both composers had reasons to pursue a boundary-crossing collaboration, yet they linked such projects with vastly different politics and professional aspirations, each oriented by his own racially defined citizenship in the United States. We glimpse the outlines of a basis for mutual interest, yet also potential for exploitation, harm, and fear—the very conditions that would provoke troubled or protective silence.

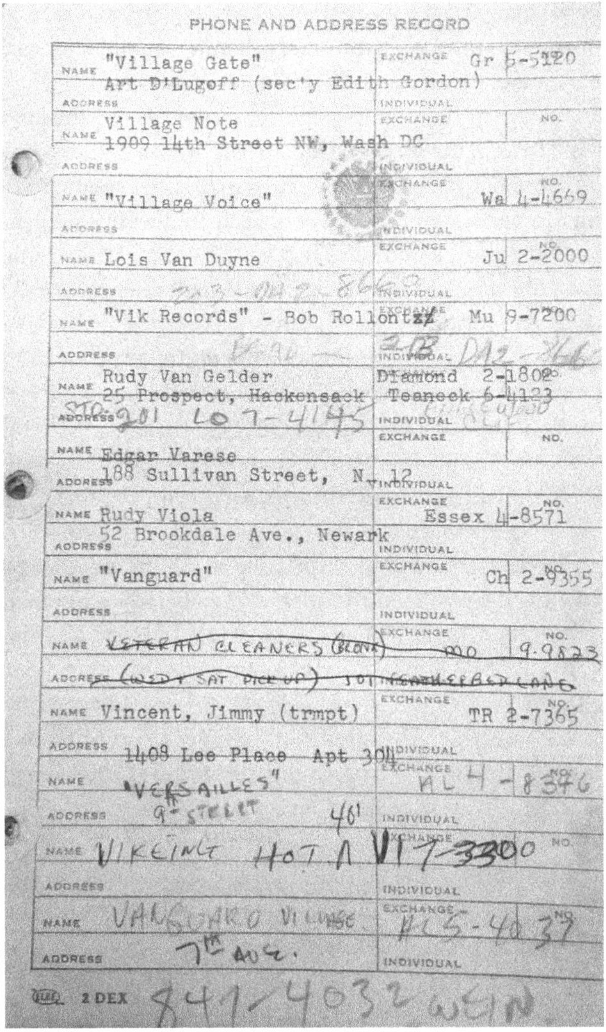

PHONE AND ADDRESS RECORD

"Village Gate" Gr 5-5120
~~Art D'Lugoff (sec'y Edith Gordon)~~

Village Note
~~1909 14th Street NW, Wash DC~~

"Village Voice" Wa 4-4669

Lois Van Duyne Ju 2-2000

"Vik Records" - Bob Rollontz Mu 9-7200

Rudy Van Gelder Diamond 2-1802
~~25 Prospect, Hackensack Teaneck 6-4123~~
201 LO 7-4145

~~Edgar Varese~~
188 Sullivan Street, N.Y. 12

Rudy Viola Essex 4-8571
52 Brookdale Ave., Newark

"Vanguard" Ch 2-9355

~~VETERAN CLEANERS~~

Vincent, Jimmy (trmpt) TR 2-7365
~~1408 Lee Place Apt 304~~

"VERSAILLES" AL 4-8346
9th STREET

VIKEING HOT

VANGUARD VILLAGE AL 5-4037
7th AVE.

2 DEX 841-4032

FIGURE 1.1. Address book of Charles Mingus. Charles Mingus Collection, Library of Congress. Used by permission.

Such concerns bring us back to the chasms that define our archive of mid-century avant-gardes. While this chapter tells the story of a fraught crossover scene in American experimentalism, it also unfolds as an exercise in how to deal with the silences that dwell within the historiography of such third-space encounters and scenes of subjection. In the case of the Greenwich House sessions, the gaps in the relevant secondary literature follow from Varèse's and Mingus's own "memory practices"—a term that describes the many ways we constantly lose, retrieve, and recompose the past through informal daily habits and other more systematic methods of preserving memory.[45] Our task therefore lies in interpreting what these silences might have meant or might continue to mean—to the musicians in the past, and to us in the present. Here we should remember that "archive" can refer, on the one hand, narrowly to a curated and sheltered collection of documents, or on the other, more broadly in the Foucauldian sense to "the law of what can be said" and this law's system of functioning.[46] The Greenwich House recordings seem to document the fact that Varèse and Mingus interacted with one another musically and socially despite their own and others' subsequent history of ignoring the encounter, downplaying it, or finding no occasion, words, or other basis through which to preserve statements about it. In this respect, the sessions' recordings reverberate as a historical testimony that countervails the "dead spots" of the archive, in both the limited and the expansive senses of that term.

Indeed, Mingus's voice asserts itself on the recordings as a vivid emblem of their testimonial power, speaking to his presence there despite the fact that his name, like most others remembered in the sessions' oral history, appears nowhere in Varèse's archive at the Sacher Foundation, and thus risked losing its place in this history of music making. In attending both to the recordings' status as "positive" evidence and the "negative" obscurity in which they dwell, my own account thus works "with and against the archive."[47] I try to interpret whatever clues remain in the historical record while also attending to the limits of that record. Following the words of Hartman, this account "advanc[es] . . . speculative arguments and exploit[s] the capacities of the subjunctive" in an effort to "displace the received or authorized account [by imagining] what might have happened or might have been said or might have been done."[48] Articulating arguments that blend primary source research with musical listening, I seek never to lose touch with the silence of unspoken situations that makes the evidence meaningful.

The Greenwich House Recordings

The Greenwich House recordings stand in a metonymic relationship to the sessions as a piece of history: they index and document them, but they cannot represent them as a whole or open a transparent window onto them. At first listening, they seem to illuminate the "real-world" texture of third space in stunning detail—revealing misunderstandings, background noises, laughter, the acquisition of unfamiliar musical skills, and subtle negotiations of authority. They may even invite a "sonic paleography" of the kind described by Michael Gallope, a study that brings the "politics [of] close reading" to "a mode of listening that is attuned to latent backgrounds (against, or in counterpoint with, the artist's intentions)," combining a sensitivity to poetics with an attentiveness to "social and historical life."[49] Yet our eavesdropping remains partial, limited by chance circumstances and choices in recording and preservation, as is true of any archival material. No scholarship to date interprets the sound preserved on the recordings in depth or discusses the reels as physical artifacts, despite their clear importance as documentary sources.

Though the labeling of the recordings is vague, it nonetheless provides glimmers of insight into the sessions and their relevance for Varèse. Sounds from the Greenwich House sessions are included on three quarter-inch tape reels in the Edgard Varèse Collection at the Paul Sacher Foundation, each contained in a shallow square box.[50] The cover of one box is inscribed "Jazz Graphs Varèse Orig." in an unfamiliar hand—indicating that musical "graphs" or charts were used on at least one occasion. Another box is labeled "Jazz," written diagonally in what appears to be Varèse's hand with fancy block letters stylized in red crayon with pink crayon shadowing. Decorated in this flamboyant way, the recording appears as a fetish object, or at the very least a thing charged with enthusiasm. A third box has "Sources" casually scrawled on the spine, in a hand that is probably Varèse's, a label that suggests that the jazz recordings served as possible sources for electronic composition. The reels were in the possession of the composer Chou Wen-chung before their acquisition by the Sacher Foundation. There are altogether about forty-three minutes of recorded sound from Greenwich House on the three reels, about twenty-seven minutes of which have been made available (with lower audio quality) on the Internet. We can establish the temporal sequence of recording excerpts on individual reels, but not from reel to reel. We know from Varèse's weekly planners that at least five jazz improvisation sessions at Greenwich House were scheduled between March 31 and August 4, 1957. Some of these were specifically identified in his weekly planner as recording sessions, while at least some must not have been recorded, as we know from Crow's attestation.[51] The personnel could have varied from session to session, but neither the players' names nor the recording dates are documented on the reels or elsewhere in the Varèse Collection, with the exception of the dates that appear in Varèse's weekly planners.

At this point it is important to remember that the recordings do not simply document a reality but operated in that reality. The tape recorder was part of the social setting and the power dynamic of Varèse's compositional practice. To be sure, electronic recording technologies have been implicated in the appropriation of colonized and minority cultures ever since their invention.[52] In the 1950s, Varèse's compositional aesthetic depended, in his words (and in keeping with the tape label "Sources"), on the collection of recorded sounds as "raw material to be treated electronically."[53] The jazz excerpt on the "Sources" reel immediately precedes recordings of what sound like West African talking drums and industrial sounds—the latter of which became integrated into the *Poème électronique*. The fact that none of the reels document or credit the individual jazz musicians reinforces the idea that their music making was treated as "raw material," in accordance with the colonialist dynamics of musical exoticism. Varèse showed himself "eager to 'discover' the sounds of living bodies and submit their raw material to composers for aesthetic refinement and technological elaboration," to invoke Amy Cimini's description of late twentieth-century US musical experimentalisms more broadly.[54] Whatever Varèse's initial expectations may have been, however, his terms of engagement were renegotiated in musical and social dialogue with the jazz musicians—a manifestation of the sessions' character as a third space. With this idea in mind, let us consider three contrasting episodes of musical interaction documented on the recordings.

RECORDED EPISODE 1: "IT'S LIKE ASKING YOU
TO PLAY TENNIS WITH NO NET"

The first excerpt on the tape reel labeled "Jazz Graphs Varèse Orig." provides a sense of the contrasting terms of engagement that musicians such as Varèse and Mingus would have brought to the sessions.[55] I will discuss musical aspects of the excerpt in relation to developments in jazz of the period before turning to the words of jazz bassist Bill Crow, who attended one of the sessions and who, in a recent interview, responded to hearing this music with memories of Varèse's interactions with the group. Crow's account suggests that Varèse approached the sessions with primitivist expectations, and this may have rankled the musicians, who themselves prized techniques that debunked ideas of jazz as an unschooled and primitive mode of expression. For this reason it is worth dwelling on the details of their musical performance.

The excerpt of approximately two minutes shows the musicians using techniques associated with Mingus's Jazz Workshop, its antecedent the JCW, and innovations in modal jazz. The ensemble in the recording comprises approximately ten players, including tenor and alto saxophone, two trumpets, trombone, tuba, drum set, vibes, piano, and bass. As recalled by

Brown, Macero, and Crow, the vast majority of these musicians had participated in the JCW, the loose group—clustered around Teddy Charles, John LaPorta, Macero, and Mingus—that coalesced in late 1953 to foster exchanges between concert avant-gardes and post-bop jazz.[56] The size of the improvising ensemble in the 1957 session would have been familiar to JCW veterans: the group had made its name in an unrecorded 1954 Carnegie Recital Hall concert with a nine-piece ensemble, and Teddy Charles had subsequently recorded a ten-piece ensemble with JCW regulars for his 1956 album *The Teddy Charles Tentet.*

What differentiates the midsize ensemble in this Greenwich House recording, however, is the fact that the musicians seem to be playing without score, whereas the JCW emphasized intricate, score-based compositions skillfully combined with improvisation. Earle Brown later recalled that at Greenwich House, he and Varèse would initially provide "very minimal information" about what they wanted from the musicians in a given session, but that "as the afternoon went on Varèse and I kept introducing subtle controls. You know, like let's have a thing, a three-part counterpoint between the trumpet, tenor saxophone . . . the trumpet[,] saxophone, and trombone."[57]

Given that Varèse offered the musicians little guidance as to what to play, it is no wonder that they relied on experimental techniques familiar to the JCW and the Jazz Workshop, using the idioms of modal jazz to bring a sense of shape and structure to their free-form simultaneous improvisation. Abjuring standard harmonic changes, they selected modal scales and a wide range of note values (sometimes within melodies evocative of "exotic" musics) within a tangled texture of multilayered pulses and riffs. The improvisation takes the shape of three distinctive sections, points of articulation emerging when one musician interrupts the flow with a boldly new "feel" that changes what the others are doing—a follow-the-leader approach that would not rely on a score. Most of the improvisation is in F Aeolian, with a strong blues inflection (less emphasis on the flatted sixth), putting it in a family of F-minor-mode improvisations that characterized signature compositions by Mingus at the time, including "Pithecanthropus Erectus" and "Tonight at Noon" (as performed with Teo Macero at the Newport Jazz Festival in 1956).

Close to a minute and a half into the improvisation the musicians build to a climax of exuberant, ornamented melodic lines outside the Aeolian mode of the opening, with a distinctive allusion to classical Arab musics characteristic of other avant-garde jazz of the period. The melodic style, with sustained ornamented pitches against a static harmonic background, recalls the opening of Mingus's "Tonight at Noon," alongside a heritage of older exoticist standards like Duke Ellington's "Caravan." (We will return to this question of exoticism and its significance in the postwar jazz context.) After a sustained climax of trumpet and saxophone wailing on C^6 and E-flat—the excerpt's registral and dynamic highpoint—the saxophone winds down this mini-duet with a leisurely oscillating A-flat^5–G^5 figure, a variation on a prominent riff from the opening, as the trumpet persists with some fanfares and running figures until the drums and vibes hit a strong downbeat. At this point the rest of the ensemble drops out, with the exception of one quiet, stray horn that lingers for a few seconds. The rhythm section closes the number with a series of largely octatonic, widely ranging sequences in the vibes, a nuanced drum solo accentuating those sequences, and sporadic, high-register timbral effects in the bass (likely Mingus). While the musicians succeeded in crafting their improvisation with a strong sense of shape—with distinctive opening, middle, and closing sections—they do not sound as smooth and confident in their playing as they might under more familiar conditions of performance.

When I played this musical excerpt to Bill Crow, it sparked memories of his own participation in one of Varèse's sessions, an occasion on which, as he recalled, no score had been used. He thought it unlikely that the recording featured his own playing, but said that it reminded him of the sound made by the ensemble at the session he had attended. At the time he had been struck by how little direction Varèse gave the players: "All he wanted to control was how long and who played together, and then you could just do whatever you wanted, with no form at all." In response to the recording, Crow contemplated the disparity between the musicians' techniques, on the one hand, and Varèse's lack of initiation into their world of training and knowledge:

It was a funny circumstance because I got the feeling he wasn't really clear about what he wanted to happen. I think he felt that classical musicians were not free enough to do this. And so he tried to get guys that had jazz experience. . . . And he didn't understand at all that jazz musicians are very formal. . . . If you're uninitiated, they may sound like they're playing randomly, but they're really playing—I mean, except for the really avant-garde—they're playing according to harmonic structure, with their own sense of melody and that whole sort of thing. He was looking for something more primitive, I think. I probably told you that line of Art Farmer's. [Varèse] said, "That's fine [what you're playing], but be more free. High, low, loud, soft, explore the full range of your instrument." Then Art said quietly to me, "I've been playing this instrument for eighteen years and I haven't played the full range of it yet. Now he wants me to do it in three seconds!" . . . But everyone was really trying to be thoughtful about it. We respected him, you know, and tried to do what he had in mind, but it wasn't anything that any of us would have chosen to do without having the game designed that way for us to see if we could play it. It's like asking you to play tennis with no net.[58]

Crow characterized Varèse here as a curious but misinformed jazz listener. He returned to the anecdote about Farmer multiple times in our conversation. "That was the joke!" he said. For Crow, Farmer's quip captured the ultimate irony: that the eminent composer did not recognize that discipline was required of jazz musicians if they were to improvise with imagination and virtuosity.

Crow's remark about playing tennis with no net—a reference to Robert Frost's oft-repeated metaphor for writing free verse[59]—highlights racially coded stereotypes of jazz that were common among the uninitiated in the downtown avant-garde and beyond. As many scholars have shown, the legacy of primitivism cast a long shadow over jazz reception, criticism, and history from its inception. By mid-century it was commonplace for outsiders to stereotype jazz musicians as embodying a spontaneous, libidinal creativity "charged with emotion, but largely devoid of intellectual content," and the jazz musician as "the inarticulate and unsophisticated practitioner of an art which he himself scarcely understands."[60] Racialized processes of listening and auditory imagination police such stereotypes along the "sonic color line," as Jennifer Stoever puts it.[61] Bill Crow's words pointed both to the lack of direction Varèse offered the players in setting the musical terms of the improvisation, and to the primitivist stereotypes underlying the belief that jazz musicians required no rules and would not even be able to follow them. Like other jazz musicians of the period, Crow bristled at the racialized assumption that jazz musicians perform at their best without disciplined techniques, ideas, idioms, and history. As a white musician dedicated to performing in interracial ensembles and committed to civil rights politics, Crow appears to have been alert to the damage inflicted by everyday primitivist stereotypes. Later in our interview, he summed up Varèse's reaction to the jazz musicians as "Well, that was nice, but I was hoping for something wilder." Crow's words evoke the double bind enforced by stereotypes: the musicians were expected to be wild and free but judged to be neither wild nor free enough.[62] In an interview from 1965, Varèse seemed to make just such a judgment when he declared, "With jazz [musicians], the ones who could have been good become very conventional," before reminiscing about his encounter with

Charlie Parker as an example of someone who to his mind exemplified this trajectory.[63]

Considered in relation to such primitivist expectations, the music on the recordings becomes more meaningful. From the opening excerpt, we can hear that the musicians brought their own "net" to the sessions—a set of rules and strategies that included the newest techniques of modal jazz. In this regard it is important to remember the political and social significance that some jazz musicians attributed to modal jazz improvisation. George Russell—one of the composers most associated with the emergence of modal jazz, who played with many of the musicians at the Greenwich House sessions—saw it as an antidote to the kinds of primitivist stereotypes that Crow identified in Varèse's reactions. With its emphasis on a knowledge of music theory and specialized technique, modal jazz partook in the modernist legacy of bebop by attempting to "convince—to try again to convince small-minded people that if you have any kind of sensitivity at all, you can see that this music does not come from someone who lacks complexity."[64]

Interpreted within this wider political and social frame, modal jazz's allusions to Global South musical cultures assume a heightened relevance. These allusions speak to a history of jazz as "partially rooted in and routed through the wealth of transformations undergone by extraterritorial sonic materials" afforded by the status of the United States as an imperial and neoimperial power, as described by Jairo Moreno.[65] Yet they also amount to more than a merely sensationalist exoticism that disavows colonial and postcolonial realities. Cultivating transnational identifications within the imperial metropolis of New York, musicians such as Russell believed themselves to have found, as Monson puts it, "kindred musical spirits in the improvisational, melodically rich classical musics of India and the Middle East"—a musical interest that also resonated with "a broader interest in India and Africa on the part of the developing civil rights movement."[66] Jazz's expanding intercultural dialogues drew strength from a politicized African diasporic and anticolonial consciousness, animated and circumscribed by "the world *as* that which is possible to experience and understand from the perspective of empire's center," in Moreno's terms.[67] For his part, Mingus made his own brand of politicized African diasporic and anticolonial consciousness explicit in works like "Haitian Fight Song." None of this is to say that the Greenwich House improvisation carried a straightforward political meaning. But it is to say that the style and techniques of improvisation bore significances quite different from the common primitivist assumptions that shaped Varèse's approach—a disparity that deepens as we consider the following examples.

RECORDED EPISODE 2: "THAT ONE FEELS GOOD!"

In this second excerpt, which immediately follows the improvisation discussed above on the reel labeled "Jazz Graphs Varèse Orig.," Varèse and his associates (likely Brown and Macero) repeatedly ask the tuba player (likely Don Butterfield) to produce a particular timbral effect.[68] This recording provides a clue as to the shifting purpose of the sessions and their relation to Varèse's *Poème électronique,* which incorporated sounds similar to those produced on the tuba alongside other sound samples that Varèse captured on tape. The excerpt also documents the verbal social interactions of the musicians, providing insight into the way the sessions' initial terms of encounter became transformed.

For a second we hear the jackhammer-like sound of a low-register, flutter-tongued tuba. At least two indistinct voices respond, followed by static in the recording. Someone says, "Shh!" Someone else (not Varèse) commands, "Now *hit* it!" The flutter-tongued tuba sound returns for four seconds. "All right, stop guarding that." "Shh!" The sound returns for five more seconds. Voices mumble in the background. "Shh!" Another musician (Butterfield on tuba?) asks, "Is he taping it?" Varèse replies, "Yes, yes, *yes!*" Another musician with a strong, nasal East Coast accent (perhaps Macero) insists, "You're *on,* you're *on!*" Three more seconds of fluttertonguing follow. Another voice enters, possibly that of Earle Brown: "It's gotta be *quiet* in here, because we're gonna *use* this, fellas!" A chorus replies, "Yeah, yeah, yeah." We hear rustling and movement. "Shh!" Then the tuba flutter-tongues for five seconds more, followed by a pause and four more seconds of the same rumbling sound. After the sound dies away, the musicians burst into applause. "*That* one feels good!" someone calls out.

This excerpt reveals the mixture of humor and earnestness with which the musicians approached the task of producing, listening to, and recording a relatively humble sound. Varèse's compositional practice depended on a discipline of "attentive listening," which sought to "coax novelty from the banal, insignificant, and arcane" in "the very monotony of sustaining, repeating, restriking, and replaying."[69] What remains fascinating about this sound excerpt is the way such a personal discipline of attentive listening *resituates* itself within a collaborative setting—itself an openended "experiment" or "try" at something. Musicians other than Varèse (most likely Macero and Brown) tried to direct the scene, but they hardly seem in control of it. Though the musicians agree that it is important to "be quiet in here" ("Yeah, yeah, yeah"), the group's overall noisiness precludes a hushed listening and recording environment (as did the space's poor soundproofing). In a buzz of activity and excitement, the musicians attend to the flutter-tongued sounds with an "attentive listening," so that the right sound might be captured on tape. The colorful proof of their attentiveness lies in their applause—their apparently unanimous judgment of the last flutter-tongued sound as superior. Someone (probably Brown) insisted that they were going to "*use* this," so we know that the musicians must have had some awareness of a purpose for the sessions, however vague it might have been.

This recording's most likely intended fate was inclusion in a collection of sound sources for electronic composition. The rumbling noise of the tuba bears a striking similarity to the sound of square waves produced by oscillators of the period, though the tuba sounds timbrally richer. The sound of the flutter-tongued tuba, moreover, specifically resembles the square-wave tone that is layered with machine sounds at 1:10 in the *Poème électronique,* which, as noted above, Varèse would compose at the Philips Corporation headquarters at least a couple of months after this recording took place. Other sound excerpts in the Varèse Collection consist of jazz instrumentalists playing glissandi and wah-wah sounds in various registers across extremely wide intervals. These examples also resemble sounds producible by oscillators while recalling Varèse's long-standing interest in sirens as instruments that destabilize the distinction between sound and noise.[70]

These sound effects raise the question of whether Varèse experimented with jazz musicians as instrumentalists capable of producing sounds analogous to those generated by the electronic instruments of the day—the unwieldiness of which he publicly lamented.[71] This question resonates with Varèse's history of exploring analogies between electronic and acoustic instruments in *Déserts,*[72] alongside his admiration of Charlie Parker's indefinable tone color ("You could not know if it was an angelic double bass, a saxophone, or a bass clarinet").[73] It also raises the specter of dehumanizing mechanical stereotypes that frame appropriations of Black culture more generally (even in the case of this tuba sound, played by the white performer of a Black-coded music). As Bill Brown and Louis Chude-Sokei show, such mechanical stereotypes are rooted in the "ontological scandal" at the heart of slavery, the slippage between person and object.[74] This ontology persisted and continued to persist after Reconstruction, materializing itself concretely, for example, in the kitsch of wind-up toys and mechanical banks depicting minstrel characters.[75] It also atomized the Black body in antebellum and postbellum medical experimentation, as described by Hortense Spillers: "The entire captive community becomes a living laboratory."[76] We will return to such questions of captivity and objectification, with specific attention to Varèse's creative circles and French technoprimitivism.

Ultimately, neither this excerpt nor any other recording from the sessions entered into the textures of Varèse's electronic composition. The recording is notable not for capturing a clean sound sample ready for incorporation into electronic music, but for documenting a vividly interactive scene. The musicians' vocal responsiveness precluded an "ideal" recording environment. To be sure, I would not describe this circumstance as evidence of a deliberate resistance to Varèse's recording project on the part of the jazz musicians. But I would describe the scene as an intensely dialogical one, in which the composer's opening terms of engagement became renegotiated over the course of the musicians' shifting interactions. It resembled third space as the "emergence of a dialogical site—a moment of enunciation, identification, negotiation—that was suddenly divested of its mastery or sovereignty in the midst of a markedly asymmetrical and unequal engagement of forces."[77] Ultimately, the tape could not function as a clean source for the jackhammer-like sounds we hear in the *Poème électronique*, and it lay dormant for many years—evidence of a garrulous but fraught site of encounter.

RECORDED EPISODE 3: "THIS IS NOT *NATURAL* FOR ME!"

The final excerpt to be considered (also from the reel labeled "Jazz Graphs Varèse Orig.") provides more elaborate documentation of the way in which such scenes unfolded, with divergent expectations for musical engagement and unforeseeable creative outcomes.[78] Alongside the sounds of musicians likely reading from a graphic score, we hear something that sounds like a subtle contest of leadership between Varèse and Mingus, which shapes the exchange of knowledge on all sides.

After some ambient noise (a plane flying overhead) and a false start, Varèse announces, "One second! . . . All right! . . . Four!" at which point the instrumentalists play continuously for about twenty seconds. Led by the trumpet, the texture quickly comes to include tenor saxophone, trombone, bass, and tuba. The musicians are experimenting in an unfamiliar idiom, and their playing reflects the strain of this challenge, with little room for nuance in phrasing, tone, or dynamics. We hear a thick and busy texture of oscillating lines across all parts, without a clear sense of meter or harmonic center, and with no complete breaks in texture. Against a relatively muddy background in the bass, tuba, and trombone, the trumpet repeats and varies a downwardly inflected midregister motive within a single scale, while the tenor saxophone plays erratic, ascending run-

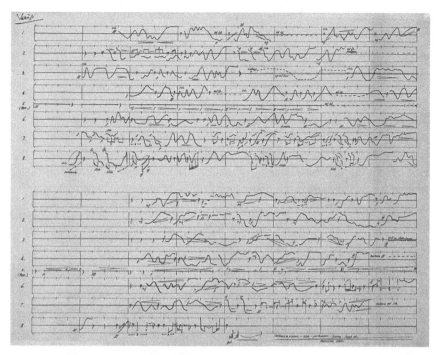

FIGURE 1.2. Edgard Varèse, fragment of a graphic score for a jazz improvisation (1957), fair copy by Chou Wen-chung. Edgard Varèse Collection, Paul Sacher Foundation. Used by permission.

ning figures, moving into the treble register. The musicians tend to orient themselves around B-flat, but they nonetheless do not play in a single key, scale, or mode. Frequent glissandi also characterize the instrumental parts, further destabilizing any sense of tonal center.

Given the character of this texture and its instrumental parts—together with Varèse's reference to measure numbers—it seems likely that the musicians were reading from a graphic score similar to a fragment found in the Varèse Collection, a fair copy attributed to Chou Wen-chung (figure 1.2). The fragment is labeled for jazz instruments and features unpitched, oscillating melodic contours across eight instrumental parts in four-beat measures, with fine-tuned dynamics and occasional expressive markings.[79] (The contours do not readily correspond to any of the passages of improvisation preserved on reels from Greenwich House, indicating that performance of the fragment may not have been recorded, that musicians may have ignored the score's contours in performance, or that recordings may have been lost.) The fragment resembles Varèse's manuscript score and sketches for electronic sounds in *Déserts*.[80] Indeed, as

Mattis observes, the very same score was later used as a sketch for electronic sounds in the *Poème électronique*—a fact that again leads us to question whether Varèse imagined jazz musicians as producing sounds that might resemble (or improve upon) those of electronic instruments. Chou Wen-chung recalls that the score was made "after some of the sessions" had already taken place. "Varèse showed [Chou] a sketch that he did but he [Varèse] was not happy with it," so Varèse asked Chou "to recreate it in the style of Chinese calligraphy which he admired."[81] This detail vividly speaks to the postwar tendency of "artists and intellectuals within hip culture [to] put [African American] symbols in play with others from European and Asian literary and intellectual traditions," in the words of Phil Ford.[82] Chou believes that musicians in the sessions "played from the multi-part chart when they did the recording," though he did not attend the sessions and cannot be sure.[83]

More than any other excerpt from the session recordings, this one captures the musicians' verbal exchanges as they work through the problems of performing in such an unfamiliar idiom, format, and setting. The first twenty-second fragment disintegrates into noncohesion and then silence, after which someone says, "No, you were one bar ahead," prompting some muttered responses. A baton taps on a stand, after which a distinctive voice with a French accent announces, "Once more, please! Once more we play! . . . Four . . . one!" (The unity of these sounding gestures reveals Varése wielding the baton.) The musicians produce a texture similar to the one just heard, but with greater transparency in the bottom register and some altered note choices and rhythmic variations. About twenty seconds into their playing, following a saxophone and trombone exchange, Varèse yells, "No, *no!*" The trombone keeps playing, and someone exclaims over the trombone, "Jimmy's right, *Jimmy's* right!" possibly referring to trombonist Jimmy Knepper, who had recently become a regular in Mingus's Jazz Workshop.[84] Varèse: "Eh?" Another musician chimes in, "We were out, *he* was right!" Another quietly mumbles, "Yeah, yeah, he was right." And then Varèse tries to command the scene again, announcing, "Once more!" Someone interrupts, "We was a voice short!" A chorus of others responds, "Yeah, yeah, yeah!" Another player adds, "I was takin' a breath like a beat too long, ya know!?," erupting into laughter. Varèse announces, "All right, we'll do it again. It doesn't matter! . . . All right . . . ," and we hear the flipping of pages. At this point a voice that sounds distinctively like Mingus's interjects, "And look, look, uhh . . . this is not *natural* for me!" "All right?" Varèse asks in a higher, strained voice. We hear the sound of stands moving and pages rustling. The player (Mingus) asks his fellow musicians, one by one, "Is this okay with you?" as he noisily rearranges the stands and they casually reply in the affirmative, "Sure." Varèse adds, "For me, I don't care. I'll turn a little bit that way, eh."

In two subsequent excerpts, separated by the stopping and starting of the tape, we hear the musicians rehearsing the same passage from the score, each time sounding better, with greater ensemble cohesion and textural transparency, and a stronger sense of dynamic and articulative contrast in the profiles of individual gestures.[85] At one point, in the penultimate recorded rendition of the passage, Mingus interrupts, "I'm sorry!" after a falling, down-bow glissando from the bass. Varèse insists, laughingly, "No! You were right, you were right on time!" Another musician owns up to having been wrong, and Varèse resumes, "All right, one more time," tapping his stand with the baton. A voice that sounds like Earle Brown's points out, "You know, this would be much easier slower, so we could . . ." and the tape cuts off.[86]

Though not explicitly identified, Varèse's and Mingus's voices are readily discernible, not just because of their distinctive timbres and accents— which are well documented in historical recordings—but also because of the contrasting social roles they commanded with these voices, which enacted a duel of authority. Varèse assumed the role of the conducting maestro. As a bandleader with an increasingly formidable reputation, Mingus wielded authority through his masterful knowledge of music in its most adventurous forms. Within a group of musicians who responded to Varèse with alacrity, Mingus took his engagement even further: he intervened to clarify the ensemble's mistakes in score reading, and rearranged the player's positions so as to improve their sight lines, asking their permission.

At the beginning of the session, the musicians' stands may have been positioned concert-style to face the conductor—the setup that was "not *natural*" for Mingus. In rearranging the stands, Mingus improved conditions for improvising the music as a conversation—the fundamental model and metaphor for jazz performance that would have been less familiar to Varèse.[87] With this move, he challenged the limitations of Varèse's initial vision while altering the musicians' conditions for engagement. We hear the musical implications of these third-space transformations in the two subsequent takes, which improve upon the previous ones. At the same time, a changed social dynamic becomes audible: as others make suggestions and provide leadership, Varèse becomes somewhat divested of sovereignty as "maestro" while he also enters *into* the group through his own laughter.

In light of this innovative music and unusual collaboration, the paradox of the musicians' relative silence on the sessions deepens. The music testifies to the singular creative nature of the sessions, an unpredictable amalgam of Varèse's poetics and those of the jazz musicians who formed the recorded ensembles. Many of the additional recorded performances show a distinctive preoccupation with noise, timbre, and effects of articulation, with little emphasis placed on harmonic and melodic cohesion or regular meter.[88] Silence and transparent textures dramatically set off the music's particularized gestures, which often relate to one another through call and response. This unique approach to form and improvisation stands out from other experimental jazz of the period, and is perhaps comparable only to the free jazz currents of the subsequent decade.[89] In the improvisatory setting of Greenwich House, the ossified categories of "classical" and "jazz" loosen in a flux of creative play. It is possible that such experimentation would have provided creative rewards for the musicians, although these would have been inseparable from the stress that resounds in Mingus's words, "This is not *natural* for me!" These words may be heard as responding to more than just performer sight lines in a narrow sense, but also to the whole scene of interaction oriented by Varèse's primitivist gaze.

Varèse's and Mingus's muteness about the sessions as a historical event jars with the exceptionality of their collaboration, positioning the scene as a zone of conflict and ambivalence. In the remainder of this chapter we will further excavate these two musicians' backgrounds in order to consider why they might not have wanted to take ownership of the innovations at Greenwich House, setting the conditions for their silence. We will also consider Brown and Macero's participation in more depth. The purpose of this exploration is not to enter narrowly into "the minds of great men," but rather to recognize the conflicted identifications, affect, and agendas that characterize such encounters and present singular challenges for a historiography of music in the imperial metropolis. Mingus's and Varèse's shared musical-experimental sensibilities ultimately risk signifying as "false cognates" because of the civil rights politics that powerfully animated Mingus's creative vision and militated against Varèse's primitivism.

Primitivism, Disavowal, and the Palimpsest

Throughout his career, Varèse's feelings toward jazz vacillated between repugnance and desire. During the 1920s, at the height of negrophilia in the Parisian avant-garde, Varèse expressed a decidedly negrophobic and nativist antipathy toward jazz, all the while embracing primitivist tropes of the New World "noble savage." Varèse's seeming "change of heart" about jazz followed the increasing legitimation of the genre in American culture at mid-century, particularly among a younger generation of composers (including Brown and Macero) who came to see Varèse as a forefather of American concert traditions, in which they also envisioned jazz playing a role. Such legitimation embodied the illusory "vision of color-blind American democracy" officially promoted in American cultural diplomacy, a message to which Varèse may well have been attuned in pursuing professional opportunities of cultural ambassadorship at the Brussels World's Fair.[90] Varèse's turn toward jazz remained riven by the ambivalence that attends ideals of white purity.

The historical record shows that Varèse avowed such ideals of purity, at least from the late 1920s onward, and that these ideals connected him with nativist New York music circles. In July 1928, after fourteen years in the United States, Varèse made the following statements about race, music, and American identity in an interview published in *Le Figaro hebdomadaire* on the subject of the "American musical avant-garde": "Jazz is not America. It's a negro product, exploited by the Jews. All of its composers from [the United States] are Jews. Jazz does not represent America any more than slow waltzes represent Germany. . . . I do not write jazz. . . . Jazz is without ideas. It's noise on which you hop around."[91] In one stroke, Varèse denigrated both Jewish and Black music as "noise," following a long-standing racist trope that disparages the humanity of its targets.[92] (Indeed, his use of the term "noise" here contrasts ironically with his later valorization of the term to describe his own aesthetic projects.)[93] Varèse's words amounted to more than an isolated expression of personal prejudice.[94] By 1928 the composer had spearheaded efforts to define American modernism by founding the New Symphony Orchestra, the International Composers Guild (ICG), and the Pan American Association of Composers (PAAC), in collaboration with such figures as Henry Cowell, Carlos Salzedo, and Carl Ruggles.[95] Scholars have acknowledged the anti-Semitism that characterized these groups—with a particular emphasis on Ruggles's habitual bigotry—and linked it with the secession of some Jewish ICG members and the formation of the League of Composers.[96] Mattis describes the real targets of Varèse's statements in *Le Figaro hebdomadaire* as "Copland, Marc Blitzstein, Louis Gruenberg and other Jewish students of Nadia Boulanger who adopted the neo-classical idiom and based their thematic materials on elements of jazz."[97] We cannot know with certainty which musics and musicians Varèse primarily associated with the label "jazz," but his 1928 disparagement cannot simply be read as a momentary expression of professional rivalry or aesthetic dissatisfaction with the incorporation of jazz idioms by composers—of whatever genre—who happened to be Jewish. Rather, he belonged to a creative circle that imbibed race-based, nativist ideologies that were powerful, pervasive, and thoroughly mainstream, as Rachel Mundy has described.[98] At stake was the question of *which* "indigenous" cultures could serve as legitimate sources for a thriving national composition scene, how racial exclusion should play a part, and how American musical culture should be projected onto a world stage.

Given Varèse's role as transatlantic emissary, it is striking that he positioned himself so closely to American nativists like Carl Ruggles. The choice sets him apart from some of his main creative interlocutors in Paris during the period, who tended to celebrate Black culture in exoticist terms—visual artists such as Pablo Picasso and Fernand Léger, and the composer Albert Roussel.[99] Nativism, in the defining words of historian John Higham, is the "intense opposition to an internal minority on the ground of its foreign (i.e. 'un-American') connections"—an opposition that may "vary widely" in its targets, intensity, and modes of expression while nonetheless constituting a "connecting, energizing force of modern nationalism."[100] Nativist projects seek to define American citizenry and culture in explicitly racial (rather than political or economic) terms, as exemplified in the Immigration Act of 1924. United States nativism ran parallel to similar currents elsewhere, including interwar xenophobia and anti-Semitism in France, which Jane F. Fulcher describes as treating race "not as a synonym for nationality . . . but as a synthesis of both culture and blood."[101]

Varèse in the 1920s may be understood as a "nativist modernist" because he participated in national aesthetic efforts that refracted nativist impulses, as described by literary theorist Walter Benn Michaels. Noting that definitions of aesthetic modernism vary widely, Michaels nonetheless stresses that many accounts "acknowledge its interest in the ontology of the sign—which is to say, in the materiality of the signifier, in the relation of signifier to signified, in the relation of sign to referent."[102] Some modernisms enact a fantasy of escaping the contingency of this relation, of "turning the sign back to the bedrock of World/Nature/Sensation/Subjectivity" (in T. J. Clark's words) or showing how the sign "might function, in effect, onomatopoetically, without reliance upon a system of syntactic and semantic conventions" (in Michaels's words).[103] Although these accounts focus on literary and visual modernisms, we should note that Varèse's compositions persistently explored such lines of inquiry in musical ways. Dissatisfied with the abstract and "arbitrary subdivision of the octave," he sought to combine unpitched sounds that indexed their own physical origins in the noisy actions of a material world—working with a musical kind of onomatopoeia, or a direct linkage of sound and sound source.[104] Michaels posits a "structural intimacy" between this kind

of modernist aspiration—to render the sign and referent nonarbitrary—
and nativist fantasies about culture, community, family, and the nation.[105]
Both seek alternatives to contingent relations, whether chancy syntac-
tic/semantic/formal ones (in artworks) or nonfamilial/nonbiological/
nonracialized ones (in national citizenship). These twinned nativist-
modernist impulses helped to motivate Varèse's projects before and
during World War II.[106]

Indeed, Varèse periodically expressed attraction to fascist movements,
and his futurism mingled with strands of racism, xenophobia, and ho-
mophobia in Parisian and New York avant-gardes.[107] Take, for example,
his relationship with his student William Grant Still. The Varèse Collection includes a defaced clipping of Still's 1937 article, "Are Negro Composers Still Handicapped?" Around the side of Still's image, Varèse scrawled,
"What a pitiful ham and poor cunt, in the end a poor bastard. THE
END of being the Good Samaritan."[108] These high-handed words of hatred targeted Still for speaking out in print about racial inequality, denigrating Still's race while denigrating his masculinity. In a similar vein,
Varèse would write to Carl Ruggles in 1944, "Christ, it seems impossible
to get help and support for something healthy and white. But use your
arse as a prick garage—or your mouth as a night lodging (look Copland
open day and night [sic], not to speak of his competing boyfriends—
what a fine virile-spiritual group you sent me!) and (to start with): N.Y. is
yours."[109] Such words show how Varèse drew from a nexus of anti-Semitic,
homophobic, anti-Black, and white-supremacist attitudes to strengthen
bonds of allegiance and affiliation in his professional world. That these
communications transpired in the late 1930s and 1940s—at the height of
the anti-lynching campaign and the Holocaust—is striking.

Because of Varèse's transatlantic background, he spoke from a peculiar cultural and national position: as an outsider-cum-insider representing the "inside" to the "outside" from a nativist ideological perspective as
a non–native-born American citizen. One might question whether his
nativist positions drew animus from an impulse to compensate for his
own French nonnative status in the United States, or indeed in compen-
sation for his partly Italian heritage.[110] As Mundy describes, composers
and critics in the twentieth century sometimes used "French" as a code
word indicating a feminized, mixed-race Jewishness—with Aaron Copland and George Gershwin as primary targets.[111] In 1932, for example,
Henry Cowell distinguished between "'Tin-Pan-Alley' New Yorkers of
Hebrew origin" who had "studied for the most part in Paris" with those
"Yankees" like Ruggles and Ives who "really succeeded in creating a distinctively American style from the soil up."[112] In the face of this racialized

and sexualized binary, Varése benefited professionally by aligning himself with the latter camp. He counts among the "ethnic whites" who, as Matthew D. Morrison describes, demonstrated their bona fides through acts of anti-Black denigration and involvement in "Blacksound."[113]

In seeking to demonstrate his masculine American whiteness, Varèse drew on a wealth of ideological resources from his earliest education in Italy and France. He had long been fascinated by the figure of the "noble savage," a trope that has historically fed into primitivist conceptions of jazz.[114] According to Varèse, the juvenile project that precipitated his serious aspirations to compose was his opera *Martin Paz*, based on the novella by Jules Verne, which featured a noble-savage protagonist in the Americas.[115] This European idea also dovetailed with United States–based nativist modernisms, which sometimes celebrated American "Indians" as a "vanishing race" and thus a sign for "racial integrity."[116] Heidy Zimmermann and Ernst Lichtenhahn have traced Varèse's early Amerindian fascinations in his later composition *Ecuatorial* (1932–34), a tone poem inspired by passages from the *Popol Vuh*.[117] As Mattis observes, Varèse's vision of America from the 1910s onward combined celebrations of primitivism and machine-age modernity—an image that jibed with popular representations of the United States in French high art and vernacular cultures.[118] *Ecuatorial* invested in these dual tropes by combining primitivist chant with state-of-the-art theremin sounds.

Varèse's trailblazing pursuit of electronic musical instruments in the early twentieth century should not be considered contradictory to, or separate from, primitivist aesthetics. Rather, it participated in "technoprimitivism," an aesthetic that reveled in discovering the supposedly archaic in the contemporary, and vice versa.[119] This concept sheds light on some peculiar aspects of the Greenwich House sessions—Varèse's use of jazz musicians to produce sounds analogous to oscillator square waves and his expectation that they read from a style of graphic notation he otherwise reserved for electronic instruments. Jazz became "a sign and sound of [primitive] Africa and [of] the machine," as Chude-Sokei has written about technoprimitivist aesthetics more generally.[120] Within this dehumanizing framework, there was no need to record jazz musicians' names, because their work simply served as a "source for . . . regeneration" within a technoprimitivist colonialist imaginary.[121]

Varèse's collaboration with Le Corbusier on the *Poème électronique* project for the Philips Pavilion at the Brussels World's Fair assumed paramount importance in relation to this technoprimitivist imaginary. Many accounts of the *Poème électronique* stress the independence of Le Corbusier's and Varèse's creative visions, and their lack of coordination in the project.[122] Yet, as their correspondence demonstrates, Le Corbusier initiated Varèse into the project's themes as early as December 1956, and Varèse received plates of primitivist images used as sources for Le Corbusier's film by June 1957.[123] This timing, which coincides with the Greenwich House sessions, allows us to situate Varèse's primitivism around 1957 within a specific creative exchange, rather than simply frame it as a symptom of French or American modernisms more generally.[124]

The architect assigned profound cultural and social significance to jazz.[125] For Le Corbusier, jazz exemplified the redemptive possibilities of a utopian "second machine age"—an idea highly relevant to the *Poème électronique* project.[126] Le Corbusier rhapsodized in stereotyping, technoprimitivist terms: "Negro music has touched America because it is the melody of the soul joined with the rhythm of the machine."[127] Tap dancers moved "as mechanical as a sewing machine."[128] Jazz contained "the past and the present, Africa and pre–machine age Europe and contemporary America."[129] For Le Corbusier, as Chude-Sokei writes, "the negro's supposedly innate ability to swing and jive [were] seen and heard as machine-age spectacles, as elaborate rituals of the submission of art to the logic of the machine."[130] Such technoprimitivist imagery betrayed multiple anxieties. It registered "an old Romantic fear of dehumanizing, depersonalizing technology" in the midst of industrialization, while also suggesting "a much more specific and explicitly American fear: that of an increasingly humanized—which is to say liberated—African-American social, cultural, and political presence."[131] Technoprimitivism put that presence "in its place" by infantalizing it in the process of idealization and spectacularization. Evoking the noble savage, Le Corbusier idealized African Americans as citizens with "virgin ears" and "fresh curiosity," constantly renewed by their music and dance cultures.[132] In the early 1960s, Varèse echoed his colleague's primitivist ideas about jazz musicians when he claimed that his mid-century encounter with Charlie Parker revealed the jazz virtuoso to be "like a child. . . . He possessed tremendous enthusiasm."[133]

By the 1950s, many of Varèse's interlocutors expressed a passionate interest in jazz that ran parallel to the music's increasing public legitimation as an art form. Perhaps the most powerful sign of jazz's changed status was its official inclusion in US projects of cultural diplomacy.[134] In his correspondence with Le Corbusier, Varèse showed a decided awareness of the importance of the Brussels World's Fair—the first full-scale version of the fair since World War II—in the Cold War competition for soft power.[135] The Philips Corporation intended its pavilion to signal their Marshall Plan–fueled resurgence as a multinational corporation following wartime exile and dismemberment. Such celebrations of capitalist revitalization assumed heightened significance in the spirit of the fair's binary ideological competition.[136] In two letters to Le Corbusier, Varèse included clippings of *New York Herald Tribune* and *New York Times* articles that discussed US efforts to "show the spiritual and cultural side of America" and build a pavilion to "counteract exhibits from Iron Curtain countries."[137] Though Varèse expressed no opinion on Cold War politics in his correspondence with Le Corbusier, he wrote approvingly of the publicity it generated for the fair. Meanwhile, at least one official at the State Department questioned Varèse's friendly colleague Vladimir Ussachevsky about ways to amplify the American musical presence there.[138] In his reply, Ussachevsky praised Varèse's participation and recommended others for sponsorship, including Teo Macero, Varèse's collaborator in the Greenwich House sessions.[139] It is impossible to know whether jazz's prominent role in musical cultural diplomacy during this period influenced Varèse's decision to experiment with jazz musicians, but the imprimatur bestowed on jazz by the US government through its cultural diplomacy projects—a government effort that Varèse appeared to value, largely for its side effects of publicity and patronage—may have directed his attention toward the music in the lead-up to his own World's Fair project.

Of equal importance, Varèse's circle at this time included a younger generation of composers who saw him as both a forefather of and a transatlantic spokesman for a maverick American experimental tradition, and who increasingly turned to jazz to redefine that tradition. Earle Brown was one of these composers. A member of Cage's circle and the Eighth Street Artists' Club, Brown met with Varèse on a nearly weekly basis during the the mid- and late 1950s and encouraged the older composer's interest in jazz.[140] As mentioned above, Brown worked as a tape engineer with Capitol Records in 1957, and he used his roster of contacts to help assemble the personnel of the sessions in collaboration with Teo Macero, who also inspired Varèse's interest in the project.

Unlike Cage, Brown described his experiments in graphic notation and "open-form" composition not as a pursuit of chance methods, but as an effort to encourage classical musicians to experiment with improvisation. "I came out of jazz," he explained, "so improvisation and flexible relationships among scoring, performers, and notation were very natural to me."[141] He later characterized his explorations of open-form and graphic notation as an effort to "bridge . . . some aspects of classical music and jazz."[142] One of the most prominent examples of this effort is his composition *Hodograph* (1959), which included a blank space that Brown filled in with calligraphic contour markings roughly comparable to the graphic notation used by Varèse in the Greenwich House sessions, though Brown varied his interpretation of those markings over the course of his career.[143] Brown's white privilege afforded him the power to come "out of jazz" and enter the world of classical music—while continuing to borrow selectively from jazz—in ways that would not have been available to Black musicians like Mingus, with similar aesthetic inclinations. At the same time, Brown privately expressed concern about the power dynamics at the Greenwich House sessions in his correspondence:

> Varèse [is] still having jazz musician sessions but I don't go any more. . . . It seemed to be an obsession with Varèse . . . a substitute for his own writing and inventiveness . . . rather an exploitation of the musicians so I withdrew. . . . Jazz musicians have tried this before themselves and a notation for this sort of thing is implied by Morty [Feldman]'s graph. . . . It's certainly a valid thing but I'm not interested in doing it.[144]

Brown saw his own engagement with jazz as transpiring on a more serious register than that of Varèse, and his concern with questions of exploitation certainly distinguished him from the older composer.

Brown's strong attraction to jazz was shared by the visual artists at the Eighth Street Artists' Club, which he attended alongside Varèse, Cage, Morton Feldman, David Tudor, and Stefan Wolpe. The club was known for its racial and gender exclusions in membership, though select exceptions were made. It featured regular speakers and panel discussions on jazz. The club's fetishization of jazz put on a show of "white hipness" by appropriating Black culture, in Monson's terms, "as a symbol of social conscience, sexual freedom, and resistance to the dominant order"—though with perhaps less emphasis on "social conscience," given that many in the club avoided explicitly political discourse.[145] The artists' avowed affiliation with jazz helped to shape their reception. For example, Jackson Pollock, as art historian Ann Eden Gibson has noted, could be compared "not only to the cowboy, but also to the jazzman, another heroic American image, inventing his composition as he went along."[146] The artists' masculinist heroization of jazz often projected a primitivist sensationalism onto the music, or denigrated the music as "folk art" inspiration for "higher" Euro-American art, differentiated in a racialized hierarchy of value.[147] Jazz worked as a marker that helped to set downtown New York creators apart from the European modernist traditions from which they simultaneously sought legitimation and distinction.

Like other artists and composers at the Eighth Street Artists' Club, Brown envisioned their avant-garde innovations as participating in a specifically American tradition, though he eschewed heavy-handed or overt expressions of nationalism.[148] According to him, the downtown scene centered at the Eighth Street Artists' Club was a "tremendously powerful American art movement. . . . We were all in a kind of creative soup together"—a melting pot that included jazz.[149] The terms under which white musicians at the Eighth Street Artists' Club engaged with jazz varied widely. Stefan Wolpe, for example, developed abiding friendships with both Black and white jazz musicians. Unlike Varèse, Wolpe tended to be more inspired by jazz's formally heterogeneous textures and its civil rights politics than by primitivist fetishes; he also grew disenchanted by the club's white machismo.[150] In addition to Wolpe and Brown, other younger composers in the downtown scene also performed or took an interest in jazz, including James Tenney.[151]

Brown's claim of Varèse as a forefather to the "American iconoclastic tradition" echoed Cage's gesture toward Varèse in his 1950s definition of "American experimental music"—a fact that speaks to the urgent and energetic discursive construction of this tradition within their circles from the 1950s to the late twentieth century. Indeed, Varèse was the only non–native-born composer included in the 1959 essay "Fifteen Composers in the American Experimental Tradition," by Peter Yates. In it, Yates singled out "fifteen fighting names of American composers" who had been "central to the growth in American music of a continental individuality."[152] All of the composers on the list were white and male, with only one of Jewish descent (that one being Aaron Copland, whom Yates also described in the anti-Semitic trope of the Jew who lacks inborn talent but compensates through "sophistication").[153] Locating his "fifteen fighting names" within an American mythology of anti-institutionalism and outsiderdom, Yates included a "maturer understanding of jazz" as a central feature of his fifteen composers' musical thought and creation.[154] Jazz represented "a separate, special part" of "American creative musical experience"—his fifteen composers had "seldom borrowed from it," but had "assimilated it."[155] Such words simultaneously evoke ideas of racial segregation and white mastery. Showing characteristic nativist-nationalist bravado, Yates privately labeled his essay "a classic, a paean of defiance, an American über alles."[156]

Significantly, Yates capped his discussion of Varèse with a techno-primitivist allusion to the composer's electronic composition and interest in jazz: "A fully equipped electronic sound laboratory has been placed at his disposal to explore what he calls 'shaped sound' in a diversity of styles, including jazz."[157] It is not clear whether the "laboratory . . . placed at his disposal" was a reference to the Philips Corporation Studio or the newly founded Columbia-Princeton Electronic Music Center (CPEMC), where Varèse also worked occasionally. What is clear, however, is that Varèse's laboratory-driven interest in jazz placed him within Yates's canon of white American music. Moreover, Yates's essay was intended for—and found—a large global audience. In addition to its publication in the bulletin of the New York Public Library (NYPL), a revised version also became the preface to the first volume of *Some Twentieth-Century American Composers: A Selective Bibliography* (1959–60), also published by the NYPL and widely distributed by the US State Department abroad.[158] As Amy Beal describes, Yates wrote the essay in dialogue with John Cage and NYPL curator John Edmunds.[159] Cage delivered his own famous essay "History of Experimental Music in the United States" (1959) at Darmstadt the same year, elaborating a genealogy that also included Varèse, though he excluded jazz and articulated his arguments in less overtly national-chauvinist terms. The close timing of Cage's Darmstadt lecture and Yates's globally distributed publication helped to crystallize the status of "American experimentalism" as a familiar genealogy—with Varèse as forefather—that gained currency well beyond the New York art and music scenes.

In this context, Yates and Cage's circle and its discourse of American experimentalism both enhanced and benefited from the revival enjoyed by Varèse's music during the 1950s. The émigré's public profile resurged after the release of the commercially successful first volume of the *Complete Works of Edgard Varèse* by EMS in 1950, his long-awaited and much-fêted entry into electronic music composition, and the culmination of this experimentation in the heavily publicized premieres of *Déserts* (1954) and the *Poème électronique* (1958). Mid-century popular depictions of the composer celebrated him in hyperbolic terms that combined a reverence for the great European traditions of high art with pride in an American spirit of modernity, invention, pragmatism, and scientific ingenuity.[160] For example, a 1954 profile of Varèse published by the magazine *High Fidelity* characterized him as "a genius within the Great Tradition of Beethovenian iconoclasm," who "pressed the 'start' button of his Ampex 401-A, with the confidence and determination of a Beethoven rapping out the germ-motif of the Fifth Symphony."[161]

It is significant here that *High Fidelity* paired this profile of Varèse with a piece by Nat Hentoff titled ". . . Jazz in Mid-Passage," which posed the following question: "European music-lovers long have accepted jazz as a major American contribution to Western culture. Now, are we going to, too?"[162] In this article Hentoff praised jazz's growing "utilization of contemporary classical techniques," making reference to the Jazz Composers Workshop's recent performances at Carnegie Recital Hall and the Museum of Modern Art under the leadership of Macero, Mingus, and others.[163] For a composer like Earle Brown, who similarly wanted to "bridge . . . classical music and jazz," it would seem natural to try to interest his mentor Varèse in this endeavor. Meanwhile, Varèse was acquiring a growing reputation among jazz musicians, enhanced by his 1950 record release and subsequent media coverage (a subject to which we will return). Brown recalled Varèse as "very flattered, easily flattered" by jazz musicians' admiration, a circumstance that further prompted Brown and Varèse to organize the Greenwich House sessions.[164]

Equally important was Varèse's friendship with Teo Macero, who devoted his compositional career to integrating avant-garde jazz and classical musics. Like Brown, Macero recalls having met with Varèse on a nearly weekly basis from the mid-1950s; their friendship became so close that Macero came to see the émigré as a "second father."[165] Macero probably met Varèse through his composition teacher Henry Brant, with whom he studied at the Juilliard School until 1953 while experimenting with electronic tape. He joined Columbia Records as a tape editor in 1957 and later enjoyed a long career there as a producer, celebrated for his intensive collaborations with Miles Davis, Dave Brubeck, Thelonious Monk, Charles Mingus, and others. At the time of the Greenwich House sessions, however, he was still best known as a tenor saxophonist and composer, finding fullest expression in his work with the Jazz Composers Workshop and his collaborations with Mingus, including their jointly led Newport Festival sets of 1954 and 1955. Again like Brown, Macero experimented with graphic notation as an outgrowth of jazz performance. His piece *Fusion* (1958) used contour graphs similar to Varèse's in order to indicate melodic profiles for jazz musicians to play.[166] Indeed, Varèse had apparently given Macero a page of graphic notation used in the 1957 sessions, inscribing it with the words "Here is the first sketch of our experiment. Cordially, Varèse."[167]

Such questions of graphic notation bring us back to the role of jazz in the conception and precompositional materials of the *Poème électronique*. In addition to the already discussed "jazz" graphic notation used as a sketch for electronic sounds in *Poème*, Mattis also describes some sound objects in the piece that Varèse labeled in his manuscript as "jazz-spurts"—a term that "might well refer to the many 'spurts' of percussion music heard throughout the work."[168] Perhaps Varèse turned to jazz as an inspiration for percussive sound effects, though we should note that the percussion "spurts" in the *Poème électronique*—mostly written for snare drum, with some claves and conga drums—do not sound strictly jazz-like in either instrumentation or feel. Varèse's association of these sounds with jazz might indicate that he had familiarity with Afro-Cuban jazz, or it might suggest a generalized conflation of African diasporic and Latin American cultures, characteristic of the French negrophilic milieus to which he belonged.[169]

Moreover, Varèse wrote, circled, and energetically recircled the phrase "chant-jazz-perc" in what appears to have been an early sketch for the Poème—a previously unnoticed sketch annotation worth interpreting in relation to his primitivist aesthetics.[170] Though Varèse did not bring excerpts from the Greenwich House recordings into the composition, he did incorporate multiple sound samples of vocal music in addition to percussion sounds, which he carefully notated, rehearsed, and recorded in the year prior to the World's Fair. The notated sketches and source sound samples for the Poème électronique contain more chant and percussion textures than are found in the final composition. If we think of "chant-jazz-perc" as a conceptual and musical grouping—a three-part compound of sonic topoi that were linked together in Varèse's conception of the piece—then it is all the more fascinating that jazz is the one element of this compound that eventually disappeared from the piece's audible final rendering. To be sure, percussion and chant had long featured in Varèse's music as emblems of his primitivist aesthetic, Ecuatorial serving as a prime example. The Poème électronique therefore returned to familiar ground at its most blatantly primitivist moments: at 4:17, for example, when a snare-dominated percussion texture precedes and accompanies a nonclassical male voice chanting nonsense syllables in a stereotyped "tribal" style; or at 6:00, when a claves-and-conga ensemble cuts in and out, leading to a section that intersperses electronic and recorded percussion sounds. At the Philips Pavilion, Varèse's music and Le Corbusier's projected images interacted with one another in a counterpoint of references that were meaningful within a shared primitivist imaginary. Yet this imaginary also remained strikingly far from the world of jazz that Varèse encountered at the Greenwich House improvisation sessions. The distance between these worlds might help to explain why Varèse eventually erased "jazz" as a concept or sound world in his final rendering of Poème électronique.

Rather than trying to use the recordings of his new jazz experiments as a sound source for electronic composition, in the Poème Varèse returned to familiar primitivist tropes and sounds. Perhaps, as Bill Crow suggested, the composer entered the Greenwich House sessions with primitivist expectations of jazz that his actual encounters failed to confirm. The reality of his collaboration—with its messy cultural translations and negotiations of authority—may have remained both too threatening and too distant from his stereotypes of what jazz should symbolize for his collaboration with Le Corbusier. The available evidence suggests that Varèse's notion of jazz was probably informed by the idea that rhythm—as opposed to melody or harmony—was its most salient parameter, as suggested by his reference to jazz in connection with percussion in the *Poème* sketches;[171] by the notion that jazz provided otherwise inaccessible timbral resources, in keeping with Varèse's words about Charlie Parker; and by a negrophilic conflation of diverse African diasporic traditions, which dovetailed with Varèse's long-standing attraction both to Latin American sounds and to the trope of the New World "noble savage."

Varèse's subsequent silence about the Greenwich House sessions contributes to jazz's palimpsestlike presence-in-absence within the *Poème*. Whatever interest in jazz he showed early on in the composition of the *Poème* became, as it were, "overwritten" by other primitivist fascinations exemplified by the chant and percussion sounds he sampled and actually incorporated into the work's textures. Signs of Varèse's engagement with *actual* jazz—rather than vague negrophilic ideas about jazz—would arise only later, resurfacing in the traces of the archive and in oral history.

Avant-Garde Ambivalence

Charles Mingus's silence in relation to the Greenwich House sessions calls out for sustained attention, because it would seem out of sync with his habitually trenchant outspokenness. Aside from Macero's oral account, the recordings, and the presence of Varèse's address in Mingus's address book, few clues speak to the jazz composer's participation in the sessions, let alone his reactions to it. Yet while Mingus had almost nothing to say about Varèse in the published and unpublished words that have been preserved for posterity, a rare exception is provided by a recently published interview with the jazz critic John F. Goodman from 1972. This interview—filled with protective silences and rich observations on Mingus's part—provides an opportunity for reflection on the composer's ambivalence toward the avant-garde and on the feelings of rejection he experienced in response to primitivist stereotypes. As we will see, this ambivalence also infused his participation in the emergent third stream genre and his composition of "Pithecanthropus Erectus"—the musical innovations of which loosely prefigure those of Varèse's experiment at Greenwich House.

In the interview with Goodman, Mingus made a passing reference to having listened to Varèse's music within a larger discussion of his critical discussion about ideas of the "avant-garde."[172] In jazz settings, "avant-garde" is often used as a near synonym for "free jazz" in reference to a stylistic category or movement, following Ornette Coleman's eponymous album of 1961. Yet in Mingus's conversation with Goodman, the term assumed fluid and changeable meanings. Among other things, it designated experimentalist jazz-classical crossover trends that predated *Free Jazz*; downtown New York concert music, and visual art scenes associated with Varèse; and progressivist notions of history in the arts more generally, which tended toward both color-blind universalism and anti-Black primitivism, as Kwami Coleman shows.[173] If the capacious term "avant-garde" designated common ground between Mingus and Varèse, then Mingus's critiques show just how shaky this ground was from his perspective. As we have discussed, the third space is an anxious, power-ridden, transitional scene of translation. In the case of the Greenwich House sessions, "avant-garde" is a problematic term of translation that helped to motivate and characterize that ambivalent scene.

Mingus's candid, freely associative conversation with Goodman is worth following in detail, because it shows the composer's attunement to racialized power dynamics that shaped ideas of the avant-garde in jazz and classical music in the 1950s. Goodman recalled that much of his free-flowing interview with Mingus revolved around the term "avant-garde," which they discussed as "cultural, artistic (formal), critical (categories), and [in] economic terms."[174] Whereas Goodman had "grown to detest" the term "avant-garde"—with all of the "confusions over where and how it applied"—Mingus seemed eager to debate it further, though he balked at its identification with his own music.[175] As Eric Porter has stressed, Mingus recognized early on that the categories "jazz" and "classical" were "informed by racialized ideas about virtuosity and genius that . . . contributed to inequality in the music business."[176] This awareness permeated his discussion of ideas of the avant-garde with Goodman. At the time of the interview, Mingus was in the middle of an artistic comeback after years of depression and relative professional inactivity, and the interviews show him energetically reflecting back on the years in the 1950s that had established his reputation as a major innovator. He remembered that the critic Barry Ulanov had characterized his music—alongside that of Macero and fellow JCW veteran John LaPorta—as "avant-garde," and he asked Goodman for his perspective on the history and connotations of the term. Ulanov's critical writings had celebrated jazz's growing engagement with classical concert idioms, which, in the critic's view, "elevated" jazz's intellectual values.[177] In keeping with this, Mingus wondered whether Ulanov's use of "avant-garde" implied that "Coleman Hawkins and Charlie Parker were all behind Teo Macero and John La Porta and myself," an idea to which he objected.[178] This remonstrance echoed Mingus's wider concern that the mid-1950s jazz boom—with jazz's growing legitimation as a national art form—had contributed to, and become rooted in, a historical narrative of jazz that tended to write out the contributions of Black musicians—including the legacy of bebop.[179] The reality of segregated market conditions surely informed Mingus's avoidance of the term "avant-garde," which often reinforced racial bias by positing European traditions as more advanced than African American ones.

In responding to Mingus's question about the meaning and history of the term "avant-garde," Goodman invoked Varèse as an exemplar of the avant-garde, as somebody doing "really new things."[180] Mingus interjected, "Varèse! That's the composer, that's the one I was telling you I was listening to, when I was listening to Red Norvo," referring to an earlier conversation not published in the interviews.[181] Mingus had toured with vibraphonist Red Norvo's sextet and trio from 1949 to 1951, a time frame that corresponds to the 1950 release of Varèse's commercially successful EMS album.[182] In the interview, Goodman went on to praise what he perceived as Varèse's nonchalant attitude toward being labeled "the most avant-garde composer around," while criticizing the term's use as a marketing handle.[183]

Crucially, at the mention of Varèse's name, Mingus turned the conversation toward a critique of primitivist tropes within the Euro-American avant-garde—without explicitly acknowledging that he had met Varèse at the Greenwich House sessions or identifying him as a perpetuator of primitivist tropes. Instead, he made reference to popular depictions of the Eighth Street Artists' Club and Abstract Expressionism, complaining of artists who "take a big bucket of paint and splash it on the canvas." Their conversation then touched on the colorful artistic practices of baboons and children, after which Mingus concluded, "finger painting, it's beautiful for kids.... But it's not beautiful for adults. They should grow up."[184] In presenting a caricature of Abstract Expressionist painting techniques, he took aim at a recognizable aesthetic orientation in the downtown avant-garde that has since been described as a "culture of spontaneity" infused with aesthetic primitivism.[185] Mingus's own musical innovations with Macero in the JCW had been compared to such "modern painting"—a comparison at which he bristled.[186] In a litany of artistic statements in the Goodman interviews and beyond, Mingus sought again and again to counteract racist stereotypes of jazz as a primal and naive release of emotion devoid of knowledge, discipline, or skill.[187] Given the prominent place of such primitivist misrepresentations in the downtown art scene, it is no surprise that Mingus associated the term "avant-garde" with such dangers. Moreover, it is highly suggestive that Varèse's name, in particular, triggered that troubled turn of thought about aesthetic primitivism, though Mingus characteristically refrained from acknowledging their encounter.

At the same time, Mingus did express identification with the term "avant-garde," though he worried about the economic consequences of that label for Black musicians. "But [our] avant-garde is out of work, man," he complained to Goodman, and then added, "That's me, I'm out of work."[188] Jazz vanguardists found themselves caught in an economic no man's land, unable to rely on either the declining, club-based entertainment economy of jazz, or classical music institutions and foundation support.[189] And as Porter notes, few African-American experimentalists who pushed boundaries between jazz and classical music received the "substantial critical support" that their white counterparts did in the mid-1950s. The example of Dave Brubeck's 1954 *Time* magazine cover story emblematized this disparity, and galvanized debates about racial inequality in jazz reception and remuneration. As Monson has written, the *Time* story "employed a discourse of respectability as it celebrated Brubeck and his contemporaries while marginalizing the contributions and experiences of black musicians," especially the innovations of bebop.[190] Classically trained musicians like Mingus may have found this all the more galling given Brubeck's relative lack of training and poor sight-reading ability.[191] The reality of segregated market conditions, reinforced by media bias, powerfully informed Mingus's hesitation to fully espouse the term "avant-garde," a concept that evoked Western concert traditions in a way that undervalued African-American contributions.

In keeping with this concern, Goodman and Mingus also made reference to a prior exchange Mingus had had with Duke Ellington on the same subject, a line of discussion that led again to Varèse. As recounted in his essay "Open Letter to the Avant-Garde," Mingus had proposed putting together an "avant-garde" album in the late 1960s or early 1970s with Ellington, Macero, Thad Jones, Clark Terry, and others, partly in response to the music of Ornette Coleman and free jazz.[192] When he approached Ellington with the idea, the older composer reportedly replied, "Why should we go back that far? Let's not take music back that far, Mingus. Why not just make a modern record?"[193] Ellington's words showed an ironic awareness of the nonprogressive connotations "avant-garde" may hold, especially those ideas of "avant-garde" that downplay Black innovations in favor of European concert traditions, or those that play into primitivist stereotypes (which Mingus may have associated with the critical reception of Coleman's music). Ellington's preference for the term "modern" probably reflects that term's more extensive history of application to African-American-led aesthetic movements, including bop.[194] In his 1972 interview with Goodman, Mingus claimed, "I like Duke's word better than the other guy's [Varèse's]," favoring "modern" over "avant-garde." But then he added, "No, they're both just as good" before again expressing doubts about the term "avant-garde" and the economic realities facing Black experimentalists.[195] His reference to Varèse as "the other guy"—in contradistinction to Ellington—suggests a neutral to negative tone that captures the smart and world-weary ambivalence infusing Mingus's entire discussion of the term "avant-garde."

In his interview with Goodman, Mingus returned to one of the most central concerns of his life and career: his "second-class citizenship" in the United States. His resistance to incomplete citizenship arguably informed almost every major aesthetic turn and career move he undertook from the 1940s onward, including his eventual affiliation with third stream and his legacy as a pioneer of hard bop.[196] His drive for civic equality would also have provided a powerful motivation for collaborating in the Greenwich House sessions with Varèse, while nonetheless setting the stage for troubled feelings about it. From the 1940s, Mingus had combined elements of classical music and jazz in order to undermine racially coded categories, establishing a universalist agenda under the motto "It's all one music."[197] (Such an approach led him to critique—and in many cases to avoid—the label "jazz" as a racialized commercial category.) By the late 1950s, Mingus's "hybrid musical vision" had brought him into alliance with Gunther Schuller just at the time when third stream began to take shape as a critical category and creative ideal. The 1955 Newport Festival planners selected Mingus (along with Brubeck and Macero) to perform musical examples for a panel devoted to exploring relationships between classical music and jazz, which included Schuller as a speaker.[198] In 1956, Mingus and Schuller both spoke on a musicological roundtable on jazz at the Music Inn, a cultural venture in Lenox, Massachusetts, that included the "first-ever school dedicated to treating jazz as a legitimate art form," run by John Lewis, with his Modern Jazz Quartet in residence.[199] (By that time, Lewis and Schuller had already cofounded the Modern Jazz Society—later the Jazz and Classical Music Society—with a concert in New York's Town Hall in 1955.) All of this preceded Schuller's historic commissioning of Mingus's *Revelations* for the Fourth Brandeis Festival in 1957.[200] Mingus's collaboration with Varèse—a friend of Schuller's—was arguably of a piece with each of these exchanges in seeking to fuse elements of jazz and classical musics. By the summer of 1957, Mingus had expanded on this vision with plans to create an "Arts Workshop" that would not only bridge avant-garde classical music and jazz, but also experiment with all manner of multimedia possibilities.[201] In this spirit, he famously pursued collaborations involving spoken word art, dance, and written narrative in "The Clown," "Ysabel's Table Dance," and "Scenes in the City."

Yet during this period Mingus also articulated a growing disillusionment with color-blind ideals of musical creation, and an even sharper critique of racial inequalities in classical music, the music industry, and US society at large. As he later put it, he and other African Americans would never stop playing the blues until they achieved "first-class" citizenship: "Only time you drop the blues is when you drop saying 'nigger' or saying 'black.' If you call us Americans, the blues might be gone. . . . When they start calling us *first-class* citizens—which will never be, I gotta figure—then there maybe won't be no reason for the blues."[202] In keeping with his words about citizenship, his music doubled down on qualities he perceived as particular to African American traditions by stressing blues, improvisation, and a stronger rhythmic drive in line with hard bop currents of the time.[203] This musical turn, exemplified in the albums *Pithecanthropus Erectus* (1956) and *The Clown* (1957), contributed to his surging critical recognition within and beyond jazz circles.

In preparation for these albums, Mingus communicated his complex formal schemes orally to musicians over the course of many hours of rehearsal—a method he discussed in the liner notes for *Pithecanthropus Erectus*. Given the all-consuming attention he devoted to his new workshop methods in 1957, it seems reasonable that he would have taken an interest in Varèse's own experimental rehearsal practices, which alternated between the use of no notation and the use of unconventional notation. Mingus developed this oral composition and rehearsal method as an alternative to what he saw as Eurocentric traditions of score-based composition. He singled out the Jazz Composers Workshop for having undervalued African American traditions of improvisation.[204] He claimed that his new approach provided more room for dialogical feedback from musicians, which enhanced the overall creative strength and innovation of the work.[205]

Mingus conceived this difficult process as nothing less than a revelatory—even utopian—mode of social interaction. "Pithecanthropus Erectus" built temporally open-ended improvisations into its chorus structure so that soloists would have the freedom to explore their individual expression as deeply as possible. Mingus framed the Workshop's creative process as a metaphor for larger social collectives on a path toward self-knowledge and equality. As in any such utopian project, however, the reality proved far more difficult, as musicians struggled with the challenges of Mingus's temper and perfectionism. Sue Mingus, later his wife, recalled that in the early 1960s, "You never knew who was going to be screamed into submission or humiliated, or wooed and loved into playing what Charles wanted him to play."[206] With all this in mind, one might argue that the dramas of cultural translation and authority at the Greenwich House sessions, which Mingus seemed eager to enter, had a more volatile precedent in his own agonistic Jazz Workshop methods.

Perhaps ironically, a substantial point of connection between Varèse and Mingus in 1957 might have been Mingus's own use of primitivist musical tropes in "Pithecanthropus Erectus" (1956)—tropes that may have attracted Varèse, who owned a copy of the album—even though Mingus intentionally wielded such tropes in defiance of racist stereotypes. This possibility complicates our understanding of Varèse's and Mingus's projects as "false cognates." *Pithecanthropus Erectus* marked a major turning point in Mingus's career, as his first record released by a major label featuring himself as bandleader and composer. Critics have interpreted the work's C sections within a repeated ABAC chorus structure as evoking a "'jungle-style' primitivism" in their exploration of experimental extended form, scaffolded only by a repeated i–IV vamp and 6/8 meter.[207] Beginning with J. R. Monterose's rhythmically unpredictable tenor saxophone wails and shrieks, these sections become increasingly dominated by cacophonous layers of simultaneous improvisation, with screaming, trilling, and guttural sounds across the ensemble at registral extremes.

Mingus conceived the piece as an ambitious "jazz tone poem" with a specific narrative of slavery—comparable in its ambitions to Ellington's *Black, Brown, and Beige* (1943).[208] "Pithecanthropus Erectus" performs an "interrogation of the concept of progress from the standpoint of the slave," performing a critique seen by Paul Gilroy as fundamental to Afromodernisms more generally, and as relevant to progressivist notions of the avant-garde.[209] The title (which translates roughly to "upright ape man") refers to famous fossil excavations made in Java in the 1890s, which the paleoanthropologist Eugène Dubois controversially claimed revealed the missing link between apes and humans on the evolutionary tree. Mingus described the tone poem's program in the album's liner notes, blending ideas from anthropology and psychology:

This composition . . . depicts musically my conception of the . . . first man to stand erect—how proud he was, considering himself the "first" to ascend from all fours, pounding his chest and preaching his superiority over the animals still in a prone position. Overcome with self-esteem, he goes out to rule the world, if not the universe, but both his own failure to realize the inevitable emancipation of those he sought to enslave, and his greed in attempting to stand on a false security, deny him not only the right of ever being a man, but finally destroy him completely. Basically the composition can be divided into four movements [within each chorus]: (1) evolution, (2) superiority-complex, (3) decline, and (4) destruction.[210]

This vivid program was given visual representation on the album's cover, designed by Julio de Diego. The image foregrounds an abstract, large, upright hominid—inspired by prehistoric cave paintings—standing powerfully to the left of three smaller figures representing successive stages on the evolutionary path from all fours. The four figures float against a grey-toned backdrop covered with black splatter marks, simultaneously evoking furrowed cave walls and Abstract Expressionist poetics.

With this composition and album, Mingus contributed to what Michael Leja has called the mid-century "Modern Man discourse"—texts and practices that turned to popular psychology and anthropology to understand the experiences of "modern man" through the tragic and terrifying foil of primitive ancestry.[211] These themes played out prominently in downtown art and intellectual scenes, not least among the Abstract Expressionist painters. Such "Modern Man discourse" responded to specific anxieties of the postwar period, despairing of traditional progress narratives in light of recent experiences of fascism, the Holocaust, and the Cold War threat of nuclear annihilation.

Yet "Pithecanthropus Erectus" entered this public conversation from the perspective of race and enslavement, turning modernist primitivism on its head. Mingus later summarized his conception of "Pithecanthropus" more bluntly, focusing on the moral barbarity of enslavement and white supremacy: "I had this imagination going. Since the white man says he came from the evolution of animals, well, maybe the black man didn't. The white man has made so many errors in the handling of people that maybe he did come from a gorilla or a fish and crawl up on the sand and then into the trees."[212] These provocative statements invert dehumanizing tropes that link Black Americans with animal imagery and ideas of primitive ancestry. They also invite us to interpret the "jungle style" in "Pithecanthropus Erectus" as a politically conscious inversion of primitivist musical tropes. At the same time, this music clearly bears kinship with the performances on the Greenwich House tapes, especially in its F-minor harmonic modality, its open-ended durations and rhythmic and harmonic structures, and its noisy, pitch-indeterminate sound effects. The musicians at the sessions appear to have replicated aspects of Mingus's

Jazz Workshop sound, whether intentionally or not—a fact that speaks to Mingus's collaborations with Macero and his history of performing with other Jazz Composers Workshop veterans at the Greenwich House sessions. By virtue of its musical innovations, "Pithecanthropus Erectus" in particular may have served as a point of reference for the musicians confronting the experimental situation at Greenwich House.

In the context of Mingus's creative output we should finally note that "Pithecanthropus Erectus" enacts an autobiographical psychodrama of modernist creation as much as a political allegory of enslavement, evolution, or revolution. *Pithecanthropus erectus* resembles the Promethean, antiheroic models of genius that have animated many modernist projects of world-making. This interpretation brings another layer to our understanding of Mingus's conflicted identification with a European modernist heritage. Having become deeply immersed in psychoanalytic therapy and study in the 1950s, Mingus frequently described his musical practice as a mode of self-expression sensitive to his own vacillating identities: "I'm trying to play the truth of what I am. The reason it's difficult is because I'm changing all the time."[213] Mingus's music embodied a self-revelatory spirit that extends ideas of psychic exploration and aesthetic self-expression.[214]

From an autobiographical perspective, one might associate the programmed themes of subordination, revolt, and devastation in "Pithecanthropus Erectus" with Mingus's daily scenes of conflict, negotiations of authority, and creative invention in his Jazz Workshop, in wider New York music circles, and beyond to his experience of incomplete citizenship more generally. Indeed, his description of *Pithecanthropus erectus*'s "superiority-complex," overwhelming self-esteem, and "greed in attempting to stand on a false security" resonates with the deep self-examinations and analyses of human relationships found in his memoir *Beneath the Underdog.*[215] In all of its themes and resonances, "Pithecanthropus" evokes a Black lyricism akin to Fred Moten's "erotics of the cut, submerged in the broken, breaking space-time of an improvisation. Blurred, dying life; liberatory, improvisatory, damaged love; freedom drive."[216]

The earliest unpublished drafts of Mingus's autobiography, which date from around 1957,[217] evoke themes of damaged love in the drive for freedom. Vilde Aaslid has described Mingus's lifelong engagement with literary poetics, like his music, as a "figurative resistance" against primitivist stereotypes.[218] The memoir's draft preface and introduction present the dual sides of his avant-garde ambivalence: his desire for a color-blind and universalist musical culture on the one hand, and his anger and humiliation as a second-class citizen in institutions of classical music on the other. The first line of the draft preface is telling, reading with a significant correction: "Jazz music [^should] means integration of the human race."[219] Bringing a theological dimension to this universalist aspiration, the preface goes on to describe Mingus's search for an "omnipotent all-conscious music of the eternal soul" that will "live God in the act of creation." "It is all my life, my knowledge, my epitaph." "It is my Bible." Combining this spiritual vocabulary with psychoanalytic and cosmological imagery, Mingus goes on to express identification with the European male genius—exemplified in the figures of Beethoven and Bartók—in his feeling of estrangement from a world of commercialism and popularity polls. Mingus then links the struggle for racial integration with the pursuit of a transcendent spiritual harmony beyond worldly sensations and concerns: "Living[,] dead[,] alive are joined in harmonic pitch, unseen, unheard, one to the other, the gathering together as all creation sings for your sacred moment of your shared tuning to[,] *with* the infinite."[220] In light of these words, it is not difficult to see why Mingus might have gravitated toward a racially integrated collaboration with Varèse, an icon of the modernist high art heritage, which could, in an ideal world, represent a station on the path toward a music of true integration and spiritual harmony.

The draft introduction of the memoir, however, paints a bleaker picture: it focuses on the racially segregated world of classical music, telling the story of a Black protagonist who enters through the back door of Carnegie Hall. Dressed to the nines in a "French suede jacket with turned-up llama-knit collar," he is humiliated by a white, female uniformed attendant, a friend of a friend, who refuses to recognize him.[221] The Black protagonist follows the white attendant as she walks away from him. "She looked so frightened. She turned white, not as a sheet, but transparent in her cream-colored uniform. I felt for the [elevator] doors but they had closed behind me." In the rest of the introduction, the narrator works through his anger about his nonrecognition by the attendant, and their painful separation. This story represents perhaps the earliest example of what became Mingus's characteristic autobiographical conceit: to compress "events and people into fictive and symbolic moments that have little to do with linear narrative or standard revelations about the life of a musician," as Nichole T. Rustin-Paschal put it.[222]

The scenario of Mingus's story clearly substitutes for power structures in the classical music world that in fact were largely male and homosocial—like those at Greenwich House. As Rustin-Paschal has argued, Mingus treated his autobiography as a site in which to work through deeply painful problems of Black masculinity in relation to "the public he inhabit[ed]," pervaded by objectifying fantasies of Black sexuality.[223]

Within the memoir, Mingus described his own sometimes aggressive and even violent behavior as a reaction to such racialized trauma. If, following Mingus, we choose to interpret "Pithecanthropus Erectus" as an autobiographically inspired Promethean account of creation and self-invention, then this work also articulates an extremely vexed identification with the modernist traditions that perpetuated demeaning primitivist fantasies.

This ambivalence could have fueled his silence about Varèse and the Greenwich House sessions, a project that combined elements of liberation and humiliation. The mixed implications of such music making would likely have been felt all the more acutely by a creator like Mingus, who conceived of notions of personhood and civic representation as constructed via sound and musical performance.[224] The statement "This is not *natural* to me!," which resounds on the recordings, compounds in significance as a protest against being objectified or dehumanized. The sessions speak to a whole history of racialized and intimate interactions among musical experimentalists in New York at mid-century, the memory of which remains caught in ambivalence and unspoken words, yet still calls out to be written. Mingus's creative practice responded to that scene through a politics of transfiguration, in Gilroy's sense—"a counterculture that defiantly constructs its own critical, intellectual, and moral genealogy in a partially hidden public sphere of its own."[225] Agency and self-protection depend here on a mixture of speaking out and expressing oneself on the level of the unsaid.

The Metropole as Third Space and Scene of Subjection

I have conceptualized the Greenwich House sessions as both a third space and a scene of subjection, providing an alternative to narratives of exchange or appropriation that oversimplify and ignore the ambivalent fissures of race, citizenship, and power that traverse the scene of music making. This argument found meaning in the limits of the archive, a task necessary to the study of any such encounter, the terms of which defy standard rubrics of historical documentation while confounding words of remembrance.

The scene at Greenwich House shows how ambivalence infused New York's changing ideologies of race during the Cold War. In preparing for the Brussels World's Fair collaboration, Varèse appears almost to have jumped on board the US cultural-diplomatic agenda, as Penny von Eschen has written, to "foreground the importance of African American culture, with blackness and race operating culturally to project an image of American nationhood that was more inclusive than the reality."[226] Caught

in the labile vicissitudes of his anti-Black negrophobia/negrophilia, however, Varèse finally backed away from a project that may have demanded
more of a concession of power than he was willing to give. Varèse appears
to have preferred the easy-to-control, made-up sounds of his own primitivist imagination—exemplified in the choral and percussion sounds
of *Poème électronique*—to the difficulty of engaging collaboratively with
Black cultural production on the terms of equality that a musician such
as Mingus demanded. Mingus's own protestation, "This is not *natural*
for me," may well have played a role in that outcome. The chancy course
of the third-space encounter—beyond the control of any individual—
finally ensured that the jazz musicians' sounds would not be captured as
signs for such a hypocritical display of "inclusivity."

The story of the Greenwich House sessions also provides insights into
the uneven distribution of resources and prestige during the fat years
of empire in New York. Even though Varèse never used the Greenwich
House recordings in his premiere at the Brussels World's Fair, he benefited professionally from the sessions, which were remembered in the
haze of legend as a sign of his white hipness.[227] Their informal memory
helped to solidify his place within a canon of American Experimentalist composers that congealed with the proliferation of US power during
the Cold War, as demonstrated by the circulation of Yates's writings via
the State Department. Supported by intersecting structures of US empire and white privilege, Varèse leveraged a persona as a genius "citizen of
the world"—a publicly celebrated representative of both European and
American cultural traditions—and as a mediator of transatlantic cultural
solidarity that also had political value in the framework of Cold War soft
power. Mingus could never have benefited in the same way from these
structures of canon formation, which remained infused with white supremacy and nativism. In this light, his strategic and ambivalent silence
about Varèse speaks volumes. It may be understood, in George Lewis's
terms, as quietly resisting "racialized notions of classical and jazz meth-
odology" that treat jazz as "a junior partner."[228]

Yet the Mingus of "Pithecanthropus Erectus," "Haitian Fight Song,"
and "Fables of Faubus" did more than just protest such hierarchies of legal and symbolic citizenship. His music also articulated powerful citizenly allegiances premised on related political struggles—domestic and
international—across a spectrum of difference. Conceived in New York
as an imperial metropole, his work implicitly asks us to "translate" among
mythologies, memories, and historical moments of subjugation and rebellion. As we have already seen, Mingus hardly shied away from the
fraught uncertainties, ambiguities, and self-critique implied by such an

endeavor—thus suggesting a way of imagining "world citizenship" very different from that of Varèse. In Shana Redmond's terms, Mingus's citizenship might be understood as one "that labors to document . . . multiple allegiances," or a "curious citizenship, that remembers."[229] Mingus's and Varèse's personae, situations, dispositions, and goals prove so disparate that it remains hard to fathom the musical conversation between a composer who uttered, "Jazz is not America. It's a Negro product," and another who eventually declared, "When you call us American, the blues might be gone." But the imperative remains to try, because their histories illuminate worlds of thought and feeling in moments of musical crossing that were exquisite and extreme—fine-tuned moments of citizenly contestation in the metropole.

✳ 2 ✳

Cold War Acropolis I

USSACHEVSKY, THE ROCKEFELLER
FOUNDATION, AND THE CPEMC

In 1958, the composers Milton Babbitt, Otto Luening, and Vladimir Ussachevsky founded the Columbia-Princeton Electronic Music Center
(CPEMC) on the Columbia University campus with the support of a massive $175,000 Rockefeller Foundation (RF) grant. Together with Roger
Sessions, who provided nominal support, this trio of composers became
the directors of the first institutionally supported electronic music center
in the United States, working in collaboration with Peter Mauzey as lead
engineer. The founding of the CPEMC testifies to an era when public and
private agencies scrambled to provide New York City with a cultural infrastructure befitting its global status as a symbol of ascendant US power.
At mid-century, Columbia University's longtime nickname, "the Acropolis," gained new value and currency in public discourse, manifesting not
least in Rockefeller-funded projects of philanthropy and urban planning
in the university's neighborhood of Morningside Heights and Harlem.
Within these public-private ventures, the term "Acropolis" captured the
desire to transform Columbia University and its environs into the "spiritual, cultural, and intellectual center of the world" and to thus inherit the
mantle of "Western civilization" from the traditional learning centers of
Europe.[1] With hubris, the classical metaphor figured uptown New York
as a cosmopolitan center and fortress—a contradictory emblem for democracy and dominion.

Recent accounts of the CPEMC celebrate its "international" personnel,
which in its early years included such foreign-born composers as Bülent
Arel (Turkey), Mario Davidovsky (Argentina), Halim El-Dabh (Egypt),
Michiko Toyama (Japan), Edgard Varèse (France), and Ussachevsky (the
disputed borderlands of Manchuria).[2] From the 1950s to the 1970s, some
composers came to the CPEMC as already naturalized US citizens (e.g.,
Varèse and Ussachevsky); others settled in the United States and became
naturalized after their affiliation with the CPEMC (e.g., Arel and Davi-

dovsky); others became naturalized and then left the United States, only to return (e.g., El-Dabh); and still others left to settle elsewhere after their research stay (e.g., Toyama). As Robert J. Gluck describes, upwards of thirty-two mostly male visiting composers studied at the CPEMC on long- and short-term stays from 1958 through the 1970s, having come from such countries as Argentina, Brazil, France, Germany, Ghana, Iran, Israel, Italy, Japan, Korea, Mexico, Peru, Spain, Turkey, and Yugoslavia.[3] In the 1960s and 1970s the CPEMC hosted a particularly sizable Latin American contingent, which grew through the studio's informal association with the Centro Latinamericano de Altos Estudios Musicales (CLAEM) at the Instituto Torcuato Di Tella in Buenos Aires, founded in 1963 as another Rockefeller-supported project.[4] The involvement of such figures as Robert Moog and Wendy Carlos at the center testifies to its connection with popular music currents despite its art music orientation. Although the CPEMC's personnel remained overwhelmingly male, it also incubated women's leadership in electronic composition through the work of both native-born composers (e.g., Pril Smiley, Alice Shields) and women who came from other countries (e.g., Toyama, Alida Vázquez).

Gluck and others' emphasis on the CPEMC's internationalism brings a welcome alternative to existing historiographies by highlighting a vast, stylistically eclectic roster of composers from outside the United States whose work has often been obscured in accounts of New York musical avant-gardes. While scant secondary literature documents the CPEMC from a detailed, critical-historical perspective, the studio's reputation often looms largest as the emblem and institutional achor of the uptown scene—a stronghold for pitch-oriented composition oriented around serial techniques, fully notated scores, reverence for Austro-German classical traditions, and university-supported initiatives including the journal *Perspectives of New Music* and the Group for Contemporary Music. This "uptown" image of the CPEMC evokes the transatlantic adaptation of Second Viennese School composition in the United States via Babbitt and a younger generation that included Charles Wuorinen and Mario Davidovsky; it presents a competing lineage to the "downtown" American experimentalist one that solidified in the late 1950s (as described in chapter 1). Working against such dualities, Gluck's itemized list of visiting and immigrating composers explodes the coherence of any account of the CPEMC as a genealogically unified "school," "scene," or "camp" rooted primarily or exclusively in European heritage. The task remains, however, to move beyond descriptions of previously overlooked "diversity" to examine the cosmopolitan space as a conduit for Cold War imperial configurations of power.[5]

The CPEMC's experiments in electronic music and sound must be understood as artifacts of the imperial metropolis, just as the personae connected with those experiments cannot be understood apart from that setting and history. As an institution, the CPEMC served manifold purposes. It was a studio—a space for more than just musical composition but also for *study*. More specifically, the CPEMC operated as a laboratory for experimentation—a "machine for making the future" with experimental systems set up to provide answers for questions not yet fully formulable in the present.[6] As such, the CPEMC participated in the burgeoning Cold War military-industrial-educational complex, depending upon the technologies, patronage, and expertise generated within this complex while also enacting a cultural diplomacy mission premised on the postwar prestige of modern technoscience.[7] The CPEMC served power in a manner comparable to earlier imperial sound laboratories such as the Wilhelmine-era Berlin Phonogram Archive: it broached questions about the psychology of human subjects, the limits of human perception, the character of human-machine interface, the boundaries of culture, and intercultural modes of transcription, perception, cognition, and communication through sound and music. Toward this end, composers at the CPEMC recorded, manipulated, and composed with sounds that were perceived as culturally "other" (similar to Varèse at Greenwich House)—the sounds, for example, of Chinese, Japanese, and Egyptian instruments. In the studio at Columbia, they shored up ideas of "Western culture" through the "interchange between the academic and the more or less imaginative meanings of Orientalism," in Edward Said's terms, via electronic composition.[8]

In contrast with early twentieth-century sound laboratories, the CPEMC hosted a large contingent of personnel originating from many different regions of the globe—creative actors embodying composerly personae outside the white, masculine Euroamerican norms of "Western" art music institutions. Visiting, immigrant, and minoritarian creators emerged as key figures at the CPEMC, helping to project U.S. soft power abroad while nonetheless remaining subject in the US domestic space to unequal citizenship statuses defined by race, gender, ethnicity, sexuality, national origin, language, and so on.[9] Such a dynamic is characteristic of imperial formations, as described in the introduction to this book. Accordingly, chapters 2 and 3—conceived as two parts of a whole—address the emergent CPEMC as an institution characterized by Cold War expansionist agendas permeated by repressive, exclusionary mechanisms. Chapter 2 focuses on the cultural diplomacy mission of Vladimir Ussachevsky, whose fruitful alliances with the RF and Otto Luening were also conditioned by his previously unexplored Red Scare persecution and surveillance by the FBI—a circumstance inseparable from his immigrant background. Chapter 3 examines the cultural-diplomatic aspirations of Michiko Toyama and Halim El-Dabh, two early guest composers who sought with varying degrees of institutional sponsorship to make the U.S. their home while confounding expectations of *whom* a composer may be. These cases compel a narrative of the CPEMC virtually absent in existing scholarship on the studio: a story of immigrant acculturation, citizenly naturalization, cross-cultural translation, and culturally amalgamated approaches to composition in the Rockefeller-supported program. They invite examination of the ideological contradictions that characterized such projects at the CPEMC as an artifact of the military-industrial-educational complex during the Cold War. Acropolis emerges as an emblem for tensions at the heart of the CPEMC as an "imperial" space: it evokes, on the one hand, a crossroads for the world, and, on the other, a defensive citadel for restrictive notions of citizenship and "Western civilization."

As a "crossroads," the CPEMC aimed to strengthen transnational professional networks, to foster cross-cultural communication through tape composition, and to produce knowledge about cultural difference and identity through exchange. These goals intersected with the RF's mid-century turn away from so-called disinterested scholarship toward a more direct engagement with international relations by creating or strengthening relevant university programs. The RF's lasting contribution to the U.S. academic system through the establishment of "area studies" programs exemplifies this shift in foundation policy, which aimed to deepen "cultural understanding" and diplomacy through new interdisciplinary curricula and exchange on university campuses.[10] These initiatives sought both to study cultural differences and to create an internationalist space for the production of knowledge that would bridge or transcend divides.[11] Electronic music spoke to the dream of an intercultural approach to composition and knowledge production—an aspiration of the RF Humanities Division in the 1950s—because it could bypass Western notation and treat pitch as well as timbral and temporal values of music with singular flexibility. As we will see, Ussachevsky spelled out the goals of this vision in the Rockefeller Foundation grant application materials that authorized the founding of the CPEMC as a "program of cultural technical exchange," the "aim of [which] is reciprocity."[12] In its early years, the CPEMC stressed the importance of exchange with the Middle East and Asia, echoing the longstanding Asia-centric priorities of the Rockefeller family. The CPEMC's subsequent emphasis on Latin America also replicated established patterns of interest within the Rockefeller family and its enterprises, exemplified not only in the RF-supported establishment of CLAEM in Argentina but also in Nelson Rockefeller's directorship as coordinator of the Office for Inter-American Affairs in the 1940s.[13] During the Cold War, the RF worked in tandem with the State Department to extend the nation's "sphere of influence" within these decolonizing regions of heightened military and economic interest, in competition with the Soviet Union.[14]

If the term "Acropolis" asserts an outward-facing stance as "center of the world," then it also implies an inward-facing, defensive posture, equally important to the soft-power mission of the electronic music studio and its founding statements. As a citadel, the CPEMC would protect "serious" culture rooted in the "great traditions of the West" from the degradations of commercialism and populism, articulating a critique of mass culture associated with antifascist and anticommunist programs of the era.[15] "A democratic society lives and grows on the resiliency of a few, a divergent few; other societies bend with the winds of doctrine," John Marshall (assistant director of the RF Humanities Division) wrote in a confidential 1958 report to the RF Board of Trustees, titled "Adventuring in the Arts."[16] Looking back on the promise of such a mission, CPEMC cofounder Milton Babbitt described the ideal role of the university as that "of the mightiest of fortresses against the overwhelming, outnumbering forces, both within and without the university, of anti-intellectualism, cultural populism, and passing fashion."[17] The electronic music studio would reimagine and improve upon a culture of high art derived from nineteenth-century Europe within the postwar American university and its technocultures, surpassing established European competitor programs to enhance the US reputation abroad. Such a "movement [of courage]—a new vitality—in the arts in the United States is perhaps most strikingly exemplified in music," Marshall enthused in his report, which was aimed at gaining RF support.[18]

As a metaphor, "Acropolis" invites us to understand the CPEMC through its gatekeeping mechanisms. Systems of inclusion and exclusion in musical institutions resemble structures of citizenship.[19] Who could belong to the CPEMC, in connection with what musical idioms, and under what terms? Embedded in "Acropolis" is *polis*—a site of plurality where unexpected hybridizations may emerge. Yet the *polis* remains circumscribed by *acro*, a fortified boundary. As a fortification for the preservation of Western culture, the CPEMC would exclude all but the narrowest slices of culture and personae defined by the gendered and racialized institutions of Euroamerican high art—an ivory tower of "terminal prestige," in Susan McClary's formulation.[20] Many established accounts of "uptown" modernism tell their story as such a tale of fortification. Yet the dual sides of "Acropolis"—indicating both citadel and crossroads— must be accounted for. My own account of the CPEMC as an Acropolis probes the ambivalence between its *acro* and *polis* functions within a narrative of American soft power. To recognize the CPEMC as an Acropolis is to treat it as an institutionalized "third space"—a "site of intercultural enunciation" across an emphatically uneven field of power as described in previous chapters.[21]

The CPEMC was more than just an electronic music studio that existed under conditions of empire; it thrived as an institution *of* empire. The powerfully overlapping referents called upon by composers at the CPEMC and an administering elite at the RF testify to its status as a quintessentially "imperial" institution: "exchange," "East-West divide," "fortress," "resiliency of a few." Pluralism meets with heirarchy, horizontal expansion meets with postures of defense. These images and their applications suggest "the force field in which [empire] operates, the breadth of its metaphoric extensions," in historian and anthropologist Ann Laura Stoler's terms.[22] The density of shared vocabularies between creative workers and policymakers is what helped to create this force field for operation. It is not every day that a figure like RF president Dean Rusk—a future secretary of state—designates a survey of American musical life as "one of our most interesting [Foundation] Monthly Reports," as Rusk wrote in 1958 after reading Marshall's above-cited "Adventuring in the Arts: Music."[23] Yet this occasion reveals how eagerly the policymaking elite solicited solutions to social and political problems from the musical arts. From the first years of their collaboration in tape experimentation, Ussachevsky and Luening successfully animated the interest and imagination of the officers at the RF. They did so by capitalizing on the waxing prestige of scientific research cultures at mid-century while appropriating a language of humanist mission, as Rachel Vandegriff has suggested.[24] At the same time, they emphasized their project's merits as an exercise in cultural diplomacy that could facilitate cross-cultural understanding by bridging musical idioms of the "East and West."

Far from spontaneous, Luening and Ussachevsky's alliance with Babbitt formed at the urging of the Rockefeller Foundation after they had independently approached the foundation, soliciting funding for electronic music laboratories at Columbia and Princeton respectively. Equipped with mathematics training, Babbitt would come to elaborate the scientific research mission of the CPEMC, developing relationships with RCA in order to secure for the studio the Mark II synthesizer—an early and relatively successful total music synthesizer. Luening and Ussachevsky would emphasize the studio's role as a hub for cultural diplomacy, in keeping with their prior experience in related fields: Luening had organized cultural exchange efforts in occupied Germany in 1948, and Ussachevsky had worked as an "area man" specializing in Central Asian studies in the Office for Strategic Services (OSS) and the State Department during and after World War II. Ussachevsky's wife, Elizabeth Kray—a veteran of cultural diplomacy who had worked at the Institute for Pacific Relations (IPR)— credited herself as an unacknowledged cofounder of the CPEMC who helped to smooth relations with the RF.[25] Roger Sessions, too, provided support by lending his name to the masthead of the CPEMC as codirector.

In the late 1950s, the team at Columbia and Princeton scrambled to outflank other US composers in the effort to establish the first institutionally supported electronic music studio in the country. In a conspiratorial letter from 1958, Luening exulted in his RF-supported triumvirate with Babbitt and Ussachevsky, which sidelined an alternate possible coalition with John Cage in their venture to secure funding within a hypercompetitive professional scene:

Cage was really nasty. I was tough but left the door open. . . . [Babbitt] was cleverly lining up power for himself. . . . I made the jesting observation [to Babbitt] that it sometimes seemed to me as though I were being used, which I thought was quite all right as long as people didn't push me around, get clever, or try to outmaneauver me in various ways. In any event, I would slug back hard, meet cleverness with cleverness, or do some maneouvering of my own. . . . Only you and I and [electronic music composers Louis and Bebe Barron] have really worked as a team.[26]

Luening's pugilistic language speaks to a wider culture of one-upmanship and mistrustful deal making within the composers' communities—a white, masculine social space where individuals acted out of fear of humiliation or desire for public recognition within the city's rapidly expanding patronage networks and arts infrastructure.

The notion of an uptown Acropolis emerged from a broader history of New York urban planning and cultural diplomacy that is also worth interrogating. As the historians Joel Schwartz and Samuel Zipp show, the metaphor of the "Acropolis" served as a banner under which the Rockefeller-backed expansion of the university and redevelopment of the neighborhood transpired in the 1950s and 1960s, under the notoriously undemocratic authority of Robert Moses.[27] In the words of a Columbia University faculty panel in 1947, this urban regeneration would make Morningside Heights "the educational and cultural counterpart of the political Capitol [sic] of the World" and "a community whose facilities can be available without restrictions as to race, color, or creed."[28] The drive toward urban renewal drew on New York's liberal political circles, which, in Zipp's words, "often imbued slum clearance and rebuilding with lofty ideals," seeking to rebuild along "modern, discrimination-free lines" while linking their efforts to the dual struggles of their era against fascism and communism. "Acropolis" embodied the image that city officials, university administrators, philanthropic officers, and other vested agents sought to project globally of Columbia University and its neighborhood.[29] In a similar spirit, Luening and Ussachevsky's 1959 Rockefeller Foundation grant application argued for establishing the CPEMC on the grounds of a very specific soft-power mission: to demonstrate American cultural and techno-scientific leadership within a field perceived to have been dominated by Europe, while opening that field up to a spirit of ecumenicism through "reciprocal" international exchange. This goal dovetails with the mission of other prominent institutions expanded or newly founded in Morningside Heights in the 1950s—from Columbia University's scientific research laboratories to the Rockefeller-supported Riverside Church and International House.[30]

From the beginning of its application in Manhattan, the metaphor captured not only Columbia's rocky escarpment foundation and neoclassical architecture, but also mechanisms for creating hierarchies of citizenship. At the 1894 dedication of the Teachers College, Columbia University president Seth Low first broadcast this image onto the uptown campus that Columbia College and Barnard College would soon join: "By their [Morningside Heights] configuration they offer precisely the conditions which such institutions need—accessibility to a large population, together with *a certain retirement from the noise and disturbance of surrounding life* and the promise of permanent occupancy. This hill is really the Acropolis of New York."[31] In its subsequent Cold War popularization, the Acropolis metaphor provided a justification and apologia for "slum clearance"—the Robert Moses–era approach to securing "retirement from the noise and disturbance of surrounding life" following decades of immigration-fueled population growth that massively increased the city's density and pushed tenement sprawl northward. "City's 'Acropolis' Combating Slums," announced a 1957 *New York Times* headline, echoing the press's repeated use of the classical metaphor in its coverage of the neighborhood's transformation over many years.[32] These headlines responded to both the first wave of Puerto Rican migration to the city and the second wave of the African American Great Migration—migratory flows of citizen groups who were then forcibly displaced from the neighborhood and largely excluded from the benefits of the university. This history remains highly relevant to the CPEMC, itself a hub for immigrants. Whereas the dispossessed local residents of color in Harlem and Morningside Heights experienced second-class citizenship through their eviction, participants and visitors at the CPEMC faced more limited challenges of citizenship status that mixed with the privileges of their affiliation with the high culture institutions of the Acropolis. To study these conditions and the creativity they made possible is to narrate a history of imperial subjectivities in and around a music-technocultural institution.

In its aspirational guise, "Acropolis" describes the ideologies that smoothed over contradictions between principles of democracy and hierarchy in Manhattan as a capital of empire at mid-century. I define the word "ideology" here not as a conscious set of beliefs but rather, in the spirit of Louis Althusser, as those ways of being, feeling, and thinking that "intermediat[e] [and ensure] a (sometimes teeth-gritting) 'harmony' between the repressive State apparatus and the Ideological State Apparatuses."[33] We can see this "harmony" between hierarchy and democracy—between institutions of repression and cultural production—when we follow Ussachevsky's trajectory as a founder of the CPEMC who walked a fine line between FBI surveillance on the one hand, and cultural diplomacy and institution-building as an electronic music composer on the other. He acclimatized himself as a "good immigrant" while seeking protection from Red Scare persecution within the RF-supported institutions of the Acropolis. In Althusser's sense, the RF "hailed" Ussachevsky, and he apprehended himself in that hail just as he had at prior stations on his path toward Americanization. These stations included the American secondary- and higher-education systems he had entered as a refugee teenager from Manchuria in 1930 (eventually attaining a BA from Pomona College in 1935 and a PhD from the Eastman School of Music in 1939); the US Army, into which he had been drafted in 1941; the OSS and the State Department, where he had served from 1944 until 1946; and at Columbia University, where he had worked as a composer, teacher, and technician from 1947 onward.

While Ussachevsky's membership in these institutions facilitated his acculturation as a US citizen, his citizenship status nonetheless remained laced with uncertainty—a vexing ambiguity that operated as a silent motivator for his early career as a composer and institution-builder. At the height of the postwar Red Scare in 1953, the State Department denied him a passport—precisely at a time when he sought to extend US residency and citizenship to members of his transnational family still in danger. He remained under investigation by the FBI from 1945 until 1965. Ussachevsky's deepening relationships with Columbia University, the Rockefeller Foundation, and Otto Luening in the 1950s provided shelter and respectability at a time when Ussachevsky found himself vulnerable to repressive state power. Luening himself, a German-American educated abroad, had long projected an all-American persona, which he leveraged as a consummate insider and liberal-democratic activist in numerous music-bureaucratic organizations from the 1930s onward. He proved an ideal ally for the younger Ussachevsky. Working as a team, Luening and Ussachevsky articulated the CPEMC's program to "integrate" the human psyche and to bridge cultural divides. They also treated composition as a matter for bureaucratic administration within a quasimissionary program for exporting values of "freedom" abroad.[34] All of these tendencies rooted them in epistemologies distinctively articulated by RF Humanities policy platforms, which also provided a basis for the cultural exchange programs that supported El-Dabh and Toyama.

A Proposal by "Good Immigrants"

Luening and Ussachevsky's 1958 Rockefeller Foundation grant application harnessed the intersecting desires of engineers and composers at RCA, Princeton, and Columbia to institute a US-based center for electronic music that would capitalize on the newest electronic sound technologies developed within commercial-military partnerships during and after World War II. The grant, which was administered in 1959, arrived as the culmination of a long-standing funding relationship Ussachevsky and Luening had established with the RF, which had awarded two prior grants in aid to the composers' incipient studio. The first, in 1953, had funded the purchase of two Ampex tape recorders, a mixing panel, and an amplifier, while the second, in 1955, had supported European travel for the purpose of surveying electronic music developments in Cologne, Baden-Baden, Eindhoven, Gravesano, Milan, and Paris.[35] Luening and Ussachevsky's report on their 1955 survey formed an effective justification for their 1958 proposal.[36] Over the course of their courtship in the 1950s, RF officers had arrived at a remarkably mutual understanding with Ussachevsky and Luening of electronic composition's mission within the wider humanities conceived on a global scale, as represented in a long trail of correspondence and bureaucratic documents. This mutuality should be understood as more than just a superficial agreement on paper. Ussachevsky and Luening's relationship with the RF profoundly oriented their professional and creative objectives in the 1950s—even their manner of knowing and being in the world. Likewise, Ussachevsky's and Luening's agendas inflected the mission of the RF arts program as it took shape over the course of the decade.

As already noted, Ussachevsky's relationship with the RF took root under conditions of duress. For two decades, the FBI investigated Ussachevsky for subversive activities and espionage in connection with his employment in the OSS and State Department on the basis of no credible evidence—a situation the composer managed with supreme discretion. Having immigrated to the United States as a teenager in 1930 and acquired citizenship in 1931, he had made the country his home, together with his brother Leonid and mother Maria, both of whom were musicians. Separated from them in the chaos of the 1929 Sino-Soviet War, his father Alexei had died in Soviet detention in 1937, while his sisters Natalia and Ksenia had lived in Leningrad and Harbin, respectively, during the early period of his FBI surveillance. The family's dispersal lay at the heart of the composer's troubled citizenship status. Ussachevsky's family abroad made him more vulnerable to suspicions of disloyalty—as OSS, FBI, and INS documents indicate—heightening the need for him to demonstrate his status as a "good immigrant." He and his family endeavored to facilitate his sisters' immigration to the United States, a cherished long-term effort jeopardized by the composer's troubles with the FBI after 1945. As we will see, this crisis came to a head in the spring of 1953, when the State Department denied Ussachevsky a passport—an event that immediately preceded his first solicitation to the Rockefeller Foundation for support in electronic composition.

Eventually Ussachevsky and Luening's deepening affiliation with the RF would help to solidify Ussachevsky's professional standing at Columbia University and ensure the institutional backing he needed to shore up his own citizenly rights. In other words, Ussachevsky being ensconced in the Acropolis provided protection and power during his twenty-year period of shadowy state persecution. Premised on conspiracy theories, clandestine activities, and xenophobia, the character of this persecution will require considerable explication below—explication absent in existing accounts of Ussachevsky and the CPEMC. For now, we should note that FBI surveillance operated continuously in parallel with Ussachevsky's fruitful partnership with Luening, the RF, and their cultural diplomacy programs. The risky character of Ussachevsky's situation casts new light on these affiliations: it shows how they emerged partly to compensate and provide protection for a citizenship constrained by the Russophobia of the Red Scare. To be sure, Ussachevsky held many structural advantages on the basis of gender and race, which allowed him to enter into a leadership position at Columbia in the 1950s. By restoring the role of state repression to his story, however, we may understand his oeuvre and career as an exemplary case for the study of Acropolis as an ideological formation of "(teeth-gritting) 'harmony.'" The relative success of Ussachevsky's career despite his years of surveillance exemplifies this "harmony" between ideological-cultural and repressive state institutions. Under these conditions, his electronic composition served as an imaginative space in which to work through related problems: his music foregrounds questions of "dehumanizing" technopower in relation to the human psyche, historical violence, secrecy, and dilemmas of acculturation. Meanwhile, his affiliations with Luening, Columbia, and the RF thrived on the mutual production of epistemologies and concepts—articulated at a level of national-strategic significance—that justified the proliferation of their institutional apparatuses. "(Teeth-gritting) 'harmony'" was perhaps the star under which his entire work of composition and institution-building transpired: Ussachevsky lived with, worked through, and papered over the contradictions between democracy and hierarchy, expansion and exclusion, that characterized his career and citizenly status.

Before considering Ussachevsky's compositional practice and history with the security state as both agent and target in depth, we should explore the RF's postwar humanities agenda—the force that profoundly oriented and made possible Ussachevsky's unique persona, career, and livelihood. After World War II, the officers of the RF overhauled the rationale of its humanities program along the following lines: they articulated a distinctive epistemology of the humanities that queried the human subject in its capacity for psychic integrity; they posited modern technologies and media as a threat to the very stability of that subject—a danger that required adaptation, domesticization, or "humanization" of those technologies by humanist specialists; and they framed the stakes of these projects as underwriting a US-led postwar project to reestablish global peace and stability. The program assumed a "first in Europe, then elsewhere" geospatial temporality of diffusion, in line with popular modernization theories of the time and other Eurocentric discourses of modernity.[37] It aimed to strengthen intellectual exchange via personal contact between the "Anglo-Saxon world" and "the continent"; this newly revitalized and reunified Western "reservoir of brains"[38] would then foster "intercultural understanding" throughout the globe as societies struggled to "humanize" new technologies and media under conditions of rapid modernization, as RF officers Burton Fahs and John Marshall explained.[39] This logic justifies the sequencing of Luening and Ussachevsky's own RF grants— the fact that the composers' RF-supported studies and networking in Europe preceded RF support for the CPEMC as a US-based global hub serving creators from both "Western" and "developing" nations in 1958.

For foundation officers, electronic music promised to enroll wartime sound technologies in a global project of cultural renewal; European humanist traditions, transformed by American democracy, would provide a basis for redeeming modern technologies that had been exploited by totalitarian governments. In addition to supporting academic institutions, the RF premised its work on the sponsorship and cultivation of exemplary individuals. In Marshall's words, "New materials, new methods [such as photography, microfilm, and sound recording] require new men—or humanists whose view is renewed in the time they work in."[40] During this period, the RF became the "first institution to begin granting large-scale amounts of money to music projects in the United States."[41] Ussachevsky and Luening presented themselves as humanists who fulfilled the mission set forth by the RF; their incipient studio reclaimed for "human values" those technologies, such as the tape recorder, that had previously been directed toward wartime use, including the dissemination of propaganda in Nazi Germany.[42] Director of the humanities Charles Burton Fahs defined "human values" as those that promote individual psychic "integrity" and "harmony," which in turn would improve "social health" and "efficiency" to instill "strength, poise, and resilience" in members of a democratic society.[43] While Fahs posited the stakes of the humanities in these terms of social hygiene and scientific management, his deputy, Marshall, located the vitality of the humanities more specifically in a Cold War critique of mass culture—the idea that the humanities in American democracy would foster "the resiliency of the few, a divergent few" that would fend off the dangers of totalitarian "doctrine" and its dissemination through mediatized mass cults such as those of the Nazi and Soviet propaganda machines.[44] Luening enthusiastically echoed such concerns, describing the relationship between "new men" and "new materials, new methods" in even more Manichean terms: his own work in the studio was "to determine whether man can use & dominate the machines he has created in the field of music or vice versa."[45] To reclaim electronic sound technologies for the purpose of "Western high art" would have answered Marshall and Fahs's most fundamental policy agendas at the RF.

The Acropolis's dual postures of defense and expansion show up in Marshall and Fahs's words: the reinvigorated humanities would "fortify" citizen-subjects just as their global dissemination would foster "intercultural understanding and thereby sound improvement in international relations."[46] By way of this vision, officers articulated an epistemology of the humanities grounded in psychological understandings of the self and in bureaucratic management techniques, both understood as salvific for Western civilization. Armed with this working agenda and knowledge, the RF Humanities Division would serve as a separate but coordinating partner with the US government to reinforce a new Pax Americana through its funding activities.

The affective tenor of the officers' bureaucratic work resonated in fraught terms of traumatic remembrance and redemption. As former RF president Raymond B. Fosdick set forth in his 1944 mandate:

> To those who in this last terrible decade have kept this faith [in freedom of thought] alive, to the universities and laboratories where on hidden altars the fire has never gone out, we in the Western hemisphere pay tribute of admiration and homage. What Pericles said of the Athenian dead can even more truly be said of these men and institutions in Europe and Asia [who fought totalitarianism]: "Their glory survives in everlasting remembrance. . . . Far away in alien lands their memory is set in the hearts of men."[47]

Such an homage participated in the hubris surrounding Cold War cultural infrastructure projects such as the expanding Acropolis of Morningside Heights. Fosdick reclaimed the words of Pericles for the officers of the RF, who "even more truly" remembered the dead of Asia and Europe in a new imperial capital, "far away in alien lands" in America. The "glory" of the dead lay in their citizenly sacrifice, which the statesman-humanist would dedicate to the glory of a greater political whole with expansionist ambition.[48] Fosdick invoked Pericles to support American power as the supposed guarantor of world peace; guided by Fosdick's postwar mandate, the RF's proliferation of soft-power programs is what enabled Ussachevsky and Luening to find sponsorship for electronic composition and projects in global exchange. What transpired within the intimacy of the studio in Morningside Heights could be seen as assuming world-historical significance.

While the CPEMC's 1958 founding formed an intervention in cultural diplomacy, it also unfolded as a powerful exercise in American self-fashioning, especially for the foreign-born Ussachevsky. The RF humanities agenda, with its emphasis on the "integration" of human subjects, served as an ideological platform through which immigrants like Ussachevsky could integrate themselves within the nation-state. The studio's legacy in cultural diplomacy has just begun to find visibility in a growing historical literature on tape experimentalism that foregrounds questions of foundation patronage in relation to the rapidly changing technocultures of the Cold War.[49] Its status as a project in American self-fashioning, however, remains obscure. No existing scholarship probes the relationship between Ussachevsky's and Luening's backgrounds in migration and their mid-century institutional alliances in New York.

Yet the CPEMC's role as a site for both cultural diplomacy and American acculturation is hardly unique in the history of Cold War institution-building in the United States. In fact, the studio can be understood as typical in the following regard: it found fierce advocates in uprooted creative workers drawn to the project of "becoming American" via modernist aesthetics and official state- and foundation-supported institutions. As long-standing scholarship has shown, mid-century US cultural and political institutions co-opted modernist aesthetic movements (such as Abstract Expressionism, bebop, and post-tonal composition) as ideological weapons to demonstrate "American" values of freedom, difficulty, individualism, and plurality in supposed contradistinction to Soviet cultural policy.[50] Aesthetic modernism formed a realm in which ideas of Americanness and Western culture could be clarified and brought into positive equation with one another, helping to bring order to disrupted world histories and individual fates. It formed a grid through which heroic ideas of America as the leader of "the liberal West" could be made intelligible both in institutional projects of cultural diplomacy and in life narratives of successful American acculturation. As Greg Barnhisel writes,

> The international character of modernism, like the military and economic alliances being forged through the North Atlantic Treaty Organization and the Marshall Plan, served to knit the West together, with the United States leading the way. Many of the artists whose works were on display in these exhibitions were also either immigrants or the children of immigrants; their Americanness and "Americanism" were thus suspect. In using freedom and individualism to "Americanize" modernism, then, Cold War modernism Americanized these artists.[51]

Luening and Ussachevsky prided themselves on their ability to work as a team.[52] Their special symbiosis was rooted not only in complimentary approaches to tape composition, professional networking, and institution-building, but also from their shared citizenly dispositions as "good immigrants," which facilitated these projects.

Luening belonged to a generation of German-Americans who needed to demonstrate their American loyalties after both world wars—a responsibility that may have loomed especially large in Luening's case, because his family had undertaken recurrent remigrations between both homelands over the course of two generations. His memoir, *The Odyssey of an American Composer* (1980)—supported with a grant from the Rockefeller Foundation—narrates a life story amply documented in interviews and extensive archival collections he painstakingly organized.[53] As a memoirist, raconteur, and self-archivist, Luening promoted a narrative that brought European high-art bona fides into communication with American mythologies of utility, industry, frontier exploration, personal responsibility, and freedom. From this history he fashioned a persona conducive to the ideological purposes of American soft power, developing vocabularies and narratives that dovetailed with languages of national mission and foreign policy: "utility," "craft," and "service" remained his watchwords rather than "genius." In his many autobiographical statements, Luening emphasized what he saw as the morally salubrious qualities of his American background, particularly in the context of the rural Midwest farm setting of his early childhood in Wisconsin: he was taught a "'do it yourself' style of instruction, taught not to rely on anything but what I could learn myself."[54] Indeed, Luening had made a fateful coming-of-age decision in 1920 to remigrate to America alone, after his childhood immigration with his parents to Germany in 1912. This remigration had been encouraged by Edith Rockefeller McCormick, who served as his patron and mentor during a three-year period when Luening had escaped with his sister from Germany in order to avoid the German draft. From 1917 to 1920, McCormick came close to being a substitute parent for Luening— whose parents had stayed in Germany in the 1910s—in Switzerland, where he also played flute in the Tonhalle Orchestra, studied composition with Philipp Jarnach and Ferruccio Busoni, and performed in James Joyce's theater company. Astonishingly, Luening's own path toward Americanization (or re-Americanization) had been bound up with the Rockefeller family from the very start through his connection with McCormick, who encouraged him to return "home" from Europe.[55]

The significance of Edith Rockefeller McCormick for Luening's musical projects extended into the core of his compositional philosophy of music, which he described as a mode of "self-realization." An early proponent of Jungian psychotherapy, McCormick would also shape the ideas of her father (John D. Rockefeller) and husband (Harold Fowler McCormick), whose correspondence reveals the adaptation of Jungian ideas to burgeoning notions of scientific management that came to characterize the business and philanthropic endeavors of Rockefeller and his milieu.[56] Edith Rockefeller McCormick had moved to Zurich to pursue treatment and training with Carl Jung after having suffered debilitating agoraphobia over many years.[57] Luening's correspondence with her, which persisted until her death in 1932, shows the extent to which her Jungian vocabularies permeated his own portrayal of himself and his composerly vocation to her:

By loving what I thought was all [composition] in order to stay true to my ideals, I found that I had gained everything that could be gained. I am a peaceful and contented man ... I take the attitude that life consists of pleasure and pain, success and failure and knowing this I am not affected by either the pleasant or unpleasant. I take things as they come, pursu[ing] that course of action, which I believe to be of the greatest value for the human race in an absolutely dispassionate manner. I can do no more than this.[58]

Luening's adoption of Jungian images of duality and balance cannot simply be dismissed as a strategy to flatter his patron, although that surely played a role, at least in part. By mid-century, Luening continued to wield a similar vocabulary to explain his "ideas about composing" in his personal correspondence with Varèse: "Humanly, I feel that music should in some way and for someone, animate or quiet the intelligence and awaken or soothe the emotions, so helping man discover a greater realization *of his nature and being* than he had before and perhaps even a semblance of balance within himself."[59] Luening's understanding of music as a vehicle for self-realization prompted his interest in music therapy, in accord with his generally pragmatic understanding of music's significance to society. It also fueled his efforts in cultural diplomacy, which brought him into partnership with the Rockefeller Foundation in the late 1940s.

By this time, Luening had established himself as a power broker in American musical institutions, well attuned to the patronage opportunities of cultural diplomacy. His transatlantic background had served him well toward this end. In 1920 he had chosen to migrate to Chicago, likely in anticipation of McCormick's planned return to the same city. McCormick continued to support Luening upon his move from Zurich to Chicago, where he conducted and composed opera and chamber works, wrote music for movies, and performed flute before eventually landing positions at the Eastman School of Music, the University of Arizona, Bennington College, Barnard College, and Columbia University.[60] A return trip to Germany in 1928–29 allowed him to strengthen ties to such musicinstitutional figures as Jarnach, Heinrich Jalowetz, and Hermann Scherchen, even enabling a brief meeting with the Cologne mayor and future chancellor Conrad Adenauer.[61] As Mario Davidovsky recalled of Luening, "He was not a Jew, but he was a *Macher*."[62]

It was in the late 1930s and 1940s that Luening cofounded the American Composers Alliance (1937) and the American Music Center (1939), and first began to serve on the Pulitzer Prize committee (1943–70). His outward-facing energy also fueled a liberal, center-left politics articulated in a steady stream of typed letters to congressional representatives, which he preserved alongside petitions and pamphlets on issues ranging from civil rights to jukebox royalties. Cultural diplomacy remained a vital preoccupation throughout his career. The American Music Center (AMC) established a library and information bureau for promoting American concert music globally, working together with the State and War Departments; it eventually served as a bridge to the RF when Luening called upon the foundation to support an AMC-organized tour for American classical and folk musicians in Germany and Austria in 1948.[63] General Robert A. McClure, known as the "Father of Psychological Warfare," opined that the tour's "enthusiastic reception . . . by the Soviet press and officials offers one of the few means of contact and possibility of improving international relations."[64] Following these successes, Luening emerged as a key specialist referee for RF funding proposals, a position that surely brought an insider's advantage to his own funding applications.[65]

The archive of the CPEMC's founding testifies to the soft-power mission Ussachevsky and Luening realized as a team. Over the course of multiple proposal drafts completed in dialogue with RF officers, they honed persuasive arguments for their project's relevance for US state objectives, with Ussachevsky taking the lead as the document's author. Elizabeth Kray, who knew Fahs from her days in the IPR, helped to smooth relations with the RF by joining in on meetings; she also typed and retyped many dozens of pages of proposal documents—an early instance of the invisible female labor that kept the CPEMC running.[66] Babbitt, who joined the effort in the late 1950s, supported them through further communications with RF officers and RCA executives concerning the Mark II synthesizer, which would form the technological centerpiece for the CPEMC. For our purposes, we should pay particular attention to an extended proposal draft that articulated foundational arguments about mission.[67] This document, which circulated at the RF, preceded and justified a pared-down, five-page final proposal that responded to RF feedback regarding details of equipment, personnel, and services that would require funding.[68] As articulated in the draft proposal, the CPEMC's "first program" would be to develop "the means by which an interested composer can speedily come to grips with the creative tape music medium" in a manner that could compete with "the success of our talented European colleagues."[69] The "second program," closely related to the first, would be to "provide a more idiomatic 'instrument for composers'"; it would "undertake to solve the problem of sound cataloguing to overcome the composer's persistent problem of accessibility to sound materials."[70] In elaborating this mission, the draft proposal emphasizes the CPEMC's status both as a scientific research center and as a site for cultural diplomacy. The studio would build upon "past and present scientific inquiries into the physical nature of sound and its psychological and physiological effects," with the aim of serving "the needs of electronic music" as a high art, just as it would bring "mutual fertilization between the music of the West and the East."[71]

These vaunted goals aligned well with those of the Rockefeller Foundation as they continued to develop over the course of the decade. Building upon the basis of humanities policy documents already discussed above, the RF created a new mandate for arts funding in 1953, administered by the Humanities Division. It supported this mandate with a number of surveys on arts production in the United States to be included in the RF trustees' annual confidential reports. In his 1958 report, "Adventuring in the Arts," Marshall emphasized the extent to which "American performing organizations have become, within a few years, an important commodity in the international relations of the nation."[72] The report also drew attention to the expanding role of new magnetic recording technologies in popularizing "good music" as opposed to commercial cultural products—a development that would help to counteract images of the US public as "addicted to the popular fare of radio, television, and motion pictures. . . . the country of technicolor, spectaculars, and comic books."[73] (Marshall's reference to electronic tape may well have been a response to Ussachevsky and Luening's repeated insistence upon its importance over the course of their years-long relationship.) As Marshall further explained, the US was "in the midst of a culture boom" that would democratize and Americanize traditions of high art inherited from Europe while wielding them in the service of cultural diplomacy.[74] This 1958 report built on Fahs's 1951 confidential report to the trustees that had justified "a few small and experimental projects" in the funding of "non-verbal arts" on the basis of familiar themes of universality, social hygiene, and psychic health: "[The non-verbal arts'] presence in almost every known culture, and their use in modern psychotherapy, gives some evidence that experience of them is essential for individual well-being."[75] "That experience has importance as something that can be internationally shared without the interference of linguistic barriers," he argued. "We believe, therefore, that Foundation interest in the non-verbal arts may also be justifiable."[76] Fahs's goals for orienting the RF funding decisions were that musical studies and experimentation should contribute to "the problem of integration of humanistic experience" and "interdisciplinary studies of cultures" in colleges and universities through the "exchange of personnel." Working toward this vision of cultural diplomacy, Marshall worked together with Fahs to shepherd Ussachevsky's proposal through the RF funding process. The final proposal—backed by the loan of the Mark II synthesizer from RCA and a financial commitment from Columbia University—appears to have sailed through RF board vetting in the November 1958 meeting.[77]

"A Cross-Grain to My American Acculturation"

Although the agendas of Ussachevsky and the RF overlapped in part, the stakes of their interventions were different. For Ussachevsky, the idea that electronic music might bring "mutual fertilization between the music of the West and the East" was more than just a strategic argument for funding or a project for improving the image of the United States in the world. Rather, it pertained to the challenges of his own immigrant adaptation in the United States. Similarly to how cultural diplomacy may bring coherence to an immigrant's divided past, magnetic tape can bring culturally disparate aural objects together in montage; such an assemblage is conducive to culturally hybrid notions of creativity and being. The divided self emerges here as an object of knowledge open to sustained inquiry via tape and its musical manipulations. Resonating with the RF's own emphasis on psychic integrity and well-being, Ussachevsky's work extended ideas of psychic exploration and self-realization found in many domains of mid-century American culture, including the downtown art and poetry scenes (as discussed in chapter 1).[78]

The goal of his tape music, Ussachevsky confessed, was to "integrate" the "mutually hostile ambiences" of his uprooted life. In a pair of late-life handwritten manuscripts uncovered by music scholars Carl Rahkonen and Ralph Hartsock, Ussachevsky described the difficulty of navigating his American acculturation through a range of competing traditions of musical composition after World War II. In these papers he explained, "I have lived longer in the United States than in China, and I usually react, especially politically, as an American." Nonetheless, his migrant background prevented him from feeling culturally "American" in a way that stimulated his creativity as an electronic composer:

> The deep imprint of my early life in a Russian community in Northern Manchuria produced an underlying cross-grain to my American acculturation. After the war when returning to regular life, I found myself resisting the currents of the American musical idiom, not wanting to go along

with the prevailing experiments, feeling to do so would implicate me in mere imitation; but neither did I want to return to my musical roots— Russian 19th-century music, in which my musical family had trained me. An alternative way had to be found that integrated these mutually hostile ambiences. Serialism was too far removed from the reminiscences of my Asian background to be of interest. I turned to the explorations of sound resources, experimenting in my living room with a tape recorder, and discovered the alternatives in electronic music.[79]

Ussachevsky's words speak both to a sharply divided mid-century American composition scene—famously split between "Americanist" tonality and European-derived serialism, among other trends—and to Ussachevsky's experience of migration as cultural fracture. Rahkonen and Hartsock convincingly suggest that the composer wrote this statement in 1984 in preparation for a grant proposal for an autobiographical project to be completed in partnership with his wife, the poet Elizabeth Kray. Referring to Ussachevsky's words as a "smoking gun" with respect to his motivations as an electronic music pioneer, Rahkonen and Hartsock conclude that Ussachevsky turned to electronic music in order to create a sound world that "utilized sounds of his native Manchuria" including gongs, bells, and sounds that approximated the resonant timbres of those instruments.[80] Electronic music, in their view, afforded Ussachevsky a wider timbral palette, which could accommodate and combine sounds from the disparate continents of his heritage. From my perspective, the resulting compositional aesthetic hovers between established conventions of musical Orientalism on the one hand, and a migrant cosmopolitanism that commemorates the disparate affiliations of a refugee's uprooted life on the other. This tendency brings Ussachevsky's work into proximity with the German-Jewish-American composer Stefan Wolpe, a friendly acqaintance of Ussachevsky's who built an entire universe of compositional concepts, rhetoric, and montage-based form around notions of migrant testimony.[81] This tendency also reminds us of the fact that Ussachevsky's and Wolpe's primary interlocutors were their poet wives—Elizabeth Kray and Hilda Morley, acquaintances of one another—both immersed in a world of poetics antithetical to the supposed nonreferentiality ascribed to high modernist musics. Such unexplored proximities remind us of the ongoing need to develop historiographies conducive both to migrant histories and to male-female partnership.[82]

While Rahkonen and Hartsock's discussion of "Chinese timbres" and "Asian instruments" tends toward generalities, their focus on a specific set of objects and historical associations that captivated Ussachevsky's musical imagination seems apt. In contrast with Pierre Schaeffer's ideal of acousmatic listening, Ussachevsky often attributed significance to the provenance of objects whose sounds he manipulated on tape.[83] As a prominent example, Ussachevsky spoke of the gong- or bell-like sounds that appear at the end of *Poem in Cycles and Bells* (1954) as having been produced by striking Chinese dinner plates. His sister Ksenia, a pianist, had given him the plates upon their reunion in the United States in 1953, long after they had become forcibly separated in the political turmoil of the 1929 Sino-Soviet War. Ussachevsky recalled: "I am not sure whether she dragged them all the way from Manchuria to Hong Kong where she stayed for a number of weeks before she managed to get to this country. [The plates] have this beautiful sound about them which I immediately then recorded."[84] (The success of Ksenia's immigration to the United States contrasted with that of Ussachevsky's father Alexei, who was "disappeared" following incarceration in Soviet Russia after Ussachevsky and his mother Maria had unsuccessfully campaigned to obtain for him a visa to the United States.)[85] The sounds of the dinner plates struck by a mallet emerge from the triumphant orchestral finale of *Poem in Cycles and Bells*, an electronic-acoustic piece cocomposed with Luening that premiered with the Los Angeles Philhamonic. The prominent placement of these sounds at the very end of this formative composition invites critical attention, as does their connection with a cathected object of memory.

These sounds, in fact, lead to a place where Romantic musical aesthetics, cultures of experimentation, and migrant poetics meet. As a stand-in for the gong, the struck dinner plates evoke music-theatrical traditions rooted in the nineteenth century: the gong served as virtual curtain raiser, curtain closer, or the marker for plot developments of "dramatic essence," such as murder, mortality, damnation, or revelation.[86] At the same time, this sound's prominent placement in an early experimental tape composition links up with a nineteenth-century legacy of clinic- and laboratory-based experimentation. (On the one hand, gongs attracted interest by virtue of the absence of a fundamental tone that characterized their acoustic sound spectrum.[87] On the other hand, they came to be used as a tool in clinical experiments, most prominently in Jean-Martin Charcot's neurological clinic at the Salpêtrière Hospital in Paris, where the struck instrument was used to induce catalepsy.)[88] The substitution of a struck Chinese plate for a gong draws attention to the Chinese provenance of both—a provenance made personal by Ussachevsky's anecdote about long-lost family. As such associations suggest, the struck dinner plates have the potential to gather meaning variously as dramatic markers, objects of memory, objects of inquiry, and instruments within experimental systems.

In order to appreciate the plates' multivalent significance in *Poem in Cycles and Bells*, let us consider the music in more detail. *Poem* consists of four separate sections, two of which recycle short electronic studies—Luening's "Fantasy in Space" (1952) and Ussachevsky's "Sonic Contours" (1952)—which electronically modify the sounds of a flute and a piano respectively (see Luening and Ussachevsky together in figure 2.1). Luening "dressed up" the electronic studies, as Ussachevsky put it, with orchestration in a lushly Romantic tonal idiom reminiscent of mid-century film music.[89] These orchestrated sections bookend, connect, and slightly overlap with the two embedded electronic studies. The orchestration works to counteract the montage-like construction of the piece with strong effects of textural, harmonic, and motivic continuity. Orchestral sounds tend to mimic electronic ones in call-and-response and *Klangfarbenmelodie* figures. A high-register shimmering activity of trills, runs, and ostinati links the recycled musical material from "Sonic Contours" with the orchestral finale, which plays with jaunty, dotted-rhythm major-mode melodic fragments in the upper strings. The contours, rhythms, and intervallic content of these snippets recall the opening theme of the piece—a singable D-major tune, simple in style, compressed within the interval of a fifth. Its tonal, folklike character locates *Poem* firmly within an Americanist style of composition, with Aaron Copland as an audible influence. The finale proceeds as a continuous accumulation of texture and sound: ostinati, melodic fragments, trills, runs, and blocks of sustained chords layer upon one another as the dynamics and instrumental activity build to a climax. The music erupts with a trumpet fanfare, which finally leads to a registrally expansive, overtone-rich electronic gonglike sound from which the concluding intonations of the struck dinner plates emerge, layered with trilling high Cs in the violins. On the one hand, these final soundings function as a celebratory curtain closer that heightens the preceding exultation while marking its end. On the other hand, the reiterative soundings of the recorded dinner plates suggest a tone more interrogative than conclusive. The sound of the plates disappears with a fade.

The apparatus of the sound laboratory effectively manipulates and magnifies a seemingly inconsequential object—the reverberations of a struck dinner plate—in order to direct human attention in new and possibly estranging ways. If the CPEMC sought to further "scientific inquiries into the physical nature of sound and its psychological and physiological effects," then Ussachevsky's own studies may loosely be understood to

FIGURE 2.1. Vladimir
Ussachevsky and Otto
Luening, early 1950s. Vladimir
Ussachevsky Collection,
Library of Congress.
Used by permission.

interrogate sound's status as an object of memory and a token of personal bonds lost and preserved. From this point of view, the composition registers the divided, uprooted self as an object of knowledge open to sustained inquiry through taped sound and its musical manipulations. It is in this sense that the work reveals an inconclusive process of "study" or "laboratory experimentation" in the act of "composition."

The ending of *Poem in Cycles and Bells* also suggests a tension in mood between strains of jubilation and of self-critical uncertainty. As the first large-scale public showcase of Ussachevsky's electronic collaboration with Luening, *Poem* announces the team's successful entry into a classical music mainstream. The celebratory tone of Luening's orchestration anticipates this triumph. A premiere with the Los Angeles Philharmonic is precisely the sort of elite public validation the RF valued for its sponsored musical-humanistic projects. If Luening sought, in broad strokes, "to determine whether man can use & dominate the machines he has created in the field of music or vice versa,"[90] then *Poem's* relative success would seem to answer with an affirmation of human mastery.

Yet, when read in conjunction with Ussachevsky's words from later in life, *Poem in Cycles and Bells* also suggests a narrative less triumphalist, more questioning, riven by incompleteness. How do the struck Chinese dinner plates of Ussachevsky's anecdote function as objects of knowledge in their repeated intonations? As fragments of reality, they commemorate not only a precarious family reunion and escape, but also situations of civil war, detention, incarceration, death, and mourning—conditions that foreground the limits of human autonomy and self-determination. The reiterative temporality of the plates' sounding suggests an inconclusive process. Such a striking mixture of tone as we find in *Poem*—a strange amalgam of triumphalist celebration and the unfinished business of critical interrogation—permeates Ussachevsky's creative practice. Public and private codes intermingle uneasily. The liberal citizen-subject emerges as something not quite as "free" or "masterful" as might have been hoped. Before we return to Ussachevsky's biography—especially the question of his persecution by the Justice Department and his compensatory reliance upon Luening and the RF—it is worth considering his electronic composition practice in more depth. It is here that we apprehend how his work harmonized with RF objectives while also realizing itelf in extremely particularized self-interrogatory ways.

In contrast with Luening's Manichean scenario of "man and machine," Ussachevsky understood his relationship with the technologies of the studio as cooperative: "What is the difference between manipulation of the machine and collaboration with it?" Ussachevsky rhetorically asked of his

FIGURE 2.2. Vladimir Ussachevsky at the CPEMC studio space in Prentis Hall, 1960s. Vladimir Ussachevsky Collection, Library of Congress. Used by permission.

compositional process.[91] The composer consistently described his musical activities in the studio as "intuitive" and "improvisational"—a manner of tinkering with equipment to produce unforeseeeable results in reiterative engagement with the machines. Figure 2.2 shows Ussachevsky in this process. Such an approach is comparable with Hans-Jörg Rheinberger's description of an experimental system as a labyrinth: it "cannot be planned. It builds itself. It forces one to proceed by 'groping' and 'grasping.'"[92] Joseph Pfender evocatively descibes Ussachevsky, in the latter's tactile and intuitive engagement, as

> connect[ing] up his nerve endings with his mechanical collaborator. Rather than producing an exteriorized media trace, he joins his own intentionality with the already exteriorized mechanism. This action suggests a parallel between the received mode of composition as intensive, solitary activity, and the routinization of composition that locates creativity somewhere between the machine and its user.[93]

This creativity, of course, involved multiple human actors working in the studio. From 1951 onward, Peter Mauzey worked with Ussachevsky to modify or invent equipment to generate the specific sounds he imagined.[94] By the late 1950s, Columbia University undergraduate work-study students assisted in the modification of equipment for that purpose.[95] Pril Smiley and Alice Shields, other composers appointed as "technicians" in the mid-1960s, helped Ussachevsky to assemble sound libraries, and even

worked so extensively on Ussachevsky's commissioned film projects as to draw his authorship into question. Smiley compared their contibutions to the invisible labor of composer-technicians who worked for Stockhausen and Varèse—a situation "that was very, very common" in electronic music studios of the time.[96] Smiley clarified that such ambiguities of authorship applied only to Ussachevsky's film scores. His "straight electronic pieces were certainly his own."[97] Indeed, I would suggest that the machine-human interface of Ussachevksy's compositional practice—located within such a dispersed assemblage of human-machine relationality—produced a remarkably lyrical voice conducive to musical narrative.

Let us consider *Wireless Fantasy* (1960) as one example of a work that thematizes the limits of human autonomy in the violent fallout of technologized modernity while leaving a trail of coded autobiographical referents. On the surface, *Wireless Fantasy* seems to celebrate a history of US-led technological advancements within a technoscape of "Western" culture—an approach that may have added virtue and weight to his account with the Humanities Division of the RF. Commissioned by the de Forest Pioneers radio enthusiast club, the composition honors the club's namesake, Lee de Forest—the American inventor of the "Audion" vacuum tube, an amplification device that enabled broadcast radio, long-distance telephony, and innumerable other modern sound technologies.[98] Ussachevsky structured *Wireless Fantasy* through the manipulation of three categories of taped sounds: (1) the 1951 Bayreuth Festival recording of Wagner's *Parsifal* (an excerpt from the prelude that features the "redemption" motive); (2) Morse-code signals by antique spark generators at the W2ZI Historical Wireless Museum in Trenton, New Jersey; and (3) short-wave radio sounds and oscillator tones created in the CPEMC.[99] All of these sounds have a strong potential to index the historical settings and objects that produced them. A consummate punster, Ussachevsky habitually referred to the piece with friends and colleagues as "de Forest Murmurs," in yet another reference to Wagner—in this case, the "Wald-weben" sequence from *Siegfried*, act 2.[100]

Wireless Fantasy plays with sonic-historical signifiers of American tech-noculture and European high art, bringing them into relationships of si-multaneity, interpenetration, and mutual transformation. From this inter-play emerges a miniature sound world of transatlantic civilization in the twentieth century with its own ghostly historiography. The work assumes a witty and affirmative tone in celebrating de Forest as an American fore-father to Ussachevsky's work. As a work of acculturation, the composition therefore locates Ussachevsky within wider currents of history and allows him to become "Americanized" in a narrative of technological progress. Yet it also features unsettling undertones that emerge from the treatment and historicity of its sound materials.

Wireless Fantasy thematizes questions of subject formation and cul-tural heritage in relation to electronic technologies from the outset. It be-gins with a gradual accumulation of layered electronic sounds—a stream of white noise, a midrange oscillating figure, and a low hum—that create steady textural continuity and a feeling of temporal suspension. At 0:14, a high-pitched sine-wave Morse code is tapped out against this backdrop. As Eric Salzman and others have noted, this code—the "DF motive"—abbreviates the initials of Lee de Forest's surname and forms a recurrent rhythmic pattern throughout the piece.[101] The sounds emerge as though from another time and place. They hark back to the early days of telegra-phy, when American exhibitioners sold the technology to the public by encouraging individuals to tap out their names or initials in Morse code.[102] Such a practice speaks to the human tendency to domesticate new tech-nologies and render them less threatening to conventional ways of life.[103] It also evokes the process by which one's name—typed into forms and/or spelled via Morse code—shapes the self in a world of technologized insti-tutions, the very process by which modern social subjects are formed.

To be sure, music also serves as a means for "humanizing" technology and as a technologized means of subject-formation. In preserving the sound of de Forest's initials, *Wireless Fantasy* transforms the long Euro-pean tradition of encoding compositional authorship and heritage in mu-sical works as motives that reference composers' spelled names or initials as pitch material. The B-A-C-H motive is the most famous example of this practice. In German nomenclature, its spelling denotes B-flat, A, C, and B-natural—a succession of notes which form the basis for compositions from J. S. Bach's time onward, and especially after the Bach revival of the early nineteenth century. Through the DF motif, Ussachevsky may be understood as declaring an American technocultural heritage for himself, with de Forest as forebear, while altering and integrating the European "great tradition" of concert composition by claiming de Forest as worthy of his own musical motive.

In keeping with such an impulse to integrate divergent technocultural and artistic traditions, *Wireless Fantasy* conjures a smooth textural continuity from disparate materials that evoke and conjoin North American and European histories within a single technologized soundscape. Following the introduction of the DF motif, the electronic textural buildup continues with noisy short-wave radio and spark generator sounds, producing variations on the opening sound materials, until all of the low- and midrange vamping drops out at 1:19 to expose a "solo" of lively chirping sounds, seemingly derived through manipulation of the original Morse code material. Beneath this chatter, the midregister drone returns to blend seamlessly into the *Parsifal* quotation, which emerges around 1:30 with its orchestral timbres filtered to resemble a ghostly choir.

As the music builds, *Wireless Fantasy* continues to handle its sonic materials in a manner that historicizes them. Just as the filtered Wagner quotation finally becomes intelligible, soft clicking sounds seem to mimic the noise of a rotating phonograph (at 1:51) while all other electronic sounds disappear to allow a clear rendering of the orchestral recording. Subsequent additional filtering of *Parsifal* mimicks the sound of an old-fashioned radio broadcast. Through such effects, *Wireless Fantasy* highlights multiple levels of mediation in historical sound production and broadcast technology. Through the *Parsifal* quotation, Ussachevsky again references de Forest, who staged the world's first radio broadcast of a Metropolitan Opera performance of *Parsifal* in 1910.[104] Yet the piece's simulation of "listening through the wireless"—which eventually superimposes *Parsifal* with a battery of Morse code tappings—also evokes Wagner's more ominous associations with Nazi propaganda and ideology. The sounds of high culture become superimposed with those of military technology. This juxtaposition of materials comes to a head at 2:45 when the Morse code appears transformed, spelling out the full name "Lee de Forest"—now heard eight and a half times in synchronic climax with Wagner's music (the "redemption motif") and the final cadence of that passage. Such a violent juxtaposition potentially brings to mind the profound relevance of de Forest's inventions to twentieth-century warfare and political domination, as documented in Carolyn Birdsall's and Roland Wittje's writings on the electroacoustic components of the Nazi war machine.[105] Ussachevsky's wartime work as an analyst in the OSS would have equipped him with ample knowledge of such technological infrastructures and their military-strategic significance.

In foregrounding the music of Wagner alongside the inventions of de Forest, *Wireless Fantasy* brings ideas of Europeanness and Americanness, high art and technoculture, into juxtaposition within an interrogation of the past and present. The fact that Ussachevsky used the 1951 Bayreuth Festival recording of *Parsifal* brings brings further complexity to his web of allusions. The 1951 recording documents the first Bayreuth Festival after World War II—a scene of denazification in US-occupied Germany. Yet, as I have shown, *Wireless Fantasy* can hardly be understood simply as a paean to US power as a redeeming force in the world, despite its use of Wagner's redemption motive in an ostentatious tribute to de Forest. Ussachevsky was known as much for his political worldliness as for his enjoyment of secrets and codes. As Pril Smiley remembered, Ussachevsky and his wife, Elizabeth Kray, were "very aware of everything that had to do with government, politics, and the world out there, but those subjects weren't the basis of conversation." She added that "Ussachevsky loved secrets, too."[106] Such a knowing but wary and secretive disposition found full expression in the curious lyrical poetics of *Wireless Fantasy*: the piece suggests a way of knowing the world in secrets and codes—an epistemology that complements the psychological and bureaucratic approaches to knowledge production that dominated Ussachevsky and Luening's joint venture with the RF.

Of course, world histories of conflict bear upon singular life narratives just as technological power impinges upon individual situations of integration and survival. Ussachevsky insisted that his electronic composition deals with "an underlying cross-grain to [his] American acculturation;" we will see that the sound of Morse code ultimately speaks at least as powerfully to the "reminiscences of [his] Asian background" as any gong, bell, or Chinese dinner plate ever could. As Ussachevsky recalled in his interview with Joan Thomson, "I think that a fascination with sounds in general was already present [from early on], because when I was back in China I used to be fascinated with the sounds of the telegraph poles along the railroad. I would stop and put my ears to the poles and listen"—resulting in the perception of "just a hum, but it's an interesting, a complicated hum which is transmitted from the wires to the wood."[107] He elaborated this image further in sentence fragments scrawled on an envelope: "Away from the souls and hearts of men, clutching the bars of a bicycle I listened to the hum of wires, resonating in the splintery round of the dead trunks of trees—made alive with the sound of electricity. Did I know then, on a Mongolian plain, devoid of sound like the craters of Mars, except for the hypnotic message of the wires, . . . the hypnotic message of the electric hum."[108] It is through such a network of autobiographical imagery that a work like *Wireless Fantasy* assumes a self-narrative character in relation to world-historical themes.

Such words show how Ussachevsky's sensitivity to questions of techno-power—deeply entangled with his self-revelatory musical poetics—would have predated his involvement in the OSS. Technopower emerges from the relations of human or nonhuman agents and technological arti-facts; it indicates a constant oscillation between technology experienced as an inert, asocial thing and as something reverberant with social and political value.[109] The "message" Ussachevsky heard when listening to the "hum" of the wooden poles would not have amounted to actual Morse code transmissions, yet the telegraph he describes so poetically surely played an outsized significance in his own family's history in Manchuria.

Born in Hailar, Vladimir Ussachevsky spent most of his childhood in Stanzia Manchouri (Manchouli), on the triple border of Russia with Inner and Outer Manchuria. (Figure 2.3 shows five-year-old Vladimir "Vovochka" Ussachevsky in Manchuria, in the military garb of gazyr breast pockets and shapka.) His father, Alexei Ussachevsky, had served as a a career military officer for the Russian Empire, settling with his fam-ily in Manchuria after the Sino-Russian War to protect the Russian sta-tions built along the Trans-Siberian Railway that were administered as a Russian concession in Chinese-occupied Inner Manchuria. During the Russian Revolution, the elder Ussachevsky's military allegiances became complicated when he solidified an alliance with Mongol forces fighting against Chinese occupiers during the Chinese Civil War, and dressed his troops in Mongolian uniforms. After the collapse of the Russian imperial army, Alexei finally sought to establish a mining business on the basis of a massive land concession granted by his Mongolian allies in the midst of the violent fallout of the Russian and Chinese revolutions. In the 1920s, Vladimir's brother was sent to the University of California, Berkeley, to study engineering for the prospective family mining business. This con-nection eventually enabled the teenaged Vladimir and his mother, Maria (a trained pianist and piano teacher), to emigrate to the United States af-ter Manchuria had become too dangerous and Alexei had finally been im-prisoned, eventually to be incarcerated in Soviet Russia.[110] With this fam-ily story in mind, Ussachevsky's memory of the sounds of the telegraph

FIGURE 2.3. Vladimir "Vovochka" Ussachevsky, July 1915, Manchuria. Vladimir
Ussachevsky Collection, Library of Congress. Used by permission.

poles summons something more than a neutral history of technology.
The Russian-Manchurian stations along the railroad and telegraph lines
erupted as a source of conflict over years of political upheaval that split his
family apart. For the luckier members of his family, they also served as a
source of communication and escape. Yet "freedom" in the United States
would hardly prove to be straightforward.

"The Grisly Detail"

Ussachevsky made reference to his troubles in the postwar Red Scare in
a 1977 interview with the musicologist and music critic Joan Thomson,
in a manner that acknowledged some facts while obscuring others. He
recounted that his first experiences as an American cultural ambassador

and publicly recognized tape pioneer were mingled with fears about his own citizenly rights and status. In 1953, as he recalled, he attended the first Congress of Experimental Music in Paris and visited the West German Radio (WDR) electronic music studio in Cologne as the sole American representative of tape experimentalism. Yet while French Radio had invited him to attend the conference and BMI had agreed to sponsor him, his plans to obtain a passport were derailed by Elizabeth Kray's employment at the Institute of Pacific Relations (IPR)—a nonprofit organization dedicated to promoting "international friendship."[111]

Ussachevsky could not obtain a regular passport, because the IPR had come under attack by Senator Joseph McCarthy, former President Herbert Hoover, and Senate Judiciary Committee chairman Pat McCarran for having been "sympathetic" to communist governments.[112] Although Ussachevsky had shown no prior activism in leftist causes, he nonetheless was denied a passport because of his tenuous connection with the IPR—despite the fact that "virtually everyone in the United States and elsewhere with expertise in the field of Asian studies was a member of the IPR."[113] Ussachevsky recalled his shock:

I after all had worked in the State Department during the war and I was in every way honorably separated from them and went simply back to music, but that didn't make any difference you see. So I had to go to a lawyer and draw up a document saying that I was never a Communist and so forth and so on. Then I had to go see somebody who gave me permission to be absent from this country for not more than ten days and go only to such places as I indicated I would go, which restricted me to Paris and Cologne, except as it may be in transit. . . . So that was the time, and that's the grisly detail.[114]

It was finally Columbia University that successfully advocated on Ussachevsky's behalf so that he could obtain a restricted passport, as his archived correspondence shows.[115] This show of institutional support, however, hardly would have made up for the troubling implications of the incident. As a result of his passport restrictions, he was forced to decline an invitation from Karlheinz Stockhausen and his wife Doris Andreae to hike on the outskirts of Cologne—a circumstance that, by Ussachevsky's account, Stockhausen himself could not understand and interpreted as a personal slight.[116] Ussachevsky's discussion of the episode highlights the contradiction between his status as the only American emissary in the European electronic music scene and his seemingly incomprehensibly restricted citizenship and mobility. The ultimate irony of the story is

that this restriction of citizenship transpired in US-occupied Germany—
the very setting that trumpeted US ideals of liberty as an antidote to the
Nazi past.

While government records amply corroborate Ussachevsky's 1977 oral
history account, this archive also demonstrates that he substantially understated the duration and severity of dangers he faced. His targeting was
hardly a short-term problem, nor was it simply an outgrowth of his wife's
employment. Two decades of FBI surveillance coincided with the critical
years Ussachevsky dedicated to career- and institution-building between
the 1940s and 1960s. Following the McCarran Internal Security Act of
1950, any suspicion of "subversive activity" could theoretically have resulted in the denial of citizenship for immigrants petitioning for citizenship, or the loss of citizenship for citizens naturalized after 1951.[117] Ussachevsky's sister Ksenia Terechovskaya (Terry), who became naturalized
in 1959, could have been subject to the act's citizenship and denaturaliza-
tion provisions if the accusations against her brother had been weapon-
ized against her.[118] As late as 1964, the Immigration and Naturalization
Service obtained FBI files on Ussachevsky for the purpose of their own
investigation in connection with his visit to his other sister, Natalia Ussachevsky, in Leningrad.[119] Upon joining the OSS in 1944, moreover, Ussachevsky had certified by signature his knowledge of the penalties for espionage under US law, which included the death penalty.[120]

It is not clear whether or how fully Ussachevsky understood the extent
of his surveillance, but we do know that he must have known more than he
admitted to Thomson in 1977, because the FBI interviewed him and transcribed a voluntary statement from him as early as 1945—something omitted in his account to Thomson. Through his work at the OSS, moreover,
he would have had an unusually detailed understanding of intelligence-
gathering techniques. Given the high stakes of the McCarran Act for him
as a naturalized citizen under suspicion of subversive activity—alongside
his literacy in government policy as a former State Department worker—
it is difficult to imagine that he would not have carefully followed these
legislative and political developments on Capitol Hill.

Ussachevsky's preserved work papers and correspondence with Luening, Kray, and others show no explicit reference to his problems during
the Red Scare—a silence that mirrors his reputation for avoiding political discussion.[121] These gaps may of course point to great fear or shame.
Such feelings would certainly have been justified: the Red Scare wielded
strength through conspiracy theories that deprived individuals of their
livelihoods and citizenly rights rather than giving them their day in court.
And Ussachevsky had had the ironic misfortune, as a naturalized citizen

of Russian background, to have worked in the Central and East Asia divisions of the OSS—a focal point of paranoid investigation during the postwar Red Scare.

Ussachevsky first came onto the radar of the FBI in 1945 in connection with his work as an intelligence analyst working on Manchuria, first in the OSS and then in the State Department. In July 1944, OSS records describe his transfer there "as one of the most important we have made for some time." The work of the Far Eastern division was under "tremendous pressure" to meet deadlines, and Ussachevsky had "three qualifications not usually found in one person": a command of Chinese and Russian languages, a high degree of academic training, and personal knowledge of Manchuria, derived from his childhood there.[122] Consequently, his OSS assignment was that of "research analyst in the Political Subdivision, Korea-Manchuria Section, Far East, Div. Cpl. Ussachvsky will be used for studies of Japanese administration and Chinese invisible government in Manchuria and will be employed in research connected with MO [Morale Operations], SI [Surveillance and Intelligence], JANIS [Joint Army-Navy Intelligence Studies], and JIC [Joint Intelligence Committee] assignments in regard to Manchuria."[123] By the end of his government career in 1946, Ussachevsky had become "head of a unit working on Manchuria in the China Political Section."[124] This career trajectory in itself made him politically vulnerable.

Running like a red thread through the history of postwar anticommunist conspiracy theories is the false claim that China's fall to communism had resulted from Soviet infiltration of the US foreign policy elite. As Ross Y. Koen, himself a victim of the Red Scare, explains, many Americans had a "tendency to believe, when their hopes weren't fulfilled, that they had been betrayed."[125] These feelings of betrayal attended the fallout of the Yalta Conference, at which the delegations of Roosevelt, Churchill, and Stalin negotiated to determine the postwar reorganization of Europe. A secret protocol from that summit stipulated that, in return for Stalin's agreement to enter the war against Japan and to join the United Nations, the Soviet Union would be allocated control of all Russian-controlled territory seized by Japan, a sphere of influence in Manchuria, domination of Outer Mongolia, and shared Sino-Soviet control of Manchurian railroads.[126] This provision proved highly consequential, because Soviet-occupied Manchuria provided a base of operations for the Chinese Communists in their civil war with Chinese nationalist forces. As such, it fueled conspiracy theories about OSS and State Department workers whispering poison into Roosevelt's ear at Yalta and hastening the fall of China to communism.

The Chinese-administered former Russian concession along the Trans-Siberian Railway had long been a place of legend in its "drama of changing peoples, of shifting social orders and races," as one cogent journalist wrote as early as 1929.[127] Richard Condon's 1959 novel *The Manchurian Candidate* exemplified such sensational depictions. After the turmoil of the Russian Revolution, Chinese-governed Manchuria garnered suspicion among white Euro-American commentators as a place "where yellow ruled white"—much like Ussachevsky's father's troops' changing from Russian imperial to Mongolian uniforms.[128] The region's bewilderingly rapid transformations in governance and social structure—and its seeming upending of white supremacist hierarchy—exacerbated conspiracy theories that thrived during the Red Scare. It was against this backdrop that the FBI began to search for communist infiltrators among the US-based "China experts" working in academia, government, and the military—the professional community in which Ussachevsky had begun his career.

Ussachevsky and Kray's names first appear in FBI records in connection with the 1945 "*Amerasia* affair," an event that helped kick off postwar paranoia. The fact that Ussachevsky's name appears at the origin of the postwar Red Scare seems to have ensured that his name would appear again and again in surveillance files, despite the lack of evidence tying him to espionage. (His name appears more persistently in the FBI files than Kray's, likely because his Manchurian-Russian ancestry marked him as suspicious, and because his higher professional status in intelligence and policy circles, underwritten by his male gender, marked him as a more serious potential threat.) *Amerasia* was an academic journal devoted to Asian affairs, oriented around the very community of Asian "area studies" specialists to which Ussachevsky and Kray belonged. The couple had met in 1943 in the Chinese Area and Language Studies program at the University of Washington, where Ussachevsky had been directed to undergo training by the US Army (figure 2.4). The Rockefeller Foundation supported this new academic initiative, aiming to promote interdisciplinary approaches pragmatically relevant to US strategic interests amid rising geopolitical tensions. During World War II, such area studies programs worked as a feeder stream for the OSS and the State Department, with personnel moving fluidly between government, foundation, academic, and journalistic settings. Following a tip in March 1945, OSS agents broke into the *Amerasia* offices, where they discovered hundreds of classified government documents, which they suspected government workers had inappropriately funneled to the journal. At this time, Ussachevsky held the rank of corporal while working at the OSS in Wash-

FIGURE 2.4. Technical Corporal Vladimir Ussachevsky in summer combat uniform, serving as secretary and organist to the chaplain, early 1940s. Vladimir Ussachevsky Collection, Library of Congress. Used by permission.

ington, DC; Kray served as the "secretary" (administrator) of the IPR in a three-room Washington office. The FBI assumed control of the *Amerasia* investigation from the OSS, seizing 1,700 classified documents and arresting six men—including the China expert John W. Service—after an illegal search.[129] As documented in the FBI surveillance of social gatherings, Ussachevsky and Kray were friendly associates of Service, along with other Chinese "area men" such as Philip Jaffe, Lieutenant Andrew Roth, and Owen Lattimore, who also came under suspicion. The FBI physically trailed Ussachevsky and Kray in connection with these colleagues, and they wiretapped or bugged phone conversations among them. In June 1945, the bureau also interviewed the couple, who insisted that they had never participated in or witnessed the inappropriate transmission of classified documents to *Amerasia*.

"USSACHEVSKY related that he considered California his home," the FBI report of his 1945 interview states. His simple bid to show American loyalty failed to convince the FBI, as did the assertion from Sam Kiser (Security and Intelligence Corps, US Army) that "the files of the O.S.S. reflect that USSACHEVSKY is known to be anti-Communist"—a logical conclusion, given that the subject's father had been killed in Soviet state purges. Ussachevsky's OSS colleagues may not have doubted his anti-Soviet sentiments, yet an OSS internal investigation in 1944 had nonetheless questioned Ussachevsky's susceptibility to blackmail, cautioning that the "Subject's sister is believed to be living in Manchuria; and the Subject, therefore, might be vulnerable to hostage pressure."[130] Although we cannot know whether the FBI entertained the same concern, we can reasonably speculate that Ussachevsky's Russian-Manchurian background and family made him more vulnerable to suspicion. His surveillance continued despite the fact that no evidence against him was found. This fact testifies to the enormous work performed by the secret police file as a "powerful biographical genre" that creates its own reality, as Cristina Vatulescu has argued.[131] Such files are interested in "*collating*, that is, 'bringing together and comparing,' different documents with the aim 'to ascertain *the* correct text,' *the* correct version of the subject. The ultimate goal is to erase all incongruities in a synthetic characterization, a characterization ideally reduced down to one incriminating sentence."[132] In this drive toward incrimination, the police file motivates bizarre actions in accordance with the alternate reality and logic it constructs. In 1947, for example, the FBI microfilmed the contents of the luggage of the Kray-Ussachevsky's houseguest Groff Conklin, a science fiction author, following the supposed "theft" of his suitcase (which would soon be "found" again by Conklin after the microfilming, in a sort of pantomime drama). By 1950 the FBI had decided to open individual cases devoted to Ussachevsky and Kray on the basis not only of their connection with the *Amerasia* affair, but also their friendship with Lattimore—who had become subject to a growing political storm—and their connection with the Yaddo artists' retreat, which had fallen under suspicion.

The *Amerasia* affair exacerbated public paranoia through its inconclusivity: it produced no convictions because of the illegality of the FBI's search, and therefore become fodder for further conspiracy-mongering that targeted Ussachevsky and Kray's professional circles. McCarthy partnered with Hoover and McCarran to posit Lattimore as responsible for the "betrayal" at Yalta, painting him as "the top espionage agent in the United States, the boss of Alger Hiss." Michaels summarizes Lattimore's situation, which led to a kind of political exile:

FIGURE 2.5. Vladimir Ussachevsky and Elizabeth Kray, mid-1940s.
Vladimir Ussachevsky Collection, Library of Congress. Used by permission.

Lattimore was a man with a distinguished career; he was a Far East Policy specialist, head of the School of International Relations at Johns
Hopkins, had, from 1933 to 1941, been editor of the journal *Pacific Affairs*
(published by the Institute of Pacific Relations), had been FDR's China
advisor in 1941, had served as US advisor to Chiang Kai-shek (receiving
a letter of praise from the Generalissimo for his work), had accompanied
Vice President Henry Wallace on a tour of China and Russia in 1944, had
been on the staff of the Office of War Information and had written many
books. But he had never worked at the State Department, and he was neither a spy nor a Communist. . . . Lattimore made some serious errors—
outstanding among these were his initial belief and public statement that
Stalin's purge trials were justified. In this instance, Lattimore was simply

and horribly wrong, yet there is nothing in his record to indicate that he was pro-Soviet; he consistently wrote and spoke against both Russian and Chinese domination of less-developed nations like those of central Asia. . . . He argued that these countries should be free of Russian domination, of Chinese domination and of American domination.[133]

Michaels concludes that Lattimore's consistently "anti-imperialist" stance, his suggestion "that the United States might be anything other than a beneficent force in any context whatsoever," is what ultimately damned him politically.[134] After twelve days of testimony in front of a combative Senate Judiciary Committee, he was indicted on seven counts of perjury that were later dismissed by a federal judge as so "formless and obscure" that it would make a "sham of the Sixth Amendment" to require Lattimore to go to trial on their basis.[135] In 1962, Lattimore finally left the United States to spend the rest of his career and retirement in the United Kingdom, working at the University of Leeds. Lattimore and his wife, Eleanor Holgate, appear to have been close friends of Ussachevsky and Kray; yet, ironically, it is only the FBI files that document their plans—for example, for a bicycling trip in Vermont—and other convivial gatherings.[136] Hardly a trace of their friendship remains documented in Ussachevsky's carefully preserved, voluminous archive of correspondence, save a 1975 letter from Emily Lattimore, their daughter-in-law, to Kray in the form of a poem.[137] This slim document reveals a potent mixture of silence, erasure, and allusive poetics that speaks volumes of their families' shared troubled history and friendship.

Ussachevsky's need for institutional protection during the Red Scare was acute. Far from being an established composer at mid-century, Ussachevsky was employed at Columbia as contingent academic labor. After having immigrated to the United States in 1929, he had, upon joining the Army, earned a BA degree in music at Pomona College and an MA and PhD at the Eastman School of Music. When he began to experiment with tape composition in the early 1950s, after his years in the OSS and the State Department, he was employed as a mere postdoctoral fellow and lecturer. The problem of his association with Lattimore and the *Amerasia* affair was further aggravated by his having become caught up in the "Lowell affair"—a 1949 effort on the part of poet Robert Lowell, along with other guests at the Yaddo artists' retreat, to have Yaddo's executive director, Elizabeth Ames, removed under accusations of communist sympathies.[138] Lowell's undiagnosed manic depression, combined with long-standing artistic rivalries, envenomed this episode, which culminated in an FBI visit to the retreat. It was in this context that Mary Townsend, Ames's administrative assistant, accused Ussachevsky, who had been a recent guest at Yaddo, of being a communist and of associating with communists.[139] Although the FBI investigation of Ussachevsky appears to have tapered off in the mid-1950s, the danger it posed persisted, as is evident in his 1964 INS investigation, precipitated by his visit to his sister Natalia in Leningrad.

A landmark 1965 Supreme Court decision finally declared the McCarran Act unenforceable—the same year as the final entry in Ussachevsky's and Kray's FBI files. This entry testifies to just how outlandish the net of surveillance had become. It consists of a memo from the CIA to the FBI, notifying them of an intercepted letter from the Columbia University musicology graduate student Richard Taruskin.[140] Writing to his "Uncle Georgiy and Aunt Nina" in the Soviet Union, Taruskin innocently mentioned his assistantship with Ussachvsky and his desire to visit his family in Russia. (Taruskin has explained that his "Uncle Georgiy" was in fact a cousin, General Georgiy Iosifovich Lieb, who served as a "*gabbai*, or president of the congregation,' of the big Moscow 'Choral Synagogue.' . . . His true role was to stand between visiting foreign Jews and their Soviet counterparts.")[141] The CIA intercepted and photocopied this letter before sending it to the FBI, which cross-listed it with Ussachevsky's file. The mere fact of having family in the Soviet Union made Ussachevsky and Taruskin targets of state surveillance and privacy violations—a danger for Russian-Americans and Russian-Jewish-Americans more generally.

The paranoid scope and duration of the FBI's investigation of Ussachevsky casts new light on his association with the Rockefeller Foundation, Columbia University, and Otto Luening—connections that assumed deepening value precisely during the acutest period of his investigation. Ussachevsky's defensive silence about politics—combined with his dedication to official US cultural diplomacy networks—roughly parallels the case of Aaron Copland, who followed a higher-profile path toward rehabilitation in American public life after he had faced passport restrictions during the Red Scare because of his leftist activism.[142] Although Ussachevsky's record as a veteran at the State Department apparently "didn't make any difference" toward exonerating him at the height of the Red Scare, it did provide a protective social network to counteract the negative professional consequences of rumor or accusation. Burton Fahs, director of the Humanities Division at the RF from 1950 until 1961, had lent his expertise to the Far East Division of the OSS during World War II before serving as chief of the division in 1945. Fahs must have come to know Ussachevsky during the war years.[143] Together with John Marshall, he remained Ussachevsky's primary friendly contact at the RF during the crucial years leading to the CPEMC's funding.

Indeed, Ussachevsky's earliest effort to enroll RF interest in his electronic music project took the form of a letter to Fahs at the height of his passport crisis in March 1953.[144] In four long, single-spaced pages, he provided a rich and imaginative account of his new electronic project to Fahs, addressing him with a tone of familiar collegiality, while requesting financial support from the RF in order to attend the Paris conference. All of the main ideological ties linking Ussachevsky's project with RF humanities policy appear in this letter from the outset: (1) an emphasis on "freedom" and "free play of a composer's imagination" that overcomes the constraints of technology; (2) a belief in the need to restore progress to "western music, and of bringing to a synthesis the new materials of the twentieth century and the musical values of the past"; (3) a differentiation of unique American innovations that will both inherit and improve European traditions, offering positive alternatives to contemporary European "mysticism and fatalism"; (4) an exhortation to "accommodate the influx of new musical ideas, some coming from non-western sources . . . to infuse all the rhythmic subtleties and tonal shadings peculiar to Oriental music"; and (5) the importance of working in partnership with Luening, a "completely well-rounded musical personality" with whom Ussachevsky presumes Fahs may already be connected.[145] This first missive did not bear immediate fruit: the RF declined both this first grant application and his later request for help with his passport. The RF had had its own troubles, having attracted heightened scrutiny from Congress and the Justice Department because for twenty-seven years it had supported the IPR with grants.[146] Accordingly, the RF acted with extreme political caution in 1953, which may well have resulted in its hesitation to stand up to the State Department on Ussachvsky's behalf. Columbia University stepped in to fill the breach.

The success of Luening and Ussachevsky's subsequent 1953 joint application for studio equipment funding set a precedent for the larger RF grants to come. This large-scale patronage of Ussachevsky's projects, in turn, helped to secure his eventual place as a full professor at Columbia University, where he would come to enjoy backing from such powerful administrators as Jacques Barzun and Grayson Kirk. During the precarious time when his passport application had been denied, however, the successive interventions from Columbia (advocating with the State Department) and the RF (granting the imprimatur of funding) meant everything: these interventions made his institutional ensconcement in the

United States possible, alongside his ability to support his extended immigrant family on their own paths toward citizenship. For Ussachevsky, the Morningside Heights Acropolis provided protection against the simmering threat represented by long-term FBI surveillance and investigation during the era of the McCarran Act. After her 1953 arrival, Ksenia received US citizenship in 1959 and changed her married surname, Terechovskaya, to Terry. Through cultural diplomacy initiatives via the CPEMC in the Soviet Union, Ussachevsky visited Natalia in 1961 and 1964 before she finally immigrated to the United States in 1966, two years before her death. Elizabeth Kray, who had gone by her married name in the 1940s and early 1950s, began to use her maiden name in the late 1950s and 1960s as she pursued a career at the heart of New York's poetry community, curating the arts series of the 92nd Street Y and serving as the first executive director of the American Academy of Poets.

As the FBI investigations of Ussachevsky show, the composer's path toward US belonging assumed a tortuous and provisional character. He leveraged security for himself and his family by navigating the cultural infrastructures of the Acropolis, which remained relatively open to him as a white male who had served in the US government, with a training in European classical music traditions. His professional ascent at Columbia required everyday exercises of personal secrecy and discretion—especially on the question of his own subjection to state surveillance and investigation. This routine itself would have produced complex ways of knowing and feeling American power as Ussachevsky undertook the administration of the CPEMC as a budding music-technocultural institution and academic unit. It seems that Ussachevsky came into his own as an "American" most especially in his capacities as a *host*, and as the administrator of a *hosting* institution. To host others is one way to feel at home and to feel empowered, even or especially when "home" itself renders refuge or security contingent. In the next chapter we will explore further how these questions of the Acropolis played out in relation to the CPEMC's first resident foreign-born visitors, who confounded the white, masculine persona of the "composer."

Cold War Acropolis II

TOYAMA AND EL-DABH AT THE CPEMC

"They were talking about me before daylight"

MIBU NO TADAMI; words set by Michiko Toyama

"People forgot me as a composer."

HALIM EL-DABH

The story of the first visiting composers at the CPEMC has never been told.[1] Michiko Toyama (1913–2006)[2] experimented with tape at Columbia from 1956 to 1959, during the period of the CPEMC's founding, while Halim El-Dabh (1921–2017) composed there from 1959 to 1962. Toyama barely figures in existing histories of music, while El-Dabh endured many years in which "people forgot [him] as a composer," before the late-life and posthumous reclaiming of his legacy.[3] Their presence in existing accounts of the studio remains shadowy at best. Like passing ships in the spring and summer of 1959, even Toyama and El-Dabh themselves appear not to have known one another, despite their remarkable similarities of practice at the CPEMC. Both composers treated electronic media as a basis for blending musical traditions from different parts of the world, espousing a project to communicate across cultural boundaries and to represent their nations of birth—Japan and Egypt, respectively—through music on a world stage. Their presence at the CPEMC responded to the studio's original Rockefeller Foundation–supported mission to create crossings between "music of the West and of the East."[4] Yet both composers also confronted the gatekeeping mechanisms of the electronic music studio as an Acropolis—a place for cultural exchange, and a fortress for restrictive notions of Western culture and progress. The two entered into a program focused on ideas of East-West encounter, yet their work remained subject to distinctively Euro-American standards of evaluation.

Their legacies remain occluded by the CPEMC's long shadow as an underexamined and vexed ideological space.

In order to enter into this scene, let us consider an anecdote El-Dabh shared with me during a series of interviews I conducted in his Kent, Ohio, home in December 2014. El-Dabh had first worked with the creative-compositional use of wire recorders in Cairo in the late 1940s, and he embarked on related projects with tape at the CPEMC.[5] He emphasized his New York colleagues' expressions of surprise in the 1950s when they learned of his early sound experiments in Cairo. Speaking of the CPEMC's founders Otto Luening and Vladimir Ussachevsky, El-Dabh recalled,

> The circumstances of Luening and Ussachevsky coming in and realizing that I have a whole wealth of experience in this, that I worked in Egypt and all this kind of stuff and . . . yeah, they didn't know about that. And I never thought of it either. It was just, like, the circumstances. But that was quite a satisfying relationship.[6]

El-Dabh's words intimate relations of both friendship and hierarchy within the electronic music studio. They portray the studio as a place that produced long-lasting bonds among visiting and immigrant composers who came from different parts of the world. Yet they also characterize the studio as a space where it was virtually unimaginable that the roots of electronic composition might have derived from any place other than Europe or North America. In El-Dabh's recollection, this "first West, then rest" mentality proved so powerful that it touched even him, he who had "never thought of it either"—that is, the fact that he had pioneered electronic music in Cairo—even though he had lived that history himself. This frame of mind proved long-lasting for the CPEMC's founders and the legacy they actively historicized. Many years after his first acquaintance with El-Dabh, Ussachevsky continued to rehearse the question of whether electronic composition had originated in Paris or New York—a narrative that implicitly denied the earlier activities of his colleague in Cairo.[7] The CPEMC's "satisfying" qualities as a social space cannot be disentangled from its function as an ideological space—a place that generated certain ways of knowing, feeling, and asserting American power and leadership in a perceived contest of Western technological and cultural advancement. El-Dabh's words speak to the dual and contradictory character of the CPEMC as an Acropolis—an agora for pluralist encounter and a bastion for "the West."

Tensions between cultural pluralism and hierarchy animated Luening and Ussachevsky's vision for the studio from the start. Their program pushed against familiar gendered and racialized norms of who the composerly subject and persona may be, yet it also harnessed categories of "West" and "East" in familiar Orientalist ways. Ussachevsky's November 1958 draft proposal, written with input from Luening, is the document that spells out this vision most fully.[8] It trumpeted the "international aspects of the program, especially in pioneering exchange with the virgin territory of the Far East and the Near East"—two decolonizing regions of strategic interest to US foreign policy.[9] "The medium of composition with recorded sound represents the most hopeful avenue of mutual fertilization between the music of the West and of the East."[10] The exchange program would train "outstanding composers and musicians" from "the Near and Far East" for the purpose of establishing "pilot programs" abroad, while opening up a new trove of non-Western musical materials and sounds to Western composers.[11] Ussachevsky singled out Turkey, the Phillipines, and Java as promising sites for electronic music studios, while noting that Japan "has already become well advanced in this respect," implicitly referencing the Japan Broadcasting Corporation (NHK) studio.[12] "The aim of this program is reciprocity," he explained.[13] The composer's emphases on "mutuality," "reciprocity," and "exchange" are typical of Cold War Orientalist discourses, which tend to camouflage the imperial and hierarchical character of US power abroad.[14] Still, Ussachevsky's description of "the Far East and the Near East" as "virgin territory" shows how he imagined this "mutual fertilization" in electronic music as flowing outward from the West, from the United States, and from the CPEMC. The program responded to an important policy objective of the Rockefeller Foundation Humanities Division to develop a Western "reservoir of brains" that in turn would foster "intercultural understanding" throughout the globe as societies struggled to domesticate new technologies and media under conditions of rapid modernization (see chapter 2).[15] This policy platform assumed a "first in Europe, then elsewhere" temporality of diffusion, as previously described.[16] Ussachevsky and Luening's proposal also resonated with RF initiatives such as the institutionalization of "area studies" programs, which aimed to anchor in US higher education the study of cultural divides.[17]

Luening and Ussachevsky celebrated technologies of electronic composition for their potential to showcase musical markers of cultural, ethnic, and racial difference within a "universal" Western compositional format. This valorization aligns with a vision of US cultural diplomacy that would spread "Western" cultural norms worldwide while acknowledging diversity within gestures of reciprocity. From Ussachevsky's perspective, tape-recording technology would bring forth "cross-fertilized" compositional forms by circumventing the limitations of Western notation while preserving the distinctive timbres and techniques of non-Western instruments:

> The tape medium surmounts the barrier of inaccessibility to most of the native instruments and the instrumental techniques, which stand in the way of the composer's incorporating of the remarkable musical heritage of many non-European countries. A non-European musician would profit from having the means to construct his music without reference to the largely inadequate Western notation should he wish to compose in larger forms more characteristic of Western music, while still retaining the essential ingredients of his native culture. A program of cultural-technical exchange would be organized, with suitable Western musicians assisting in acquainting the non-European composer with tape techniques, while in turn making use of recorded native materials for [Western musicians'] own compositions.[18]

The appropriative dimension of Ussachevsky's project appears on the surface of his words: "Western musicians" would "mak[e] use of recorded native materials" through their capture on magnetic tape. These sounds on tape would participate in a project of preservation enabled by modern technoculture. The extractivist and preservationist elements of Ussachevsky's program perpetuate the legacy of ethnographic sound laboratories such as the Berlin and Vienna Phonogram Archives, as does its fixation on West/non-West binaries. Magnetic tape enacted a "relay" of cultural practice: it performed tasks that had been associated with wax cylinders, phonograph records, and wire recorders within the disciplinary setting of comparative musicology earlier in the twentieth century.[19] Like these preceding technologies, magnetic tape recorded the sounds of cultural "others" to render them manipulable for knowledge production and compositional practice.

In line with Orientalist patterns of thought, Ussachevsky consistently conflated "Western" with "European" and "non-Western" with "non-European"—a faulty logic that foreclosed any possibility of conceiving of the US-based specialist instructors at the CPEMC as being "non-European"—which in fact most were. This hardened conflation of "Western" with "European" was likely premised on ideas of cultural, ethnic, and racial heritage suffused with whiteness. It summons a tradition of laboratory research that rejected biological racism while nonetheless remaining subject to the "ghosting presences of race and culture," as Benjamin

Steege writes.[20] Ussachevsky's own subjection to these ghosts might also be understood in relation to his childhood in the contested borderlands of Manchuria, a place that confounded fixities of ethnicity, race, nation, and East/West division. It was the very slipperiness of such boundaries that drove many Russian Manchurian refugees to hold fast to claims of authority rooted in white European identity, even if those claims were only implicit, as in Ussachevsky's case.[21] At the CPEMC, Ussachevsky's colleagues appreciated him as an exceedingly gracious and generous host to foreign-born visitors, and he devoted himself to helping composers who, like him, sought refuge in the United States. As Alice Shields remembered, "Ussachevsky was the vibrant energetic core of the Center, with a delightful personality full of humor, kindness, and a deep interest in others."[22] Known as the "life of the studio,"[23] Ussachevsky entertained collegues and students at the Shanghai Café in Harlem and the Harbin Inn in Morningside Heights, speaking with restaurant staff in a Northern Chinese dialect and delighting in the familiar foods of his childhood home, as the composer Pril Smiley and the poet Kathleen Norris remembered.[24] Yet his vision for the CPEMC remained rooted in the "first West, then rest" mentality that El-Dabh identified as permeating the studio. These ways of thinking and feeling would have been reinforced by Ussachevsky's "area studies" training during World War II, alongside his tenure as an OSS officer and State Department official.

The imperative remains to think behind and beyond the notions of American power and Western culture that were central to the sound laboratory. Toward that end, the cases of Michiko Toyama and Halim El-Dabh invite reappraisal of the studio as an imperial space that resists simple top-down narratives of ideology and power. This approach jars against the CPEMC's commonplace reputation as an anchor of the "uptown scene"—a designation that evokes, above all, the transatlantic transmutation of notated European concert traditions in North America. In New York music scenes and scholarship, "uptown" is a concept that suggests a continuity of the "great traditions" of Western high art, meshing well with the "first West, then rest" mentality. It stresses one side of Acropolis (a fortress for the West) over the other (a crossroads for pluralism). To foreground Toyama and El-Dabh as protagonists at the CPEMC, by contrast, is to reframe the institution and its significance altogether. The CPEMC figures here not so much as the home of a particular "uptown" musical style or school, nor exclusively as a crucible for the ideologies connected with that label. Rather, the studio emerges as a node in the circulation of labor and expertise in a US imperial setting. It depended on crossings between the peripheries of US empire and the metropole. As a cultural institution, the CPEMC produced and transformed subjectivities and epistemologies. These variable ways of being, feeling, and knowing emerged from conditions of geographical and cultural mobility emblematized in Toyama's and El-Dabh's personal narratives and compositional practices. To highlight their work and presence at the CPEMC is to show how cultural agents from the supposed periphery of US power grappled with, altered, and made possible the establishment of such a cultural institution at its metropolitan center.

The remainder of this chapter unfolds as a diptych portrait of Toyama and El-Dabh, which redresses their absence in existing historiography while enhancing our picture of the electronic music studio as a Cold War Acropolis. Toyama's and El-Dabh's career trajectories bring into stark relief the CPEMC's gatekeeping, modulated by the globally ambitious RF patronage network and related institutions of higher education, classical music, and technoculture. El-Dabh's and Toyama's situations present a zone of unpredictability, of flux and transformation, created in the tension between these two functions of Acropolis as crossroads and as fortress. As resident composers, El-Dabh and Toyama created novel ways of imagining, dreaming, anticipating, knowing, and desiring through their intense engagement with electronic music technologies under these conditions of ambivalent gatekeeping. As Ann Laura Stoler writes, "The shaping of common sense, and the reigning in [sic] of uncommon sense, together make up the substance of colonial governance and its working epistemologies."[25] Toyama and El-Dabh showed the potential to scramble any "commonsense" preconceptions of the white male classical music composer—at times creating an "uncommon sense" ripe for rebuke, dismissal, discipline, or management. Establishing "common sense" and reining in "uncommon sense" became the business not only of the CPEMC founders but also of the music critics and foundation officers who secured the economy of prestige that justified the institution's purpose.

Dilemmas of acculturation played out prominently in the CPEMC as a hub for visiting and immigrant composers. Similar to early twentieth-century European sound laboratories, the CPEMC's ventures included an ethnographic component rife with questions of racialized representation. For Toyama and El-Dabh to become involved in such ventures brought manifold complexities of self-representation into play. Although these topics are virtually absent in existing secondary literature on the studio, they surfaced repeatedly in Toyama's words and in El-Dabh's interviews with me. Together with Bülent Arel and Mario Davidovsky—whose work and programs deserve further attention beyond this chapter—Toyama and El-Dabh stand out as the first "non-European musicians," and the first foreign-born non-US citizens, to experience the studio's program of exchange. Unlike Arel and Davidovsky, however, Toyama and El-Dabh actively claimed musical heritages outside the Western concert tradition as a foundation of their respective practices and musical poetics. As elite cultural emissaries to the United States, Toyama and El-Dabh assumed the responsibility to represent their respective national heritages to American audiences. At the same time, they lived diasporic lives caught in between nations, languages, and identities—a condition that formatively shaped their approach to tape as a medium conducive to montagelike forms and ethnographic applications. Standard historiographic categories defined by nation and genre cannot do justice to such culturally "in-between" figures like Toyama and El-Dabh—a fact that contributes to the dearth of secondary literature about their lives and work.

"I Had a Chance to Try It Myself"

Michiko Toyama inscribed a revealing first-person account of her professional trajectory into the liner notes of her one and only album, *Waka and Other Compositions*, released in 1960 by Folkways Records.[26] These liner notes—combined with a short encyclopedia entry and a Japanese-language article by the music scholar Hiromi Tsuji—constitute the bulk of Toyama's presence in published written sources.[27] Within this sparse archive, her album stands out as a stirring public statement of composerly persona and practice, a representation of herself as an artist, intercultural subject, and music professional with a distinctive history and set of creative aspirations. In the notes, Toyama underlines her credentials as a classically trained composer in Western concert music while leveraging authority as a knowledgable carrier and translator of traditional Japanese heritage. The first page juxtaposes a list of the album's contents with a photographic portrait of Toyama, a first-person statement by Toyama about her life and work, and a third-person biography (figure 3.1). Each of these components speaks to the challenges she faced as a Japanese woman claiming the authority of composerly authorship that institutions of classical music and higher education (both at home and abroad) resisted conferring upon her. The featured headshot of Toyama depicts the composer in a kimono, her hair set in a shimada chignon, her alert eyes glancing sidelong from the three-quarter view of her face. This image plays into American stereotypes of Japanese femininity; it contrasts greatly with the Western style and dress she assumed in other portraiture.[28] Yet the sharpness of Toyama's glance, shooting daggers, prevents the image from

FIGURE 3.1. Portrait of Michiko Toyama included in the liner notes of *Waka and Other Compositions* (1960). Photographer unknown. Ralph Rinzler Folklife Archives and Collections, Smithsonian Institution.

congealing into pure objectification. Her ostentatiously traditional self-presentation in dress and coiffure resonates with the image on the album's cover—Tsukioka Kogyo's woodblock print *Sôshi-arai Komachi*, from the series *Nogaku hyakuban* (One Hundred Noh Dramas; 1898–1903), set off against a mod electric-orange background (figure 3.2).[29] The print depicts the ninth-century *waka* poet Ono no Komachi—a frequent subject of Noh drama—reading a book. The cover artwork evokes Toyama's connection with a vibrant lineage of Japanese women's literacy and cultural production. Toyama's first-person statement about waka documents her desire to study electronic composition—a desire first frustrated, then fulfilled—in a manner that foregrounds her struggle and agency. Toyama first encountered musique concrète via a demonstration by Pierre Schaef-

FIGURE 3.2. Michiko Toyama, cover of *Waka and Other Compositions* (1960).
By permission of Smithsonian Folkways Recordings.

fer at the Paris Conservatory in 1952: "It was not until five years later that I had a chance to try it myself," Toyama declared, alluding to her studies at the CPEMC. In her liner notes she credits Luening, Ussachevsky, Varèse, and the eminent Japanese mathematician Nabuo Yoneda (who also played flute for the recording) as having supported her in that endeavor after she had studied with Boulanger, Olivier Messiaen, Darius Milhaud, and Noel Gallon in Paris.

In naming her mentors in France and the United States, Toyama presents her bona fides and lineage as a Western-trained composer; she goes on, however, to extend her authority to that of an ethnographer and indigenous expert. She describes her electronic composition *Waka*, composed in the studio at Columbia, in didactic terms that explicate her classical

Japanese heritage to an English-speaking audience. She implicitly locates her work's value in the translation of that heritage:

[*Waka*] is partly inspired by "Saibara," a kind of ancient folk song of [the] 9th century, adapted to the Imperial court music, "Gagaku." "WAKA" is the name of a special type of a poetry of 31 syllables, composed in five lines. In my tape music, the poetry is taken from an ancient collection by the name of "Hyaku-nin Shu" which means "Hundred Poems" dated from the Kamakura period of the 12th century.[30]

The liner notes go on to supplement this description with English translations, by the poet Kenneth Rexroth, of *Waka*'s texts alongside calligraphic renderings of the originals by the artist Taiun Yanagita, which were also printed in Rexroth's 1955 publication *One Hundred Poems from the Japanese*.[31] Toyama's use of Rexroth's work places her in proximity with the downtown poetry scene and its Orientalist fascinations. Her reference to saibara locates her work squarely in the postwar, transnational gagaku craze, a trend illuminated by the composer Rica Narimoto and the musicologist Anthony Sheppard.[32] The album credits the Japan Society of New York for its assistance in the preparation of the recording and liner notes. That institution's mission—to improve cross-cultural understanding between the United States and Japan—may have inflected the didactic tenor of the liner notes. Folkways Records's own mission—to be an "encyclopedia of sound," as Tony Olmsted describes it—would have made the label a natural home for such an album that claimed to document Japanese classical and folk traditions.[33] Toyama assumed a similar approach to documenting the other nonelectronic works featured on the album—*Voice of Yamato* (for soprano and chamber orchestra), *Two Old Folk Songs with Koto* (for vocals, tape, and narration), and *Japanese Suites* (for orchestra)—which are also based on Japanese classical poetry and folk songs.[34]

Yet the sound of *Waka* gives the lie to any rigid claims of cultural authenticity. In contrast with saibara, *Waka*'s form actually resembles that of a lied or chanson crossed with spoken word performance (another feature that bespeaks its connection with the downtown poetry scene, alongside jazz). Like the through-composed art songs of Europe, *Waka* unfolds as a series of nonrepeating, contrasting sections strongly responsive to text painting. Saibara remains relevant to the ornamentation, harmonic language, and instrumentation of the piece—which enlists traditional court instruments such as the gakubiwa and shakubyōshi—but *Waka* avoids the heterophonic textures characteristic of saibara. Its lied- or chanson-like structure recalls Ussachevsky's vision for electronic music that would allow a non-Western composer to compose in Western forms while "still retaining the essential ingredients of his native culture" via the timbres, tunings, and subtleties of rhythm and phrasing that evade Western notation. *Waka* may be understood as "synthetic" within the musicologist Yayoi Uno Everett's taxonomy of postwar intercultural composition strategies in that it "transform[s] traditional musical systems, form, and timbres into a distinctive synthesis of Western and Asian musical idioms."[35] As such, it instantiates a "hybrid musical heritage" that is "dynamic and dialectical," to borrow Nancy Rao's terms.[36] From a related perspective, Toyama's work in the Western art song genre allows us to ask, following Sindhumathi Revuluri,

> what happens when a musical idiom that has narrated . . . Western civilization is also used to tell [an alternate history]. Is this the ultimate imperialism, the colonizing power of the Western musical language? Or does it threaten the power and autonomy of the Western idiom, revealing that it has porous boundaries and can be manipulated . . . into sounding something unlike itself?[37]

This framing of the question allows us to foreground Toyama's agency in redefining a variety of distinctive idioms in her own terms, despite the decades-long inattention critics and musicologists have shown to her composerly voice. This perspective also calls out for notions of hybridity entirely different from Ussachevsky's racially tinged idea of "cross-fertilization," which replicated imperial hierarchies of East and West. Hybridity emerges instead as third space (in Bhabha's sense)—a set of cross-cultural negotiations fraught with internal difference, transpiring across an uneven field of power and calling into question established categories.[38] We will return to Toyama's own hybrid electronic composition after picking up the thread of her prewar narrative.

"She Climbed over the Mountain and Went Back to Her Village"

By the time Toyama released *Waka* in 1960, she had already lived a peripatetic life—shuttling, from 1930 onward, between Japan, France, and the United States. As her English- and French-language correspondence shows, she routinely went by the name Françoise.[39] Toyama counts as an early protagonist of what Karen Kelsky and Midori Yoshimoto have identified as a late twentieth-century Japanese female internationalism—a movement among women of the upper middle classes who sought the personal and professional opportunities abroad that were denied them at home within oppressive political and family structures.[40] Toyama was born into a family with extraordinary geographical, cultural, and socio-economic mobility. Her grandfather Shuzo Toyama (1842–1916) was a founder of Japanese capitalism, having established modern systems of industry and finance in the Meiji state. Before serving as director and Osaka branch manager of the Bank of Japan in 1882, he had earned recognition for institutionalizing and disseminating modern bookkeeping practices while working in the Ministry of Finance. In 1892 he established Japan's first credit research system and credit-rating bureau in Osaka, five years after having researched those institutions in European countries and the United States on a fact-finding tour. In the late 1880s and 1890s, he also founded numerous banks along with a brewery (now Asahi Breweries), a chemical company (Osaka Chemistry Industry Company), an electric railway (Hanshin Electric Railway Company), and a baseball team (the Hanshin Tigers) that counted among Japan's earliest.[41] Shuzo Toyama's flurry of capitalist initiatives furthered the ambivalent Meiji project of staving off Western colonialism by instituting economic, cultural, educational, social, and political reforms partially adapted from Western models.

As Hiromi Tsuji suggests, Michiko admired her grandfather's projects and cosmopolitanism, which fueled her "strong interest in foreign cultures as a child."[42] Her own professional coming of age and European travel would commence in 1930, at a time when borders were beginning to harden, but her career benefited directly from the legacy of Meiji globalization processes from which her family's wealth and mobility were derived. The post-Meiji French mania for *Japonisme* fostered artistic milieus in Paris where she would be "welcomed," albeit on exoticist terms. Her family's attunement and access to these transnational formations provided a basis for her temporary escape from the convention of marriage.

In 1930, Toyama relocated to Paris to study piano and composition—a daring move that testifies to developments in the early Japanese feminist movement and its connection with elite women's higher education. As Tsuji writes, Toyama initially headed to Paris to study piano with Henri Gil-Marchex, but soon discovered a desire to compose her own music, and thus enrolled at the École normale to learn from Nadia Boulanger. Toyama's mother, Haru, had herself studied music at the Tokyo Music School (present-day Tokyo University of the Arts)—the first music conservatory established in the Meiji period, incorporating Japanese and Western elements[43]—but she had been forced to abandon her studies upon marriage. According to Tsuji, Haru "entrusted her dreams" to her daughter and provided "emotional and economic support" that empowered her to pursue a path to music as a profession.[44]

Their mother-daughter alliance likely thrived in music-educational experiences that nurtured aspirations for self-determination. The feminist movement in Japan had built upon the aspirations of middle- and upper-class women, such as Haru Toyama, who had graduated from the newly formed educational institutions associated with the Meiji restoration.[45] In the 1890s the Meiji state had instituted legal reforms to shore up nationalism by reinforcing and enshrining patriarchal household structures in the codes of citizenship, against which women of all classes struggled. The Meiji Civil Code of 1898, which remained in effect until after World War II, excluded women from partisan politics on the grounds that their duties as wives precluded it.[46] The code conceived the patriarchal household as the smallest unit of the state. Accordingly, like that of civil servants, women's duty was to promote the economic development of the family by managing the household and their children's education.[47] Urban upper-middle-class women felt demoted to the status of private domestic laborers in the code's aftermath.[48] The term "new woman," adopted from the West, described women across all classes who chafed at these national reforms. The appellation emerged in connection with the groundbreaking women's publication *Seitō* (Bluestocking), which ran from 1911 to 1916 despite government attempts at censorship. World literature and the arts served here as a touchstone to address the political struggles of women, highlighting such topics as forced marriage, romantic love and sexual desire, abortion, rape, prostitution, women's medical care, childbirth, women's professional and economic status, class struggle, anarchist theory, and the need for fully enfranchised citizenship more broadly.[49] As Teruka Nishikawa, Wesley Berg, and Janice Brown write, the Meiji Civil Code had ensured that for the most part there was "no question of training women for careers as professional musicians" within the "good wife, wise mother" (*ryōsai kenbo*) doctrine of the Japanese state; yet women (such as Haru Toyama) had been "among the first Japanese to be trained in Western music in the Meiji period."[50] Although Haru Toyama's exact social and intellectual connections remain unclear, it seems reasonable to associate her with ideas of the "new woman," which would have justified support for her daughter's brazen decision in 1930 to study alone abroad.

In Paris, Toyama joined a very small community of Japanese artists, intellectuals, and students who were active in French cultural institutions that had embraced exoticist *Japonisme* for more than half a century. In European music scholarship, Jirohachi Satsuma (known by the nickname "Baron Satsuma") appears as the most visible member of this community. The scion of a wealthy cotton-trading family, Satsuma became a patron of Parisian art circles, associating with such figures as Gil-Marchex (Toyama's piano teacher, who had traveled to Japan multiple times) and Maurice Ravel.[51] In 1927, Satsuma commissioned the construction of the architecturally stunning Maison du Japon, which quickly became an important cultural hub that housed Japanese students in Paris.[52] This event testifies to French-Japanese cultural exchanges that continued to deepen more than fifty years after the initial influx of Japanese art and culture on the European market following the Meiji restoration. Other members of the 1930s Japanese community in Paris included the novelist Riichi Yokomitsu, the painter Tsuguharu Foujita, the composer Kosuke Komatsu, the painter Saburōsuke Okada, and his wife, the writer and playwright Yachiyo Okada, among others. The question of Toyama's relationship with this expatriate community—and that of other Japanese women within it—deserves further attention through sustained oral history and archival research. At present, the sparse US-based record on Toyama tends to locate her more in the circles of Nadia Boulanger than among expat Japanese intellectuals, though further documentation from France and Japan could revise this picture.

A memory book given to Boulanger by her students includes an entry by Toyama that speaks to the nature of her persona as a female composer within that musical community. As I state in this book's introduction, I use the term "persona" here in a distinctive sense: in the terms of the historians of science Lorraine Daston and H. Otto Sibum, "persona" describes how individual subjects assume collective patterns of being, thinking, knowing, and feeling within social institutions.[53] The female composer may be considered such an identity, shaping as it does "the possibilities of being in the human world, schooling the mind, body, and soul in distinctive and indelible ways."[54] This persona arises from habits of thought, attention, training, affective responses, and ethics—patterns that are necessarily gendered in relation to the masculinist character that the historical category of the "composer" assumes more generally. Toyama's entry in the memory book articulates a shared persona as female composer through the invocation of a famous lullaby from the Edo area. The lullaby is a transcultural genre that involves the matrilineal voicing of aspirations from mother to child, here a gift from student to teacher. Above her signature, Toyama notated the pentatonic tune of the Edo lullaby alongside the words of its fourth and fifth lines, "She climbed over the mountain and went [back] to [her] village. What souvenir did she bring with her to the village?" The reference to the souvenir clearly pertains to the memory book, casting Boulanger as the female protagonist who had "climbed over the mountain" and returned home with a token to memorialize that achievement. At the same time, appearing above Toyama's signature, these words cannot but also pertain to her own feat of having secured a virtually unprecedented status—recognition as a Japanese woman composer of European-derived art music—made possible by traveling alone halfway across the world for an education with Boulanger.

It was in 1937 that Toyama won a major prize for her piece *Voice of Yamato* in the fifteenth festival of the International Society for Contemporary Music (ISCM) in Paris—a prize that was itself a "souvenir" to bring home. She conducted her work's premiere on the festival's opening night.[55] The ISCM archives show that their sponsorship of female composers through performance was rare at this time—let alone the granting of prizes to them.[56] Yet Boulanger appeared prominently in the 1937 festival program as a conductor and selection committee member: a reminder of her advocacy for Toyama's crystallizing professional persona and success.[57] The 1937 ISCM festival ran in parallel with that year's Paris Exposition. France's centrist parties hoped this simultaneity of cultural events would amplify the city's standing on the world stage despite unstable domestic politics and the dreaded anticipation of world war.[58] As one critic of the era put it, the ISCM was founded in 1923, when it "was still possible to believe that relations between nations could profit by the yearly meeting of men who throughout the world history have shown themselves as ambassadors of good-will. . . . It was also possible to expect that these festival rivals [at the ISCM] might reveal genius—the men or, at least, the man worthy to succeed in the royal line of artists who have commanded the admiration and gratitude of the whole world."[59] Although hopes for such goodwill in world politics had diminished by the late 1930s, Toyama nonetheless represented her nation as a cultural ambassador and a representative of exceptional achievement, despite the masculinist cast of these categories and her own position as gendered quasi-exile from Japan. Her manner of representing Japanese nationhood through music would therefore sustain deep complications.

Voice of Yamato

Before returning to *Waka* and Toyama's activities at the CPEMC, we should dwell on her award-winning *Voice of Yamato*, which looks forward to *Waka* while also adapting French musical idioms of *Japonisme* in a project that portrays female lineages of literacy at the heart of the Japanese nation. This venture was vexed in the complexities of its power dynamics, not least because Toyama's compositional voice drew fundamentally from her Parisian musical training and its *Japoniste* currents. Let us be clear about what this means: *Japonisme* generally speaks from a position of superiority by reinforcing epistemological and ontological distinctions between the West and the Orient, in Edward Said's sense.[60] As a form of Orientalism, *Japonisme* functions within larger imperial structures to dominate, restructure, and wield authority over a region and culture by generating imaginative and scholarly discourses about it. Whether in scholarship or in the arts, it plays on stereotypes of Japanese culture by vacilating between its valorization as a domain of sensuous aesthetic refinement and its denigration as essentially submissive—and therefore coded feminine. Puccini's *Madame Butterfly* remains perhaps the most iconic musical representation that plays with these ambivalent stereotypes.[61] It is well known that exoticist acts of appropriation typically decontextualize non-European musical forms and sounds from their indigenous contents and contexts, and that these sources themselves often become transformed beyond recognition. As Revuluri writes, such exoticist musical works are best interrogated in relation to issues of power, rather than from the standpoint of whether their "sounds [are similar] to those from the place imagined."[62]

Toyama's *Voice of Yamato* unfolds as a work steeped in such *Japoniste* musical idioms, disconnected from the Japanese musical sources upon which they are ostensibly based. Yet the piece hardly indulges in the wide-angle stereotypes often associated with *Japoniste* creative works. *Voice of Yamato* wields Japanese literary knowledge to enter into contested discourses about the Japanese state from Toyama's position of gendered exile abroad—an important dimension of the work that clearly distinguishes it from other works of *Japonisme* created by her European counterparts. It shows how the "performance of Japanese people abroad" evades "a simplistic binary between 'resistance' and 'complicity'" in imperial formations such as Orientalism, to borrow the words of the Americanist Mari Yoshihara.[63]

Voice of Yamato demonstrates a particular way of knowing and representing modern Japan through feminine traditions of literacy and creative production. Toward this end, it also articulates itself in an exoticist musical idiom Toyama would have associated with her new home and opportunities in France. Her choice of title and texts calls out for a historical consideration of Japanese-language literary studies in relation to modern conceptions of the Japanese state. During the 1920s and 1930s, Yamato (an ancient term referring to a "chosen people") denoted both the Japanese Imperial House and an increasingly racialized mythology of the Japanese people; in literature and journalism, the term served to unite and inspire pride in a Japanese nation with both a growing global diasporic presence and escalating imperial ambitions.[64] With a focus on Japanese Canadians, the historian Aya Fujiwara writes that the ideologies surrounding Yamato instilled "nostalgia for Japan and a joy at being part of the transnational Japanese community"; they also contributed to a sense "that the racism that Japanese Canadians were facing every day at both personal and official levels never hindered them from being proud of their racial background."[65] Written in Paris, Voice of Yamato would have participated in such a diasporic conjuring of the Japanese homeland. A historically contextualized consideration of the poetry set by the work, however, reveals gendered fault lines within such national visions. The work brings together classical texts from the Man'yōshū (the earliest known collection of Japanese poetry, dating from around 759 CE, during the Nara period) and the Kokin Wakashū (a celebrated anthology of poetry dating from around 920, during the Heian period). Within Voice of Yamato, the Man'yōshū texts highlight ideas of political sovereignty, conquest, and Japanese identity, while the waka texts of the Kokin Wakashū emphasize themes of love and yearning from an implicitly female perspective—composed by anonymous poets, who included female courtiers.

The literary scholars Robert Tuck and Tomiko Yoda both emphasize that waka (classical Japanese poetry, later exclusively associated with a thirty-one-syllable, five-line form) became a contested site for reform and even exclusion in Japanese court and academic settings from the 1890s onward, due to its alleged "feminine" qualities.[66] This circumstance informs the interpretation of Toyama's musical settings of waka, both in interwar Paris and in post–World War II New York. The problem with waka, Tuck suggests, lies in its supposedly "unmanly" themes of love, its displays of "emotional sensitivity," and its long legacy of female authorship extending from classical times—especially the Heian period—to the present day.[67] Yoda writes that, even in the work of those critics who venerated the Heian period, "the femininity of Japanese aesthetics was celebrated as long as it is grasped in an abstract, symbolic sense, remaining disassociated from the concrete figures of women."[68] The very notion of female authorship provoked deep concern. Western Orientalist stereotypes of Japanese culture as feminine and submissive exacerbated Japanese anxieties about gender and masculinity during the Meiji period of national reform. To Meiji critics and scholars, the female-coded waka genre risked feminizing Japanese men, and rendered their female counterparts "conceited," or useless for domestic tasks and childbearing—a result that could bring about "not only internal disorder but also domination by foreign powers."[69] As a court poetry central to the image of the Imperial House, waka carried particular risks. Reenvisioning the modern emperor required waka reform, to "distance him from the supposedly effeminate nobility and [foster] the image of a martially minded, powerful sovereign," appropriate to the modern nation-state.[70] Correspondingly, love poetry became marginalized, especially in connection with images of the sovereign.[71] Toyama's own era of rising Japanese militarism shared important ideological consistencies with Meiji culture. These continuities arose from the ongoing political effort to construct "the antiquity of the imperial system" and unify the Japanese people under the emperor, now construed as militarist.[72] Although Tuck and Yoda focus on the high literary culture of the Meiji period, and though masculinist waka reform was hardly uniform, their observations are nonetheless relevant to ideologies in Japanese literary production of the 1930s.[73] Against this backdrop, it is significant that *Voice of Yamato* brings love poetry and women's voices into proximity with images of Yamato and the Imperial House, adhereing to none of the rules of masculinist waka reform.

Classical Japanese poetry had already served as a source of inspiration for Parisian musical works of *Japonisme*—as exemplified in Igor Stravinsky's *Three Japanese Lyrics* (1912–13) and Maurice Delage's *Sept haï-kaïs* (1925)—but Toyama approached her selection of texts in a manner that entered into Japanese discourses about nationhood differently than did her European *Japoniste* counterparts. This idea appears all the more remarkable given her musical language's kinship with those of composers like Delage and Stravinsky. The first movement of *Voice of Yamato* sets a long poem and two envoy tankas (short poems) from the fifth book of the *Man'yōshū*—texts that highlight images of ancestral imperial sovereignty, foreign conquest, and death. (Stravinsky and Delage, by contrast, had focused on classical poetry with nature imagery.) In this first movement, Toyama enlists a woodwind-heavy instrumental ensemble, pentatonic harmonic language, and cantatalike form to portray the dramatic lamentation over the death of the poet Yakamarö, who had accompanied a military mission to "The Land of Kara" (the former state of Karak, located on what is now the Korean peninsula), which the poem identifies as "the dominion of the Imperial ancestors."[74] The music laments the death of Yakamarö, who finds his final rest between home and colony—between Yamato and Kara—on Iki Island, as recounted in the lore of the *Man'yōshū*.[75] This movement is followed by two wakas— a springtime meditation on rebirth, aging, and time, and a lamentation of love from the *Kokin Wakashū*[76]—followed by a prayer, and a final celebration of Yamato ("Oh land of reed plains / Fair land of rich ripe ears /

Oh land divine") to round out the five-movement piece. *Voice of Yamato* wields Stravinskian idioms that Toyama would have studied with Boulanger—including ostinati, running and chirping instrumental figures and calls, closely spaced chordal accompaniment, and obbligato wind instruments—although she directs them toward lyrical expressive effects that contrast with Stravinsky's models.

Voice of Yamato is distinctly Toyama's own, in its musical and textual dimensions that intimate complexities of Japanese national belonging. The work's combination of texts prevents it from playing into the masculinist fixities of national dogma on the one hand, or of Orientalist stereotype on the other. It promotes neither a simple national-propagandistic agenda, nor *Japoniste* stereotypes of decorative beauty and subservience. The work's setting of two anonymously written wakas from the *Kokin Wakashū* is signficant here, since that collection was known for including texts by female courtiers. Toyama inserted these female-coded wakas at the core of a cantata about Japanese nationhood, which begins with the intriguing legend of Yakamarö's death in a liminal space—on an island that is neither the intended site of conquest nor his rightful home. This tragic image of *stranding* evokes conditions of uprooting more generally. In broaching this theme of displacement, *Voice of Yamato* does not necessarily style itself as an overtly politicized work, nor as an explicitly feminist one. Yet it certainly counts as a work of Japanese feminism, insofar as Toyama herself emerged as the "Voice of Yamato" at the ISCM Festival by conducting her own work about questions of Japanese national belonging, feminine voices of lament, and the uncertain transitional spaces between home and empire.

The outbreak of World War II in 1939 cut short Toyama's early career, and she was forced to return to Japan in 1939 after she had completed her studies. Her success in Paris hardly resonated in her home country. As Tsuji emphasizes, *Voice of Yamato* wouldn't receive its Japanese premiere until more than fifty years later, in 1993. Tsuji attributes Toyama's neglect in Japan to the "disappointment and resentment" of a prominent group of nine male composers in Japan—including Kiyose Yasuji (1900–1981) and Matsudaira Yoritsune (1907–2001)—who had coordinated to submit their entries to the 1937 ISCM festival in a mail shipment that had arrived too late for consideration. When Toyama's work was selected, "they were met with a completely unexpected result."[77] *The Japan Advertiser* reported briefly on the critical response to her prize entry in gendered terms that dismissed the very notion that Toyama could be a composerly voice for Japan: "One critic states [that the piece] started off prettily and then dragged slowly and is uninteresting music for any country."[78]

Two years after returning to Japan, Toyama married and eventually had two children. After her husband died in combat in 1945, she began an appointment as assistant professor at the Osaka Junior College of Music in 1951, to support her family. In 1954 she finally returned to Paris to study with Milhaud and Messiaen at the Conservatoire, backed again by her mother, Haru, who cared for her two children.[79] By her own account, as we have noted, Toyama became captivated by Schaeffer's musique concrète. In July 1955, she sailed on the *Liberté* from Le Havre to New York to take up a scholarship for compositional studies with Roger Sessions at the Berkshire Music Center at Tanglewood—a position that would have been approved by the director of composition at the time, Aaron Copland.[80] Toyama's move to New York shows how her connections to Boulanger's American circle of students provided an ongoing source of professional support, while also foreshadowing Halim El-Dabh and Mario Davidovsky's own paths to the CPEMC via Tanglewood.[81] In 1956, Toyama joined the electronic music studio at Columbia University.

Waka

Waka and Other Compositions stands as the most valuable record of Toyama's work at the CPEMC. It also sheds light on the CPEMC's character as a Rockefeller-supported site of "East-West exchange," and as an incubator for women's leadership in electronic composition more generally. *Waka* shows Toyama interweaving European and Japanese classical traditions through the use of a cutting-edge technological platform. She intensified her focus on classical Japanese love poetry and female traditions of literacy, refracted through the lens of Orientalist translations. Toward this end, she channeled European art song traditions, with their narrative focus on themes of psychic exploration and inner experience. In Toyama's work, waka, chanson, and lied interacted with the downtown spoken word trend—itself associated with a self-narrative, confessional style of lyrical expressivity. Working with the technologies of the studio, Toyama produced a musical idiom fundamentally concerned with intercultural subject formation via the human-machine interface.

Waka constitutes the first episode of the CPEMC as a feminine expressive space and as a quasi-ethnographic sound laboratory dedicated to the study of cultural difference. The Rockefeller Foundation had funded the studio on the basis of a distinctive epistemology of the humanities, which resonates with *Waka*'s themes and effects. The foundation sought to enlist specialists to adapt modern technologies and media toward "humanist" ends, which would investigate questions of "psychic integrity."[82] We will see that *Waka*, in its broadest outlines, reflects such projects of knowledge production. Yet it does so in a way that produces an alternate history of the intercultural feminine subject. It turns familiar traditions inside out through their interpenetration, just as it coaxes a particular Cold War ideological space "into sounding something unlike itself."[83]

An unabashedly lyrical poetic voice and subject emerges from within *Waka*'s soundworld of globally intermingled traditions. The Romantic art song has long been understood as a genre that evokes narrative and implicit personae that arise from quasimimetic music-text interactions. *Waka* finds a close kinship with this genre in its setting of love poetry, updated in the media of tape composition and spoken word. Beate Sirota Gordon, performing arts director of the Asia Society and the Japan Society, recited the narration in the recording of *Waka*, which was intended for live performance.

Waka proceeds in two parts, each a miniature, through-composed work in itself. The texts set by *Waka I* and *Waka II* consist of five-line love poems from the twelfth-century collection *Hyaku-nin Shu*, as described in Toyama's liner notes.[84] The text's authors, indicated in the liner notes, showcase female and male authorship side-by-side. *Waka I* sets five such poems in succession, while *Waka II* sets seven. (One of the latter poems is missing from the liner notes.) In *Waka I* and *Waka II*, Toyama, by stringing together poems that dovetailed in imagery, created a more extensive narrative arc than each five-line poem would have permitted on its own. This approach took advantage of the dense intertextuality characteristic of waka as a genre. Toyama composed music that elided the individual poems: textural breaks within the music coincide not with the breaks between poems, but with transformations in imagery. The work thus dramatizes changing inner states and perceptions embodied in the voiced narrative. All of these qualities affiliate *Waka* with Romantic genealogies of through-composed song, with a female character as narrator.

In *Waka*, electronically generated sounds evoke strange qualities of interior alienation. The piece's thoroughgoing preoccupation with psychic interiority participates in a mid-century American project to reimagine human subjectivity. Such a postwar "modern man" discourse sought, in Michael Leja's words, to "accommodate and enrich developing models of the human individual" inherited from European traditions of high art and literature.[85] Yet Toyama elaborates this project through an engagement with Japanese classical love poetry that renders modern man other to itself. *Waka* foregrounds themes of estrangement and love—the very kind of forbidden love that had rendered the waka of the *Kokin Wakashū* suspect to Japanese nationalist discourses in the lifetimes of Toyama and her mother. In the same stroke, *Waka* reenvisions the genre of the European art song—imbued with a Romantic narrative heritage of love and alienation—as something compatible with electronic sounds popularly conjured as mysterious and otherworldly (à la Louis and Bebe Barron's *Forbidden Planet* sound track). Recited in succession, the short individual poems of *Waka* blend together within a longer meditation on love and its consequences. *Waka I* ruminates on the public spectacle of the narrator's love that should remain private, while *Waka II* enacts the narrator's longing for her missing lover, her disordered thoughts, her burning body, and the "falling away" of her self.

The first electronically generated sound of the piece—a high-pitched composite of sine waves—emerges at 0:47, at the critical moment when Gordon pronounces, "Yes I'm in love." After these words, the spoken voice formulates the central image of the narrative—"They were talking about me before daylight"—accompanied exclusively by the penetrating and sustained high-pitched sinusoidal tones. This sound gradually crescendoes while gathering timbral complexity through the addition of new frequencies over the course of twelve seconds—an effect that uncannily mimics the sound of a shō (mouth organ). As Gordon continues with the lines "Although I began to love without knowing it. / Although I hide it / My love shows in my face so plainly," a gakusō (zither) strums chords (0:59) to emphasize her words against the continued backdrop of the intensifying, complexifying sinusoidal sound, finally ending with an accented release.

The narrator's declaration of love amounts to a declaration of estrangement by virtue of the disconnection between her private and public worlds. The first appearance of electronically generated sound, in all its piercing intensity, marks this rupture as something perplexing and painful. The "talk" of others emerges as a threat to the female narrator's social self, to her standing in society, and possibly to her psychic integrity. This latter question of psychic integrity explicitly emerges in *Waka II* when the narrator intones, "This morning my thoughts / Are as disordered / As my black hair"—a moment that not coincidentally marks the first appearance of electronically generated sounds in the second movement. (These important lines come from a poem by Lady Horikawa, a Heian noblewoman who contributed to the *Kokin Wakashū*.) At this introduction of electronic sound (3:33), irregular pluckings give way to a quick pulse of reiterative high-pitched pings, beeps, and low thuds that accompany Gordon saying, "At last the dawn comes through the cracks of the shutters, heartless as night." The timbrally kaleidoscopic pulse accelerates to a frenzy before breaking off. Silence ensues, followed by the reentry of the resonant thuds, now slowed down, which ominously punctuate Gordon's deliberative pronouncement, "You do not come." In *Waka*, electronic sounds summon an atmosphere of suspense alongside effects of estrangement, shame, and interior unraveling.

The electronic moments of *Waka* produce disruption—even shock—in their juxtaposition with the traditional Japanese and European instrumental sounds that precede them. These highly indexical timbres mark the lyrical self in *Waka* as intercultural from the start. In *Waka I*, the opening sets up listeners' expectations to hear text-music relationships via timbre and rhythm—expectations that render the emergence of the sustained sinusoidal sound all the more resonant as a marker in the narrative. *Waka I* begins with a lone taiko cadence that loosely recalls the drum introductions of some genres of gagaku performance.[86] As the recitational voice enters with the line, "The winds rustle the bamboos / By my window in the dusk" (0:17), the kakko drum enlivens the taiko cadence with a light, pattering cross-rhythm. The flute, played by Nabuo Yoneda, floats into the texture with a series of ornamented, sustained pentatonic tones (0:26), which culminate in a syncopated, fluttering outburst akin to modal jazz improvisation. This flute line accompanies and illustrates Gordon's recitation, "Mist floats on the Spring meadow. / My heart is lonely. / A nightingale sings in the dusk." Blatant in its text painting, this music forms a backdrop to the spoken word much in the spirit of jazz-poetry experiments of the era. It is what sets off the electronic moment above: the piercing electronic sound that accentuates the narrator's words about the talk of others, rendering those words both strange and significant. After this turning point, Toyama explicitly foregrounds the techniques of the tape medium in a manner that reconfigures the soundworld of the work's acoustic introduction. At 1:17, for example, recorded, spliced, and manipulated taiko samples form a driving rhythm interspersed with deeply resonant electronically generated sounds, their composite and pulsing tumult quickening before an eventual release into a descending filigree flourish produced by a lute. Such moments demonstrate Toyama's facility with the montage techniques of the medium, while also testifying to her timbrally sensitive poetic imagination.

Electronically generated sounds come to mingle with acoustic ones in perceptually confounding ways as the tape medium facilitates a poetics of mutability and shape-shifting. In her liner notes, Toyama professed her "great admiration" for Varèse and acknowledged (in Frenchified English) his "friendly advices." Like Varèse, Toyama appears to have been fascinated by the creation of analogies between acoustically and electronically generated sounds. Unlike him, she brought this fascination into the service of a narrative of psychic exploration that was self-consciously confessional—even expressionist—in tone. While Leja describes the mid-century American "reconfiguration of the subject" within New York avant-gardes as explicitly "white heterosexual male," *Waka* participates in such a project from a different angle—one that is feminine and culturally hybrid in its embodiment. It may be compared to the "double-voiced discourse of marginalized artists" that Ann Eden Gibson has attributed to "others" working within New York's visual avant-gardes.[87]

A Studio of Her Own

By 1959, Toyama had developed a plan to found an electronic music studio in Kyoto. This project accorded with the raison d'être of the CPEMC, which had justified itself as a model that would spread via pilot programs throughout the world. This ambition echoed the policy platform of the RF Humanities Division, which argued for the worldwide distribution and adaptation of US-based programs that would adapt cutting-edge media technologies toward humanist ends in cultural diplomacy. As noted, Ussachevsky stressed the importance of "mutual fertilization" with the "virgin territories of the Middle and Far East."[88] Toyama's own plan, however, hardly treated Japan as a "virgin territory." Rather, we will see that her vision modeled itself prominently on the legacy of Shōhei Tanaka— the eminent Japanese physicist, music theorist, and inventor who himself had straddled the intellectual communities of Germany and Japan in the late nineteenth century.

Toyama's intention to establish her own studio took root after her studies at the CPEMC, when she returned to Japan to assume a position as a research fellow at the Department of Electronics in Kyoto University. The dearth of primary sources prevents us from ascertaining the exact reasons for Toyama's return to Japan from the United States in the summer of 1959. Yet we should note that, without any fellowships, she could not easily have remained in the United States or embarked on a path to citizenship, because of the severe anti-Asian quota restrictions codified in the Immigration Act of 1924 and the Immigration and Nationality Act of 1952. In 1958, the RF had declined her application for support, despite Luening's positive recommendation. This grant would have extended her stay in New York.[89] (She took residence at the Huntington Hartford Foundation in Pacific Palisades in July of 1959, but she appears not to have had funding to stay long.)[90] After her return to Japan, she quickly shifted gears. In letters to Varèse, she elaborated her dream of building an electronic music studio in Kyoto—a project for which she would again seek RF funding.

"I finally went to see this untempered harmonium in Kyoto," Toyama wrote to Varèse in 1960, "and I could [recreate] one with oscillators at Kyoto University as soon as I get a Rockefeller grant which is pretty 'hopeful.'"[91] These words demonstrate that a late nineteenth-century instrument lay at the center of her vision for a new electronic music studio. The enharmonium—Toyama's "untempered harmonium"—was a keyboard invented by Tanaka to demonstrate his theories of just intonation—a system for tuning musical intervals through whole-integer ratios (e.g., 1:2 = octave, 2:3 = perfect fifth, 3:4 = perfect fourth, etc.) rather than equal temperament's division of the octave into twelve equal semitones. While the first enharmoniums were constructed in Stuttgart in 1892,[92] a later version was built in 1936 for Duke Matsudaira Tsuneo, a diplomat and head of the · Imperial Household Agency.[93] The instrument was later donated to the Buddhist Music Association before finding its way to the Kyoto Women's University, where it was used in religious services, which Toyama could have attended.[94]

The enharmonium was both a ghost and a harbinger. In it dwelled the Meiji-era dreams of cosmopolitanism that had inspired Toyama in her grandfather's narrative. It embodied an era of global border crossing that in some respects had ended abruptly in the 1930s, as Japanese imperialist expansion accelerated. At the same time, the electronic sound of this instrument portended new possibilites for cultural internationalism in the postwar era. Tanaka had conceived of the instrument in settings of Meiji cosmopolitanism and German liberal bourgeois academe. Having acquired a degree in physics at Tokyo Imperial University in 1882, Tanaka went on to study acoustics and electromagnetism with Hermann von Helmholtz at the University of Berlin from 1884 through the 1890s.[95] Upon his return to Japan in 1899, Tanaka had worked in the railway industry as an engineer, and eventually served as director of the Bureau of Experiments of the Japanese Government Railways—a position that could easily have brought him into contact with a railway magnate such as Toyama's grandfather Shuzo.[96] The enharmonium remained for Tanaka a signature achievement, an instrument whose just intonation would foretell "a new music theory focused on global modernity."[97] As Walden writes, the tuning system

> would be modern in that it would seek to understand music as constructed by sequences of individual notes, like atomic particles, that were combined in various permutations to form both melody and harmony; it

would be globalist in that it would enable cross-cultural comparison of how these sonic particles were combined in different ways. The revolution in music theory . . . would be worldwide in Tanaka's formulation, with musical traditions from around the globe interwoven into a single theoretical just-intonation network that was in tune with the modern politics of transnational exchange.[98]

Tanaka's invention from the 1890s aimed to enhance music's potential as a universal grammar to bridge cultural divides while working as a site for comparative ethnological studies.[99]

These aspirations—the desire for a universal grammar and comparative studies—call out for analysis within the Cold War terms of Acropolis. They resonate with postwar Rockefeller Foundation objectives, just as they do with Meiji state or German high imperial ones. Toyama's aspiration to recreate Tanaka's enharmonium with mid-century oscillators reminds us, as Joseph Pfender writes, that "the technological disruptions of electricity, steam power, and industrialization in the mid to late 19th century [might be] more important to the soft underbelly of literate culture [in the middle of the twentieth century] than the harsh existential questions wrought by nuclear weapons and the Cold War."[100] These disruptions—so important to Toyama's family history—remain vibrant in her mid-century compositional practice. Although we do not yet know the details of Toyama's reconstruction plan for Tanaka's instrument, we may surmise that it likely responded to the values of "global modernity" described above, which jibed with her own intercultural compositional agendas which had found residence at the CPEMC.

Toyama's project might have seemed tailor-made for the RF's stated funding objectives, but she ultimately found no support from the foundation. The details of her proposed electronic music studio at Kyoto University remain obscure. Long considered an innovator in bureaucratic management,[101] the RF only preserved dedicated files pertaining to those funding applications that were approved. The idea of the "successful application" worked as an organizing concept for the RF archives, leading to the creation of individual files devoted to successful applicants—a paper trail for the "reservoir of brains" it sought to accumulate.[102] Thus, unlike her 1958 CPEMC proposal and proposal draft, Toyama's 1960 application does not inhabit the Rockefeller Archive Center (RAC), nor does there exist a file devoted to her case. This situation points back to the archive as a site where ideology determines patterns of accessibility and representation, reproducing power structures.

A few scattered clues concerning Toyama's application nonetheless populate the RAC. Most prominently, a tentative and partial response to her proposal appears in the diaries of Burton Fahs, who was still director of the Humanities Division in 1960 when Toyama approached him about the project during one of his many visits to Japan. Fahs's notes, likely transcribed by a secretary, immediately point to the gendered and racialized nature of the evaluation process:

> Following lunch CBF [Charles Burton Fahs] was called on at the villa by Prof. KIYONO Takeshi of the Department of Electronics of the Faculty of Engineering and Miss TOYAMA who is a research assistant under Kiyono and also a lecturer at Kobe College. Toyama is a somewhat unfeminine Japanese lady with scraggly hair and scratchy voice but apparently knows her music well. She studied electronic music in Paris and after several years there came to New York with work with Lunning [sic] and Ussachevsky.[103]

Fahs's words about Toyama's voice and appearance—"unfeminine," "scraggly hair," "scratchy voice"—register his discomfiture at confronting an Japanese female authority on electronic music. Here the gendered and racialized formulas of high imperialism repeat themselves once more, making an assessment of her racially differentiated capabilities and character. They undercut Toyama's stature by questioning her respectability embodied in the sound, comportment, and couth of her body. Fahs's mildly mocking tone evokes the world of racism, in W. E. B. Du Bois's words, "that looks on in amused contempt and pity," alongside the problem of "looking at one's self through the eyes of others, of measuring one's soul by the tape" of that world.[104] Indeed, this problem connects with the thematics of *Waka*, with its emphasis on the "talk of others" as a threat to the female narrator's social and psychic self and to her standing in society. One can only imagine the harmful dynamics of Toyama and Fahs's in-person meeting, which evokes elements of a "scene of subjection" due to the blatant racialization of the professional encounter, masked by liberal ideas of freedom and humanity at the center of the RF mission (and keeping in mind the important difference of this scene as anti-Asian rather than anti-Black).[105] Fahs's initial judgment would appear to have been damning for Toyama's suit from the start. It reinforced the RF's rejection of her prior 1958 application—a denial that had prevented her from staying in New York to continue her projects at the CPEMC.[106]

Yet Toyama's international credentials, which Fahs carefully referenced in his diary entry, may nonetheless have sufficed to fix his attention to her account of electronic music as a modernizing force in Asia.

His entry goes on to gloss Toyama's argument in favor of electronic music as a medium for making Asian music "modern" while still preserving elements of tradition:

> Believes [Ussachevsky and Luening's] approach preferable to that at either Cologne or Paris. Argues, in terms almost identical to those of [José] Maceda in the Philippines that electronic music, far from being a threat to Asiatic traditions in music offers an opportunity for the creative composer to use Asiatic timbres, moods, and ideas effectively in the creation of modern music which he cannot do if he is limited to the traditional instruments and their players.[107]

Fahs's summary of Tanaka's argument dovetails with Ussachevsky's description of electronic music as a medium for a "non-Western" composer to retain "essential ingredients of his native culture" while composing in large-scale "Western" forms. It also resonates with Tanaka's search for a "universal collection of tones enabling the transciption of global musics" into a modern notational medium. Fahs's reference to the Filipino composer José Maceda conveys the extent to which the RF cultivated an energetic conversation with "expert" informants on musical developments pertinent to questions of global exchange and cultural diplomacy. (Maceda had studied musique concrète in Paris in 1957 and 1958 before entering the PhD program in ethnomusicology at UCLA in 1961).

Fahs's diaries also register the ferment of discussion on "East-West exchange" leading up to two spectacular events devoted to that question: the 1961 East-West Music Encounter, organized by the Congress for Cultural Freedom, and John Cage's 1961 tour of Japan, partly sponsored by the Sōgetsu Art Center.[108] (It is worth noting that Sōgetsu had initially planned to invite Varèse rather than Cage in 1961, but Varèse ultimately declined due to health difficulties. Toyama served as a mediator between Varèse and Sōgetsu in a role analogous to that of Yoko Ono in the Cage tour, as described in chapter 4)[109] As reported by Fahs, Tanaka's argument for electronic music as a means to make Asian music "modern" cannily participates in the RF's own favored modernization models for understanding the evolution of societies, just as Ussachevsky's successful draft proposal did. In her pursuit of RF funding, Toyama's fluency in the norms of this discourse may have helped to counterbalance the demerits of her "inappropriate" persona in Fahs's chauvinist evaluation.

Fahs maintained enough interest in Toyama's project to record a detailed description of her specific needs:

Toyama says that the Japan Broadcasting Corporation electronic music equipment is available only to a limited group of favored composers (all twelve-tone) and then only for short periods. She has not been accepted. Unless she can get some equipment in Kyoto she will be unable to complete work begun at Columbia. Kiyono backs her in terms of faculty and student interest (Kyoto University does not have a School of Music) and can assure space. They say that what they need is quite simple—something like what Ussachevsky had with our help in the early stages of his work. Specifically they need three tape decks, nineteen oscillators and a few additional items all available through Japanese manufacturers. Minimum total cost not providable by the university is Yen 2 million, about six thousand dollars. CBF said only that he would study further; that he was hesitant to take further steps in electronic music at this time. T's tape now in CBF's office [and] can be sent to Mrs. [Beate] Gordon at the Japan Society.[110]

Fahs's account here accords with Toyama's own, suggesting that Fahs's diary entry may have rendered aspects of her proposal faithfully. Her request for nineteen oscillators comes close to the twenty digitals that Tanaka's keyboard required,[111] providing further fodder for the idea that she seriously planned to recreate a modern version of this instrument. (Perhaps the Electronics Department at Kyoto University already had the one additional oscillator required to make the complete set.) Fahs's rendering of her words about the Japan Broadcasting Corporation matches her communication to Varèse of her estrangement from the institutional elite at NHK radio.

Toyama's outsider status in Japanese musical institutions would have compromised her standing with the RF, since the foundation depended heavily on expert referees, published reviews, and institutional recognition in their evaluations. Toyama had gravitated toward music-educational opportunities—first in France and then in the United States—seeking to study European concert traditions and their contemporary compositional legacies. Like Ono, Toyama surely confronted not only massive gender barriers, but exclusion as a cultural alien in Japan because of her many years abroad.[112] As she wrote to Varèse after returning to Japan in 1959, "Life here is far from New York's. . . . I look forward to discovering all that is 'pure' Japan but alas! no one can share my feelings. As for music, it is dominated by the dodecaphonists[;] these are the ones who direct NHK Radio [Japan Broadcasting Corporation], publications, concerts, etc."[113] These words call out to be read in relation to the RF files, which portray her as isolated from the high-prestige new music circles connected with radio. "I was just disgusted with Japan and was planning to go back to New York this spring," Toyama wrote to Ussachevsky in 1959, "but my brother brought me to Kyoto Univ. and introduced me to Dr. Kiyono."[114] Her meeting with Kiyono had launched the possibility of cofounding a studio, which in turn had made it possible to imagine staying in Japan (since she had found no entry into Japan's official music institutions). Ussachevsky wrote that he "hoped the application to the Rockefeller Foundation will bring the support which is requested" and hoped too that his "efforts in that direction will do some good."[115] But Ussachevsky's recommendation could not compensate for her lack of acceptance in Japan's "new music" circles.

Toyama's quest for RF funding, which she had once assessed as "hopeful," ultimately went nowhere. Within a week of Fahs's meeting with Toyama, he consulted the ethnomusicologist and musicologist Robert Garfias, who provided a positive assessment of her ideas while casting a negative light on her troubled relationship with the Japan Broadcasting Corporation:

CBF [Fahs] asked Garfias his opinion of the argument of Maceda and Mrs. TOYAMA that electronic music is a constructive method of helping oriental musicians deal with their oriental music tradition. In general he concurs. On the other hand he speaks much more favorably of the work of the Japanese Broadcasting Company in this regard than did she—implies she is bitter because not included in their list. Garfias speaks highly of TAKEMITSU Toru, who works at NHK as perhaps the most promising composer.[116]

After this diary entry, Toyama's proposal appears to have fallen off Fahs's radar, although he referenced once more the idea "given earlier by Toyama, Maceda and Garfias—that electronic techniques offer the opportunity for modern composition with effective use of oriental resources."[117] Fahs's diaries suggest that he valued Toyama more for her contributions to an ongoing debate about "East-West" musical fusion than for her viability as a funding candidate.

Fahs's original 1960 rejection letter to Toyama appears in the Ussachevsky Collection at the Library of Congress. In his final missive to her, Fahs explained that he saw "no possibility of obtaining . . . assistance for you here," and his only "constructive suggestion" would be that "perhaps you could correspond with Dr. Ussachevsky" in the hopes that the CPEMC could contribute "modest amounts" to the Kyoto studio project. About a year prior, Toyama had confessed to Ussachevsky that she would be "so embarrassed if nothing comes out of [the application]" after she had secured the support of Dr. Ko Hirasawa, the president of Kyoto University, along with other professors.[118] Now, in January 1961, having finally received the RF's long-awaited decision, she mailed the original document (signed by Fahs) to Ussachevsky, and scrawled a note: "I am not expecting any grant but I would appreciate very much if I could have any small job around the studio. Françoise."[119] These words speak to her relationship of mentorship with Ussachevsky while also intimating the studio's longtime economy of undercompensated female labor. Although we know little of Toyama's routines at the CPEMC during her residency there, we do know from such composers as Pril Smiley and Alice Shields that the studio would later come to depend heavily upon women's work as bureaucratic administrators, instructors, and compositional assistants in a manner that tended to downplay their contributions. Ussachevsky's wife, Elizabeth Kray, complained to the CPEMC composer Mario Davidovsky of her own place in this economy of invisible labor.[120] "Any small job around the studio" might have provided for Toyama a path to return both to New York City and to the technologies on which her compositional work depended. "I am hoping to come back to New York again next fall," she wrote to her friend (and fellow Boulanger student) Louise Talma within a month of her RF rejection.[121] The CPEMC, however, appears not to have been able to offer financial support for her relocation.

Instead, the Japan Society (JS) of New York emerged as a primary, if limited, source of institutional funding. The JS, as we know, came to sponsor the release of Toyama's album *Waka* in 1960—after she had submitted her application to the RF, but prior to her rejection. By the end of that year, while Toyama's application had been declined, she benefited from the release of the album, drawing wider audiences to her work and documenting it for future generations. The JS also sponsored her for a visit to New York in the winter of 1961–62.[122] Closely affiliated with the RF, the JS dedicated itself to a mission of cultural exchange directed by John D. Rockefeller III. Fahs's April 1960 diary mentions that Toyama's tape "can be sent" from his office to the JS, and it is possible that Beate Sirota Gordon, as the JS performing arts director, took positive action on Toyama's behalf after having received her tape from Fahs. Yet Toyama may also plausibly have found sponsorship with Folkways Records and with the JS prior to Fahs's 1960 communications with Gordon. A hub for the expatriate commmunity in New York, the JS was a logical source for support. Ussachevsky, moreover, had already built a friendly relationship with Moe Asch, the owner of Folkways Records, with whom he had corresponded about the release of recordings of Mongolian songs and electronic music.[123] The Folkways album *Sounds of New Music* (1957) included early electronic works by both Ussachevsky and Luening alongside acoustic works such as El-Dabh's *Spectrum #1* and Cage's *Dance*.[124] This album would have set the stage for *Waka*.[125]

1960—the year of *Waka*'s release and of her RF rejection—appears to have brought about a negative turning point in Toyama's public career as a composer. Gordon, Ussachevsky, and Luening had been her main advocates in the United States. Over the course of the following year, however, Ussachevsky's advocacy for Toyama dwindled. He sent the recording of *Waka* to Pierre Schaeffer in Paris in the hopes that he would program it in a June 1961 concert.[126] Toyama reciprocated his advocacy by sharing tapes of CPEMC composers (Ussachevsky, Luening, Sessions, Babbitt, and Varèse) with Mayuzumi at the NHK, which successfully resulted in the FM radio broadcast programming of Ussachevsky's work in Japan (as reported by Toyama).[127] Ussachevsky, however, subsequently declined to program her work at the famous showcase concert for CPEMC composers staged at Columbia's McMillin Theatre in May 1961 (which featured music of Arel, Babbitt, Davidovsky, El-Dabh, Luening, Ussachevsky, and Charles Wuorinen). Toyama's lack of access to studio equipment prevented her from being able to refine her techniques and finish work in progress. In the fall of 1960, Luening suggested that they consider her for inclusion in the upcoming May concert, but Ussachevsky disagreed on the basis that *Waka* "suffers from the narrator and an inferior technical quality."[128] His disapprobation of the narrator may reveal differences in taste; his objection to her works' technical quality, while subjective, implicates her lack of studio access. Ussachevsky continued to hold back his support for Toyama in 1961, when Henry Jacobs of the Audio-Visual Research Foundation in San Francisco asked about the possibilty of programming her work alongside that of El-Dabh. Ussachevsky responded, "I will ask El-Dabh whether he has something recent to send," but he did not address the question of Toyama.[129] By 1961, Toyama's declining prestige, as evident in her grant rejection, and her ongoing lack of studio access appear to have dampened Ussachevsky's inclination to advocate for her. In the long run, the waning of Ussachevsky's support cemented her near invisibility in existing accounts of the CPEMC. Indeed, when her name came up in a 1978 oral history interview, Ussachevsky dismissed her with the words, "I think she came to us prior to the establishment of the Center. She worked in a studio, but I think she worked in a pre-Center studio."[130] He then resumed his discussion of male composers (those featured in the 1961 concert) and their mastery of relevant technologies.

Compounding Toyama's professional obstacles, the scholarly journal *Ethnomusicology* published a mixed review of *Waka* in 1961. (*High Fidelity*, which regularly reviewed music from the CPEMC, declined to review the album.) The fact that this solitary key review appears in an ethnomusicological journal suggests Toyama was likely taken more seriously by American scholars and critics as a ethnographic informant than as a composer. The reviewer, Ralph Greenhouse, a musician and anthropologist then employed at the Library of Congress, claimed that there was "much beauty and considerable promise in this music," but that it nonetheless became "a crying necessity" to "reject it as traditional Japanese music (*hogaku*)."[131] In Greenhouse's estimation, Toyama fell short as a cultural informant due to her Western musical education—an idea he illustrated with stereotyping imagery of passivity and dependence: "Herself an anomaly, [she has] at one time or other fall[en] under the spell of Boulanger, Milhaud, Messiaen, Sessions, and Varèse."[132] Before positively noting the album's high-quality performances and production, Greenhouse concluded his discussion of Toyama's composition with an extended quotation from the ethnomusicologst William Malm, which can be summarized in a single thesis: "To the extent that Japanese music attempts to imitate the Western nineteenth-century [and, I might add, twentieth-century] sound ideal, it will lose its own most vital elements. In such a situation it is doomed to eventual failure."[133] Toyama's reception in *Ethnomusicology* speaks to the double bind she faced as a Japanese woman creator among American critics and audiences—the trap of her work being reduced to exoticist stereotypes and being subject to denigration as a mimicry of Western models.

Despite setbacks in her critical reception and composerly opportunities, Toyama continued to work as a professional in the music world, eventually pursuing a career in acoustics research.[134] Speaking to Hiromi Tsuji, she explained, "To me, composition is something I enjoy, and something I do for myself. As much as I'm interested in having people listen to my music, I have no intention of seeking out opportunities to present my work to the public."[135] Tsuji provides a valuable interpretation of these words in relation to the professional obstacles Toyama faced:

Her reluctance to share her work might explain her struggle to leave her mark as a composer. At the same time, her experience underscores the difficulty of maintaining a successful compositional career without establishing a solid network within Japanese musical circles. It goes without saying that these difficulties are further compounded when the composer is a woman.[136]

The archival record underscores the reality of these difficulties. The "talk of others"—a threat to female social standing and psychic integrity, thematized in *Waka*—ultimately undermined Toyama's ability to pursue many of her desired creative projects in the electronic music studio. With her standing as a composer diminished in Japan, she devoted herself for a period to the invisible labor of copying scores and instrumental parts for others, including US composers. "Unless your bill is payed [*sic*], I won't be able to leave Japan!" she wrote to Talma in October 1961, with regard to her friend's copying order.[137] These words betray her painful lack of financial independence at this time, and her desire to return to the United States. (Toyama also recommended Toshi Ichiyanagi, in New York, to Talma as an excellent copyist, suggesting her likely proximity to Ichiyanagi's wife, Yoko Ono.)[138] For Toyama, the possibility of being recognized as a composer had become inextricably linked with the possibility of leaving Japan and returning to the United States. Yet she appears never to have returned to North America on any long-term basis.

Following her fellowship in the Department of Engineering at Kyoto University, Toyama eventually came to work at the University of Tokyo in the Department of Information Science at the School of Science, and in the Radio Research Laboratory at the Ministry of Post and Telecommunications. As Tsuji explains, "She encountered difficulties in continuing with her creative projects. She soon began sequestering herself in her own home, devoting most of her time to writing books on acoustics."[139] Toyama's abstracts appear throughout the *Journal of the Acoustical Society of America* and the *Journal of the Acoustical Society of Japan*.[140] These projects demonstrate not a complete severance of her creative path as a composer, but rather a continuation of related projects in knowledge production, cross-cultural communication, and cultural comparativism. In some ways, her professional trajectory mirrored that of Halim El-Dabh. After their visitorships at the CPEMC, both Toyama and El-Dabh found themselves subject to a critical backlash and limited professional opportunities as composers. They subsequently devoted themselves with great intensity to adjacent professional fields that had long been central to their compositional practice: Toyama as an acoustician, and El-Dabh as an ethnomusicologist.

New York Memories

When I met Halim El-Dabh in December 2014, I did not yet know enough about the CPEMC to ask certain questions, including whether or how well he had known Michiko Toyama. At that time I had never heard of her. Still in the early stages of researching my book, I had not yet delved deeply into the CPEMC's history, because some of its most important archives remained inaccessible or in processing.[141] Yet I knew that I would devote at least one chapter to the CPEMC, and I took interest in El-Dabh as one of the studio's less known composers. In the fall of 2014, I reached out to El-Dabh's assistant—the musicologist Laurel Myers Hurst—who let me know that El-Dabh was eager to visit with me. If I wanted to interview him at all, however, I would need to do so right away, given his ill health. In early December, El-Dabh and his wife, Deborah, welcomed me into their home in Kent, Ohio, for four long days of digitally recorded interviews interspersed with conversation-filled meals. Hurst facilitated the visit, supplementing my own audio recording with video recording of our interviews for El-Dabh's personal archive. An intensely expressive person in word, countenance, and gesture, El-Dabh reminisced and puzzled over the past with great animation.

I conjecture that El-Dabh did not know Toyama well or at all, because he made a point of naming to me his female interlocutors—including Peggy Glanville-Hicks, Martha Graham, Yuriko Kimura, Elizabeth Kray, and Alice Shields in the United States, and Bathaina Fareed and Izzy Scalada in Egypt[142]—but never mentioned Toyama. In our conversation, issues of immigrant acculturation, cross-cultural communication, and ethnographic knowledge production emerged as what he saw as the key elements characterizing the social and intellectual life of the CPEMC. Later, after El-Dabh's death in 2017, as I became aware of Toyama and immersed myself in her scattered archive, I marveled at the apparent similarities between their creative projects and professional struggles. Telling their stories together may even spur a counterhistory that imagines what would have happened if they had known one another well—keeping faith with the speculative tone of searching remembrance and futuristic imagination that characterized El-Dabh's conversations with me.

El-Dabh took the occasion of my arrival from New York as an opportunity to look back on the city he had left more than half a century before. He discussed his first, Fulbright-sponsored trip to New York from Cairo in 1950—a short sojourn in the city that preceded his studies in composition at University of New Mexico (1950–51), the Berkshire Music Center

(1951–52), Brandeis University (MM 1953), and the New England Conservatory of Music (MFA 1954). Along this path of education, he found mentorship and instruction with Ernst Krenek, John Donald Robb, Francis Judd Cooke, Aaron Copland, Irving Fine, and Luigi Dallapiccola. After amassing an impressive portfolio of compositions and reviews, El-Dabh returned to New York in 1956 to solidify his nascent career, which had been nurtured by the patronage networks of US cultural diplomacy (figure 3.3). He quickly found community and critical recognition collaborating with the Martha Graham Company on the acclaimed ballet *Clytemnestra* (1958), which paved the way for the Guggenheim and Columbia University grants that in turn funded his appointment at the CPEMC in 1959. He looked back on that time nostalgically, sitting side by side with me as he thumbed through a curated album of old press clippings. He emphasized his feelings of gratitude for the welcome he had found in New York, along with his "luck." His relatively quick acceptance within New

Halim El-Dabh, Egyptian composer, playing the derabucca

FIGURE 3.3. Halim El-Dabh, as depicted in the *Christian Science Monitor*. Photographer unknown.

York's cultural institutions seemed to mirror the spirit of sociability he had found among strangers in the city:

I go on the subway, I can talk to people at 3 o'clock in the morning. Fabulous! Somebody doesn't know me and we have coffee together. We were talking on the subway. I found that a lot. You arrive in a neighborhood, you come in, and you start having bagels, having donuts, and a whole world is there. I mean New York is an incredible city. It was like love at first sight. Everyone thought I was going to be repulsed by it [because of its reputation for rudeness]. It was love at first sight.[143]

His spirits were mounted quite up to happiness. Even amid El-Dabh's elation, however, he was acutely aware of his exotic appearance to others within his artistic circles. As he put it to me in reference to his racialized reception within the institutions of classical music and every day on the street in the 1950s: "Yes, I *am* an African."[144] Over the course of many years, he came to develop a strong sense of identification with African-Americans—the identity many white Americans casually assigned to him because of his medium-dark complexion. The institutions of US soft power had effectively launched El-Dabh's career as a composer and cultural diplomat, dispatching him from Cairo to New York, from the outer peripheries of US power to the metropole. There he unexpectedly encountered racist bigotries and structural inequalities, which drew him into the politics of the civil rights movement in the 1950s and beyond. After his work at the CPEMC, he undertook ethnographic research in Ethiopia before contributing to the establishment of Africana studies programs at Howard University and Kent State University. His time at the CPEMC represented a turning point after which he became less recognized as a composer and more recognized as an ethnomusicologist.

At the CPEMC, El-Dabh confronted the mixed gatekeeping mechanisms of the studio as an Acropolis. As an RF-supported hub for cultural diplomacy, the studio welcomed El-Dabh and his projects; but as a bastion for restrictive ideas of Western genius, it would not propel his compositional career with the same force that it did others (including its founders, Ussachevsky and Luening, and other creators such as Mario Davidovsky and Charles Wuorinen). Although El-Dabh touched on these issues of power only lightly in our interviews, they become apparent in the patterns of his critical reception. Like Toyama, El-Dabh found only a conditional welcome among white American music critics, who evaluated his work and persona in emphatically racialized terms even when they praised him. Following this dynamic, the "first West, then rest" ide-

ologies permeating institutions of classical music and technoscience obscured and continue to obscure El-Dabh's legacy. Like Toyama, he led a
peripatetic life, shuttling between nations, languages, and traditions; his
hybrid persona and oeuvre confound the standard categories of nation
and genre that so often define musical historiographies. El-Dabh's presence in existing narratives of electronic music and the New York avant-
garde scene remains faint—a circumstance compounded by the fact that
his extensive personal archive has long been inaccessible. Still, a biography by Denise Seachrist, recordings, published interviews, and a smat-
tering of journal articles and book chapters render El-Dabh's legacy more
visible than Toyama's. Unlike Toyama, El-Dabh would find the opportunity to pursue US citizenship—a path made possible by his first marriage
to Mary Hyde El-Dabh (a US citizen) and a string of professsional successes, including fellowships and commissions that were less accessible
to Toyama as a Japanese woman. My own contribution to El-Dabh's historiography builds on a growing recognition of his work that accelerated
in the years around his death.

Effendi Experimentations

By the time El-Dabh began his grant-supported work at the CPEMC in
1958, his career had already taken off with the support of a powerful cultural
diplomacy infrastructure. In Cairo in the late 1940s, he had emerged as an
attractive candidate for the newly founded Fulbright Program by virtue of
his elite background and enterprising creativity as an amateur composer
interested in cross-cultural exchange and matters of war and peace. El-
Dabh belonged to a social category in Egypt known as the *effendiyya*—the
self-consciously modern urban professionals who later came to define the
postcolonial Egyptian state, as described by the historian of science Omnia El Shakry and the literary scholar Lucie Ryzova.[145] Journeys to study
abroad in "the West" often figured as a rite of passage for Egyptians of
El-Dabh's social class, although France and the United Kingdom had
served as more typical destinations than the United States. One of El-
Dabh's uncles, Aziz Benyiamin Fam, had undertaken a rare pathway to
emigrate to the US, a relatively uncommon destination for Egyptians,
in 1904.[146] He eventually settled in Detroit, where he worked in real estate and married a Jewish-American woman.[147] El-Dabh fondly recalled
how an older sister had taken him as a child to consult "a visionary [in]
a strange house in Cairo" to divine the whereabouts of his uncle through
use of a crystal ball. "A few days later we received a letter from him from
[the United States]; we were to come and visit."[148] Such dreams of trav-

eling abroad were common to his cosmopolitan circles in Cairo, a global nexus of modern commerce and culture under successive Ottoman and British occupying regimes. Fundamental to the effendi experience was the situation of being between cultures—a consequence of French and British economic, political, and military incursions in Ottoman Egypt and the British Protectorate from the late nineteenth century onward, which exploited Egypt's strategic geography between continents and waterways. For the middle and upper middle classes, this liminal experience produced a dual imperative for European-style "Western" education and proficiency in Arab, "national," or local traditions of culture and knowledge. In Ryzova's study of effendi autobiographies, she describes these narratives as detailing rites of passage invested with world-historical import, undertaken in the service of "publicly-oriented missions" fraught with moral and political dilemmas of cultural crossing.[149]

Such a model, which foregrounds the relationship between cross-cultural education and public responsibility, resonates with the coming-of-age narratives El-Dabh shared with me. Born into a prosperous family whose income came from the grain business, Halim, as the youngest of nine children, was singled out for early access to a Western-style education that contrasted with the upbringing of his older siblings. He enrolled in a French-language Jesuit school before eventually obtaining a BS in agricultural engineering from Cairo University in 1944.[150] El-Dabh emphasized how his passion for "creative activities" extended across interests in "the ancient and the modern"—understood as encompassing Arab, Egyptian, and European traditions in art, philosophy, and religion.[151] He attributed his omnivorous pursuits to the encouragement of his oldest brother Bushra, whose own intellectual and creative ambitions had been frustrated after having been drafted into his father's grain business. It was Bushra who brought the eleven-year-old Halim to the famous Cairo Conference of Arab Music in 1932, an event that exposed the younger El-Dabh to such composers as Béla Bartók and Paul Hindemith, precipitating his commitment to musical studies. As a teenager, Halim studied oud and Arab classical musics with Bushra, and studied piano, composition, and European music theory at the Szulc Conservatory, an institution founded by the Polish-Jewish refugee Josef Szulc.[152] El-Dabh immersed himself in Cairo's rich music, literary, art, and film scenes—and even eventually contributed a score to Cairo's flourishing movie industry.[153] As Michael Khoury notes, "El-Dabh would . . . have contact with some of the more well-known Egyptian composers and performers of the time, including Umm Kulthum, Muhammad 'Abd al-Wahhab, and Abdel Halim Hafez."[154]

Together with his brother Bushra, El-Dabh entered into social circles connected to Egyptian Radio and the Young Men's Christian Association (YMCA) in Heliopolis, where men and women debated music, culture, and politics in a publicly minded spirit of civic engagement:

> The YMCA was an independent institution, didn't have any connection to America; it was a space where you went there and gathered. You talked politics, you did art, you did music performance, you volunteered. I volunteered to do literacy teaching for the neighborhood at one time. . . . You were free to do what you wanted to do: swim, play, express. I had a lot of my music played there, you know with some of my friends, with exhibits and everything, so it was really a pulsing center in the life of Cairo and its political scene too. People discussed Trotsky and Stalin's philosophy, and [the] philosophy of Karl Marx we discussed there openly. I think we were not allowed in other places. People talked about the differences; you know they were really open.[155]

Khoury describes how El-Dabh also joined "a group of French, Syrian, and Lebanese men with common interests in music. . . . They introduced him to composers such as Schönberg, Stravinsky, and Milhaud and discussed emerging ideas in philosophy."[156] El-Dabh's musical activities, however, remained a mere avocation. During his twenties, he instead pursued a career as a high-ranking administrative official responsible for managing and modernizing the agricultural zone of Middle Egypt during a period of dire constraints at the end of World War II, and amid ongoing British occupation and the revolutionary turmoil that destabilized the governments of Farouk I and Fuad II.

El-Dabh's career in agriculture entailed modes of knowledge production that remained fundamental to his subsequent work as a national emissary, cultural diplomat, and composer. These continuities arose from his early, innovative use of sound technologies and ethnographic methods of musical study in Egypt. In the 1940s he worked with magnetic wire recorders—borrowed from Egyptian Radio[157]—in an effort to develop a sound-based beetle repellent as an alternative to insecticide during a period of severe wartime food shortages and famine. Later, he would joke that his experiment with beetles and wire recorders constituted his first effort to "communicate across boundaries.")[158] He used his work trips in the Nile Valley, moreover, as an opportunity to study rural musical traditions, loosely drawing on ethnographic methods he had encountered as an adolescent at the Cairo Congress. Such efforts participated in what El Shakry has called the "romantic tradition in the human sciences" as adapted by a Egyptian nationalist elite, whose "research on the *mentalité* of the peasantry included the representation of their everyday life, manners, and customs, and the collection of folkloric material."[159] The *effendiyya* "inaugurated its own social-scientific program, in which both the uniqueness (a precondition for nationalism) and educability (a precondition for progress) of the collective national subject (e.g., the peasant, the village, the family) could be demonstrated through ethnographies, field experiments, and social-engineering projects—which would remedy the imputed stagnation of Egyptian society."[160]

Far from contradictory, El-Dabh's wide range of activities—from developing a beetle repellent to the collection of "folklore"—could be understood as contributing to the spiritual and technical development of the emerging nation that sought freedom from colonial rule. As El Shakry emphasizes, this project unfolded as a search for alternative speaking positions that would rely on internal indigenous sources of progress while "rejecting the totalizing, racialized nature of European claims to progress, reason, and the nation-state."[161] In the anthropologist Nicolas Puig's terms, a "cosmopolitan atmosphere" permeated "the emergence of a new political, modernist and reformist subject embodied by the *effendi* in the context of the progression of Arab nationalism and anti-colonial struggles in the first half of the 20th century."[162]

El-Dabh's own espousal of this mission shows up in his words as a visitor at Columbia University in the late 1950s. At the CPEMC, he articulated a compositional program that sought to undermine distinctions between "West" and "non-West," which he saw as a "demeaning political move" that denigrated cultures of Africa, Latin America, and Asia.[163] Salwa El-Shawan has described similar attitudes among Egyptian intellectuals, musicians, and audiences: "Those who describe music as being oriental at times and Western at other times are mistaken. Music is [a] language . . . without any differentiation between East and West."[164] In a Composers Forum discussion at Columbia University in 1958, El-Dabh patiently engaged with audience members who fixated on the "Oriental" aspects of his music following a performance of his works *Tahmeela* (for orchestra) and "House of Atreus" from *Clytemnestra*. He responded to their fixation by describing his projects more capaciously as encompassing "the traditions that I have lived," which included "European traditions," "American traditions," and a "history of Egyptian music [that] expands to three thousand years."[165] This response to the audience exemplifies the postcolonial struggle to establish a new position from which to speak, a struggle associated with the cosmopolitan nationalism of the effendi elite.

In the service of El-Dabh's own state-building vision in Cairo, sound recording technologies became enmeshed with questions of religion and spirituality on the one hand, and with Egyptian and US-based discourses of human rights on the other.[166] This nexus becomes apparent in El-Dabh's *Ta'abir Al-Zaar*, a sound document the composer produced in 1944 by manipulating the recording of a Zār ceremony.[167] The Zār is a centuries-old healing ritual prevalent around the horn of Africa and the Middle East. El-Dabh attributed a liberatory quality to this ceremony, because it extended across decolonizing regions and also often included women participants (as practiced in a variant by exclusively female urban groups in Cairo).[168] Central to Egypt's project of modernization, El-Dabh maintained, was the resuscitation of ancient religious sources that would unify society on a common spiritual ground free from gender discrimination: "So in my travel with the Zār I was interested also in the position of women. . . . It was part of the answer in society."[169] New technologies, from his perspective, could produce new aesthetic practices and realities imbued with a prominent "women's presence."[170]

By El-Dabh's account, however, his path *into* the ceremony as a male outsider unfolded as a story of subterfuge, transgression, detection, and forgiveness. He tried to gain entry to the all-female ceremony by cross-dressing as a woman. He admitted his male identity when the practitioners recognized his deception, and he finally confessed his need for personal healing. The women, he claimed, eventually granted him the permissions he had initially failed to seek in the first place.[171] Given El-Dabh's interest in human rights, it would seem strange that he had not respected the women practitioners' sovereignty over their ritual. Yet the episode reminds us of continuities between El-Dabh's compositional practice and his Orientalist heritage as an ethnographer. El-Dabh turned to the all-female Zār ceremony romantically, as though in search of a redemptive internal "other," and he did so in a way that maintained his positional superiority relative to those whose sounds he captured.[172] In El-Dabh's account to me, his emphasis on his own need for forgiveness emphasized the aspirations toward social unity that guided his postcolonial project.

The future-oriented mysticism of this venture participated in a long tradition of sound recording's fetishization of the spiritual and the occult. As Delinda Collier argues, it "links up to specific concepts of removal, or spirit possession as a method of performing disembodied sound."[173] El-Dabh sought to capture and enhance via sound recording the ecstatic movement and affect of the trance ritual: "Oh, there was incredible energy, it was like flying in the air, their bodies."[174] Toward that end, he transformed the ceremony through his presence with the bulky wire recorder, and produced a recorded sample of the ritual's sounding reality. Later, El-Dabh's own perception of reality was altered as he worked on the recording at a studio of the Egyptian Radio:

So I was at the radio station, [working with] the voices, and then I started hearing this other sound coming out of those voices; so then I started manipulating the tapes, the recording, into reverbs and echoes and, . . . later on, looping.[175]

In his interview with Khoury, El-Dabh further specified his technique of "using a rudimentary echo chamber and . . . bouncing the piece from one wire recorder to another."[176] As he recounted to Kamila Metwaly, "The radio station had movable walls, so I could move the walls as I ejected sound in a chamber and move the wall to change the vibration, to change the echo, reverberation, electric energy, the voltage control."[177] The composer's approach resonates with Amy Cimini's description of late twentieth-century US musical experimentalisms as "eager to 'discover' the sounds of living bodies and submit their raw material to composers for aesthetic refinement and technological elaboration."[178]

Unlike these later US practices, however, El-Dabh appears not to have considered the resulting recording a "composition" at all, despite the fact that he presented it in a gallery setting at the YMCA.[179] By his own account, El-Dabh understood the process of manipulating the sounds as an introspective experience with spiritual and political implications during a time of great political upheaval and factionalization in Egypt. "So I started manipulating my tapes in a different sense to create a new reality for me," he recalled. "Or an extended reality, a transformed reality, so that desire of transformed reality made my musical electronic process."[180] The manipulated sound generated desire for and insight into a possible future reality grounded in a renewed spirituality traversing social and cultural divides: "I felt close to this kind of expression, the mystical feeling, there is a universe, there is a connection that links us all beyond your limited views."[181] For El-Dabh, the remembrance of an ancient ritual, full of promise for the future, resonated in the reverb and echo effects of the wire recorder's manipulations.[182] Ultimately, the project's loosely ethnographic methods and sensibilities—combined with its human rights aspirations and mysticism—would also provide a basis for his work at the CPEMC.

El-Dabh's journey to the United States in 1950, and his decision to embark full-time on a career in composition, cannot be disentangled from intensified US government efforts to strengthen American economic, cultural, and political leverage in Egypt, a nation of acute strategic significance during the Cold War. The country was considered vital to supply routes in case of armed conflict with the Soviet Union, and it hosted a massive British military base in the Suez Canal zone that provoked constant conflict. Egypt's vibrant political culture had brought forth powerful revolutionary nationalist movements, which US officials worried would destabilize the entire region.[183] US policy envisioned Egypt as key to establishing stability in the entire Middle East, which officials "defined as the region being at peace, governed by leaders friendly to the West, open to American economic opportunities, and free from Soviet influence."[184]

This postwar policy objective formed the backdrop for El-Dabh's recruitment, a story that is intimately connected with the premiere of El-Dabh's solo piano piece *It Is Dark and Damp on the Front* (1949), which he performed himself. This work drew critical acclaim after its performance before an international audience at the Assembly Hall of All Saints in Cairo.[185] As El-Dabh remembered, the committee organizing the event had initially resisted programming his work in a concert that otherwise featured only Europeans; but pressure from Egyptian community members—notably, his friend Kamal Iskander—prevailed. *It Is Dark* may be understood as an affectively rich tone poem responding to the 1948 Arab-Israeli war; it highlighted the "war front" inside every person affected by the "double tragedy" of the Holocaust and the Nakba, as El-Dabh described it to me. To Khoury, he recalled, "1948, for me, was very disturbing. The whole balance of the Middle East was falling down."[186] He continued,

> I came to the realization that the front is in every human being. You have to have a balance. A balance in power and relationships. As long as someone is sitting on top of somebody, you can't have a balance. Without balance, there is no rest. Conflict has affected everyone in this world. It's perpetuating this kind of negative energy. It has a fear dimension. It perpetuates other wars. It perpetuates suffering for humanity. It's a composition of what happened. I felt a horror feeling, but I felt hope.[187]

It Is Dark drew widespread acclaim "against the backdrop of a sympathetic and shocked international community in Cairo . . . [and had] broad appeal to those in the region, the majority of whom were deeply affected by al-Nakba."[188] Its unusual musical language made expressive use of crisp, repeating pianistic gestures that resonated across expanses of silence to create what El-Dabh called "heteroharmony": "I'm not following the traditional basic European chord formation or chord motion, [but rather] get satisfaction when I hear . . . the amount of resonance that comes from a chord juxtaposing [with] another chord."[189] This effect of resonance, created through unorthodox pedaling technique, elicits from the tempered piano "the feeling [of] the instruments that are not tempered [and] carry a different relationship of intervals."[190] El-Dabh explained that heteroharmony allowed him to range broadly across sound worlds he associated with both European and Arab musical heritages: "So I feel those vibrations from a wave form feeling so they give me a way of expressing myself in a wider scope."[191] The work captured the attention of a cultural attaché of the American Embassy in Cairo, Robert S. Black, who organized a repeat performance in Oriental Hall at the American University in Cairo.[192]

Given US foreign policy objectives, El-Dabh's mobilization of public sentiment in a discourse against war and conflict likely attracted Black and his colleagues. The intercultural aesthetic of the piano piece may only have heightened its appeal for the diplomats at the US embassy, who would have idealized notions of East-West exchange in a spirit similar to that of the RF officers who socialized there. Following the critical success of *It Is Dark*'s premiere, Black convinced El-Dabh to study composition in the United States and to embark on a new career as a composer and cultural diplomat through the newly created Fulbright Program. El-Dabh had long been attracted to the United States not only by the example of his Uncle Aziz's immigration, but also by his image of "the political scene, of course, the utopia of America. . . . When I used to visit the Cultural Center in Egypt, [there were] these beautiful pictures on the wall of America, the land of honey, the land of milk, or honey and milk, whatever, how beautiful it is, promoting human rights and all that, it gives you a feeling of 'This is it,' you know? So there was a lot of temptation."[193] In El-Shawan's words, moreover, European-educated Egyptian composers who wrote in hybrid concert idioms in mid-century Egypt "were confronted with difficulties in having their works performed, recorded, and published. . . . They spent their lives fighting for recognition."[194] For El-Dabh, migration to the United States seemed very attractive.[195]

New York Metamorphoses

In describing his early transition to the United States, El-Dabh laughingly told a joke indicative of the racialized setting in which he found himself:

When I first arrived it was New York, and I was met by the Black family who took me [in] because I was part of the international institute there, part of the Fulbright, and he took me in and then I met rich white people! That was really interesting, the contrast. I had a great time.[196]

These words indicate the complicated reception El-Dabh received within a world of elite white American cultural, arts, and diplomatic circles he entered, where his Egyptian identity came to be prized as a novelty. Egyptian immigration to the United States had never been sizable, with fewer than twelve thousand Egyptians following this path between 1820 and 1969.[197] By the 1950s, Middle Eastern and North African immigration to the United States had virtually ground to a halt following the 1924 Immigration Act, and many established Arab families sought to camouflage themselves through assimilationist practices, like the Anglicization of names, in order to avoid discrimination.[198]

El Dabh belongs to a small wave of Palestinian and Egyptian elites who managed to enter the United States during the postwar period despite its ongoing severe restriction on "Asian" immigration (the category under which Middle Easterners were classified). It was not until the late 1960s—after the 1965 Immigration Act—that El-Dabh would discover solidarity with a visible and thriving Arab diasporic community. He especially credited Ibrahim Abu-Lughod's 1968 founding of the Association of Arab-American University Graduates, where El-Dabh found support and kinship.[199] In the 1950s, however, he circulated extensively in white cultural and professional spaces where his Egyptian background was regarded as intriguingly exotic: "Nobody had heard of an Egyptian in 1950, so everyone invited me to these places."[200] On some occasions he found himself subject to explicit anti-Black denigration. Especially poignant was his memory of a composition teacher who, when El-Dabh encountered difficulties transcribing a composition for piano soon after his arrival in the United States, dismissed him with the words, "Well, you're just an African." He explained that these words shocked him, but that he also made a positive decision to take the statement as a compliment: "Yes, I am an African!"[201] In our interviews, El-Dabh tended to address memories of racial discrimination with upbeat puns and jokes that worked through a spirit of reclamation. The approach echoes Benjamin Patterson's own "survival technique" as a contemporaneous Black composer of "getting through difficult situations with humor with more smile on your face" in Fluxus practices.[202] As we will see, El-Dabh's electronic music activities also provided a powerful expressive outlet and a means for self-alteration as he adapted to life in the United States.

At the CPEMC, El-Dabh confronted the gatekeeping mechanisms of the studio, as mentioned above. Ussachevsky and Luening appear to have welcomed him with genuine warmth, and eagerly promoted his electronic composition—a dynamic congruent with the cultural-diplomatic mission of the CPEMC and its sponsors at the RF. As a person ambiguously coded Black, however, he remained subject to multilayered, systems of exclusion within Western classical music, academia, and technoscience. This gatekeeping becomes apparent in the trajectory of El-Dabh's career and critical reception in the 1950s and 1960s.

El-Dabh's 1959 invitation to the CPEMC and his Guggenheim and Columbia University Fellowships all came on the heels of his acclaimed composition of the score for Martha Graham's ballet *Clytemnestra* (1958), for which he received superlative reviews. Graham lauded him in the *Foreign Press News* as "an Egyptian writing on a world theme—Clytemnestra has many sisters in the world."[203] *The New York Tribune* celebrated his "remarkable score" as having been essential to the creation of an "ageless" work that would "be as at home in an ancient Greek amphitheatre as it is in a Broadway house."[204] *The New York Times* praised his music as capturing "the distinctive color and the very bone and muscle of the [dance's] movement style."[205] The exoticism of Graham's work set the terms for critics' interpretation of El-Dabh's music as they focused on its timbral and rhythmic qualities, alongside his Egyptian origins, which were taken to approximate the world of ancient Greece. From the 1920s onward, Graham had built her career upon exoticist traditions of modern dance focused on cultures of the Middle East, Asia, and the Americas. She had cultivated an image of exoticism, burnished by a multiracial troupe of dancers and collaborators, including El-Dabh. This ensemble of color made possible her trademark ability to present as "an 'exotic' woman while remaining recognizably white" and therefore privileged to "showcase her stardom as a white woman choreographer—a woman who could do her own work," as Caroline Joan S. Picart writes.[206] El-Dabh relished the opportunity to collaborate with Graham on *Clytemnestra*, which surely resonated with his avowed feminist leanings. He also parlayed the critical success of this project into new creative opportunities through his work in the CPEMC. Yet the critical reception of his compositions after 1959 would never reach the heights of acclaim he had received in Graham's orbit, where his own "exotic" persona had seemed to make sense to white audiences and critics. It is no coincidence, moreover, that the first tenure-track academic position he landed, in 1966, was at the prestigious Howard University, a historically Black institution.

In this context, the CPEMC emerges as a fascinating way station in the transformation of El-Dabh's career and subjectivity as he navigated a path toward minoritarian US citizenship. The studio's function as a way station, however, cannot be separated from its gatekeeping as an Acropolis. In the years around 1960, El-Dabh shuttled between activities of effendi cultural diplomacy and racialized immigrant acculturation in the

United States. This dynamic effected a metamorphosis in him that both extended and altered given ways of knowing and being, reaching into questions of subjectivity and persona.[207] The institutional space of the CPEMC proved vital in this regard. The studio enabled El-Dabh to pursue a mission of research and creative production that enlarged upon his mysticist, politicized Zār project in Cairo. At the same time, as Ussachevsky and Luening proclaimed, tape's capacity to bypass fixed notation and tuning systems heralded unprecedented new modes of "intercultural" composition through the use of cutting, splicing, looping and other format-specific techniques.[208] These affordances made possible El-Dabh's "creative ethnomusicology"—what Akin Euba describes as a "transformational zone between research and composition," which treats ethnographic "fieldwork as an essential aspect of composition."[209] For the migrant composer, this transformational zone between research and composition also constituted a realm for self-alteration.

During this period, El-Dabh approached electronic composition with a speculative spirit of political and citizenly engagement that characterized his complex path from Egyptian effendi status to minoritarian American citizenship more generally. While at the CPEMC from 1959 to 1962, he appears to have grappled with the question of whether to return to Egypt or settle in the United States permanently. He even returned to Cairo for most of 1960 to serve, at President Nasser's invitation, in the Ministry of Culture of the United Arab Republic—a short-lived pan-Arab political union between Egypt and Syria.[210] (In 1947, El-Dabh had composed *Ya Gamul Ya Nasser* in Nasser's honor.)[211] There he prepared related "creative ethnomusicological" projects for the new pan-Arab state, which included his composition of music for a light show at the pyramids. The officers of the Rockefeller Foundation took notes on his activities and socialized with him in diplomatic circles—circumstances that show the extent to which El-Dabh remained caught up in a net of soft-power infrastructure intimately aligned with geopolitical strategy.[212] El-Dabh chafed at the bureaucratic routines of his position in Cairo. Disillusioned by his experiences in Egypt, he returned to New York in the fall of 1960 to continue his work at the CPEMC and to follow through on a path toward US citizenship. El-Dabh's "transformational zone between research and composition" reimagined Arab and African pasts to speculate about liberatory futures, while treating magnetic tape as a medium for reimagining his own and others' changing subjecthood during a time of political upheaval in both of his homelands. To foreground this path suggests a new way of conceiving the CPEMC's dual mission as a music composition and research center—a way that refuses simply to rein-

scribe the ideologies of the RF Humanities Division or Luening and Ussachevsky's goals as the legacy of the CPEMC.

"You Are Free! You Are Free! Unshackled!"

El-Dabh's work at the CPEMC can be understood in terms of an Afrofu-
turist poetics that also draws on traditions of Orientalism and comparative
musicology—a perspective that brings multiple domestic, diasporic, and
imperial frames into play at once. Afrofuturism pertains to El-Dabh's work
by virtue of its speculative focus on ideas of African and Afrodiasporic
modernity, its thematization of liberation and futuristic subjecthood, and
its exploration of these themes through a playful human-machine interface engaging Arab and African heritage.[213] As Alondra Nelson and others
have written, Afrofuturism disrupts linear ideas of progress that relegate
Europe's "others" to premodern temporalities.[214] The RF's subscription to
a "first in Europe, then elsewhere" theory of modernization epitomized
such attitudes, as did Ussachevsky and Luening's long-standing insistence
upon New York and Paris as the only competing birthplaces for electronic
composition. Although the very existence of El-Dabh's electronic oeuvre
generally refutes such narratives, the composer also mobilized forms of
knowledge production connected with imperialist projects. In his mission to educate US audiences about the Egyptian heritage, he assumed
the split authority of an ethnographer and an informant, occupying a dual
insider-outsider status in relation to the Arab, Muslim, and Egyptian traditions he publicly represented—traditions with which he had varying
degrees of proximity as an urban Christian elite. From this split position,
he devised a mystical, liberatory poetics, variously adaptable to the purposes of Egyptian revolutionary nationalism, Arab or African diasporic
solidarity, anticolonialism, and US civil rights.

El-Dabh's tape piece *Leiyla and the Poet* (1959) stands out for inviting interpretation along these lines, intimating how his complex poetics
of representation shifted during his time at the CPEMC. His electronic
oeuvre includes the tape pieces *Element, Being, and Primeval* (1959), *Michael and the Dragon* (1959), *The Word* (1959), *Leiyla and the Poet* (1959),
Meditation on White Noise (1959), and *Electronic Fanfare* (cocomposed
with Otto Luening, 1963). While they all deserve elaboration, *Leiyla and
the Poet* provides an unusually rich example. The composition transforms
ecstatic Arabic and Muslim traditions within a poetic setting of quasi-
ethnographic experimentalism, blending a future-oriented mysticism
with self-consciously progressive gender politics, much as the earlier Zār
project had done. El-Dabh would later link *Leiyla*'s themes with the con-

cerns of Black feminism. The work centers on a classical story of forbidden romance between the poet Qays (renamed Majnun, meaning "madness" or "possessed") and his cousin Layla, imprisoned and later forcibly married off by her family to thwart her love for Majnun. With origins dating to seventh-century pre-Islamic Arabia, this canonical narrative tradition known as "Layla-Majnun" came to occupy a prominent place in Sufi devotional poetry, where literary erotics offered a path toward God. All of this history bears profoundly upon El-Dabh's setting, which draws upon musical conventions of Sufi ecstatic ritual and places them within a modern multimedia environment. *Leiyla and the Poet* retranslates this classical literary tradition with special attention to gendered representations of desire. El-Dabh's version of Layla-Majnun focuses not on Majnun's desire for Layla and finally for God, but rather on Layla's yearning for Majnun and for poetry in her quest for liberation. At its 1961 premiere, *Leiyla and the Poet* represented Egyptian, Muslim, and Arab cultural traditions to New York audiences, working as a sort of ethnographic translation that also aspired to modernize those traditions in the electronic music studio.

The *Leiyla* performance referred to herein corresponds to the recording released on the 1964 LP *The Columbia-Princeton Electronic Music Center*—a recording El-Dabh treated as equivalent to what he had premiered in 1961.[215] We should note, however, that another, earlier version of the piece (labeled "final master revised") exists on a reel in the archives of the Columbia-Princeton Electronic Music Center; and El-Dabh later released the fourteen-part "electronic drama" called *Leiyla Visitations* on the 2001 CD *Crossing into the Electric-Magnetic*, which suggests a decades-long involvement with the theme and materials of the piece.[216] All of these versions of *Leiyla* manipulate the sounds of El-Dabh's own voice and the playing of Arab wind, string, and percussion instruments—a setup that foregrounds El-Dabh's shifting persona as cultural expert, informant, and altered subject.

Over the course of five and a half minutes, *Leiyla and the Poet* follows an accelerating slow-fast format that loosely evokes ecstatic Sufi hymnodies such as the Egyptian Madh genre. The opening draws attention to the sounds of spoken word and Arab instruments through their estrangement—instruments that El-Dabh treated as cherished belongings, carrying them with him throughout his travels.[217] With deliberate, undulating microtonal intervallic motion, the high sinusoidal sound produced by a sped-up sample of a reed flute (a ney or kawala) opens the piece, like a futuristic *taqsim*. At 0:19, El-Dabh's voice, distorted by its own echo, intones barely audible words—"Leiyla," "poet," "poet's vision of light"—while pinging sounds ricochet across a wide registral expanse defined at its uppermost limit by the whistling of the altered flute. The echoing vocal intonation sounds ambiguous in both its gender and meaning, while muted deep-register vocal exclamations respond to the intonation, evoking group participation. Resounding at the threshold of aural decipherability, these sounds have the potential to draw listeners in with their ambiguity. Over the course of the rest of the piece, the intelligibility of El-Dabh's intoned text sporadically, increasingly clarifies as the work's themes of divine light and desire unfold.

After this call-and-response opening, *Leiyla and the Poet* proceeds in three remaining sections that comment upon and transform devotional traditions of Layla-Majnun. Following a frame drum cadence, an extravagant vocal gesture initiates the next section. The invocation of the name "Leiyla" (at 0:54) moves exuberantly from chest to head voice, from low to high, on the syllable "Leiy"—only to land with a guttural accent on "la." As El-Dabh recalled, "I created my own Leiyla. It was right there in my voice: 'Eiii!'"[218] Here the voice conjures its own realities; it transforms the speaker—his very being—through the force of gesture, vowel sound, and register. Two layers of registrally differentiated text sound simultaneously, set against a background of sparse instrumental gestures (1:01). El-Dabh's doubled voice addresses Leiyla while invoking images of love, vision, and madness: "You shall succumb to your cousin, a madman," "Leiyla, my sight," "my love, my way of sight," "my desires, my heart free to love, free to love a woman," "Leiyla vision of light." As the literary scholar Lalita Sinha emphasizes, the Layla-Majnun tradition tends to mobilize sight and light as metaphors to evoke Majnun's perception at a higher level of reality through love.[219] This accords with Sufi devotional interpretations that treat Majnun's possession by love as a path to the divine—so much so, that Layla herself becomes secondary or even irrelevant to the image of the divine that resides in Majnun's inner being. Similarly, the Islamic studies scholar Annemarie Schimmel writes, "Thus Layla, as well as the other women cast as the beloved in classic Arabic literature, such as Hind and Salma, turn up in Arabic mystical poetry as chiffres, or metaphors, for the Divine Being the poet so ardently yearns for."[220] The repeated text fragments, varied in their repetition, evoke Zikr—the devotion of worshipers meditating on the name of God and his attributes as though they were prayer beads. Within this tradition, the names "Layla" and "Allah" sometimes converge in their repetition within the Islamic testimony of faith.[221] Worldly bonds and particularities dissolve in a process *Leiyla and the Poet* dramatizes through the sounds of El-Dabh's ecstatic performance—sounds that were carefully recorded and manipulated on tape.

A proliferation of pulsating instrumental layers brings great energy to the final section, which also transforms Leiyla's characterization through a concatenation and dense layering of text. An abrupt splicing of the tape (at 2:28) initiates a new texture of oud and tabla beating out a fast pulse that quickens, set against the repeating words "to love a woman, to love Leiyla." As the layered instrumental texture builds, the recorded intonation of text comes to circle around words about Layla's own desire rather than her status as a metaphor for God: "A woman desires free love, to follow a poet's vision beyond." "A woman Leiyla desires love." El-Dabh's focus on Layla's own desire and her capacity for poetry resonates with recent literary interpretations of Layla-Majnun, such as the literary scholar A. A. Seyed-Gohrab's work on the classic twelfth-century Persian poet Nizami Ganjavi.[222] As Seyed-Gohrab suggests, this interpretation has generally remained muted or silent relative to the dominant readings, which privilege Layla's status as a metaphor for God.[223] The history of Layla's representation helps to make sense of El-Dabh's claim that he sought to "make her three-dimensional, to unshackle her." "You are free! You are free! Unshackled!" he exclaimed to me, referencing both Leiyla's captivity by her parents in the narrative and her flattened representation.[224] His idiosyncratic Romanized spelling of Layla's name further supports her movement away from conflation with Allah, emphasizing instead the multiple vowel sounds of his wild diphthong cry, "Eiii!" The mystically infused liberationism of Leiyla and the Poet is probably best understood as having emerged from effendi aspirations to Egyptian and Arab modernity. Yet it also eventually came to gesture toward an intersectional Black emancipation for El-Dabh, who emphatically designated it in an interview with me as "womanist"—the term coined by Alice Walker in 1979 to theorize an "*instinctively* pro-woman" attitude rooted in Black women's cultures and spiritual perspectives.[225] The tape materials of the CPEMC archive further support the proposition that themes of liberation and shifting cultural affiliation lie at the heart of Leiyla: the repeated line "Leiyla a woman desires free love" appears prominently in an earlier version of the piece and in related taped materials, alongside meditations on "our tie to the clan" and "our place in the tribe," which come under pressure due to Layla and Majnun's struggle for freedom and love.[226]

If Leiyla and the Poet aimed to summon ideas of liberation, then it also called for an unorthodox approach to staging. At the work's 1961 premiere at Columbia's McMillin Theatre, El-Dabh placed thirty-two audio speakers throughout the auditorium—altering their output to produce a spatialized sound via remote control—and he spotlighted inanimate clothed figures onstage, who represented the title characters to be brought "to the

fullness of life" through sounding, ecstatic experience.[227] El-Dabh thus addressed the classic problem of electronic music concerts—the absence of
live performers—through stagecraft and early innovations in surround
sound. As he put it, he wanted the audience to "have body feelings" as
well as "mental feelings," so that "you can really hear the sound in your
physical body."[228] The elongated figures that stood on the stage to summon Layla and Majnun were "like stands with cloth on them, and [there
was] an openness like a desert, and . . . the lighting I made it to give this
yellowish desert feeling."[229] The multimedia presentation of *Leiyla and the
Poet* participated in an approach that Fred Turner has dubbed "the democratic surround"—"a new kind of multi-image, multisound environment"
that its practitioners hoped would "awaken [the] audiences' senses—first
of sight and sound, but soon thereafter, of their personhood and of the
possibility of belonging to an egalitarian society."[230] In El-Dabh's work,
the ideal of ecstatic bodily and mental experience carried nothing less
than profound ideas of liberation and egalitarianism. As he put it, "When
you have body feelings as well as your mental feelings, you are also able
to hear through your body, not just your ears; in the back of your head,
on the top of your head, around you, you're into it, you're kind of transformed, too. You become Leiyla or you become the poet."[231] He imagined
Layla's liberation as extending outward through a shared transmission of
ecstatic energy and love via sonic multimedia.

The audience responded to the performance with shouts, laughter, and
boos—a vocal reception El-Dabh appears to have welcomed. Referring to
the noisy audience at the premiere, Harold C. Schonberg of the *New York
Times* described the tape work as "the most interesting piece on the program, precisely because it hinted at a means of intensifying human feelings rather than complete impersonality."[232] El-Dabh remembered, "Oh I
was elated and crazy, and they shouted at me and they screamed, and that
was a serious audience who expected contemporary music."[233] The rau-
cous response disrupted "serious" modern classical concert hall etiquette,
resonating instead with Egyptian music settings, where "listeners are very
vocal."[234] Vital to the latter, as A. J. Racy describes, is the Arab concept
of *tarab*, which he defines in its broadest sense as "the merger between
music and emotional transformation," a concept "connected with in-
toxication, empowerment, inspiration, and creativity."[235] In this general
sense, *tarab* surely suggested a set of possibilities El-Dabh sought to carry
across and alter within a "contemporary music" performance space. For
the composer, every shout from the audience confirmed the work's success at transforming body and mind.

In evaluating the composer's work in the studio and auditorium, we should recognize these spaces as laboratories that served a "translational" function. They isolated and transferred unwieldy, complex elements (musical and literary material, knowledge, intuitions, concepts, and sources) from a broad social field into a space for intensive analysis, supported by specific and powerful technologies. In turn, they aimed to transform the relations and significances of those resources by breaking down boundaries between "in-house" and wider social spaces. The goal of El-Dabh's "translational" activity at the CPEMC was to transform commonplace, denigrating ways of hearing, knowing, feeling, and representing cultural, racial, and gender difference via sound.[236] This work responded powerfully to his role as an elite Egyptian cultural emissary with a sense of public mission, and as a minoritarian immigrant on a path toward US. citizenship.

The uncertain outcome of this venture depended on the gatekeeping mechanisms of the CPEMC as an Acropolis. *Leiyla and the Poet* eventually found a cult following after its CPEMC-backed commercial recording release in 1964, attracting such creative figures as Frank Zappa and Alice Shields.[237] El-Dabh eventually gained recognition as the "father of African electronic music" at the 2005 UNYAZI Electronic Music Symposium and Festival in Johannesburg—"the first event of its kind on the mother continent," as George Lewis writes.[238] Yet back in the 1960s, white critics balked at the idea that El-Dabh could truly belong to the worlds of classical music or electronic composition, and the Black press did not register his music during this period in the early 1960s.[239] As Denise Seachrist recounts, the mixed reception El-Dabh's orchestral work *Partita Poly-Obligati in Song Cycle* (1961) signaled the first negative turning point. Eric Salzman of the *New York Times* criticized the composer for writing something "not much like" his usual style, with "ostinato figures that are almost neo-classical or neo-baroque rather than neo-oriental."[240] This assessment seemed to bar El-Dabh—unlike his white counterparts—from having license to write in nonexoticist, European-derived idioms. Later reviews of the LP recording of *Leiyla and the Poet* wielded racist tropes to depict the work as licentious and barbaric, or as thoughtless mimicry. Michael Steinberg of the *Boston Globe* reviled the piece as "sheer nightclub exotica, of no musical value, and primitive in its exploitation of electronic possibilities."[241] Alfred V. Frankenstein of the *San Francisco Chronicle* blithely dismissed it as "pretentious nonsense."[242] Denise Seachrist describes how El-Dabh's "troubled" feelings about his negative press motivated his decision to abandon composition, and the United States, from 1962 to 1965.[243] Based on extensive conversations with El-Dabh, Laurel Hurst notes that marital tensions may also have motivated his and his family's move from the city.[244] Funded by the Rockefeller Foundation, the composer embarked on ethnographic studies in Ethiopia during this period, along with other travels.

As El-Dabh remembered, "After I left New York and went to Ethiopia in 1962, people forgot about me as a composer. I became known as a musicologist."[245] In Addis Ababa, he taught at Haile Selassie I University and founded the Orchestra Ethiopia—an innovative project that brought together Ethiopian soloists in an ensemble to play traditional Ethiopian melodies he arranged to convey "unity of cultural diversity," as Kay Kaufman Shelemay describes it.[246] Upon his return to the United States, El-Dabh worked as a freelance composer in Rockport, Massachusetts, before being hired at Howard University in 1966 as an ethnomusicologist and scholar of Africana studies. At Howard, he co-taught a course on politics, society, and culture in Africa with political science faculty; eschewing the classroom, they met over cocoa with students in a pottery shop.[247] In 1969 El-Dabh joined Kent State University, where he helped to found the university's Africana studies department alongside the Center for the Study of World Musics. From the late 1960s onward, he found great fulfillment contributing to the Black Arts movement and to the emerging field of Black studies through his creative ethnomusicological activities. The Black press reported approvingly of his lectures on Arab and sub-Saharan music culture, and some of his music became adapted within Black Arts movement projects. His work and teaching answered a collective yearning for a "pillars of civilization" alternative to ideas of the West.[248] In our conversations, El-Dabh expressed gratitude for the character of his career trajectory, without regret about its course. "I was so lucky!" he repeated throughout our conversations in December 2014. Nonetheless, he occasionally struck a bittersweet tone when discussing the lack of recognition he had found as a composer after he left New York and the CPEMC.

El-Dabh's mixed feelings invite us to pause on his departure from the studio, to contemplate the excitations and terrors associated with it. In our interviews, El-Dabh shared a vivid explanation for his abandonment of New York and its composition scene in 1962—an explanation that unfolded as a bracing monologue about the awesome and terrifying potentialities of the electronic music laboratory. The unrelenting intensity of his work at the CPEMC, he said, had precipitated his departure from the United. "My body was shaking," he said, regarding his response to the stimulation and stress of laboring there. With a mixture of elation and fright, he "heard the beating of sounds at such high frequencies they can't usually be heard." He told Luening, "Call the marines, the building will take off!" He needed "to go back to Africa" because he "was leading an untenable schedule," with the long hours spent in the studio obsessing over the tape and sounds, devoting himself all the harder to this work in order to refine experiments in cross-cultural communication.[249]

El-Dabh's warning about the imminent "takeoff" of the CPEMC figures the studio as a vessel of uncontainable pressure, and as a vehicle of untold power. It describes liminal modes of perception (hearing frequencies that "can't usually be heard") that anticipate technologically mediated wonder and catastrophe ("Call the marines!"). The explosiveness of El-Dabh's imagery partakes of a mystique surrounding the CPEMC and its physical location in Prentis Hall. A white terra-cotta building constructed in 1909 as a dairy processing plant, Prentis Hall housed lab spaces that were rumored in the 1960s to have been used in the Manhattan Project. ("The building I was working in had nuclear experiments!" El-Dabh would later exclaim.)[250] Regardless, Prentis Hall had the aura of a place where hard and soft power mingled. The building also literally stood on a different kind of boundary relevant to New York's history and global image as a capital of empire. At the far northern edge of Morningside Heights on 125th Street—just beyond the citadel of the central campus— the building bordered the African-American and Puerto Rican neighborhoods of Harlem that the New York Times regularly reported on as "slums" encroaching upon and threatening the "Acropolis" of the university, much to the concern of philanthropists, university administrators, and urban planners.[251] By the early 1960s, many buildings around Prentis Hall had literally been blown up in "urban renewal" projects of demolition and reconstruction that became known as "Negro removal"—a process that confirmed denizens of the neighborhood as second-class citizens.[252] On 125th Street, the international racial diversity of elite transnational exchange met with the internal racial hierarchies inherited from a long past of settler colonialism, slavery, formal empire, and the ongoing African-American Great Migration.

In his late years El-Dabh was a thinker finely attuned to these power structures. His words about the studio violently "taking off" situate the electronic music laboratory in relation to modes of state power, both internal (as exerted in the neighborhood's demolition sites) and external (as exercised in the nuclear arms race). Oblique and poetic, El-Dabh's imagery registers these important questions within a mirror of memory; it evokes ecstasies of discovery in tandem with fears of violence (and possibly fears of complicity). El-Dabh's words about the studio, and his oeuvre more generally, present an opportunity to study the peculiar dreams, dispositions, attentions, and forebodings that constitute not only the "soft undertissue" of empire but "its very marrow"—to invoke Stoler's provocative take on the character of imperial subjectivities and epistemologies.[253]

Uptown Refigured

The few chapters herein represent only a first step toward studying the CPEMC as a hub for cultural diplomacy and immigration within US-imperial ideological formations. Future work could focus on Bülent Arel and Mario Davidovsky as possible foils for Toyama and El-Dabh in the early 1960s: these CPEMC composers tended—at least on the surface—to stress continuities with European traditions of art music rather than notions of cross-cultural communication. Moreover, the studio's relationship with the Rockefeller-supported Centro Latinoamericano des Altos Estudios Musicales (CLAEM) at the Di Tella Institute in Buenos Aires also deserves a fuller accounting, following the work of the musicologist Eduardo Herrera on CLAEM's relationship with the RF.[254] By the 1970s, the CPEMC hosted a sizeable roster of Latin American composers (supported by Ussachevsky and Davidovsky's guest teaching in Buenos Aires) whose size exceeded that of any other group defined by region or continent. This cohort included, among others, Davidovsky, Sergio Cervetti, Manuel Enríquez, Francisco Kröpfl, alcides lanza, Enrique Pinilla, Alfredo del Mónaco, Marlos Nobre, Carlos Rausch, Héctor Quintanar, Edgar Valcárcel, and Alida Vázquez. Yet, as Robert Gluck shows, the CPEMC also hosted sizable contingents from the Middle East and Turkey, Eastern Europe, and East Asia, and at least one composer (Steven Agbenyega) from West Africa.

In the history of the CPEMC, Toyama and El-Dabh should be understood as the tip of the iceberg in their capacity as forerunners for what became a thriving cultural diplomatic program. The studio's reputation demands sustained reevaluation: it must come to be understood as something *other* than its current image of an "uptown" institution rooted exclusively, or even primarily, in European legacies. Ethnographically inclined compositional practice declined in the studio after the departure of Toyama and El-Dabh, but the cultural exchange program remained vibrant. Significant tensions would have arisen between the studio's status as an incubator for European-derived "uptown" composition and its role as a hub of cultural diplomacy with Latin American, Asian, Middle Eastern, and African composers. According to alcides lanza, who joined the studio with a Guggenheim Fellowship in 1965, the CPEMC had by then come to epitomize now-familiar ideas of "uptown" as they crystallized during the mid-1960s: "writing 12-tone music, rhythmically and pitch-conscious, all notated with conventional [Western] notation."[255] Lanza stressed that the CPEMC of the mid- and late 1960s offered less support for alternative approaches including "improvisation, aleatoric music, graphic music, musique concrète, jazz."[256] To make his point, he recalled that only one microphone existed at the CPEMC at this time, and it was kept in Ussachevsky's desk.[257] According to lanza, Ussachevsky practiced a compositional method, premised on the montage of recorded sounds on tape, that had lost prestige in the wider academy relative to serialism—a trend that even changed the technological setup of his own studio.

In contrast, Alice Shields makes the important observation that Ussachevsky maintained a "multi-stylist" studio with strong support and mentorship for composers, such as herself and Pril Smiley, who pioneered analog-based electronic composition in opera and theater respectively—work that could never be described in the limited terms of "uptown."[258] The center "was *the* place where you could find a big diversity of musical styles. If you wanted to see the full spectrum of what was happening from 1959 to at least 1970–75, that was where you went to hear it."[259] Yet there was no "equal opportunity" financial support to bolster Ussachevsky's advocacy for stylistic diversity in the 1960s—certainly not for the sorts of intercultural projects Toyama and El-Dabh had pursued.

Hardly serendipitous, this circumstance corresponded with shifts in RF humanities funding priorities, which in the first half of the 1960s moved away from a rubric of "intercultural understanding," and toward one of finding exceptionally "promising" individuals, as articulated by RF associate director John Marshall.[260] Marshall's language partly intersected with Babbitt's melancholic positioning of the university as the "mightiest of fortresses" against "overwhelming forces"[261] of populism, propaganda, and commercialism.[262] It also corresponds with the musicologist Anne Shreffler's argument that serialism enjoyed enhanced institutional prestige in connection with Cold War ideologies in the United States in the 1960s—an argument that has been expanded and refined by Emily Abrams Ansari.[263] Indeed, the early history of postwar RF music patronage at Columbia shows how traditional European ideas of high art and genius ultimately supported the rise of serialism's star in the academy. By 1964, the CPEMC fell under the purview of the newly created RF Arts Division, where the rubric of "exceptional promise" morphed into a fullfledged genius discourse.

After having issued the massive start-up grant in 1958, the RF continued to support the CPEMC in modest ways, by sponsoring individual composers alongside the affiliated Group for Contemporary Music performance ensemble. A language of exceptionalism rather than interculturality dictated these decisions, as is evident in the RF officers' effusive memos about Davidovsky, one of the main beneficiaries of RF support at the CPEMC of the 1960s: "When we declined general funding support to the Columbia-Princeton center [in 1966] . . . we did give an exceptional flsp. [fellowship] to Mario Davidovsky on the grounds of his exceptional genius."[264] While the studio continued to sponsor composers from all over the world, the language through which the RF reached funding decisions shifted emphatically toward European-derived concepts of high art. Michael Uy argues that Babbitt became a particularly important "arbiter" for the RF during this period, in a relationship that contributed to the founding of the journal *Perspectives of New Music*.[265] The ways in which visiting and immigrating composers navigated this altered and altering place—now popularly imagined as the "uptown scene"—should become a vital subject that may well render "uptown" foreign to itself.

* 4 *

A Counter-Discourse of Orientalism

ONO IN OPERA

"They had to think about how to think about an oriental woman."

YOKO ONO[1]

In her 1962 manifesto "The Word of a Fabricator," Yoko Ono put herself on the side of fiction, drama, and intentionality in the explicit politicization of her practice.[2] Without naming him directly, she took her friend and mentor John Cage to task for his Zen-inspired poetics of indeterminacy, which sought to liberate music from human intention and expressivity through the use of chance operations like coin tosses to derive musical scores.[3] Drawing from the *I Ching*, Cage claimed that such chance operations mimicked the nonintentional processes of nature. As Benjamin Piekut has written, nature (figured as chance) thus became the authority that grounded Cage's aesthetic practice, which, in his words responded to "Oriental philosophies in accord with the acceptance of nature."[4]

In Ono's judgment, however, a political naïveté and philosophical presumptuousness lay at the heart of Cage's project:

This is an attempt to raise man's stature to that of nature . . . by succumbing to and adopting random operations as men's own. It is the state of mind of wanting to become a weed and join the heartbeat of the Universe by entering the world of nothingness and blowing in a gentle wind.[5]

The dream to become egoless and "plant-like," she argued, is illusory and politically debilitating because "contemporary men . . . are soaked to the bones with a fabricator called consciousness."[6] Drawing on Marxist and existentialist vocabularies, she explained,

We are talking about a body of a betrayer/*l'étranger* to the natural world . . . We, "the betrayer," are so invaded by the falsehood of consciousness we cannot even become operational by using such a loose method as random operation.[7]

"Operational" appears in this passage as a surprising term that plays on Cage's "chance operations" to suggest a political efficacy she found these techniques lacked. "Operational" means "working": it suggests a politics defined as the common interest that binds individuals in efficacious action (rather than "blowing in a gentle breeze"). Ono's use of the term resonates with her designation of *AOS—To David Tudor* (1961)—arguably her most ambitious work of the period—as an "opera" about the "blue chaos of war," inspired by her own history as an internal refugee following the Tokyo firebombings.[8] For Ono, as we will see, there could be no celebration of cultural exchange between "West" and "East" without a politics of practice responsive to mutually entangled histories of violence. Accordingly, "The Word of a Fabricator" reads as a manifesto in the fullest sense of the term: a clarifying text that aims not only to interpret the world but also to change it.[9] As such, it foreshadows Ono's increasingly public artistic involvement in peace and liberation movements over the course of the decade.

In the spirit of "The Word of a Fabricator," this chapter interprets Ono's early work as the crucible for a politics of art and action that responded to New York's status as a capital of empire in the early 1960s, heralding the increasingly explicit politicization of the downtown avant-garde scene in subsequent years. The timing of Ono's manifesto was significant, coming near the end of the so-called "consensus period" of the Cold War, in which a hegemonic bloc of the government, civil society, and media supported US expansionist policies abroad, before fracturing with the escalation of the war in Vietnam. This concept of a "consensus period" tends to downplay minoritarian voices that protested empire and internal hierarchies of subjugation well before the escalation of the war in Vietnam. Unlike Cage, Ono could not find a home for her thought and work in Cold War consensus discourses or, more specifically, in the "Cold War Orientalism" that Christina Klein has identified as characteristic of the period—a mid-century US fascination with Pacific Rim cultures attending expanded US geopolitical power abroad.[10] In Klein's terms, Cold War Orientalism produced "narratives of anti-conquest" (not unlike Cage's turn away from ego) in a manner that ultimately legitimated "U.S. expansion while denying its coercive or imperial nature."[11] To locate Cage in this discursive formation is not to crudely cast aspersions on him as an "imperialist," but rather to recognize his proximity to a liberal US mainstream that embraced ideas of "cultural exchange" without specifically critiquing US neo-imperial power. This view of Cage brings him into the orbit of the founding ideologies of the CPEMC, or close to Varèse at Greenwich House. In her navigation of gendered and racialized gatekeeping in the New York avant-garde, Ono can be compared with Charles Mingus, Halim El-Dabh, and especially Michiko Toyama. Her perspectives on power were drawn from a life lived in empires on both sides of the Pacific.

In Ono's manifesto, her words about "the body of a betrayer/*l'étranger* to the natural world" speak to a particular experience of mass violence and betrayal perpetrated by each of her home nations—Japan and the United States—during and after World War II. As Midori Yoshimoto describes, the violence of the Showa-period Japanese militarized society and the US bombings in Japan hindered Ono's identification with either of the nations in which she had been raised.[12] (A Japanese citizen, Ono had moved between Tokyo and California during her childhood, due to her father's banking career.) She could not easily ignore the violent and imperial nature of either nation, just as she could not let go of the "consciousness" and "intentionality" in her practice that aspired to respond to those political realities.[13] "The Word of a Fabricator" therefore articulated an incipient politics shaped by Ono's exilic persona, conceived in gendered and national terms, and her experience of wartime trauma. Ono critiqued Cage's Zen-inspired thought from a perspective drawing on transnational German, French, and Japanese currents in phenomenology. She envisioned a new politics of practice that rejected Cage's valorization of chance and indeterminacy while further extending his challenge to traditional authorship. In the interest of politics, she threw her own body, voice, persona, imagination, and history into the public realm.

This chapter devotes sustained attention to the early performances in New York that launched Ono's transcontinental career, interpreting them in relation to the philosophical and political practice outlined in "The Word of a Fabricator." Her later celebrity and reputation in the art world might cause observers to lose sight of the specific innovations of her early career, which oriented her politics of practice for years to come. With some notable exceptions, her first works and performances have found a relatively slim reception—a fact that may seem odd given her increasing recognition as a founding mother of 1960s performance and conceptual art movements.[14] This lacuna partly arises from the ephemeral nature of those early pieces, which confounded disciplinary expectations even more intensively than many other happenings and event-based works of the period. While Ono's reception has mostly fallen under the purview of art critics and historians, relatively few visual traces remain from her early career. Moreover, unlike the oeuvres of such creators as Cage and La Monte Young, Ono's first performances eschewed formal scores and tape recording, discouraging musicological methods of interpretation. Ironically, without a consideration of her early work—due to this lack of documentation—musicology has tended to treat Ono as a follower of Cage, when in fact her frequent rejection of score-based composition sets her apart from him.[15] As she put it to her friend and collaborator George Maciunas, "Most of my pieces are meant to be spread by word of mouth [and], therefore, do not have scores. This means is very important since the gradual change which occurs in the piece by word spreading is also part of the piece."[16] Such alteration of the work through fluid transmission disperses the authority of traditional authorship within a constellation of storytellers, creating an informal community history and network within and through the work's path of travel. These "stories"— elaborated in oral history, ephemera, critical commentary, reviews, and Ono's own self-narrative—form the essential archive for her inaugural creative interventions.

Ono's early work, with its robust thematization of state-sponsored violence, can be seen as a harbinger of the increasingly vocal politics of dissent articulated in the "post-Cagean avant-garde" of the 1960s—a spirit of dissent that, as Thomas Crow describes, intensified in tandem with freedom struggles at home and abroad. Ono's work therefore also points to a gap in our historiography. The increasingly explicit politicization of this 1960s downtown community of artists, musicians, and thinkers is sometimes taken for granted as a natural accessory to Cagean poetics. Crow, for example, associates this politics of dissent with the move (via Cage and Jasper Johns) away from the "heroic model of artistic selfhood" and "spectacular self-revelation" (e.g., in the cases of Pablo Picasso and Jackson Pollock), which found parallels in the "spontaneous organization from below" that characterized "the most exciting and successful forms of dissenting politics" of the era.[17] Yet there remains the need to interrogate more precisely what made the politicization of the downtown scene around Cage possible.[18]

The need for such an inquiry becomes all the more urgent given Cage's notorious reluctance to align his musical projects around 1960 with any explicitly activist platforms—despite a nascent interest in anarchism—or to address the politics of his practice in an otherwise prolific outpouring of self-positioning words about music.[19] As he put it in 1957, his music was "an affirmation of life—not an attempt to bring order out of chaos nor to suggest improvements in creation, but simply a way of waking up to the very life we're living, which is so excellent once one gets one's mind and one's desires out of its way and lets it act of its own accord."[20] Such a statement may indeed imply its own "utopian politics" of withdrawal and silence, as Caroline Jones has written.[21] Yet we should also acknowledge how such words may suggest, as Yvonne Rainer later put it, the "total ignoring of worldwide struggles for liberation and the realities of imperialist politics, on the suppression of the question, 'Whose life is so excellent and at what cost to others?'"[22] The move toward indeterminacy, in other words, risks acting as a mask for power and a suppressor of action, especially when articulated in New York—a capital of empire at the height of the Cold War.

We will see that Ono's work bridges the chasm between Cage's indeterminate practice around 1960 and the openly dissenting, heterogeneous politics that flourished among younger generations in the downtown scene in the decade that followed. Three refreshing historiographic possibilities emerge from such a study. First, to see Ono as an "operatist/operator" is to begin to rethink the category of the "post-Cagean avant-garde," moving toward an ironically less ego- and genius-centered way of representing the fluid community at hand. Second, to grapple with the politics of Ono's practice is to recognize alternatives to the stale binary between a Cagean poetics of indeterminacy on the one hand, and traditional composerly or painterly authority and authorship—as represented in Beethoven, Picasso, or Pollock—on the other. Ono's abjuring of the score format and her notion of word-spreading as politics brought one "third way" model among many that coexisted in the downtown scene and elsewhere.[23] To study this model, I argue, is to confront Ono's poetics as shaped by a specific, gendered history of displacement. By situating this troubled narrative at the center of the 1960s New York "downtown scene," we counter many of the easy mythologies that sometimes naturalize it as a culmination of the "American Century," intimating a sense of belonging that creators like Ono could not take for granted.[24] In the remainder of this chapter, we will elaborate on these historiographic possibilities through (1) a consideration of Cold War consensus politics of geopolitical expansion, and their relationship with Orientalist downtown New York avant-gardes around Cage; (2) a discussion of Ono's philosophically informed words about her politics of practice, read in relation to Arendtian notions of action; and (3) an extended exploration of her art actions and their oral history at the Chambers Street Loft Series, AG Gallery, Carnegie Recital Hall, and Sōgetsu Art Center.

In the pages to come, my sustained attention to Ono's words and performances, alongside the afterlife of her work in the words of others, acknowledges her own serious engagement with discourse as "the power

to be seized."[25] Cold War Orientalism operates through discursive proce-
dures of exclusion that bar a person such as Ono from occupying a central position as agent of change, artist, composer, or thinker in narratives
of avant-garde history. In many accounts of postwar avant-gardes, as described above, John Cage has persisted as *the* crucial figure who tends to
occupy these positions of agency. Ono made her debut precisely in the
years when such mythologies around Cage had begun to congeal in historical and critical accounts (as discussed in chapter 1), and these mythologies benefited from his superb mastery of Cold War Orientalist
discourses. In focusing extensively on Ono's early practice—virtually a
counter-discourse to Orientalism—I take this chapter as an opportunity
to explore the creativity of her early-career response to the challenges
this situation created for her as a Japanese woman in Cage's milieu, as a
woman actively seeking to develop a politics of practice to highlight and
redress state violence in connection with multiple empires. Here Ono's
investment in the power of words, drama, and storytelling cannot be un-
derestimated.

Cold War Orientalism and Cultural Mercantilism

Before turning to Ono's words and works in more detail, we should explore the conditions that made her intervention in "The Word of a Fabricator" possible and timely. In other words, we should consider how the
downtown scene participated in a Cold War consensus politics, bound
up with Orientalist fascinations, that called out for critique. Although
Cage refrained from articulating an explicit politics of practice in the
1950s, the very concept of "American experimental music" he promul-
gated at home and abroad was deeply imbricated with Cold War American politics of geopolitical expansion. Amy Beal has shown the extent
to which Cage and his circle depended on new funding opportunities
that arose in conjunction with Marshall Plan–era reconstruction projects
in occupied West Germany, including the Darmstadt Summer Courses
for New Music.[26] She writes, "The support and publicity they received
[and acknowledged candidly], underwritten by a lavish policy of Cold
War funding for culture, allowed such uncompromising innovators to survive professionally abroad during decades of financial struggle and limited recognition at home."[27] The canon of "American experimental music," constructed and promoted by thinkers like Cage, is an artifact that
crystallized within the new patronage networks of postwar reconstruction and Cold War competition exemplified by institutions like the Darmstadt Summer Courses.

The ideologies of this canon cannot be disentangled from the geo-politics that made its formation possible. "Ideology" should here be understood in its two partially overlapping senses: in its neutral sense, as a system of thought through which one interprets the world; and in its negative sense, as "illusion, false consciousness, unreality, upside-down reality" (akin to Ono's "falseness of consciousness").[28] In the case of John Cage, these dual senses interrelate in a state of flux, just as his political consciousness changed considerably over the course of the 1960s (though our own discussion will stick to the years around 1960).

In his influential essay "A History of Experimental Music in the United States" (1959), Cage argued for the "present necessity" of a kind of globalization of musical innovations, thought, and values emanating from his own work in the United States. Delivered at the Darmstadt Summer Courses and read widely in Cage's circles, the essay defined experimental action as "action the outcome of which is unseen."[29] Here "American experimental music" came to be characterized through its use of chance operations and collage techniques, its changes in "habits of notation," which create indeterminacies in performance, and its "attachment to emptiness and silence" as an ethical, psychological and spiritual stance. Cage stressed the need to "giv[e] up control so that sounds can just be sounds," and he cited the moral authorities of Buddha and Jesus to bolster that call.[30] "America has an intellectual climate suitable for radical experimentalism" of this kind, he argued.[31] Echoing long traditions of American exceptionalism, Cage figured the United States as a crossroads for the world's intellectual, technological, moral, and spiritual developments—a nation that signals freedom and modernity "in our air way of knowing nowness":

Buckminster Fuller, the dymaxion architect, . . . explains that men leaving Asia to go to Europe went against the wind and developed machines, ideas, and Occidental philosophies in accord with the struggle against nature; that, on the other hand, men leaving Asia to go to America went with the wind, put up a sail, and developed ideas and Oriental philosophies in accord with the acceptance of nature. These two tendencies met in America, producing a movement into the air, not bound to the past, traditions, or whatever.[32]

Receiving streams of thought and experience from Asia and Europe, the United States in turn had a responsibility to send its cultural innovations abroad, just as the world—in this case, Europe—had a responsibility to accept this importation as a spur for self-transformation. On the question of music, Cage explained,

The silences of American experimental music and even its technical in-
volvements with chance operations are being introduced into new European music. It will not be easy, however, for Europe to give up being
Europe. It will, nevertheless, and must: for the world is one world now.[33]

Cage's globally expansionist vision for "American experimental music"
would seem unmistakable in this lecture at Darmstadt—a lecture that
also found a popular readership after its 1961 publication—yet this hu-
bristic dimension of Cage's project largely goes unnoticed in secondary
literature.

Christina Klein has interrogated the relationship between the expansion of US power during the early Cold War and "the simultaneous proliferation of popular American representations of Asia," such as those
that animated Cage's lecture.[34] Drawing from Raymond Williams, she
describes Cold War Orientalism as participating in a "cultural formation": texts and artifacts—like the Darmstadt lecture—generated meaning through their interaction with other "meaning-making discourses and
activities," taking shape "in relation to particular cultural institutions, to
the political commitments of their authors, to the legal structures regulating race and statehood, to the ebb and flow of social attitudes, and
to the shifting political discourses and policies that defined Asia."[35] In
Klein's account, cultural texts "perform a hegemonic function to the extent that they legitimate a given distribution of power, both within and
beyond the borders of the nation."[36] Cultural hegemony works by elaborating "structures of feeling" in which "the ideological principles that
support a given arrangement of power are translated into regularized patterns of emotion and sentiment."[37] Klein defines Cold War Orientalism as
a sentimental structure of feeling that ostensibly upheld ideals of cultural
tolerance, inclusion, and racial equality within an increasingly intercon-
nected world.[38] Repudiating the violent exploitations of European high
imperialism, Cold War Orientalism celebrated such global interconnec-
tion as anticolonial and reciprocal. Yet these representations ultimately
belied the very real forces of racialized coercion—through proxy wars,
clandestine service activities, trade policies, and other strategies—that
characterized the US neo-imperialist presence in the Pacific Rim and elsewhere. Klein's argument keeps faith with Williams's characterization of
structures of feeling as showing "a false consciousness, designed to prevent any substantial recognition" of "deep and central connections with
the rest of the general [social] life," including imperial life.[39]

In addition to Williams's work, Klein's Cold War Orientalism draws
on Mary Louise Pratt's study of European imperialism, specifically the

"narratives of anti-conquest" Pratt defines as "the strategies of representation whereby European bourgeois subjects seek to secure their innocence in the same moment as they assert European hegemony."[40] For Klein, Cold War Orientalism retranslates these strategies in a US neo-imperialist setting. Cage's Zen-inspired exhortation to "giv[e] up control so that sounds can just be sounds"—which attended his insistence that the world accept its own transformation by "American experimental music" and chance operations—may be read as precisely such a strategy. Under the banner of noncoercive exchange ("giving up control"), he demands acceptance of a new world order (experimental music everywhere, including Europe!); this strategy enlisted East Asian thought as its vital resource in promulgating a vision of American exceptionalism. Cage's words can therefore be read as a Cold War consensus discourse that generates positive sentiment around US expansionist projects without explicitly backing a specific set of foreign policy objectives. In Williams's terms, such a structure of feeling does not necessarily operate consciously, but rather concerns inchoate "meanings and values as they are actively lived and felt" but are not yet articulated as a system of beliefs embodied in "more formal concepts of 'world-view' or 'ideology.'"[41]

In advocating US-led cultural transformations on a global scale, Cage's words replay familiar strategies of modernism associated with colonialism and empire. Here we should note similarities and differences between Cage's words at Darmstadt and what Ming Tiampo has called the "cultural mercantilism" of Euroamerican avant-gardes—an idea that brings us back to the dilemmas Yoko Ono would have faced as a Japanese woman in the downtown New York scene around Cage. The term describes a center-periphery ideology permeating modernist and avant-garde cultural production, an ideology that conceives "modernism as a closed system, located in the West and perpetually disseminated to its periphery."[42] For Tiampo, cultural mercantilism can be compared "to economic policy such as the Ansei treaties, which gave the European metropole cheap access to raw materials while at the same time allowing the export of metropolitan manufactured goods to captive markets that were prevented from developing industries of their own."[43] Artists in the "West" would draw on elements of "Eastern" practice as raw materials in order to develop cultural products and concepts for exportation. This system flowed in only one direction, shutting down any reverse motion and thus restricting who could successfully lay claim to originality in arts production: "Europeans borrowing from Japan are considered inspired, whereas Japanese borrowing from Europe are seen as derivative."[44]

This logic jibes with long-standing racial stereotypes that have constricted European and North American ideas about East Asia from the late nineteenth century to the present, as described by historian Bruce Cumings: "For Westerners accustomed to think in racial terms, Japanese success was inexplicable because they were 'yellow' and not white (although they soon became honorary whites). . . . Westerners usually explained ['the untiring industry of the Japanese'] through a combination of Japanese sweating of labor and shameless copying of foreign models."[45] As W. Anthony Sheppard notes, Cage followed a long line of European and American cultural authorities who urged Japanese musicians to preserve their traditions, which they saw as a precious resource for their own practices.[46] Along these lines, Cage famously encouraged Toru Takemitsu not to appropriate Western models, but rather to shift his attention toward his own Japanese heritage.[47] This advice finds kinship with the attitudes of cultural mercantilism that permeated the downtown avant-garde at the Eighth Street Artists' Club, to which Cage belonged—a scene highly cognizant of its role in heralding the "American Century" by inheriting the supposed mantle of arts leadership from the capitals of Europe.

Tiampo interrogates how cultural mercantilism shaped the reception of Japanese artists in New York during the 1950s, detailing particular instances that likely would have made their impression on Ono as a newcomer to the scene. There is the case, for example, of Kenzō Okada, who "became one of the most successful of the Japanese émigrés who painted in the milieu of Abstract Expressionism" after he moved to New York in 1950.[48] In a "country that was both hungry for Japanese exotica and wary of letting foreign elements burrow too deeply into the fabric of 'American-type painting,'" Okada's work was "praised for its qualities of restraint, assumed to be an essential part of Japanese character . . . [and] he was eulogized for his use of empty space, nothingness, an evocation of the Zen that had been so popularized by figures like D. T. Suzuki and Alan Watts."[49] As Tiampo writes, "The only way to succeed as a foreign artist in this context was to visibly differentiate oneself by one's foreignness (raw materials) or to become accepted as a full-fledged American, as did Willem de Kooning."[50] (Here we should note that Ono herself never even applied for US citizenship.) The latter option of assimilation would prove impossible for Asian Americans because of the racial component of American citizenship that was enshrined in law.

Japanese artists based in Japan faced similarly daunting challenges in their US reception. The case of the Osaka-based Gutai group, founded by Jirō Yoshihara, deserves special attention here, because it incorporated performative elements of practice that prefigured Ono's later art actions. The group initially found favorable US publicity in a nuanced and provocative article by Ray Falk, the *New York Times* correspondent in Tokyo. "These artists are not bound to brush and canvas. Anything and everything may be utilized. . . . Still not satisfied, the Gutai-ists turned to the theater and gave action to their art."[51] But the American reception of Gutai became contemptuous after the group's first show outside Japan, at the Martha Jackson Gallery in New York in the autumn of 1958. This show focused on Gutai's paintings rather than its actions and performative elements. Working alongside Martha Jackson, the French critic Michel Tapié (associated with France's Art Informel movement) authored the show's publicity materials. As Tiampo writes, these materials "marketed [the show] in a way that obscured Gutai and perpetuat[ed] cultural mercantilist assumptions about center and periphery. . . . While Tapié framed Gutai as radically Other and therefore regenerative, Jackson's publicity situated the group within the gallery's larger project of promoting the New York School."[52] Reviews for the show tended to dismiss Gutai as an unsuccessful imitation of American models, or to use the art as an opportunity to celebrate US global leadership in spreading ideals of democracy and freedom in Japan. "Gutai was caught in the same trap as Okada," Tiampo writes, "but was unwilling to offer audiences the Orientalist rhetoric that they yearned for."[53]

Michiko Toyama would have presented another model for Ono, potentially a source of both inspiration and warning. It is very likely that the women knew one another, because Toyama studied side by side with Ono's first husband, Toshi Ichiyanagi, at Tanglewood in summer 1956, and later referred to him in her correspondence. Toyama and Ono also shared Beate Sirota Gordon, the arts director of the Asia Society and the Japan Society, as a supporter. Toyama's diasporic life of professional independence—distinct from the "good wife, wise mother" paradigm of female citizenship in Japan—may well have served for Ono as a model to emulate. Yet Toyama's reception in the United States and Japan would have presented a cautionary tale. Ralph Greenhouse's negative review of Toyama's *Waka*, which took her to task for supposedly imitating Western models, came out in May 1961, before Ono's debut at Carnegie Recital Hall.[54] That year, Toyama also experienced gendered ostracization within the very Japanese new music circles, associated with Sōgetsu Art Center, into which Ono entered upon her 1962 return. Toyama's compositional career had begun to suffer in palpable, public ways precisely in the years when Ono was making her debut.

All these precedents—Okada, Gutai, and Toyama—speak to the double bind to which Ono would become vulnerable as an emerging artist: the trap of her work being reduced to exoticist stereotypes, subject to denigration as a "mimicry" of Western models, or being used implicitly to justify US geopolitical hegemony in East and Southeast Asia despite the antiwar commitments that have remained a constant in her career. Ono thus confronted a dual imperative: to distinguish her work from that of Cage and the downtown scene around him, and to articulate a robust politics of practice reinforcing this distinction. She needed to resist Cold War consensus politics and find alternatives to the cultural mercantilism as a model that threatened to restrict the meanings and "operational" potential of her work.

Ono as Phenomenologist

In "The Word of a Fabricator," Ono described how she could not let go of intention and consciousness as a creator, but rather found herself "groping in a world of stickiness."[55] Her work would ideally "operate" by setting off unforeseeable transformations in the minds and actions of other people with whom her life was connected. The challenge lay in how to open herself and her work up to this altering and alterable web of others—to the "world of stickiness," with its murky and messy materials, actions, feelings, and words—to break through her own limited viewpoint and isolation as a creator.[56] Ono's word-spreading model of art as politics was a response to this challenge. As she later put it, her events had no "script," but rather had "something that starts it moving—the closest word for it may be a 'wish' or 'hope'"—a gift from the artist that transformed in the hands, minds, and words of others.[57] These transformations fundamentally altered the identity and structure of that "work," and revised notions of authorship. Ono's focus on audience response connects her with Marxist theorists like Bertolt Brecht and Jean-Paul Sartre—whom she later credited—while her move away from strong notions of authorship distinguishes her work from that same tradition.[58]

Another way to frame Ono's thought—particularly her emphasis on intentionality within a web of unforeseeably altering actions and after-effects—is via her connection with a German-Jewish diasporic milieu in New York that entertained similar concepts. As I have shown elsewhere, Ono befriended the refugee composer Stefan Wolpe and his wife, the poet Hilda Morley, in the mid-1950s:

I loved the intellectual, warm, and definitely European atmosphere the two of them had created. Stefan immediately showed me his musical scores. I was surprised how complex, precise, yet emotional his works were. I don't know of any other composer of the time who represented atonal music so brilliantly.[59]

Their friendship blossomed during a time when each self-consciously sought to formulate a creative response to their diasporic and refugee past. Wolpe was also a friendly acquaintance of Heinrich Blücher, the husband of Hannah Arendt, and the composer developed theories of action closely connected with Arendt's own work, which she had developed in dialogue with Blücher's theories of art.[60] Wolpe valued music as a locus for metaphors of human life and action. He conceived of his own composition as a play of multiple agents that "make connections, bump up against one another," pursuing "immediate, delayed, distant, shifting, single, many, similar, dissimilar, direct, vague, and opposite goals."[61] He conjured particular sets of notes or pitch classes as entities that acted within the limits of a musical texture seen as a world. In analogy, he described his own life as playing out in a "Meschennetz von Verantwortlichkeit und Besorgtheit" (human net of responsibility and concern), producing unforeseeable consequences in its flux of interaction.[62] This concept is remarkably close to Arendt's notion of the "web of human relationships"—the "inter-est" that binds individuals to one another and differentiates them in their concerted actions: "The stories, the results of action and speech, reveal an agent, but this agent is not an author or producer."[63] Wolpe's and Arendt's projects were by no means abstract, but rather responded to experiences of physical and psychological violence, in the wake of genocide, that led them to question established notions of autonomy, individual powers of self-determination, and related notions of human development and progress. For Wolpe, music served as an imaginative realm to work through these questions and to model the wonder of fragile beginnings in the midst of dire constraint and unfathomable loss. Given Ono's proximity to Wolpe, there is an aptness to the kinship of her imagery—her "world of stickiness" and her "word-spreading" theory of action and new beginnings—with Wolpe's. Her compositional practice, however, contrasted tremendously with his.

Such diasporic connections bring new meaning to the philosopher Cecilia Sjöholm's argument that Arendt's work illuminates the politics of contemporary performance art. Although Sjöholm focuses on the works of Marie Fahlin and Ana Mendieta, her arguments also resonate provocatively with Ono's word-spreading model of art as politics. Sjöholm elaborates on fictionalized rituals of burial in Fahlin's and Mendieta's work, comparing them to classical tragedy (*Antigone* in particular). Burial here is not closure, but rather the "beginning of something new," the "claiming of a new order," the heralding of unforeseeable consequences in the minds and actions of the audience as witnesses.[64] (These observations also illuminate Ono's *AOS*, which displays bodies like corpses.) The shared ritual forms the basis for politics, the notion of which Arendt derived from the classical polis, which is

> not the city-state in its physical location; it is the organization of the people as it arises out of acting and speaking together, and its true space lies between people living together for this purpose, no matter where they happen to be. . . . Action and speech create a space between the participants which can find its proper location almost any time and anywhere. It is the space of appearance in the widest sense of the word, namely, the space where I appear to others as others appear to me, where men exist not merely like other living or inanimate things but make their appearance explicitly.[65]

Human subjects differ from other natural or inanimate objects because they disclose themselves within a web of relationships constituted by action and speech. This vision of Arendt's roughly accords with Ono's insistence on humans' separation from other natural phenomena—their inability to discard consciousness and simply "become a weed and join the heartbeat of the Universe." Another point of connection between Ono and Arendt lies in the exilic or diasporic elements in their respective projects. For Arendt, politics does not derive from ties to a "physical location," but rather arises in the "in between" space of action and speech among agents, wherever they happen to be.

Such resonances surely arose not only from Arendt's and Ono's overlapping social circles, but also more broadly from a common intellectual heritage and a shared investment in politically oriented philosophical projects that revised transnational legacies of phenomenology during and after World War II. To appreciate the fullness of this connection, let us consider Ono's personal and educational background. Born into a noble family and merchant dynasty in Tokyo in 1933, Ono was disowned by her parents when she made the unconventional choice as a woman to pursue a career as an artist. She had spent her childhood shuttling between Tokyo and San Francisco, but after the trauma of the 1945 firebombings, she and her family endured starvation conditions in the countryside around Nagano—an experience she later cited as securing her unusual path to follow a life of the imagination.[66] As her first adult step in this pursuit, she entered Japan's prestigious philosophy program at Gakushuin University in 1951 as its first female student—a study that left a lasting imprint on her thought. This decision represented a serious challenge to Japanese female citizenly expectations. Post–World War II legal and political reforms, mandated by the US occupiers, granted women the rights to vote, hold office, choose their own spouses, and access education with equal opportunity. Yet young women admitted to elite universities faced harassment from fellow students.[67] Moreover, because Ono had been born into a family of prominent national standing, she was expected to lead an impeccably conventional life as a woman in the public eye—an ideal that precluded pursuing a career as a philosopher or intellectual.

After two semesters, she withdrew from the program at her family's urging, to study poetry and music at Sarah Lawrence College, close to their new family home in Scarsdale, New York. Nonetheless, she continued to find her family's expectations unbearable. She finally dropped out of college in the mid-1950s to elope with the composer Toshi Ichiyanagi and embark on a career in the arts, at which point her parents broke off contact. Ono made ends meet by teaching classes in tea ceremony, calligraphy, and other traditional arts at the Japan Society in Manhattan, supported by Beate Sirota Gordon, while Ichiyanagi helped her gain access to New York's avant-garde composition scene. The first semipublic and public performances that made her name took place in New York in 1960 and 1961, beginning with the Chambers Street Loft Series organized with La Monte Young, and culminating in her November 1961 debut at Carnegie Recital Hall—after which she embarked on a performance tour in Japan with Ichiyanagi, Cage, and the pianist David Tudor. She wrote "The Word of a Fabricator" after returning to Japan in 1962, while trying to decide whether to reestablish herself there—a difficult decision, since she was often treated by critics there as a female novelty act, a copycat of Cage, an affront to *ryōsai kenbo* ("good wife, wise mother") ideals, and a cultural alien because of her many years abroad.[68]

It was therefore at a precarious moment in her early career, as she was living between two nations, that Ono turned to the resources of her hard-earned philosophical training to articulate a politics and philosophy of artistic practice. At Gakushuin University, Ono had immersed herself in the phenomenological tradition, studying such thinkers as Kierkegaard, Husserl, Heidegger, and the French existentialists.[69] Ono saw this study as vital to her self-invention after World War II. As she explained, "My strength at that time was to separate myself from the Japanese pseudo-sophisticated bourgeoisie. I didn't want to be one of them. I was fiercely independent from an early age and created myself into an intellectual that gave me a separate position."[70] From the 1880s onward, the Japanese academy had hosted enduring dialogues with German phenomenology, spear-headed by the nationally influential philosopher Kitarō Nishida, who encouraged many of his students to study with Husserl and Heidegger in Freiburg, bringing phenomenology further into conversation with East Asian Buddhist strains of thought (which had arguably already influenced Heidegger).[71] A postwar generation of Japanese scholars of philosophy built on this foundation via French existentialism, which resonated with the imperative to create a "new society" in renunciation of Japan's recent authoritarian and militarist past, without resorting to naively progressive notions of history or heroic ideas of the human subject that had become untenable after Auschwitz and Hiroshima. By the early 1970s, Japanese was the only language into which Heidegger's *Being and Time* had been published in five different translations.[72] Thus, Arendt's immediate philosophical heritage was also vitally important within Ono's postwar Japanese intellectual setting. This Japanese philosophical tradition needed to contend with the shadows of nationalism and authoritarianism in which Nishida, like Heidegger, had been implicated.[73]

Due to elements of conceptual kinship, Arendt's postwar critical engagements in the phenomenological tradition shed light on Ono's own. Arendt's ideas also help us to put a finer point on Ono's simultaneous embrace of the politics of intentionality on the one hand, and her abjuring of traditional authorship on the other. Like Sartre, Camus, and others of their generation, Arendt found in Heidegger's work an unprecedented opportunity for philosophy to access political questions—an opportunity that she argued Heidegger had himself let slip by. As is well known, for Heidegger, what differentiated humans from the rest of the natural world was the significance for humans of the question of being, or *Dasein*. Heidegger questioned what it means for humans to be situated in time and space, given that they are always already in-the-world, in an *Umwelt* or environment constituted by their concerned involvement with things. Within this world, "appearances" shine forth as the phenomena that orient this concern. The word "appearances" here refers not exclusively to visual images, but to the entire registering of sense perceptions as a whole, which fit humans into the reality and world that surround them.[74] This "world" of human concern, phenomena, appearances, and being-with-others (*Mitsein*) is precisely where Arendt and others located the political, even though Heidegger himself tended toward a different set of questions concerned with human individuation and freedom from the world through death. As Sartre put it, human reality is "in the world" via its practical concerns, and we are responsible for this world as the horizon of meaning in which we operate.[75] As Nishida formulated it in his later writings, the world is a "topos" that arises with acting individuals through their creative interactions—individuals who see things anew with a sense of "moral responsibility."[76] And as Arendt wrote, "To live together in the world means essentially that a world of things is between those who have it in common, as a table is located between those who sit around it; the world, like every in-between, relates and separates men at the same time."[77] The political comes into being when humans assemble in speech and action in responsibility for this shared world.

Such notions of "world" as common interest imply an emphatically relational vision of art as politics; indeed, Ono and Arendt conceived of action as so highly relational that it tends to resist strong notions of the sovereign subject or traditional authorship. Within Arendt's model, art is political because it appears in public and solicits unforeseeable responses and consequences in the web of human relationships. This idea resonates with Ono's assertion that her work would *operate* through its transformation in word-of-mouth remembrance, which itself fundamentally alters the "original" and undermines traditional notions of authorship. For Arendt, the human agent initiates action, yet she is never sovereign in her actions. Moreover, she cannot claim authorship of the stories that her actions provoke—an important means through which she "appears" in public. As Arendt famously put it, "It is because of this already existing web of human relationships, with its innumerable, conflicting wills and intentions, that action almost never achieves its purpose; but it is also because of this medium, in which action alone is real, that it 'produces' stories with or without intention."[78] Accordingly, Arendt valorized art practices that exist "only in sheer actuality" rather than those that produce a reified "work," noting the examples of "healing, flute-playing, [and] play-acting" in ancient history.[79] In other words, the "work" to Arendt "is not what follows and extinguishes the process but is imbedded in it,"[80] recalling Ono's idea that "the gradual change which occurs in the piece by word spreading is also part of the piece."[81] For Arendt the work was part of the altering process of action, while for Ono the altering process was part of the work. These strong similarities between Ono's and Arendt's aesthetics exceeded their immersion in a common phenomenological tradition. Both partook of the cult of action and spontaneity that dominated downtown New York art circles at mid-century, and both took their ideas in strikingly similar directions, holding onto the artist as intending agent while turning away from strong notions of authorship and reified work products. While Arendt looked to ancient Greece for inspiration, Ono found models in Japanese traditional arts like flower arranging and tea ceremony—resulting in actions that scrambled gendered divisions of labor and traditional European boundaries of media in the high arts.

Storied Actions

Ono's earliest "works" may be interpreted as actions producing stories in the spirit of Arendt's sense. Take, for example, Ono's earliest performances in the Chambers Street Loft Series, of which no publicly accessible documentation in the form of photography, scores, or recordings remain. Ironically, even though Ono conceived the idea of renting the loft of the hundred-year-old Italianate commercial building in Tribeca for the performance series, and paid the $50.50 monthly rent, her works did not appear formally on the series program—a circumstance she has attributed to gender bias in the downtown art and music scene.[82] From the beginning, Ono found herself denied credit for her role in organizing and producing the series, which La Monte Young claimed as solely his own in the series invitations, programs, and oral history. Ono has recalled that gender bias even fueled a sensational rumor that she was merely a "kept woman," housed in the loft by a "wealthy Chinese man"—a rumor that originated in some artists' dim-witted joke that Young's name sounded Chinese.[83] As Ono bluntly put it, "Most of my friends were all male and they tried to stop me being an artist."[84] This situation was likely complicated by Orientalist assumptions animating the cruel joke that Ono was La Monte Young's concubine. As Ono later rather generously stated, "They had to think about how to think about an oriental woman. I think it was very difficult for a lot of people who never had to deal with anybody oriental before."[85]

The Loft Series featured artists who had met in Cage's class at the New School and who continued their activities through a new sponsoring organization called the New York Audio Visual Group. As Dick Higgins, a key member of this group, recalled, the Loft Series provided a forum in which to witness the "results" of work they termed "research art," which focused on the use of "systems, charts, randomizations" in the production of music and sound—a reference to the kinds of indeterminate scores and systems Cage had taught.[86] The concerts were not public; rather, Ono and Young sent invitations only to a small circle of interested parties, labeled with the emphatic disclaimer "THE PURPOSE OF THIS SERIES IS NOT ENTERTAINMENT." As Higgins recalled, Young and the series not only scorned entertainment but also "very much rejected the idea of dramatic or theatrical value."[87] Philip Corner—whose work Ono tried to have performed in her loft, before being thwarted by Young's objections—observed how zealously Young policed the boundaries of his circle: "He was against everyone—except a few friends held over from California. . . . [It got back to me] that he considered me a reactionary because I still used crescendos."[88]

Ono responded to the challenge of her own noninclusion by staging characteristically dramatic guerilla performances. On one evening, for example, she could be found flinging her hair and throwing dried peas from a bag at visitors. By her own account, this composition—which she called *Pea Piece*—transformed a ritual she remembered from her childhood, the rural spring custom of throwing soybeans to ward off *oni*, which in Japanese folklore resemble devils, demons, or trolls. The sounds of the scattered peas delighted Ono, which she heard, in the spirit of Cage, as a kind of music in itself.[89] But unlike Cage, Ono also deliberately staged *Pea Piece* as a dramatic gesture that transforms actions from personal childhood memory, translating them within a contemporary setting. In the context of the Loft Series, the downtown artists who excluded her from her own programs could themselves stand in as the devils she needed to ward off. It is also relevant that World War II–era Japanese children's literature and films specifically depicted Western men as *oni*, foreign devils—a history that brings another layer of richness to Ono's hybridizing translation of this ritual to catch American downtown artists off guard.[90] Her gestures of hair flinging and pea throwing worked strategically to ensure that she would be remembered and talked about, despite being omitted from the official program of her own Loft Series.

Oriented by Ono's later words, we can interpret her avoidance of the traditional score format as dismantling authorship even more radically than Cage's indeterminate practice. At the same time, her embodied performance—and her insistence upon concrete experience and personal memory—conferred a different kind of authority to her work. This authority was not sovereign, because she asked that her pieces be talked about and refigured by others, whether in real life or in the lives of their imaginations. The circumstances of the initial event—the initial "hope" and "wish," as she put it, that brought it into being—were simply "something that starts it moving," as it transforms in the hands and minds of others.[91] Her work is thus distinctive in claiming a kind of embodied authority of witness while also dispersing authority among others to retranslate her work collaboratively in relation to their own memories and settings. Needless to say, this approach was far from the exotic fare expected from East Asian artists in the downtown avant-garde. Instead, it referenced Ono's personal background and past while attempting to implicate others and their memories in a mutual, unfolding future.

In accord with Arendt's model, Ono's actions could not reach a targeted objective on their own; nor did they necessarily communicate the growing ambitions she intended. For Ono, the Loft Series was a site of tremendous uncertainty. Would her intercultural projections of nonauthorial authority find a savvy reception, or would they pass without serious notice? Would the stories circulating about her and her work help to secure her professional footing, or would they undermine her? Her actions in the Loft Series bring into sharper focus the dilemmas of her "appearance" in public.[92] In addition to staging dramatic guerilla happenings, Ono displayed visual traces in the loft of actions already performed. She called all or most of these works "instruction pieces," writing instructions for actions or rituals: texts that existed in a hybrid space between poetry and score—eventually published in *Grapefruit* (1964). Yet unlike some authors of word-based scores in her circle (e.g., Young and George Brecht), she did not share her texts publicly at the time of the Loft Series. Rather, Ono's instructions were personal texts that, by her account, had originated as a kind of therapy following a method that first emerged with her refugee experience in 1945: "We had no food to eat, and my brother and I exchanged menus in the air. We needed new rituals in order to keep our sanity. We needed our powers of visualization to survive."[93] While "survival" in 1945 referred to brute physical and psychological resilience, the same word in 1961 addressed her need to protect and perpetuate a precarious, newly emerging artistic identity and career in a downtown scene resistant to her authority as a creator and thinker.

The story of *Painting to Be Stepped On* (1960–61; figure 4.1) exemplifies how Ono's early work met with uncertain reception at this time, despite the rich associations it later accrued through the words with which she surrounded it. This work follows a simple imperative: "Leave a piece of canvas or finished painting on the floor or in the street."[94] At the time of the Loft Series, Ono left a swath of linen on the floor to collect the footprints of her visitors. Like *Pea Piece*, Ono saw *Painting to Be Stepped On* as translating a historic ritual within a contemporary setting—this time, though, with attention to a specific episode of violence. As she later explained,

This painting stems from *fumie*, meaning "stepping painting." In the 15th century [*sic*] in Japan during the persecution of the Christians by the feudal lords, suspected Christians were lined up and asked to step on a paint-

FIGURE 4.1. *Painting to be Stepped On*, from *Paintings & Drawings by Yoko Ono*, AG Gallery, New York, July 17–30, 1961. Gelatin silver print.iImage 14¹³⁄₁₆ × 15⁹⁄₁₆ in. (37.7 × 39.6 cm). Sheet 19¹³⁄₁₆ × 15⁷⁄₈ in. (50.3 × 40.4 cm). Photograph by George Maciunas. Gilbert and Lila Silverman Fluxus Collection Gift, 2008, Museum of Modern Art, New York, 3202.2008.16. Digital image © The Museum of Modern Art / Licensed by SCALA / Art Resource, NY. By permission of Billie J. Maciunas.

ing of Christ or the Virgin Mary. Those who would not step on the painting were crucified.[95]

These later-life words about *Painting to Be Stepped On* locate terror at a site of cross-cultural encounter. They also raise questions of inclusion and exclusion that resonate with the community dynamics of the Loft Series. Both of these themes are notably absent in the critical literature on this work.[96]

Nonetheless, *Painting to be Stepped On* has in recent years invited more notice than any of her other works in the Loft Series, by virtue of an oft-recounted anecdote involving Marcel Duchamp. This story merits retelling because it foregrounds the dilemmas of intelligibility and authority

Ono faced in the months prior to her Carnegie Recital Hall debut. As Bruce Altshuler explains (following correspondence with Ono), "Marcel Duchamp had attended a concert in Ono's loft in 1961 during which she waited with anticipation, and eventual disappointment for him to notice and to step on her *Painting to Be Stepped On*."[97] Yoshimoto explains that Ono "was aware that Duchamp was her predecessor in using chance elements to complete a work, [but] she took one step further than Duchamp toward the demythologization of art by requiring others to participate in its making."[98] Ono's excitement about this idea exacerbated her disappointment that he failed to participate in the "making" of the work by stepping on it. From today's standpoint, this story speaks with humorous irony of one iconic vanguardist's nonrecognition of another. But in 1961 this failure may have pointed more direly to the irrelevance or obscurity into which Ono's work risked falling. Unlike Duchamp, the cellist Styra Avins, a sympathetic acquaintance of Ono's, recalled something that may have been an early version of *Painting to Be Stepped On* at the inaugural concert of the series.[99] She remembers "footprints spaced a pace apart painted in white [against black] on the floor" in Ono's loft.[100] Yet Avins does not recall that Ono shared any words about her inspiration or intention for the piece, and without such contextualization Avins found herself at a loss for what to make of the encounter, other than that "it was very far out, that much was clear!"[101]

Given the challenges she faced in the Loft Series, Ono could not have anticipated that a more important connection than Duchamp would emerge through her actions there: a friendship with George Maciunas. Ono would help to catalyze Maciunas's subsequent career as founder and impresario of Fluxus, just as Maciunas would help to assemble the conditions through which Ono would make her work more public. Inspired by the Loft Series, Maciunas established his own series at his newly created, and short-lived, AG Gallery on Madison Avenue in 1961. In contrast to Young, Maciunas advertised AG Gallery events widely in newspapers, though the space remained intimate, with largely insider attendance. Having met Ono at her loft, Maciunas invited her to stage her first solo show in July 1961 before the gallery's closing. It was in this setting that Ono finally made her texts public, displaying her verbal instructions (handwritten by her husband, Ichiyanagi) with the material traces of their execution, while remaining on hand at the gallery to provide further explanations to visitors. Her presence, in the manner of a guide or docent, heralded a new way of acting in the "space of appearance" at the gallery. She surrounded the instruction pieces with narrative while encouraging others to develop their own narratives and to participate in the work's creation. Her presence and words saved the "instruction pieces" from obscurity, while conferring authority to her actions through their rootedness in personal experience and memory. Other than Maciunas's photography, no physical objects document the instruction pieces from the period of the show. Ono destroyed the associated materials after their exhibition, at which point the gallery also closed. But she set a precedent for her practice that continues to this day, surrounding her work with layers of commentary that remain remarkably consistent in their imagery and concerns throughout different stages of her career, while inviting the alteration of those works through public participation.

Carnegie Recital Hall

"I feel a strange attraction to the first man in human history who lied," Ono wrote as the first line in "The Word of a Fabricator." A sustained inquiry into the relation between truth and lies in the fabrication of art animated her earliest works, including those at Carnegie Recital Hall.[102] When Ono argued against Cage's chance methods as a misleading representation of chance and nature as truth in art, she characterized the human condition as "soaked to the bones with a fabricator called consciousness."[103] Rather than attempting to discard her own consciousness, choice, and history, she would use them to fabricate works of fiction that create their own "conceptual reality."[104] Ideally, her fabrications would operate through their transformation in the minds and hands of others.

Ono similarly stressed the importance of such mental exercises to initiate action with material consequences in the world. From her perspective, the reality of the work would become a "concrete matter"—something beyond a mere mental construct—once others enacted and altered it, by the creator's own invitation.[105] This is the process that allows the artist to break through her isolation as a creator with a limited vantage point and consciousness: "It is nothing more than the obsessive act of the driven, attempting to make one's own fiction a reality by allowing others to cut off pieces of the romanticism that inevitably enwraps fiction."[106] "Romanticism" here refers to established notions of expressivity that designate fiction as the manifestation of a unique subjectivity. In keeping with postwar existentialists and phenomenologists, drama, via Ono's idiosyncratic take on opera, would provide a medium par excellence for reaching beyond romantic solipsism toward public engagement and action.

At Ono's 1962 Carnegie Recital Hall concert, she put such ideas to the test before an audience of around 250.[107] Remarkably, she compared her works to the "excessive illusions and dramas" of medieval ritual: "At its bottom lay an endless pessimism that only a fictional order can rescue us from death."[108] For Ono, contra Cage, the contemporary moment was no time for "blowing in a gentle wind"; it was a time for "rescue." Her work would not accommodate consensus politics, and instead reckoned with haunting memories and anticipatory fears of state violence. Ono's own life experiences would form the basis for narratives and dramas that would become altered in the throes of spontaneous performance and in the words and memories of witnesses. These performances at Carnegie Recital Hall can only be reimagined through a conflicting assemblage of oral accounts, written documents, reviews, and ephemera. Before exploring the works performed, let us dwell on a few visual documents that vividly demonstrate Ono's conceptualization of the concert.

"A WORLD OF STICKINESS"

The Silverman Fluxus collection includes three black-and-white photographs by George Maciunas intended to advertise the 1961 concert. Although they never served their original purpose, the photographs read more importantly as a kind of visual manifesto articulating concepts that defined Ono's debut "recital." Carefully preserved by Maciunas, the photographs show Ono behind, beside, and bursting through the concert program, which is written in her own calligraphy on a massive surface of pasted-together newspapers (figures 4.2a–c). As in her Loft Series performances and her AG Gallery show, Ono's work at Carnegie Recital Hall continued to emphasize her own body, voice, persona, and life story—specifically, her experience of violence during World War II. The posters dramatize such self-disclosure by juxtaposing her body with the signature gestures of her own hand. In one photo (figure 4.2a), the camera captures her from above, looking earnestly upward while kneeling directly upon the poster with paintbrush in hand, as though signaling her authorship in real time. In the other two photos, Ono stands behind the newspaper-canvas program held upright as a screen, her face appearing behind a rip in the upper middle of the poster. Maciunas manipulated lighting to create different effects. A backlit version shows Ono's figure wavering behind the tissuelike paper, her right hand opening the tear through which she peers (figure 4.2b). In the alternate, frontlit version, the contrast between Ono and the program appears more solid, and the décollage effect of the ripped paper more vivid: Ono gently draws back the sliced paper to reveal her direct gaze, as though revealing the person behind the program (figure 4.2c). The image evokes with visual directness her desire to access a public world, to cut through and fold back

FIGURE 4.2A. George Maciunas, photograph of Yoko Ono with her *Poster for Works by Yoko Ono*, Carnegie Recital Hall, New York, 1961. Gelatin silver print. Image 7¹⁵/₁₆ × 7¹³/₁₆ in. (20.1 × 19.9 cm). Sheet 10¾ × 8⅞ in. (27.3 × 22.5 cm). Gilbert and Lila Silverman Fluxus Collection Gift, Museum of Modern Art, New York, FC1118. Digital image © The Museum of Modern Art / Licensed by SCALA / Art Resource, NY. By permission of Billie J. Maciunas.

the screen of her poetic program. As Natilee Harren writes, in this image "it remains unclear what constitutes the inside and outside; what is important is rather the status of the hole as a passageway, an architecture of transition."[109] Related notions of translation joined Ono and Maciunas in their collaboration (chapter 5).

These photos broach questions concerning the nature of authorship, public appearance, and intermediality in art by bringing Ono and Maciunas's creative dialogue front and center. Neither Ono nor Maciunas can claim authorship of these photographs/programs/(non)advertisements as a whole. Ono set something into motion with her visible persona, program, and paintbrush, but the afterlife of this "thing" moved beyond her

FIGURE 4.2B. George Maciunas, photograph of Yoko Ono with her *Poster for Works by Yoko Ono*, Carnegie Recital Hall, New York, 1961. Gelatin silver print. Image: 7½ × 7⁹⁄₁₆ in. (19.1 × 19.2 cm). Sheet 9¹⁵⁄₁₆ × 7¹⁵⁄₁₆ in. (25.3 × 20.2 cm). Gilbert and Lila Silverman Fluxus Collection Gift, Museum of Modern Art, New York, FC3175. Digital image © The Museum of Modern Art / Licensed by SCALA / Art Resource, NY. By permission of Billie J. Maciunas.

own authorship in a chain of intermedial commentary (a photograph reflecting upon a calligraphed program and its creator). The pasted-together newspapers suggest that this dialogue aspired toward something more than a coterie exchange. As the print media par excellence of imagined nations, and the classic found-object source material for engagé art, newspapers bring a whole "world" into the picture.[110]

The glue used to paste together Ono's newspapers as emblems of a public world brings to mind her words about "groping in a world of stickiness." Like the photographs, these words suggest a straining of perception. They show a typically phenomenological concern with a "starting point" from which one apprehends and accesses a world of appearances.[111]

FIGURE 4.2C. George Maciunas, photograph conceived as poster for works
by Yoko Ono, Carnegie Recital Hall, New York, 1961. Gelatin silver print.
Image 7½ × 79⁄16 in. (19.1 × 19.2 cm). Gilbert and Lila Silverman Fluxus
Collection Gift, Museum of Modern Art, New York, 2598.2008. Digital image
© The Museum of Modern Art / Licensed by SCALA / Art Resource, NY.
By permission of Billie J. Maciunas.

Following Sartre, "stickiness" (or "viscosity") signifies as a threatening
and female-gendered term evoking the vagaries of how the human body
connects with the world.[112] Ono's "groping in a world of stickiness" serves
as a provocative foil to Arendt's "acting in a world of appearances," suggesting that action is not smooth and appearances not clear. In her Carnegie Hall Recital Concert, drama was the medium for working through
the implications of these ideas.

All of the works on the program—*Grapefruit in a World of Park*, *Piece
for Strawberries and Violins*, and *AOS—To David Tudor*—were enacted
by an ensemble of performers who mimicked the actions and sounds of
fictional or historical events. The program, set almost entirely in a dark-

ened concert hall, dealt dramatically with themes of loss, gender, and violence. The production included a roster of now-celebrated collaborators belonging to a younger downtown generation, who performed movement, voice, and instruments: George Brecht, Trisha Brown, Joseph Byrd, Philip Corner, Richard Maxfield, Jonas Mekas, Yvonne Rainer, and La Monte Young.[113]

Produced by Norman Seaman, the concert owed much to Charlotte Moorman, who was Seaman's apprentice and also served as the concert's production assistant. Moorman had recommended Ono to Seaman after having seen the premiere of early versions of her works *Grapefruit in a World of Park* and *AOS* at the Village Gate in an April 8 program titled "An Evening of Japanese Music and Poetry," which Ono headlined with Toshi Ichiyanagi and Toshiro Mayuzumi.[114] Seaman would eventually become known as "a niche impresario" who produced more than three thousand performances, exposing adventurous audiences to new performers during off-times in summer or midweek.[115] For a relatively small fee, he would book a performance space, put an ad in the newspaper, sell tickets, manage staff, and invite reviewers. "If enough tickets sold that a profit was to be had, Mr. Seaman and the performer split it."[116]

Philip Corner paints a vivid picture of Ono's debut concert, full of messy uncertainty: "I arrived in mid-afternoon at Carnegie Recital Hall—I was holding down a job in Brooklyn—to find that they were waiting for me. A somewhat chaotic situation." He saw that Young was "sitting in a corner with a friend" doing a "rhythmic repetitive ritual," and that "Yoko [had difficulty] getting order." By Corner's account, Moorman helped to corral the performers and bring efficiency to the proceedings. She took Corner backstage, saying, "We have an insensitive toilet flusher"—meaning that the person Ono had enlisted to play that "instrument" was insensitive in timing and execution. "[The toilet] was 'rigged up' [with a contact microphone], and on cue I flushed. That was my introduction to that avant-garde cliché."[117] Ono turned an avant-garde cliché into a central part of the work's poetics, using the newest technologies in sound amplification (contact microphones) to create something that would become a leitmotif throughout the program. With tongue in cheek, she later explained that her use of toilet flushing was inspired by Cage's own use of "water sounds" in such works as "Water Music" (1952), which alternated the shaking of water vessels with the shuffling of cards, the blowing of bird whistles, and the playing of piano and radio. Yet Ono turned to this water trope in a decidedly unromantic way, insisting upon a confrontational poetics dealing with the violent and unsavory rather than beautiful randomizations of natural order.

GRAPEFRUIT IN A WORLD OF PARK

Grapefruit in a World of Park combined poetic text recitation with musical improvisation, bringing a familiar format of the Greenwich Village
club and coffeehouse scene into the recital hall. (Indeed, as already mentioned, the work had premiered at the Village Gate the previous April.)
Bearing a loose kinship with the politicized poetry-jazz experiments of
Amiri Baraka, Allen Ginsburg, and Charles Mingus, *Grapefruit in a World
of Park* consisted of poetry read against a sonic backdrop of amplified toilet flushing, electronic sounds, and recorded "mumbled words and wild
laughter."[118] Richard Maxfield coordinated the electronic sound production. The *New York Times* review glibly summarized this sonic backdrop
thus: "Musicians in the corner made their instruments go squeep and
squawk." Of the program more generally, Jonas Mekas recalls that each
participant largely "did their own thing," and he fondly remembered playing bayan—a Russian chromatic button accordion—off and on during
the evening.[119]

Although we cannot reconstruct the full soundscape of this performance, we do have access to the recited text, which reads as an extended
set of stream-of-conscious fragments of seemingly internal dialogue, set
in a park with intimations of violence lurking within and beyond the
edges of the scene. It begins: "WHERE IS THIS / THIS IS THE PARK /
I CAN SMELL METAL IN THE AIR / NO ITS THE CLOVERS / ARE THEY
BLEEDING / NO ITS THE SUNSET / IS THIS THE ROOM / NO ITS THE
SUNSET / WOULD YOU LIKE TO SPEAK TO THE DEAD / OH NO / I ONLY
CAME HERE TO PEEL GRAPEFRUIT / IS IT TOO COLD / ITS TOO WARM
/ THE SKYS TOO HIGH / PEOPLE TURNING UP THEIR STOMACHS CON-
TENTEDLY TO THE SKY."[120] Thus, the piece begins as a phenomenological description of the world unfolding from a particular standpoint and
orientation—"the 'here' of the body and the 'where' of its dwelling," as
Sara Ahmed has put it.[121] This "here" and "where" of the park, however, is
hardly stable, with consciousness hovering between past and present, the
living and the dead, between the "world of park" and other places. The
text's uniformly capitalized script and lack of punctuation suggests a flattened delivery—something that might have had an estranging effect on
the vocal narration, especially when coupled with the affectively charged
laughter and mutterings of the background recordings.

It is worth dwelling on Ono's opening question and answer: "WHERE
IS THIS / THIS IS THE PARK." The literary scholar Paul Saint-Amour
notes that the deixis of linguistic shifters like "this," "here," and "now" not
only discloses "some lustrous and essential property of the object [and

moment] in question," but also has the potential to link "present luminos-ity" with "present disaster."[122] It concerns itself not only "with *immanence* but also with *imminence*."[123] In the work of Virginia Woolf, for example, deixis creates a sense of looming expectation, structuring perpetual sus-pense or dread: "What Clarissa Dalloway calls the 'this, here, now' may place us not in the corona of the moment but in its crosshairs."[124] Saint-Amour links these literary techniques and effects with Woolf's reflections on total war and her phenomenological accounts of air raids. Given her own history of surviving the Tokyo firebombings, Ono's references to "metal in the air," "bleeding," and "the dead" hardly seems far from such a world of experience. In *Grapefruit in a World of Park*, the sky vacillates in its value and significance: it promises safety, as the placid blue vastness toward which people "contentedly turn up their stomachs"; but it also triggers unfathomable terror, as something "too high" that reeks unnatu-rally of metal. The text reads as a dialogue of questions and answers: the narrator asks anxious questions about "this" world of park, only to be an-swered in the negative with reassurances asserting the normality of the park scene. Incongruous peacetime and wartime imageries compete to designate the place.

The text continues with an eerie assemblage of sensuous park ele-ments, snatches of dialogue, culinary and picnic imagery, and evocations of death. American commerce brands the scene: "DRINK PEPSI COLA YOU'LL LIKE IT IT LIKES YOU." This antimetabole brings people, ob-jects, and corporations into an unsettlingly symmetrical relation with one another. The second stanza begins with repetition: "LETS COUNT THE HAIRS OF THE DEAD CHILD / LETS COUNT THE HAIRS OF THE DEAD CHILD"—a line that even the dismissive *New York Times* reviewer noted. After this repeated provocation, the dialogue begins to assume the char-acter of an exchange between parent and child: "NOW DON'T HURT YOUR FINGERS / NO I WON'T." This intergenerational exchange broaches the question of the future, dwelling in past, present, or anticipated experi-ences of death and destruction.

Ono's emphasis on themes of maternal loss—including taboo sug-gestions of abortion or miscarriage—revives established tropes of Jap-anese feminism dating back to the early twentieth-century publication *Seitō* (see chapter 3). In *Grapefruit in a World of Park*, these themes blend with a warlike atmosphere of foreboding. Midway through the work, its text doubles down on such images of childhood and death: "WIPE YOUR FINGERS ON THE GRASS ITS / STICKY / THE LOLLIPOPS ARE GETTING SOFT / DO YOU LIKE MY BABY CARRIAGE / OH ITS SIMPLY WONDER-FUL / THE CURVE THE SHINY WHEELS / EVERYTHING JUST RIGHT /

IS IT EMPTY / I SHINE IT EVERY DAY WITH VINEGAR AND TAKE OFF THE SMELL WITH PERFUMES." This passage resonates with the text's earlier ambivalence about the status of grapefruit: "EVERYTHING SEEMS SO RIGHT IN THE PARK— / YES DOESN'T IT / EVEN THE GRAPEFRUIT OH NO NOT THE / GRAPEFRUIT YES EVEN THE GRAPEFRUIT. / WHY DON'T YOU THROW IT AWAY ITS / WRINKLED / ITS WRINKLED." As Chrissie Iles observes, the grapefruit in the text could "represent a child, a womb."[125] Ono's focus on the flesh of the fruit, with repeated references to peeling and wrinkles, would support such a reading of body parts in birth and decay. From this perspective, the sound of toilet flushing is all the more disturbing, suggesting a crude disposability of life. Barbara Haskell and John G. Hanhardt designate the entire poem as an "aria," which should be understood as a lyrical interlude within a larger drama or opera. This larger drama, however, is implied by the text as an object of the imagination, rather than being literally performed. It is a drama dealing with a gendered space of loss and violence, oriented from the embodied standpoint of peeling a grapefruit "in a world of park."

Following Saint-Amour, the text also demands a historical analysis that treats "expectation, anxiety, prophecy, and anticipatory mourning as serious objects" of study within the Cold War's phenomenology of "perpetual interwar." The term "interwar" here denotes "not just 'between wars' but also 'in the midst of war' . . . what one subject, community, or population experiences as an interval of peace another may experience as a time of intermittent or even continuous violence, whether in the shape of small wars, colonial occupation and policing, anticolonial uprising, civil war, or the psychic violence of war anticipation."[126] Likewise, to take for granted the "interval of peace" in consensus-period New York, circa 1960, would depend upon a particular subject position and embodied point of view, which Ono and many others could not so easily assume.

PIECE FOR STRAWBERRIES AND VIOLIN

Piece for Strawberries and Violin continued to juxtapose domestic culinary imagery and terrifying sounds, beginning with Yvonne Rainer sitting at a chair in front of a table of dishes, backed at a distance by a cluster of chanting men. As critic Jill Johnston described,

> Not much happened. Yvonne Rainer the dancer was nice to look at as she sat still on the chair, also as she did an "exercise" in excruciating slow motion of bending the knees, contracting the abdomen, and grimacing the facial muscles. I like the ending of this piece. Miss Rainer and another girl

[Trisha Brown] had been eating uneventfully at a table center stage. A man from the huddle joined them. They began spitting their pits closer to the mike—concealed somewhere on the table—and breaking or cracking table litter over it. Another man walked round the table tearing off pieces of newspaper, and pretty soon the table was a scene of muted carnage.[127]

Ono's *Piece for Strawberries and Violin* featured neither violin nor strawberries, but it did showcase violence and stone fruit. Together with *Grapefruit in a World of Park*, it abounded in images of vulnerable skin and flesh, suggesting situations of precarious birth or strained life within a banal scene of material destruction. For Trisha Brown and Yvonne Rainer, such an emphasis on everyday task movements formed the basis for the Judson Dance Theater they formed in 1962. *Piece for Strawberries and Violin* provided an occasion to make repetitive physical gestures evocative of domestic routines on the one hand and childbearing on the other. Susan Rosenberg has described Trisha Brown's earliest work, *Trillium* (1962), as applying "tasks as a structure to generate movement as material, producing a new understanding of what constitutes dance"—which Brown saw as an analogue in dance to Cage's endeavor to transform everyday sounds into music. *Piece for Strawberries and Violin*, however, brought task movements into relationship with specific props to evoke gendered narrative or contextual associations resonant with Ono's entire program.

To be sure, the table at the center of the performance cannot be overlooked in relation to Ono's wider constellation of words and symbols. As Ahmed and Ann Banfield observe, tables appear in philosophy as special objects—the "things nearest at hand for the sedentary philosopher . . . the furniture of that 'room of one's own' from which the real world is observed."[128] They also work as "orientation devices," providing "a surface on which we place things and do things," similar to Arendt's use of the table as a metaphor for "the world" of common interest.[129] Kitchen tables in particular fill this role as "kinship objects" that orient family members in particular relations and determine, in effect, who has "a place at the table."[130] As Ahmed points out, a tension emerges between the writing table (as a traditionally male space set apart from domestic family concerns) and the kitchen table (as a site of women's domestic labor, or as a space to be "cleared up" for other kinds of work, intellectual and political). This tension would appear highly pertinent to Ono's practice, which agitated against professionally debilitating gender boundaries. Johnson's account of *Piece for Strawberries and Violins* suggests a stark divide between the women who perform difficult physical work—their muscles twitching in labored contraction—and the men who join the table to create the

"muted carnage" characterized by amplified cracking, spitting, and ripping sounds, leaving the mess of food debris and torn newspapers at the
end. In the spirit of Ono and Maciunas's program/advertisement photographs, newspapers hold a special status as the media of imagined nations
and public life. In light of the brutal actions at the table, *Piece for Strawberries and Violin* might suggest a denigration of public space that intersects
with gendered violence in a domestic sphere—without a clear separation
between inside and outside, home and world.

AOS—TO DAVID TUDOR

Ono has repeatedly and pointedly called *AOS—To David Tudor* an "opera." By her account, the title combines the Japanese word "*ao*," designating an untranslatable blue-green color, with the word "chaos" to evoke its
subject matter: "the blue chaos of war."[131] Its dedication honors the virtuosic pianist most closely associated with Cage, whose works, in Ono's
words, "came to existence only because of your [Tudor's] playing." (Ono
wryly told Tudor, "I thought you could use a piece that you cannot take
part in," offering a gift that asked no favor in return.)[132] I have discussed
AOS—To David Tudor elsewhere with respect to its thematization of failures of translation in relation to "the blue chaos of war"—failures immediately evoked in its title.[133] For our present purposes, however, I would like
to foreground *AOS*'s status as an opera—or as an expressively vocalized
(if not sung) drama—because it is through this genre that Ono enacts
her politics of practice. Her opera reworks the conventions of that genre
almost beyond recognition. Yet the generic category "opera" is close to
Ono's world, since it designates qualities characteristic of her early work,
namely a heightened affective register and sense of dramatic structure
thoroughly at odds with a Zen-inspired placidity and indeterminacy.[134]
As noted, Ono also used the term "opera" etymologically (activity, effort,
labor), as something meant to work in a spirit of public involvement.[135]

AOS consisted of five contrasting acts set in a fixed sequence intimating the skeleton of a narrative. It took as its starting point Ono's own consciousness and memory, but it also brought structured opportunities for
the ensemble and audience to "finish" the work in their own ways. While
no score exists, Ono's previously unpublished notes on the work have
become publicly available in recent years.[136] According to the account,
the opera would begin in darkness with the sound of performers reading
aloud from newspapers in various languages, aided only by the light of
matches, lighters, and flashlights. As individual lights extinguished, the
performers would stop reading, or would turn to other performers' lights

to continue. With the help of the composer Richard Maxfield, Ono had fitted the performers' bodies with contact microphones, which would catch the subtle sounds of rustling newspapers, flicked matches, and clicking lighters—the kinds of sounds that "almost don't come out."[137] At Carnegie Recital Hall, the dim lighting and murmuring soundscape likely strained the performers' perceptions as they tried to read from the newspapers in their hands. The scene enacts a public world of human concern, complete with the challenges of perceiving, communicating, and acting in that world when it—or the space of appearance, in Arendt's sense—becomes diminished, and speech indecipherable.

In dramatizing these themes, the slow temporality of *AOS* apparently encouraged a mixed response of boredom and suspense. As the *Village Voice* critic Jill Johnston put it, "I was alternately stupefied and aroused, with longer stretches of stupor, as one might feel when relaxing into a doze induced by a persistent mumble of low-toned voices."[138] Jonas Mekas has recalled that George Maciunas insisted on meticulously timing each segment of the program.[139] This precise timing of the opera's acts could have targeted such a response, which might be compared to Sianne Ngai's concept of "stuplimity"—an affect or aesthetic experience "in which astonishment is paradoxically united with boredom."[140] Yet *AOS* likely also proceeded with a tedious but tragic air of foreboding. Ono later explained that she "wanted to deal with the sound of fear and of darkness, like a child's fear that someone is behind him, but he can't speak and communicate this."[141] This dire suspense resembles the "uncanny temporalities . . . of wounding anticipation" that Paul Saint-Amour associates with war and its aftermath.[142]

The second act would seem to have confirmed the gist of this interpretation: it erupted in brutal action, as human bodies came to be treated like trash. Rather than fully discharging the suspense of the previous scene, the violence of act 2 would likely only have amplified it.[143] In act 2, performers tied one another up with rope and gauze, attaching to their bodies objects like old beer cans, chairs, a table, and a toilet bowl. The contact mics would have picked up the troubling sounds of performer's constricted movements and panting. Johnston saw humor in the scene "when three men rushed in and out alternately piling up and removing a toilet bowl and a weird assortment of boxes."[144] But the onstage imagery also would have appeared brutal. One group of performers dragged the bound bodies across the stage, piling them up one by one as a "mountain of human bodies," while illuminating them with matches and cigarette lighters.[145] Ono's notes suggest that performers should optionally pull off the bound performers' clothing, or use matches to burn their skin while simultaneously performing banal actions like drinking or reading; but no accounts confirm whether this happened.

Even without such extreme measures, the scene juxtaposes images of dehumanization and terror with the everyday. The mountain of human bodies brings to mind a mass grave, made all the more macabre by Ono's suggestion that "the piled up performers should try their best to move around as much as possible."[146] It brings to mind Sjöholm's Arendtian interpretation of "rituals of burial" in performance art. In these terms, we might say that Ono created a common space through the exposure of living bodies, with burial figuring not as closure but as "the beginning of something new."[147] But this space likely responded to specific images and concepts connected with the atrocities of World War II, which informed the mimetic fictional actions onstage. Act 2 also follows as a seeming consequence of the linguistic confusion and failed public assembly of act 1, intimating the barest rudiments of a narrative by virtue of their sequence.

Lights finally illuminated the entire hall in act 3, the midpoint of the opera, while audio recordings of the previous two acts played on loudspeakers, filling the hall with the audible memory of the work's opening while all action onstage ceased. These recordings were mixed with other recorded sounds, which Ono stipulated in her notes "should be all in voice," whether "the voice of animals or other living things." In the subsequent performance of the piece, in 1962 at the Sōgetsu Art Center in Tokyo, Ono played recordings of Hitler, Hirohito, and the Japanese general Hideki Tojo, though it is unclear whether she played them at Carnegie Recital Hall as well.[148] The Sōgetsu version clearly situated AOS in relation to a recent totalitarian past. This move recalls how Ono asserted the singularity of human consciousness in her critique of Cage in "The Word of a Fabricator," declaring the need to assume responsibility for "the body of a betrayer/l'étranger to the natural world."[149] With the lights dimmed once more, the last two acts continued to juxtapose mundane images and sounds of terror. Performers conducted a banal conversation against the backdrop of an expansive torn canvas held upright like a screen. (The screen was cut from the same cloth as the Painting to be Stepped On.) Behind the cloth, performers pierced the fabric and jutted their extremities through it, waving their limbs around like dancing, dismembered body parts. This image connects with the newspaper screen of Ono and Maciunas's photo advertisement, while moving into the realm of the grotesque.

In an unusual finale, Ono appeared at center stage and, in the words of Johnston, "concluded the work with amplified sighs, breathing, gasping, retching, screaming—many tones of pain and pleasure mixed with a jibberish [sic] of foreign-sounding language that was no language at all."[150] As Ono later put it, "I wanted to throw blood."[151] Trisha Brown, who participated in the Carnegie performance, noted that Ono described her "aria" as responding specifically to a childhood memory of hearing a woman give birth. (As in her show at AG Gallery, Ono continued to surround her work with self-narrative words and sounds.) In Brown's recollection, Ono learned her "aria of high-pitched wails" by tape-recording her own simulation of remembered birthing sounds, and then playing that tape backward and imitating the backward rendition. Although not confirmed by other accounts, Brown recalls this part of the performance at Carnegie as "accompanying a rhythmic background of repeated syllables [and] a tape recording of moans and words spoken backward."[152] This extraordinary technique would have brought forth a layered multiplicity of voices, live and recorded, that scrambled or reversed time and memory. Ono's performance centered on her own voice, body, and persona as it dramatized the birth of something new from traumatic, bloody memory following unmistakable scenes of human brutality. It was thus that Ono rendered opera and fiction, or sympathized "with the first man who lied"—differentiating her work, with its tragic five-act sequence and final birthing aria, from a poetics of indeterminacy. Haunted by the violence of the past and by anticipated wounds of the future, Ono's opera sought to build ties of solidarity in a project of rescue.

Sōgetsu Art Center

Ono published "The Word of a Fabricator" six months after her Carnegie show. Originally published in Japanese, the essay was timed to coincide with her *Works of Yoko Ono* show and performance at Sōgetsu Art Center in Tokyo on May 24, 1962. With this professional coup, Ono became the first woman to stage a solo show as part of the official Sōgetsu activities at a time of considerable cultural and political ferment. In "The Word of a Fabricator," Ono surely anticipated the need to fend off common gendered and culturally mercantilist assumptions about her work—a concern that the critical fallout of her Sōgetsu performance finally justified. As Yoshimoto reminds us, Ono belonged to a small wave of Japanese artists who made careers outside Japan that would not have been possible in Japan because of the "good wife, wise mother" citizenship model that oriented institutions in the arts. Ono's ambivalent return to Japan in 1962, and her critical reception there, provide further insight into her practice and its relationship with gendered imperial power formations in both of her home countries.

Founded in 1958 through private sponsorship, Sōgetsu Art Center (SAC) emerged as the premier hub in Tokyo for artists, musicians, composers, and poets to collaborate, congregate, and show their work in the postwar period. As Miki Kaneda describes, "With a performance hall, regularly scheduled performance and film series, and its own arts journal, the SAC was a space where artists could collaborate and speak across disciplinary boundaries in ways that would have been impossible in traditional museum, concert hall, or academic contexts."[153] Sōgetsu was also a portal for the importation of American and European modernisms: its auditorium displayed prestigious, mural-like canvases by the Abstract Expressionist painter Sam Francis on one side and the Art Informel painter Georges Mathieu on the other, symbolically announcing this import function and arguably emblazoning culturally mercantilist principles in the performance space.[154] Sōgetsu also became a site where intellectuals hotly contested matters of Japanese government and nationhood in the shadow of American occupation. In the midst of fierce protests in June 1960 over the renewal of the US-Japan Treaty of Mutual Cooperation and Security, which gave the United States the right to station troops in Japan, musical societies gathered at Sōgetsu to plan antimilitarist, pro-democratic protest actions with a membership 580 strong—an unprecedented event that continued to influence Sōgetsu programming in the early 1960s.[155] These conditions defined Ono's debut as the first woman to stage an official solo show at Sōgetsu.

Ono left New York in March 1962 to join her husband, Toshi Ichiyanagi, in Japan, where they planned to use their professional connections to organize a national tour with John Cage, Merce Cunningham, and David Tudor (though plans with Cunningham fell through).[156] Ono's last major performance in New York was a contribution to a benefit concert at the Living Theatre for *An Anthology of Chance Operations*—a publication edited by La Monte Young that featured contributions from many of the artists who had participated in the Chambers Street Loft Series. The circumstances of Ono's move suggest the ambivalence of her attachment to the downtown art community that had both nurtured and frustrated her talents. Ono apparently planned only to stop over in Japan for a few weeks, but she ultimately stayed for two years. As she later put it, "Had I stayed in New York I would have become one of those grande dames of the avant-garde, repeating what I was doing."[157] If Ono found her circumstances in New York unpropitious for growth, her return to Tokyo brought no easy homecoming or sense of belonging.[158] As she confessed in correspondence with Tudor, "[Toshi and I] feel closer to you [David Tudor, John Cage, Merce Cunningham, and Tudor's partner M. C. Richards] than to our parents or any Japanese. . . . Since we were in N.Y. for the past ten years without ever coming back to Japan, we are finding ourselves rather foreign in this country."[159] Nonetheless, the couple's connections and reputations were strong enough to secure her show at Sōgetsu and to ensure the participation of "thirty luminaries."[160]

Works of Yoko Ono featured all of the pieces from the Carnegie Recital Hall, supplemented by an even wider range of media accentuating themes, materials, and actions from her previous work. The program defined and organized itself around four multimedia elements: events, music, poems, and instructions for paintings. The former two composed the performance program, while the latter two remained on exhibit for a longer period of time. The "music" included *Grapefruit in a World of Park, Piece for Violin and Strawberries, Piano Piece to See the Skies, Pulse,* and *AOS—To David Tudor. Piano Piece to See the Skies* probed at the limits of audibility across a disjunctive three-part structure—juxtaposing tiny sounds barely discernable to the human ear, banging piano sounds "that can be heard all the way up to the sky," and amplified breathing sounds resulting from the exertion of performance.[161] In *Pulse*, Ono directed performers to make heterogeneous sounds after solving mathematical problems by hand on paper, a game that might be described as a tongue-in-cheek parody of the Cage-inspired "research art" of "systems, charts, randomizations" practiced by her friends in the New York Audio Visual Group. The "events" of the concert comprised *A Piece for Chairs I–X*, which brought people into varying relationships with chairs—for example, reading newspapers in chairs while the chair legs were cut from under them with a saw, or wrapping bodies in gauze and stacking them on chairs like corpses.[162] This piece foreshadowed *AOS*'s treatment of human beings as objects—a theme that became even more overtly historicized and politicized in its Sōgetsu rendition. As mentioned above, it was here that *AOS*'s third act included the amplified playback of speeches by Hitler, Hirohito, and Hideki Tojo. Responding to *AOS*, one critic highlighted Ono's themes of dehumanization and objectification, which played out all the more chillingly in spontaneous interactions: "This is not an art that is created beforehand, but an art where the audience experiences the process of performers creating nonsensical actions in front of their eyes, and receives something through this. What is interesting about all this is that it seems that humans are treated materialistically."[163]

Following blatant references to a recent past of atrocities, *AOS* at Sōgetsu concluded in a more self-consciously interactive way than *AOS* at Carnegie, with the performers lining up at the front of the stage and staring into the eyes of audience members. Each time an audience member averted his or her glance, the performer would glare into a new set of eyes, following this procedure indefinitely. The performers' laser-beam stares seared through through the fourth wall of the theater, in the style of Brechtian theater. Ono called this set of actions *Audience Piece to La Monte Young*—a work that could be performed independently or as the conclusion to *AOS*. Its confrontational final gesture can be read as an effort to jolt audience members so that they would become self-conscious actors responding to worldly dilemmas presented onstage. The dedication to Young may figure both as a clever challenge to him—as a creator who himself avoided explicit politics—and as an homage to his penchant for musical works of long duration.

As an interactive laboratory for both performer and audience member participants, *Works of Yoko Ono* produced unforeseeably tragicomic results. Informed by the accounts of Théo Lésoualc'h and Yoshiaki Tōno, Yoshimoto explains: "While most of the audience left quickly, some people remained for a long time. One of them abruptly came up to the stage to pinch the nose of all the performers, which caused a fight with one of the performers."[164] At Sōgetsu, *Audience Piece* lasted several hours, with the performers and a handful of audience members finally leaving the building only when the building manager secured the premises for the night at 1 a.m.[165] Given Sōgetsu's status as the hotbed for a politically engagé artistic vanguard, it should come as no surprise that Ono's work drew the sustained fascination of a devoted cadre who stayed to the bitter end.

For those audience members who wanted more, the exhibition would have provided a bounty. Sōgetsu displayed Ono's *Touch Poems*, including a handmade book with Ono's dark hair and the red locks of a friend glued between the pages, interspersed with strips of cut white paper arranged in an abstract design.[166] This work, previously exhibited at the Living Theater *Anthology* benefit concert, gestured toward an embodied poetics of intimacy quite different from the depersonalization of artistic persona then associated with Cage's circles. The Sōgetsu exhibit also spotlighted Ono's *Instructions for Paintings*, with calligraphy by Ichiyanagi, in the same vein as the instruction pieces featured the previous summer at Maciunas's AG Gallery, which were eventually to be published in *Grapefruit* (1964).

Despite the engrossed response of the audience, critics were harsh. Looming over the reception history of *Works of Yoko Ono* is a hatchet job written by the American expat critic Donald Richie—a piece that encapsulates Ono's struggles with Cold War Orientalism and cultural mercantilism exacerbated by gender bias in both of her home nations. Scholars and critics have described the reception of Ono's 1962 Sōgetsu show as "unfavorable" and "mixed"—qualifiers that respond specifically to Richie's review, which also appears to have made a strong impression on Ono.[167] The review echoed and reinforced Japanese-language criticism of the time, which treated Ono as an imitator of Cage and an affront to *ryō-sai kenbo* ideals of Japanese femininity.[168] Published in the respected visual arts monthly *Geijutsu Shinchō*, the review launched a personal attack against Ono that also condemned Sōgetsu and its Japanese audiences. According to Richie, Ono was deluded in thinking herself "modern" because she had lived in New York, and her works "sought to give the appearance of avant-garde."[169] But, he claimed that all of her ideas were in fact "borrowed from John Cage," and that she "did not demonstrate any originality." The fact that Sōgetsu sponsored Ono's program reveals that "it hardly lives up to [its] reputation [for presenting the finest of Japanese avant-garde art]. The works it shows are actually mostly old-fashioned. Yoko Ono's program . . . epitomizes this." As evidence of Ono's supposedly infantile creativity and amateurism ("on the level of an elementary-school sports day"), Richie interestingly singled out the slow-moving duration of her pieces, the very device for inducing a mixture of shock and stupor that had so intrigued the *Village Voice* critic Jill Johnston. Ono's alleged misuse of time—her performance of a piece "which took forever"—"exposed the very nature of the Japanese," who mistakenly believe "that great and important works are those which take time." From Richie's perspective, Ono's insistence on performing such a slow and boring piece as *AOS* "deceived," "disrespected," and "insult[ed] the intelligence" of her audience, who, in his view, "deserved" this treatment since they never "complained" and remained in their seats. Compounding the insult, Richie denounced Ono's reference to the violence of the recent past: "Ono incorporated speeches of Hitler at Nuremberg and Hideki Tōjō during the war. It was such a tacky idea. It was cheap non-sense. No one clapped, even after it lasted over twenty minutes." Richie closed his review by again repeatedly asserting the obsolescence and unoriginality of Ono's art, insulting the largely Japanese audience who attended—"They were glued to their seats, as immobile as cows"—and confessing regret that Ono could not show the "brilliant magic" and wit of a Francis Picabia or an Erik Satie.

The tone and argument of this review followed established patterns in Richie's journalistic oeuvre. Having moved to Japan in 1947 with the American occupation forces, he pursued a decades-long career as a film critic and travel writer interpreting Japanese culture and mores for a mostly though not exclusively English-language readership, helping to shape the sentimental "structures of feeling" of Cold War Orientalism. For example, his 1971 travelogue *The Inland Sea* ruminates on the status of the "floating world" of Japanese service professionals, from "bar-boys to . . . geishas," who display a "purity" and "innocence" incomparable to their American counterparts.[170] He saw these qualities as fundamental to Japanese character. From Richie's perspective, the Japanese public at Sōgetsu was trying to be something different from their nature, aspiring to a "Western" sophistication of which they were incapable. Ono's ethnicity and gender doubly determined her own exclusion from this avant-garde lineage and future. She could never be Cage, Satie, or Picabia. In trying, she relinquished her main supposed virtue: the "innocence" that was the birthright of Japanese women.

Ichiyanagi came to Ono's defense with a robust response to Richie's diatribe, insisting on the originality of Ono's work. Ichiyanagi's argument unfolded around a dense assemblage of direct quotations from Ono, so much so that the essay reads as a cowritten document. He insisted that "each artist has a language of his/her own, which sometimes cannot be understood solely through already formed sensation"—a characteristic that applied even more thoroughly to Ono's idiosyncratic work, the philosophy of which differed entirely from Cage's.[171] Ichiyanagi pointed not only to the uniqueness of Ono's conceptual world, but also to the generosity with which she shared her ideas with others, including Cage. The fact that ideas "flow endlessly from her, and she gives these to other people," made it all the more ironic that she was "criticized for having stolen other people's ideas."[172] Echoing Ono's "word-spreading" idea of the work, Ichiyanagi insisted that she "employed the 'unreliable [*futa-shika*]' format of oral transmission" rather than scores.[173] In my own interpretation, this oral transmission not only undermines traditional notions of authorship—as we have already discussed—but also creates potential for the wide-open temporalities embedded in *Audience Piece to La Monte Young*—at which point Ono's "initial wish" moves into the hands and minds of others. Drawing on Ono's diction, Ichiyanagi linked this transmission process with a "very 'unreliable' and 'ambiguous' use of time" rather than a "beautiful use of time"—taking direct aim at Richie's criticism of the long durations of her work. Ono's ambiguous use of time responds to her belief that a work "does not communicate, but must be discovered by others," a belief that demands "active participation and highly sophisticated reflexes from the audience, in a different way from works of chance operation."[174]

Getting to the heart of her politics—with its thematicization of dehumanization—Ichiyanagi further interpreted her words: "'I can't stand the healthy honesty of Picasso or Pollock. I need a fictional world whose setting is much more complicated.' This is a world in which a chair and a human being are transformed into something of the same order."[175] Ono's reference to the "healthy honesty of Picasso and Pollock" showcases her dark irony. She could find no comfort or belonging within a canonical avant-garde lineage implicated in culturally mercantilist politics. Nothing is innocent, everything is complicated, and relations in a world of humankind and objects demand extraordinary feats of imagination for their transformation.

Ichiyanagi's essay went on to imply that Ono's work would not allow for the escapism of mid-century consumption, entertainment, or Orientalism. In her own words, she found "candy-like art that is dedicated solely to sensual pleasures . . . bleak." The same with "watching baseball."[176] Pointedly, Ichiyanagi further explained to his readers that "Ono's work lacks the so-called 'Japonica' aspect, and therefore it was utterly despised in New York by foreigners well-versed in Japan who love Japonica." Rather, she devoted herself to creating "works that dealt with 'unreliable transformation' and 'time.'"[177] In line with these concerns, Ichiyanagi pointed to a work on display at Sōgetsu—*Painting That Shakes Hands*—that he believed explicitly demonstrated "the character of her art":

"All that remains is for it to shake hands with everyone"—Ono says with a hint of self-mockery. But this work, which has a lengthy subtitle "Painting for Those Who Must Wear a Fake Smile," creates a beautiful world of new rules that sublimates and stylizes her philosophy. Only a hand pokes out from the back of a white canvas. And it is grasped by many unknown hands in unknown spaces.[178]

This piece points to a charade of fake smiles and endless handshakes—a potentially electrifying image for Japanese audiences up in arms about the US-Japan Treaty of Mutual Cooperation and Security. The piece may be understood as a parody of the Cold War Orientalism's masking sentiment: the idea that the United States' overseas expansion of geopolitical power is a mutually beneficial, noncoercive enterprise. At the same time, however, *Painting That Shakes Hands* also gestures toward the highest aspirations of Ono's practice, the idea that her initial hope or wish might set something meaningfully in motion beyond the control of the initiator, enacting a politics of its own in "many unknown hands in unknown places."

To Spread by Word of Mouth

It has been the task of this chapter to demonstrate how Ono's early work fought against modes of cultural evaluation that restricted who could lay claim to artistic originality in a closed system privileging the "West" over the "rest." In doing so, it resisted any sentimental discourses that mapped innocence and reciprocity onto the expansion of US power in East Asia and elsewhere during the consensus period. To be sure, the Cold War Orientalism of John Cage differs from that of, say, Donald Richie; and Cage himself articulated a changing, more explicit politics of practice over the course of the 1960s.[179] Yet we cannot overlook the extent to which *any* form of Cold War Orientalism conflicts with the strong anti-war commitments implicit in Ono's work from the start—commitments she has described as entangled in personal memories of violence during World War II.

Ono embraced Cage's call to *open up* the musical work—to make it permeable to unforeseeable elements and actions—while rejecting his abnegation of intention, consciousness, and personal history in the compositional process. While she envisioned her work as starting from a place of intention and memory, she also invited its refiguring in the consciousness, words, and actions of others—moving beyond her original "wish." These transformations would constitute more than a secondary layer of interpretation and commentary, becoming part of the work itself. As we know, Ono wanted her unscored works "to be spread by word of mouth," a process that was "also part of the piece." Her works at Carnegie Recital Hall and Sōgetsu—staged as a fiction or drama—would thus ideally unfold a politics, defined as a common interest that binds citizens in public assembly, deliberation, speech, and action. This politics responded overtly to the past—offering the possibility to connect personal with collective histories, while linking the problems of the past with the demands of the present and future. In this respect, Ono's highlighting of war, peace, and violence in her idiosyncratic, personalized poetics was not for nothing. Rooted in personal experiences of trauma and gendered exile, her early work is a touchstone for understanding how New York avant-gardes became politicized through internal critique in the 1960s, and how they mediated larger networks transnationally.

Ono's work opens the question of whether engagé artists like herself could leverage transnational circuits of exchange in the 1960s to circumvent, even oppose, the "official" US-based global patronage networks that had emerged at the start of the Cold War and had since flourished. What would it mean to create an art transnationalism in resistance to US empire? How would this transnationalism stand as a foil to the State Department's prolific public diplomacy and cultural reconstruction projects abroad, to the CIA's secret (and sometimes not so secret) sponsorship of liberal elite art vanguards throughout the world, and to major foundation patronage that strategically allied itself with State Department goals? These questions resurface in the discussion of Fluxus, the sponsoring organization founded by George Maciunas that itself offered an "ambiguous temporality" and "world of stickiness" through which Ono's work would become discovered and altered by others.

The Haunting of Empires

MACIUNAS, FLUXUS, AND THE BLOODLANDS

"I use a stomach pump to rid the instrument of any foreign bodies."

BENJAMIN PATTERSON, *Stars and Stripes*, August 30, 1962[1]

"Don't we believe in death anymore?"

GEORGE MACIUNAS, playing himself,
in Jonas Mekas's *Guns of the Trees*, 1960[2]

In a 1993 written reminiscence, the experimental poet and Fluxus creator Emmett Williams touched on George Maciunas's unspoken history:

In late 1962 or early 1963 George picked me up in Darmstadt in one of his famous used—or overused cars. I forget where we were headed, to one Fluxus festival or another (there were so many of them in the beginning it's hard to keep track), but I can remember very well that as we approached Frankfurt-Höchst he called my attention to a large industrial complex. *"That's where my father worked during the war,"* he said, pointing. "Was he a . . . a slave laborer?" I asked, in a sympathetic, understanding tone. *"No, he was an electrical engineer. He had a job with Siemens-Schuckert."* And that was that. Of course there was much more to it than that, but I didn't dare ask. The subject was still taboo. I wish now that I had asked. Had I been bold enough, I might have learned then and there the answer to a question that worries a lot of would-be biographers of George Maciunas. Some hazard to guess that George's father was a collaborator.[3]

The story of the Maciunas family, who fled Lithuania in 1941, emerges from the time and terrain of the "bloodlands"—the region between Berlin and Moscow, where the Nazi and Soviet regimes killed some fourteen million people in the middle of the twentieth century. As the historian

Timothy Snyder writes, this terrorizing and morally ambiguous zone has often evaded comprehension and articulate memory.[4] Embedded within this chapter on Fluxus is the history of the Maciunas family, which haunts the scene of Fluxus's founding in Wiesbaden, Germany, in 1962, yet remains taboo.

Under these conditions of occluded remembrance, George Maciunas figures with a mixture of brilliance and obscurity in histories of the postwar New York avant-garde. When he founded Fluxus in 1962, he launched a transnational sponsoring organization for artists, musicians, and writers dedicated to questioning boundaries between art and life. This organization helped to coalesce disparate strands of artistic experimentation that had developed across East Asia, Western Europe, and the United States. At the time of Fluxus's founding, Maciunas had just moved from New York City to Wiesbaden to work as a graphic designer in the US Air Force. From Wiesbaden he launched the series of far-out festivals that made Fluxus's name in Western Europe, while hatching plans for tours in Eastern Europe, Siberia, and East Asia. It was in Wiesbaden that he also first lambasted US imperialism, capitalism, nationalism, and militarism in a series of letters, manifestos, and newsletters that sought to define Fluxus as a movement and community. Making ample use of Air Force resources, Maciunas's practice came to be defined by a flamboyantly heterodox use of media: the IBM typewriter, tape recorders, digital adding machine tape, and contact microphones came into communication with older, mundane technologies like tabbed card files, maps, charts, bowler hats, umbrellas, duck calls, and classical instruments in outrageous, vaudeville-like performances laced with dark humor. As Julia Robinson has written, Maciunas's mixed artistic persona and roles—as Fluxus's founder and leader, impresario and jokester, graphic designer of flyers and leaflets, organizer of concerts, documentary photographer, compiler of editions and multiples, and so on—has resisted categorization by virtue of "a complex and hybrid 'authorial' model that would suspend the term *artist* or reveal it to be irrelevant."[5] Maciunas's bewilderingly mixed persona and practice may indeed contribute to his inadequate scholarly and critical treatment. Yet the gaps in his story also exceed this circumstance.

While secondary accounts of Fluxus fiercely contest what Fluxus is, who its central figures are, and how to tell its legacy, they are generally united in ignoring a central fact. When Maciunas moved from New York to Wiesbaden in 1962, and planned further trips east, he reversed the direction of refugee flight he had taken as a child with his family from their native Lithuania to Germany in 1944, and finally to the United States in 1948. Wiesbaden was only twenty-eight kilometers from Frankfurt-

Höchst, the place of his father's employment at the Siemens Corporation in Nazi Germany. Maciunas's background under conditions of totalitarianism and uprooting would appear significant to Fluxus's famed antinationalist, antimilitarist character. His father's employment as an architect and electrical engineer working for the Nazi war machine would also appear relevant to Maciunas's preoccupation in Fluxus with the specific technologies of the US military base where he himself worked. Yet, with few exceptions, the secondary literature on Fluxus generally turns away from Maciunas's background, in keeping with Williams's words about the worries of "would-be biographers."[6] This silence renders traces like Williams's anecdote—and the scant other primary sources and oral histories testifying to this past—all the more valuable.

As such sources attest, histories of violent uprooting abide in the present even when the chroniclers of history—and the displaced actors themselves—turn the page to start a new chapter. The experience of exile, Edward Said wrote, apprehends multiple settings in relationship with one another: "Both the new and the old environments are vivid, actual, occurring together contrapuntally."[7] Williams's anecdote illuminates such contrapuntal experience, showing how Maciunas's memory of Nazi-era Frankfurt-Höchst shadowed his 1960s Fluxus road trips and festivals. The central burden of this chapter is to show how memories of occupied Lithuania and the Third Reich appear to have animated Maciunas's experience of American neo-imperialism in early-1960s Germany. To recognize this contrapuntal experience is to refine our understanding of Maciunas's influential politics of practice.

Yet the implications of such contrapuntal experience reach beyond the individual creator's biography, opening the history of Fluxus up to broader questions of nation, race, militarized expansionism, hierarchies of citizenship, guilt, and responsibility. Maciunas's story, in other words, works in tandem with others to evoke the hauntings that bind scenes of empire across divergent times and places. It bears a close kinship with the oeuvre of the Lithuanian-American filmmaker and poet Jonas Mekas, whose work selectively dredges up "painful feelings of guilt and complicity" in autobiographical projects concerning World War II and the Holocaust, as Michael Casper writes—feelings insufficiently acknowledged even in the public presentation and words of Mekas himself.[8] It connects with Yoko Ono's early interventions, which foregrounded the entangled colonial violence of both of her "home" nations (as discussed in chapter 4). It also links up with Benjamin Patterson's powerful and implicit engagement with racism as a Black American exile in Wiesbaden and cofounder of Fluxus—another story that has generally been obscured within Fluxus historiography, as described by George Lewis.[9] In bringing these stories together, I join Alexander G. Weheliye's call to "emphasize the family ties between political violence and suffering" and to "bring into focus the relays betwixt and between [different but related genocides] to design novel assemblages of relation" without reducing them to a hierarchical "grammar of comparison."[10] As Snyder writes of the "bloodlands," "Often what happened to one group is intelligible only in light of what happened to another."[11] In this chapter, I rethink Fluxus as producing such "intelligibilities" and "assemblages of relation" in the study of empire and genocide. As I show, Fluxus projects scrutinized these things by treating them as objects of study and by "playing" at them mimetically, whether consciously or unconsciously—parodying the processes, personae, technologies, and symbols of empires past and present. In exploring this dynamic, I treat the protagonists of my narrative not as ciphers for liberation, suffering, or resistance, but rather as everyday subjects whose lives played out in webs of choice and constraint.

Here we should remember Fluxus as a tumultuous "third space" where languages and personae of vastly different backgrounds entered "a translational space of negotiation [that] opens up through the process of dialogue" across an uneven field of power, as described elsewhere in this book.[12] Third space exceeds the mastery of its participants: in the transitional flux of translation, actor's intentions become caught in uncertainty and ambivalence, disjunct from their aftereffects. These translational dynamics often remain hidden from the historical actors themselves. Yet they also bring forth unexpected modes of remembrance and anticipation in the upheavals of dialogical encounter. My account of Fluxus tracks how its community worked through traumas of state violence—victimhood and perpetratorhood—in its poetics of performance. This working-through varied in the explicitness of its articulation. Maciunas's contribution to this legacy appears most pronounced via his agonistic collaborations with other artists—among whom Jonas Mekas, Yoko Ono, and Ben Patterson feature most prominently in this narrative. Framed this way, Wiesbaden signifies not only as a vexed site of return for Maciunas, but also as a site of newfound power within an "infrastructure of prestige" for US art abroad during the Cold War—a system anchored in the US cultural-diplomatic, economic, and military presence in Germany, which Maciunas and his fellow travelers both depended upon and railed against.

Before returning to Maciunas's family history and the scene of Fluxus's founding, let me spell out in greater detail how my approach differs from current accounts of Maciunas within Fluxus historiography. The Museum of Modern Art's acquisition of the Silverman Fluxus Collection has virtually assured Maciunas's enduring canonical status in the annals of art history. At the same time, the question of "Maciunas the migrant"—how his status as a displaced person figures within literature—shows strange patterns of erasure. A good amount of scholarship flags his uprooted background in order to bolster Fluxus's claims to transnationalism. Yet such references typically conceal or minimize the story of "the bloodlands" that gave rise to his uprootings.

As an extreme example, Hannah Higgins peculiarly *rewrites* Maciunas's history when she describes him as "not an 'American impresario' [but rather] a Lithuanian expatriate who by 1962 had lived only briefly in New York."[13] Referenced more than once, her assertion that Maciunas is "not American" marginalizes his presence within the implicitly American origin story of Fluxus she constructs—a pragmatist, "experiential" genealogy centered on John Dewey and John Cage—which, she argues, found fullest expression within transnational networks of collaboration that were "inherent in the work" of Fluxus.[14] Her description of Maciunas as a "Lithuanian expatriate" misrepresents his relocation to the United States as a matter of choice, just as it denies his naturalized US citizenship and the fact that he had lived his entire adulthood in the United States until his return to Germany in 1962.[15] Higgins defines Fluxus as a movement that generated, in John Dewey's terms, an "active and alert commerce with the world . . . complete interpenetration of self and the world of objects and events."[16] We will see how Maciunas's childhood experiences, under conditions of double genocide, would likely have contributed to a decidedly ominous vision of what such "commerce with the world . . . complete interpenetration of the self and the world of objects and events" may mean—a vision incongruent with Higgins's benign picture. Here the haunting of earlier empires—suggested by Maciunas's story, which Higgins disavows—would risk spoiling a celebration of American innocence implied by Dewey's words as a motto for Fluxus's US-based genealogy and global presence. This haunting whispers: *Not all cultural experience is broadening; not all border-crossing is liberating; and the modern 'American' present perpetuates the oppressions of the past.*

Within Fluxus historiography, Higgins has sought to deemphasize the importance of Maciunas and his radical politics; yet even those accounts that privilege Maciunas and his politics ignore the conditions of forced displacement that defined his early life. The effect of this historiography is to locate Maciunas within a canonical history of white European avantgardes intersecting with radical left-wing politics. Meanwhile, it erases histories of genocide. This erasure may be understood as reinforcing Marxist narratives of class struggle while downplaying questions of race and ethnicity. For example, Astrit Schmidt-Burkhardt and Cuauhtémoc Medina have each brilliantly specified the character of Maciunas's Marxism as it evolved in the early and mid-1960s. Schmidt-Burckhardt considers the far-left politics of Maciunas's *Atlas of Russian History* and other "learning machines" (maps, charts, etc.) as technologies for the production of knowledge.[17] Medina "reconstructs" Maciunas's mid-1960s "political intentions" in seeking to defect to the Soviet Union and launch Fluxus there as an anti-art program consonant with official cultural platforms—a plan he never fulfilled.[18] Yet neither Schmidt-Burckhardt nor Medina considers Maciunas's history in the "bloodlands" as pertinent to his studies of East European political geography and history, let alone his dreams of boundary crossing in that region. Similarly, Mari Dumett examines Maciunas's engagement with ideas of "corporate culture" as an important object for historical and political study across multiple centuries, yet she declines to explore the genocidal, state-dominated capitalism at Siemens that would have shaped his coming of age in Nazi Germany.[19]

We should note that such erasures actually echo Maciunas's own silences. As Williams's anecdote suggests, Maciunas tended to be quiet about this history: he certainly did not thematize genocide in his written programs and manifestoes for Fluxus in Wiesbaden in the early 1960s, despite the later foregrounding of them in his 1967 poster *U.S.A. Surpasses All the Genocide Records!*, made famous in the peace activism of Yoko Ono and John Lennon (see figure 5.5). Rather, like Schmidt-Burkhardt and Medina, Maciunas located Fluxus within a more stable, linear historical narrative—a genealogy of politically radical aesthetic avant-gardes originating in the European "capitals of modernity" in the early twentieth century. Like Higgins, Maciunas also stressed the primary importance of John Cage, even designating him as a "root" and a "spiritual father."[20] In line with this chosen paternity, Maciunas embraced a light, ironic tone in his words and work, which may ward off interpretations weighted by tragic history.[21] He also valorized Fluxus as a collectivist and anonymous form of cultural production, an orientation that might discourage autobiographically informed readings of his projects. This chapter reads against the grain of Maciunas's self-narratives and genealogies, treating his desire for paternity, continuity, levity, and anonymity as an effect of uprooting, rather than as a reason for ignoring that displacement. These self-narratives express a desire for home. "Dwelling" here becomes "the artificial, achieved hybrid 'figure' against the 'ground' of traveling, movement, and circulation," as James Clifford has written of migration studies more generally.[22]

In consonance with this position, I maintain that it is virtually impossible to provide a vivid account of Maciunas's politics and poetics of practice, with its signature objects and techniques, without understanding Germany as a vexed site of remigration. Indeed, Maciunas's anti-imperialist politics found its fullest expression in a critical engagement with media technologies of empire essential to the administration of subjugated populations through hard and soft power—the very technologies his father had helped to develop as an architect and electrical engineer. Similarly, techniques at the very core of Fluxus can be freshly understood as strategies of survival that emerged from the "bloodlands" and other terrains of violence, including racial terror in the United States. I have already gestured toward two of these techniques. The first is *erasure*. When regimes change or people flee, some facts are best forgotten or simply removed from the record for the sake of survival, whether that survival is conceived existentially or psychically. The second technique is a kind of *skeptical mirroring*, which produces effects of irony and parody that range in tone from ambivalence to derision. Totalitarian regimes (and other situations of violence) produce among their subjects behaviors of mimicry as a camouflaging mode of self-defense. For those who cannot trade in straight talk for fear of persecution, the "affected ignorance" of irony lightens the burden of oppression. This is an idea suggested by the artist's wife, Billie Maciunas, and his friend Jonas Mekas.[23] The third technique is *economy of means*. More than a modernist design principle, this strategy amounts to a way of life under conditions of scarcity and terror when efficiency means everything. In Maciunas's hands, it aimed to produce a superabundance of knowledge and efficacy with minimal materials and gestures. The fourth and fifth techniques, equally central to my arguments, are *sabotage* and *translation*. Both usually recede into the shadows of anonymity; both scramble boundaries between the inside and outside of languages and institutions. But, as we will see, sabotage burns bridges while translation builds them. Before addressing Maciunas's practices in depth, we will examine the totalitarian occupations and migrations of his past, two conditions that themselves confound the inside and outside of nations, communities, and power.

Postgenocide Personae

To see George Maciunas as haunted by his father's wartime occupations is not to search for superficial psychoanalytic explanations for his life's work in Fluxus, or to rehearse simplified Oedipal dramas. Rather, we should remember Edward Said's observation of the special place of *family in exile* as an essential unit that provides life-saving shelter from the torrents of geopolitical violence while circumscribing the life of its members to a point of claustrophobia in that very protection: "I felt that a whole world was held at bay, ready to tumble in, engulf us, perhaps even sweep us away, so protected and enclosed was I inside the little world my parents created."[24] From one generation to the next, family passes on strategies of survival. From one generation to the next, family perpetuates, changes, or simply endures a social and political order with the help or hindrance of those adaptive techniques.

It is significant that Maciunas appeared to follow in his father's professional footsteps—pursuing training as an architect and professor—before he flamboyantly tossed these career paths aside to enter New York's avant-garde scene in 1960, and subsequently moved to Wiesbaden. It is no small thing to undertake academic training at three prestigious institutions as Maciunas did—acquiring degrees in art and architecture from Cooper Union (1949–53) and the Carnegie Institute of Technology (1952–54), with a minor in musicology, and then making progress toward a PhD in art history at NYU (1955–60)—only to abandon the secure career paths those credentials would have facilitated.[25] When Maciunas jettisoned the idea of becoming a professor or architect, he also rejected a set of personae that were far from neutral within his family history.

"Professor" and "architect" were more than just professions; they were a way of being in the world, managing a family legacy, and perpetuating or changing social and political regimes. As cited in the introduction, Lorraine Daston and H. Otto Sibum note that intermediate

> between the individual biography and the social institution lies the persona: a cultural identity that simultaneously shapes the individual in body and mind and creates a collective with a shared and recognizable physiognomy. The bases for personae are diverse: a social role (e.g. the mother), a profession (the physician), an anti-profession (the flâneur), a calling (the priest). . . . Personae are creatures of historical circumstance; they emerge and disappear within specific contexts.[26]

In Daston and Sibum's terms, personae are molded by techniques that "shape selves from within: sharpening the senses, channeling attention, expanding or contracting the credible, fixing emotional allegiances, training patterns of inference and argument, bending personalities, instilling an ethos."[27] "Personae are as real or more real than biological individuals, in that they create the possibilities of being in the human world, schooling the mind, body, and soul in distinctive and indelible ways."[28] In accord with this formulation, I would suggest that the inherited personae

Maciunas "tried on" in early adulthood eventually revealed themselves as uninhabitable ways of "being in the human world," with unbearable costs for the "mind, body, and soul." As we will see, Maciunas's dilemmas of "persona" had everything to do with the historical circumstances under which Alexander Maciunas occupied the "intermediate space between the individual biography and the social institution" under conditions of genocide in Lithuania and Germany in the 1940s. The ways in which modern personae shape the body and mind depend, after all, upon how these personae work in tandem with state power and administration.

As we will see, George Maciunas's difficult and agonistic fashioning of self went hand in hand with resisting a sense of national identification, whether Lithuanian, American, or Lithuanian-American—sidestepping significant conventions of masculine identity, and embracing a far-left, pro-Soviet politics that targeted US imperialism, understood as a category that also refers to the power of US-based capitalism and its globalizing effects. While Maciunas apparently resisted inheriting the personae his father had inhabited under unbearable moral conditions, he held onto specific techniques through which his parents had navigated their family's survival within totalitarian societies. Indeed, these techniques provided a basis for Fluxus and for the new hybrid persona Maciunas attempted to craft in a critical relationship with the institutions of technology, industry, education, and empire that had defined his father's career. Under these conditions, Fluxus emerged ambivalently in Maciunas's hands and mind as its own institution, and perhaps as a make-believe empire in itself.

Alexander Maciunas's story "between the individual biography and the social institution" was a typical one of collaboration and survival in the bloodlands. As Snyder has written, the legacy of multiple occupations in Lithuania from 1940 onward proved particularly brutal:

A single occupation can fracture a society for generations; double occupation is even more painful and divisive. It created risks and temptations that were unknown in the West. The departure of one foreign ruler meant nothing more than the arrival of another. When foreign troops left, people had to reckon not with peace but with the policies of the next occupier. They had to deal with the consequences of their own previous commitments under one occupier when the next one came; or make choices under one occupation while anticipating another.[29]

Alexander trained as an electrical engineer and architect at the Technische Hochschule in Berlin-Charlottenburg. Before the war, he had served as associate dean of engineering at the Institute of Technology in Kaunas, and as a high-ranking representative at Siemens Corporation. The company had established itself in the country immediately after its 1918 national independence and became central to its infrastructure. Working from the Siemens office in Kaunas, Maciunas helped to construct and maintain Lithuania's first power plants, telephone wire systems, and overland electrical networks for the operation of vital modern infrastructure such as streetlamps and trams.[30] After the Soviet occupation of Lithuania in 1940, he worked in the Energy Department at Siemens.[31] Alexander's early professional persona—engineer, as an agent of Lithuanian autonomy and modernity—utterly transformed under conditions of occupation. During this time, about twenty-one thousand Lithuanians, many of them elites, were deported to Siberia and other distant parts of the Soviet Union.[32] Benefiting from Alexander's collaboration, the Maciunas family moved into a spacious villa vacated by victims of these deportations, which then drastically escalated in the weeks right before the Nazi invasion in June 1941.[33]

The matriarch of the family, Leokadija Maciunas (née Saikowska), recalled how her husband, Alexander, finally also came under threat when he refused to denounce colleagues that summer. An outspoken and flamboyant former opera ballet dancer, she had come from a background vulnerable to scrutiny by the Soviets. Born into an upper-class and likely impoverished Russian family that had migrated across the Russian empire from Latvia to Armenia to Georgia to Lithuania, Leokadija was the daughter of an officer in the Russian imperial army.[34] In her extraordinary, archivally preserved typescript "My Son," written after her son's 1978 death, she described the Soviet threat of 1941 with indignation: "[The Soviets] suggested my husband spy on his friends and denounce his colleagues every day. He so sharply refused this vile role then that they noted it down."[35] With dark humor, she added, "Fortunately a few days after this offer the Germans occupied Lithuania in one day and the Soviets didn't succeed in arresting my husband."[36] Her ironic use of the word "offer" reveals the cost of the provisional benefits they had enjoyed up to that point—similar to the conditionality of such benefits under the next occupation. When the Germans arrived, Alexander resumed his work with Siemens and received permission to remain in the same appropriated villa, but he now shared it with a German general and his mistress. According to the daughter of the family, Nijole Valaitis (née Maciunas), this arrangement lasted until the general grew uncomfortable with the family's presence, at which point the Maciunas family moved to their dacha.[37]

Already, this story of shifting occupations suggests the vitality of two survival techniques. One glimpses a scene of erasure via the "forgetting" of violence that literally had secured the family home, appropriated as it was from deportees, alongside the strategic silences and obfuscations that would have been necessary for Alexander to cooperate with successive terrorizing regimes. (Leokadija omitted any reference in her account to the home appropriated from detainees; her daughter preserved this information for memory.) One also detects a skeptical mirroring in Leokadija's use of irony, which speaks to the fragile nature of her husband's association with occupying powers that would have required him to blend in and mimic the actions, attitudes, and words (like "offer") of those around him when in public, while thoroughly probing their meanings in private.

Born in 1931, George Maciunas—then known as Jurgis—was nine years old when the Nazi occupation and genocide began. When the Germans arrived, as Snyder emphasizes, many non-Jewish Lithuanians welcomed the Germans as liberators—as evoked in Leokadija's relief at the Soviets' departure.[38] The Nazis capitalized on the recent Soviet purges to win Lithuanians over to their cause, assembling Lithuanian units to exterminate the country's Jewish population, which they scapegoated for the Soviet deportations and massacres. One German *Einsatzkommando* reported the Lithuanian "Jewish problem" resolved after only six months of occupation, when nearly 115,000 had been massacred in killing fields.[39] In Maciunas's hometown of Kaunas, 3,800 Jews were murdered on the streets in the span of a few days in late July.[40] In subsequent weeks in Kaunas, the Lithuanians and Germans systematically rounded up and killed approximately 5,000 more Jews in a nearby fort.[41] Lithuania ultimately came to attain the highest "kill rate" in Nazi-occupied Europe, with 96 percent of the Jewish population—those who had not fled immediately after the invasion—murdered.[42] Hitler even "cited [this] as an example of how inciting local populations was a most effective way to achieve Nazi goals."[43]

The Maciunas family could hardly have avoided witnessing effects of this genocide. The art historian Giedrė Jankevičiūtė argues that genocide-inciting images of "Bolshevik terror" permeated the propagandistic press in Lithuania so thoroughly in 1941 that children would readily have been exposed to this graphic violence, alongside "rumors about the mass killing of Jews" if not actual killings.[44] Firsthand German accounts describe children as spectators to brutal street killings in the city of Kaunas. In one particularly notorious episode at the Lietūkis Garage on Vytautas Boulevard, a sixteen-year-old Lithuanian murdered dozens of Jewish men: "After every blow of the iron bar, [the crowd] applauded and when the murderer began to play the Lithuanian anthem, they began to sing it to the accompaniment of the accordion. In the front row of the crowd, there

were women with children in their arms, watching all that was happening."[45] The historian Robert van Voren shows that only a "very small minority" of the Lithuanian population directly participated in the exter-
mination of their Jewish neighbors, yet "the largest contribution to the
massacre was . . . an indifferent population and, most importantly, a com-
pliant bureaucracy. From the Provisional Government in Kaunas all the
way down to local mayors and police officers, all looked the other way,
fulfilled orders and did what they were asked to do."[46]

Recalling this period of the war, Leokadija remembered that "all of a
sudden without rhyme or reason [young Jurgis/George] started to make
faces; he blinked his eyes and tightly shut his eyelids. During this time
his face and especially his mouth changed his expression [into a constant
grimace]." Within her otherwise detailed account of her son's childhood,
Leokadija referred to this period of German occupation only with this
suggestive image of her son's changing facial expression, which she associated with his "nerves," his "so-so" performance in school, and his "feeling
of not being fully valued or that he was worse than others."[47] Such words
may indicate the everyday problems of any child, or they may camouflage
(and betray) a response to violence: feeling "worse than others" could
even be a response to the Soviet ideologies of class difference that threatened bourgeois families like the Maciunases, or to the Nazi ideologies of
racial difference that likewise turned Lithuanians into victims and perpetrators, inserting them into a racial hierarchy below Aryans but above
Jews. "I lightly massaged his forehead daily according to the doctor's advice," Leokadija wrote. "It gradually got better and the boy stopped gri-
macing. Then the Soviet Army was getting nearer and we had to flee." The
family practiced economy of means: "Travelling lightly we took only the
most necessary so that we could carry our bags ourselves if we had to."[48]

When the Maciunas family escaped to Germany in 1944, they resettled
near Frankfurt in Bad Nauheim, a spa town that had been repurposed as
a massive wartime infirmary. They chose this site, within commuting distance of Frankfurt, because young Jurgis/George had long suffered from
severe asthma and a heightened susceptibility to infections. In Williams's
account, Maciunas's linguistic and national identity began to split when
he entered the violence of the Nazi educational system: "George—or Yurgis—or Jürgen Matschunas, as his name was Deutschified for the record
books—and his sister Nijole were enrolled in the Ernst-Ludwig Schule
(today the Ernst-Ludwig Gymnasium) in Bad Nauheim for the duration
of the war."[49] As Thomas Kellein writes (drawing from a conversation with
Nijole Valaitis), "When they did not stand up instantly at the beginning
of a lesson and cry, "Heil Hitler!" like their classmates, they were smacked

on their fingers with a ruler."[50] Leokadija recalled a telling scene of severe schoolyard bullying:

> Once at school one of the vulgar boys argued with Yurgis and hit him with his fist. Yurgis, seeing the unjust fist in his face, covered his face with his hand, and the other hitting hand, broke his hand. Nijole (his sister and my daughter) brought him home after they had helped him first at school. She was indignant at the vulgarity and the impudence of ignorant German children. Not one of them knew that Lithuania bordered Germany. They all hated foreigners.[51]

This anecdote speaks to the top-down objectives of the Nazi educational system: to indoctrinate pupils within its system of racial hierarchy and, especially among boys, to strengthen "the will to fight" and "to prepare for killing as well as for dying."[52] At school, both Nijole and Yurgis Maciunas would have been exposed to a genocidal cult of masculinity that equated German "men of steel" with hardness, self-denial, sadism, and death, as described by Klaus Theweleit—an image to which we will return as a foil for Fluxus's own imagery.[53] This state-disseminated ideology, which eroticized violence, could not permeate every classroom uniformly.[54] Under cover of secrecy, family units also provided potential shelter from or contestation of this ideological system,[55] exemplified in Leokadija and Nijole's tone of aristocratic affront at German ignorance.

Faced with debilitating stresses at school, Jurgis/George entered into a greater closeness with his father by assuming professional activities as his informal apprentice—a situation of protective enclosure within family, in Said's terms. Paraphrasing conversations with Nijole Valaitis, Thomas Kellein explains, "Each day after school, George would help his father at work, for which he was rewarded with a hot meal."[56] Frankfurt-Höchst was the site of a massive IG Farben complex where Siemens technical employees performed contract work. Given his technical background, Alexander Maciunas would have been well suited to maintaining or expanding the electrical plan of the complex; but the precise nature of this work remains obscure because the archival record is "remarkably poor."[57] Still, the general working conditions at Höchst are well known. Like other German-controlled industrial sites during the war, Höchst exploited forced laborers, including foreign nationals from occupied territories, Jews, Roma, Sinti, and prisoners of war. Approximately two-thirds of IG Farben's investments had become militarized by 1944, focusing on materials needed for the production of munitions like explosives, synthetic rubber, and poison gas.[58] One of the largest departments at Höchst was pharmaceuticals, which developed drugs tested on human subjects deliberately infected with typhus in Buchenwald, Auschwitz, and Gusen/Mauthausen—a crime that was unsuccessfully prosecuted at the Nuremberg Trials.[59] The Höchst complex survived the war with remarkably little damage, despite the constant threat from Allied bombing raids.[60]

During these war years, IG Farben's corporate culture had descended into paranoia, social disconnection, and abysmal moral incapacity. Managers and employees at the firm kept one another in the dark about their activities. An IG Farben executive named Georg von Schnitzler recalled, "A survey of what IG really did make or not make for the Wehrmacht became more and more pure guesswork, and one abstained from asking in order not to put one's technical colleagues in a difficult position."[61] The Nazi regime required the company to conceal many of its activities, just as the company sought in many cases to conceal its activities from the state.[62] According to the historian Peter Hayes, this dynamic produced a corporate culture not only of obfuscation but also of atomization among managers and technical specialists. In her canonical work *The Origins of Totalitarianism*, Hannah Arendt identifies social atomization as a characteristic outcome of totalitarian terror when the bonds of ordinary human interaction dissolve in paranoia—a process that also breaks down any sense of shared reality and responsibility.[63] Similarly, Hayes writes that the "professionalism" of the men who ran IG Farben worked as an apologia for moral cowardice:

> Their sense of professional duty encouraged them to regard every issue principally in terms of their special competences and responsibilities, in this case to their fields and stockholders. In obeying this mandate, they relieved themselves of the obligation to make moral or social judgments or to examine the overall consequences of their decisions. . . . The professional spirit, with its glorification of partial, even tunnel vision, helped Farben's leaders to evade these difficulties.[64]

Hayes's study of IG Farben's corporate culture pinpoints how the personae of its business and technical leadership transformed in response to their totalitarian settings, shaping mind, body, and soul, in Daston and Sibum's sense. Though we cannot know exactly how this corporate culture shaped Alexander Maciunas, we do know that the focus on technical proficiency at the expense of moral, social, or political questioning would have been a requirement for any employee in the workplace. At the same time, Alexander could not have demonstrated loyalty to the regime by joining the Nazi party, as it prohibited membership of foreign-born noncitizens such as himself.[65]

The nature of Jurgis/George's apprenticeship with his father would have differed according to whether they were in the workplace or at home. According to Nijole, as Kellein writes, "at the age of thirteen, [George, assisted by his father] started building an exact balsa-wood model of their country house in Kulautuva."[66] Leokadija, by contrast, remembered that her son had built such a model of their Lithuanian dacha soon after they immigrated to New York in 1948: "All the measurements were precise according to the directions of his father, my husband."[67] The model dacha— one of his first work products— retained a heightened significance for Jurgis/George. Regardless of whether the model was built in Germany, the United States, or both, this adolescent project registers the survival techniques his family required for daily living. It would appear obvious that the Maciunases' lives depended upon various practices of translation, understood in the narrow linguistic sense. (While Alexander had already spoken fluent German from the time of his student days, Leokadija and her children studied the language at home in Bad Nauheim, while generally speaking Lithuanian among themselves.)[68] Yet translation also signifies more broadly in its etymological sense of "carrying across": it refers to modes of historical continuance that depend upon cultural crossings and their unpredictable play of difference. Like the Maciunas family, the dacha—as an idea—*moved across* geography and time to enter radically new surroundings. As a material object and miniature, it was easy to handle, comprehend, and carry—and perhaps even traveled from Germany to the United States as a cherished object under a constant state of refinement and elaboration. It materialized memory, and in doing so, it transformed the "original" that it translated. For the family, it provided a tangible bridge to a lost home and sense of security.

It also testified to the technical skills of the father as they were being passed on to the son; indeed, it testified to these skills as *dedicated to family life rather than to occupying powers*—a slippery line of demarcation. If, as Nijole Valaitis had it, Yurgis began to construct the model in Germany, then the balsa wood—a valuable import—likely would have been pilfered or scavenged, perhaps even from Alexander's workplace. Such activity would have bordered on sabotage, both by redirecting material resources away from the war effort and by countering the ideology of German racial supremacy through the construction of a Lithuanian cultural symbol with those very redirected resources. (In a similar spirit of covert resourcefulness, Nijole recalled that Yurgis developed skills as an electrician, "repair[ing] broken radios that his father had brought home.")[69] Whether it was built in Germany or New York, the model dacha epitomizes the spirit of pride that Leokadija, ventriloquizing Nijole, projected in her words about the "ignorant" Germans with their hatred of foreigners, the kind of words she would presumably have hidden within the shelter of their family circle and the Lithuanian language (like the dacha). The model also evokes the erasures necessary for the family's psychic and existential survival—the forgetting necessary for Leokadija's later pronouncement that her family had always lived "carefully, happily, pleasantly," and that her husband had "never bowed to anyone."[70]

During the immediate postwar period, when Alexander once more adapted to new occupying forces by working for the US military, the Maciunases had the opportunity to immerse themselves more openly in their Lithuanian heritage at their new makeshift home in the Displaced Person's Camp in Hanau, which abounded in arts activities organized by refugees eager for ethnic self-assertion and community.[71] Within this setting, Jurgis/George rediscovered his passion for classical music, organizing a musical quiz show. The project signaled an about-face for the teenager, who had previously renounced piano during wartime with the dictum that "music was for women rather than men."[72] The format of the quiz show would have been an ideal medium for spontaneous interaction and humor, the very space of human bonding that the paranoia of Nazi governance had largely precluded.

After the Maciunases' charity-supported immigration to the United States in 1948, Alexander quickly found employment in the private sector while also teaching at City College of New York. He founded the Association of Lithuanian Engineers and Architects in Exile and served as its first president (1949–54).[73] Like other national professional associations, this organization sought to foster Lithuanian identity-based camaraderie, which would have been impossible under totalitarianism. The organization asserted a kind of dual symbolic citizenship: it advertised the social respectability and economic usefulness of an immigrant group in the United States while also setting its sights on Lithuania as an imagined site of return. In reasserting his Lithuanian identity, Alexander's professional association ventured into a new beginning apart from the ethical distortions of working under successive genocidal regimes. Yet these new foundations in exile also depended on strategic "forgetting" that had long become a fact of life, reinforced by corporate cultures like those at IG Farben. In 1959, the *Lithuanian Encyclopedia*—a massive, thirty-five-volume national-exilic project organized in Boston—published an article on Alexander Maciunas that stressed his Lithuanian nationalist political orientation while omitting any reference of his work for the Nazis.[74] The fact that Alexander had worked at Siemens and likely IG Farben during the war—corporate leaders in the Aryanization of German industry and the use of slave labor in the service of munitions and genocide—was unmentionable. The difficulty of such "remembering" in the postwar period, according to Arendt, remained a powerful legacy of Nazism's systems of organized lying, which destroyed subjects' ability to distinguish facts and take responsibility for reality.[75]

In the face of this challenge, Jurgis/George (who now spelled his name "Yurgis" in English) appears in college to have immersed himself in a fact-oriented study of historical violence. Indeed, Leokadija attributed her son's failure to pursue a stable and respectable career to his eccentric attraction to academic pursuits, exemplified by his masterwork, *Atlas of Russian History* (1953), which he completed at University of Pittsburgh and valued as a major achievement throughout his life.[76] The *Atlas* shows how Maciunas's refusal to follow in his father's footsteps amounted to a selective but powerful attention to historical facts. Responding to a course he had taken on Russian history—a staple of the Cold War curriculum—the *Atlas* reached far beyond that course's purview: it initiated Maciunas's lifelong pursuit of "pictorial methods to systematize knowledge" with efficiency, "to learn by taking in as much information as possible at a glance."[77] (Maciunas also supplemented his *Atlas* with two charts, *Chronology of Russian History: 867–1950* and *Chronology of Russian History: 1917–1934*.) Like Maciunas's model dacha, the *Atlas of Russian History* created a tangible bridge to the geography and events of his family's past. Unlike the dacha, the atlas was meant to produce knowledge about power, violence, and political geography. The first of many such "learning machines," the *Atlas* consisted of thirty-seven superimposed translucent pages inscribed with pen-drawn maps, which outlined important geopolitical events, military incursions, and movements of populations in Russian history from 700 BCE to the late nineteenth century. Its layered structure compensated for discontinuities of historical experience. Its efficiency of design may have responded to Maciunas's anxiety that there would never be enough time for the immensity of study that living required.[78]

Schmidt-Burckhardt provocatively describes the *Atlas* and its associated charts in the terms of Claude Lévi-Strauss's "small-scale model": it involves a "quantitative transposition [that] extends and diversifies our power over a homologue of the thing, and by means of it the latter can be grasped, assessed and apprehended at a glance."[79] I would add that the violence of this "thing"—Russian imperial history—may render miniaturization all the more necessary as a way to master and take hold of it. The physical presentation of the *Atlas*—with its covering of delicate, inscribed leaves of paper—brings to mind Walter Benjamin's exilic words about the nineteenth-century European craze for encasing miniature objects in the bourgeois home, which produced a sense of dwelling and protection against the violent contingencies of modernity: "pocket watches, slippers, egg cups, thermometers, playing cards—and in lieu of cases, there were jackets, carpets, wrappers, and covers."[80] Within Maciunas's oeuvre, the *Atlas* stands out within a whole world of encased miniatures that similarly created a sense of itinerant dwelling in the same stroke as producing knowledge. These included not only his later Fluxkits, but also intricately detailed filing systems that organized information on all manner of topics, such as his studies at New York University on European and Asian arts, crafts, and architecture in migration.[81]

Following Schmidt-Burckhardt, we should understand systems like the *Atlas* as generating new understandings of subjects like migration and empire. Yet we should also recognize these technologies as tools *of* empire, the very means through which imperial administrations operate and generate power. As a response to the US Cold War classroom—indeed, as a tool that mimics epistemic models that have historically served American power—the *Atlas* figures its own relationship to power ambiguously, suggesting ethical and political dilemmas. It is unclear, for example, whether Maciunas sees Russia in the *Atlas* as a land of ancestry to be regarded with pride or with horror. The same could be said of the US educational system that provided Maciunas with the classroom tools and ways of knowing that made the *Atlas* possible. While the *Atlas* tells a history of violence, it also depersonalizes that violence. By conveying a continuous succession of military conquests and population movements, moreover, it risks portraying violence and volatility as the "primordial character" of a people, nation, or region as a legacy without beginning or end—a move that potentially reinforces Cold War Russophobic prejudices.[82] The historiography of the *Atlas* stops short of narrating the Russian Revolution and genocidal events of the "bloodlands" in the twentieth century, while nonetheless gesturing toward it via a prehistory of conflict. In doing so, it minimizes Maciunas's personal encounter with state violence to a mere ripple in an endless stream, articulating a pessimistic vision of the future. Macuinas's cultural entrepreneurship of the early 1960s can be seen as providing an outlet to mitigate the bleakness of such a picture while continuing to experiment with new modes of remembrance and forgetting.

Lithuanian Beat Bohemia

The founding of Fluxus can be told as a story of young, exiled Lithuanian-Americans coming of age in the politically engaged bohemia of late beat-era New York City. It was in this setting that Maciunas sought to consolidate a new hybrid persona as impresario, knowledge worker, cultural and political agitator, and mediator of transnational art communities. To emphasize the Lithuanian refugee side of the Fluxus story is to accentuate one facet of the "assemblages of relation" among histories of trauma that Fluxus partially remembers. Maciunas's friendship with Jonas Mekas is decisive here. A Lithuanian-American writer and budding filmmaker nine years Maciunas's senior, Mekas had spent the last year of the war working as a forced laborer in Hamburg after he fled Lithuania. The Holocaust scholar Michael Casper has recently disclosed that, prior to his confinement, Mekas had spent three years writing for Lithuanian nationalist publications that advocated pro-Nazi, anticommunist positions—a fact that highlights the dilemmas of complicity that have haunted Mekas's own work.[83]

After graduate studies in Germany and immigration to the United States, Mekas met Maciunas through Nijole, who described Maciunas as "her crazy brother."[84] Together with the gallery owner Almus Salcius, Maciunas and Mekas eventually engaged in a kind of left-wing rebellion against the powerful anticommunist politics of the Lithuanian-American community in which they had first found their footing as new immigrants in the United States. Their rebellion spurred them in the late 1950s and 1960s to depart from Lithuanian-American enclaves into a wider world of avant-garde arts entrepreneurship in Manhattan and beyond. Yet their rebellion could never fully "move beyond" their Lithuanian past. More specifically, it took the form of a peculiar poetics of memory—simultaneously vague and accusatory—that responded to the moral and political obfuscations of the "bloodlands" without finding itself capable of fully naming or analyzing traumas of victimhood and perpetration. This indistinct but intense poetics of memory found voice in such a question posed by Mekas in his Lithuanian journal entry: "Isn't a not-small part of the curse and guilt of what you did also on me?"[85]

A similarly evocative but ambiguous memorial poetics of genocide finds expression in Maciunas's naming of Fluxus—a term that describes a purging tide. As numerous firsthand accounts recall, Maciunas coined the name at a 1960 meeting of young Lithuanians in New York, where he floated *Fluxus*—with its connotations of "flushing," "flowing," and "bodily

discharge"—as the name for a possible group publication.[86] The far left–
leaning group, which included Mekas and Salcius, apparently infuriated
the anticommunist Lithuanian Society, which had initially agreed to host
their meetings and had provided Maciunas with the IBM Executive typewriter that would provide the signature font of his subsequent career and
persona.[87] (Maciunas would have had an entrée with the Lithuanian Society, which his father had helped to lead before his death in 1954.)[88] Under the umbrella of the Lithuanian American Council, the primary political goal of most Lithuanian-American organizations of the period was to
rally support for an independent Lithuania—a goal that also led organizations to take a hard line against diplomacy with the Soviet Union, even
protesting against Eisenhower's 1958 invitation to Khrushchev to visit the
United States.[89] According to Leokadija, when Lithuanian Society board
members got wind of the leftist orientation of Maciunas and his friends,
they banned the group from their auditorium space. "To them, who had
fled from the communists, it seemed blasphemous," she remembered.[90]

Despite the inchoate nature of the significance of the term "Fluxus" to
Maciunas and his Lithuanian-American friends in 1960—it was, after all,
only *proposed* as a title for a *possible* periodical—its charge nonetheless
proved so powerful that both "a dutiful Soviet apparatchik" and a CIA officer reportedly contacted Mekas about the group's activities.[91] Maciunas's
FBI file shows that the New York office conducted a six-month investigation of the incident, interviewing numerous members of the Lithuanian-
American community who suspected that the emerging magazine was
being funded by the Soviet Union.[92] When the FBI finally interviewed
Maciunas himself, the artist put the officers at ease by stating that he and
his collaborators "could not agree on many items connected with publish-
ing this magazine[;] he had lost interest and as far as he know the magazine will never be published. . . . He stated that he does not know any Soviet Nationals and has never been in contact with any Soviet nationals."[93]

To appreciate the full nature of the explosive charge of "Fluxus" as a
name, we should consider not just its evocation of revolutionary leftist
politics, but also how it scrambles ideas of nation, gender, and sexuality
through its image of amalgamation and lack of purity. Leokadija recalled
the Lithuanian Society's ban as having infuriated her son so thoroughly
that he switched his name entirely from Yurgis to George—a move she
saw as signaling his separation from the Lithuanian-American community more generally.[94] During this period, Maciunas also distanced himself from a United States–based national identity, consistently referring
to "Americans" as a group apart from himself in his correspondence—a
distinction also reflected in his "foreignized" English that persistently re-

fused the grammatical use of articles.[95] (Ideals of "anationality" would emerge as central to his cultural platforms for years to come.) As I have already suggested, the imagery of the term "Fluxus" holds weight as a powerful counterpart to the racist, nationalist cult of masculinity Maciunas had endured in Nazi-occupied Lithuania and Germany. Klaus Theweleit's classic analysis of German fascism describes its "emotional core" as a revulsion against women that intersected with racism, xenophobia, and paranoia over the "Red Flood" of communism. He locates this revulsion in popular fascist images that valorized hard bodies while expressing horror at the "dirty" bodily liquids that destabilize their boundaries.[96] Maciunas's terror at this masculinist cult may partly have inspired the image of "Fluxus"—a "morbid or excessive discharge" associated with nausea, diarrhea, or fear—while evoking solidarity with revolutionary left-wing politics in a language of Duchampian iconoclasm. ("Like toilet flushing!" as he put it to Ono.)[97] In New York City, Maciunas's new ideas sought "a public that was the new youth, overgrown with hair and slovenly dressed," according to Leokadija, who consistently expressed a mixture of pride, amusement, and alarm at her son's activities.[98]

If the idea of Lithuania as a homeland—complete with the shelter of the family and its personae—had once provided a stabilizing point of reference, then the very name "Fluxus" represented an unmooring from those fixities. Although the Lithuanian-American exile community aimed to restore Lithuanian national independence in the name of democracy, members of the Lithuanian exile community had contributed directly or indirectly to the Nazi assault on democracy and to genocide. This central paradox destabilizes all manner of sacred boundaries: between victim and perpetrator, native and foreign, occupier and occupied, Lithuanian and Nazi, democracy and totalitarianism, capitalist enterprise and state domination, patriotism and terror, new world and old world. In the midst of these ambiguities, a trail of strategic forgetting and obfuscation—moving from the East European bloodlands to postwar America—appears to have provoked a spirit of rebellion in Maciunas and his friends. The generalized intensity of their rebellion was like hurling an accusation that could not fully name its target. Immersing themselves in Greenwich Village counterculture, Maciunas and his friends hit their elders where it hurt by refusing to be "good immigrant" citizens in the United States, eschewing a particular persona of political benignity, social respectability, and economic usefulness. In doing so, they sought new ways of being, acting, and knowing. In the early 1960s this search touched on questions of complicity in acts of intensified aesthetic utterance that usually fell short of explicitly naming Jewish victims or Lithuanian perpetrators.[99]

Maciunas's performance in Mekas's first feature-length film, *Guns of the Trees* (shot in 1960 and released in 1962), provides insight into how a "perpetual interwar" phenomenology of the Lithuanian bloodlands intersected with Greenwich Village's radical dropout culture, with its persistent critique of US nationalism and imperialism via the antiwar and civil rights movements.[100] The film evokes "assemblages of relation" with regard to histories of violence, an evocation that begins with a gesture of displacement: the film never names Lithuania, but rather focuses on racial violence in the United States as a scene of continuous violence akin to "perpetual interwar."[101] It was with *Guns of the Trees* that Mekas established his signature memoiristic style of cinema, which expanded upon the extensive practice of journal-keeping he had maintained as a mode of testimony and survival while subjected to forced labor.[102] Mekas has described the film as a series of improvised sketches. A nearly continuous voiceover characterizes the film's impressionistic narrative,[103] which meditates upon state terror and the responsibilities of a younger generation via the lives of two young couples, one white and the other interracial. The question of national violence—internal and external—emerges in the film's insistent juxtaposition of images of antiwar and civil rights protest, police brutality, military armaments, and a modernizing New York City infrastructure that separates the poor from the rich. When one of the white characters chooses to commit suicide, the voiceover articulates a complaint reminiscent of Snyder's discussion of the hazards of double occupation in Lithuania: "Tell me, do I have a choice? My only choice is between one corruption and another, between one lie and another, between one pretension and another." The film's imagery and voiceover repeatedly highlight relations between internal and external modes of subjugation within empire. They showcase racialized inequalities of citizenship enforced by mob violence and militarized police, alongside subjects' unequal stakes within an ownership culture of global capitalist enterprise bound up with the hard-power footprint of the United States in the Cold War.

Maciunas, playing himself, enters the film at a key moment of impasse for the interracial couple, played by Argus Spear Juillard and Ben Carruthers, as they confront a crucial dilemma: They must provide for their coming child, yet they find a complacent life of "normality" in the pursuit of white-collar careers morally untenable. Lucia Dlugoszewski's jarring soundtrack—consisting of loud and sustained, dissonant, high-pitched woodwind tones—hinges together a static medium shot of the Black mother-to-be in a visual rhyme with another medium shot of Maciunas. The camera frames the seated Juillard leaning back in a chair, her eyes looking upward in apparent anxiety, adjacent to a teacup and a blown-up photo of her suicidal friend resting on a table. The next shot observes Maciunas from behind, leaning over his desk littered with open books, and then pans across his meticulously arranged modular shelving unit—with its clean display of vertical files, audio equipment, and Renaissance musical instruments and woodblock prints—to arrive at the image of a medium-complected man standing awkwardly in the doorway. This man is the father-to-be, played by Carruthers; he appears in a checked, double-breasted suit that contrasts with the beatnik style of his earlier appearances in the film. When Maciunas fails to notice him knocking at the door, the father-to-be addresses "Mr. Maciunas" by name, stumbling over its foreign pronunciation to ask if he would be interested in buying life insurance. Maciunas, delivering the scripted lines written for him by Mekas,[104] swivels around to riposte in a deliberate, Lithuanian-accented English: "Don't we believe in death anymore?" The father-to-be smiles sheepishly as Maciunas begins to show him items from his shelves. As their voices fade out in the audio mix, we hear a voiceover of Allen Ginsberg reciting his poem "Death to Van Gogh's Ear." The film then cuts to a close-up of the father-to-be pensively watching young children playing in the park, set against Ginsberg's resounding words: "petroleum mongers in Texas—jet planes streak among the clouds— / sky writers liars in the face of Divinity—fanged butchers of hats and shoes, all Owners! Owners! Owners! with obsession on property and vanished Selfhood! / and their long editorials on the fence of the screaming negro attacked by ants crawled out of the front page! / Machinery of a mass electrical dream! A war-creating Whore of Babylon bellowing over Capitols and Academies!" The film flashes back to a scene of Maciunas, pale and pucklike, demonstrating to Carruthers how to play the krummhorn, as though refusing the present and its social order through absurd and anachronistic performance practices.

Maciunas's cameo in Mekas's film commemorates his own break with a white-collar, straight male persona, a break that arrived most definitively in 1960, the year of the movie's filming. As such, the scene unfolds as a kind of commentary by Mekas on the fragmentation of Maciunas's life trajectory. According to Leokadija, George was expected to—and tried to—fill his father's shoes as breadwinner and head of the family when Alexander died unexpectedly in 1954, leaving the family with no savings. But Maciunas had strayed from this path, toward an eccentric lifestyle immersed in the arts and the study of the past, while making ends meet by working off and on as an architect, designer, and draftsman.[105] After his sister Nijole had married an architect, George resisted his mother's suggestion that he marry a ballerina (like her) to complete the intergenerational symmetry: he "was able to be completely absorbed in his work" and "[w]omen didn't interest him."[106] According to Leokadija, he responded to her concern by citing "the example of monks" in their pursuit of scholarly studies to justify his unconventional lifestyle: "the most learned people were there [in monasteries], and he wanted to know more."[107] Some of Maciunas's friends referred to his queerness as "asexuality," because it included an apparent aversion to sexual and romantic relationships.[108] But his defiance of gender norms also included cross-dressing, which became semipublic with his 1966 self-portraits in drag and then routine in his late-life partnership with Billie Hutching, culminating in their famous drag wedding ceremony a month before Maciunas's death in 1978.[109]

Keeping in mind the complex conditions and character of Maciunas's queerness, it is nonetheless difficult to separate his gender identity from the violent cult of masculinity to which he had been exposed in childhood. Indeed, *not* growing up to become a "man" under the moral and political terms of Nazism arguably constitutes a survival technique in itself. Playing the comically phallic krummhorn in Mekas's film (with music figured as a "feminine" pursuit) can be understood as precisely such a refusal. In 1952, the Selective Service System made the following judgment of Maciunas: "After an interview with a service psychiatrist the subject was classified as 4-F because of psychopathic reasons, to wit his actions, manner and appearance indicated that he was not fit for armed forces service. Also that from his appearance it seemed that he *might* be a drug addict."[110] Although the conjecture about drugs was in all likelihood wrong, the overall pronouncement ("unfit for service") seems to fit.

Of course, Maicunas's voicing of Mekas's ironic question, "Don't we believe in death anymore?" works as a provocation to know the past and present. The question emerges from the space of their friendship—from the negotiations between a "privileged," villa-dwelling, former child apprentice at Siemens, who had benefited from his father's collaboration, and the former young adult slave laborer, who himself had collaborated with Nazism as a Lithuanian nationalist propagandist before his dispossession and enslavement. The question can be understood to interrogate the past from a standpoint of complicity, uncomfortably conjuring a time when we *did* believe in death, to the point of eradicating millions. (This question could be asked, for example, of the families in the Lithuanian Society.) It may also target the denial of violence, as though asking, "Don't we believe that this death happened, or that death is still happening? Why do we not believe this?" (These questions could be asked of anyone, including New Yorkers living at the epicenter of American empire.) It may also express yearning for a long-ago time when a theology premised on fear of death would have inspired moral behavior, in keeping with Maciunas's emulation of monks—a persona also prominently featured in Mekas's film—and with Ono's fascination with medieval ritual. This yearning seeks an alternative to the corrupt present. In the musicologist Kirsten Yri's terms, it articulates a nostalgia for "the Middle Ages . . . as a utopian Other," its music a "people's music" inspiring "a critique between the elitist division between 'fine arts' and crafts.'"[111]

Following a long tradition of leftist thought, Maciunas sought alternative forms of community in music making outside the "elite" common-practice-period concert hall or the "commercial" world of mass-produced sounds. In 1960, before moving to Wiesbaden, he even went so far as to manage a twelve-person early music ensemble for several months. He was, as he put it, "interested in musical polichrony, or color in music," and this led him not only to explore early music, but also to lean toward "electronic music and [the] music of John Cage," having first become attracted to a performance of prepared piano at the Carnegie Institute of Technology.[112] He was drawn to heterogeneous timbres because they speak to the sounds' conditions of production, and therefore to material history.[113] In 1960 Maciunas enrolled in Richard Maxfield's composition course at the New School, which Maxfield had taken over from John Cage and subsequently devoted exclusively to electronic composition—the first such course taught in the United States. It was there that Maciunas met La Monte Young, who invited him to the performance series Young was cocurating at Yoko Ono's Loft.

Equipped with a newfound circle of acquaintances, Maciunas established the institutional space in which his new persona was formed: the AG Gallery on Madison Avenue. Maciunas founded the gallery together with Almus Salcius after the Lithuanian Society debacle in the winter of 1960–61. Inspired by Ono and Young's Loft Series, the gallery operated in an art deco storefront on the Upper East Side from approximately December 1960 until its final show, *Paintings & Drawings by Yoko Ono*, in August 1961.[114] As Maciunas himself later explained, "This whole idea of the series [at Ono's loft] gave me sort of an idea to imitate it and make it [an] even more extensive series at our new gallery."[115] Many dimensions of Maciunas's AG Gallery deserve attention—from its experimental, early music, and electronic music programming to its poetry and film series to its sparse interior design to its meticulously designed brochures. I will focus here on Maciunas's collaboration with Yoko Ono, to show how his rebellious politics of memory found amplification in her own. Their politics—which turned the inward shame of violence outward—tentatively reconfigured the terms "public" and "private" in a way that

Michael Warner has described as characteristic of 1960s countercultures and counterpublics more generally.[116] Ono and Maciunas's collaboration helped them not only to launch their careers but to fashion for themselves new personae as ways of being in, acting in, and knowing the world.

Speaking of Maciunas in 1961, Ono recalled him as "very political": "I was also very political, so we got on very, very well."[117] To be sure, their politics included shared leftist, anticonsumerist, anti-imperialist commitments. But their connection also inhered more specifically in a politics of memory concerning mass death and complicity with Axis power in Frankfurt and Tokyo. Both channeled unwieldy and intimate sentiments into confrontational, ironic modes of public address. In chapter 4 we saw the passage of Ono's creative work from "private" to "public" via her collaborations with Maciunas, including the Carnegie Recital Hall performance of her opera *AOS—To David Tudor*. This major early work dealt with the "blue chaos of war" from the perspective of Ono's own refugee experience after the Tokyo firebombings. Ono is one creator who would have been profoundly attentive to the multilayered irony of Mekas's and Maciunas's question, "Don't we believe in death anymore?" The public voicing of that question, which intimates the most shameful aspects of personal history, enacts a politics of memory that calls out for counterpublics, in Warner's sense, which are "structured by alternative dispositions or protocols, making different assumptions about what can be said and what goes without saying."[118]

Ono has consistently described her creative practice as a means "to survive," a practice that originated in her experiences as a wartime refugee. Many "techniques of survival" that thread through my discussion of Maciunas's history appear to have been prominently thematized in Ono's AG Gallery show, perhaps reinforcing their place within Maciuans's emerging vision of the organization that would become Fluxus. There is, for example, Ono's *A + B Painting*, which stands out for its articulation of a logic of translation (figure 5.1). The work responds to the following instructions:

> Cut out a circle on canvas A. Place a
> numeral figure, a roman letter, or a
> katakana on canvas B on an arbitrary
> point. Place canvas A on canvas B and hang
> them together. The figure on canvas B may show, may show
> partially, or may not show.
> You may use old paintings, photographs, etc.
> Instead of blank canvases.[119]

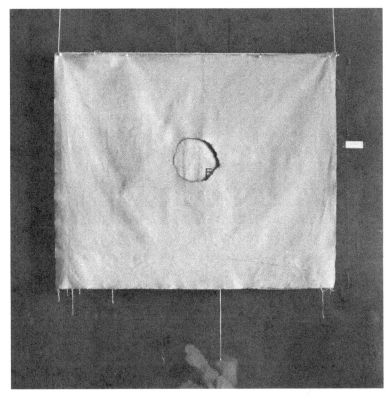

FIGURE 5.1. *A Plus B Painting* (1961) from *Paintings & Drawings by Yoko Ono*, AG Gallery, New York, July 17–30, 1961. Photograph by George Maciunas, 1961. Gelatin silver print. Image 15½ × 15½ in. (39.3 × 39.4 cm). Sheet 19¹³⁄₁₆ × 15⅞ in. (50.3 × 40.4 cm). Gilbert and Lila Silverman Fluxus Collection Gift, Museum of Modern Art, New York, 3203.2008.7. Digital image © The Museum of Modern Art / Licensed by SCALA / Art Resource, NY. By permission of Billie J. Maciunas.

Ono marked "canvas B" with a graphic referent, which then became obscured, framed, or modified by the layering of "canvas A." *A + B Painting* shows how a new frame recontextualizes a preexisting sign, just as, for example, the downtown avant-garde scene framed and brought new meaning to a Japanese ritual to ward off *oni* in Ono's *Pea Piece*; or as the totalitarian setting of 1944 Germany reframed the value of a Lithuanian dacha in memory; or as a past in wartime Tokyo or Frankfurt acquires new significance—and becomes partly occluded—in the Cold War metropolis of New York. *A + B Painting* showcases a logic of translation that would prove vital to Ono's and Maciunas's poetics in its many disparate incarnations. Ono envisioned her "instruction pieces" as incomplete works to be carried forward by audience members, as though being moved from one source language into another, or from one history into another.[120] Following an ethos that stressed concept and process over art object, Ono did not preserve her artworks after the gallery closed. But Maciunas carefully stored the photos he had taken of most of the works, having translated them into a new medium for future rediscovery in the early 1990s.[121] While Ono's instruction pieces at AG Gallery have garnered considerable critical attention, we should also consider the other component of the exhibit: calligraphic pieces that Ono and Maciunas deemed with irony to be "salable" because they "reinforced the natural association of Ono with Japan and more importantly with Zen Buddhism, much in vogue within the American avant-garde."[122] These works may arguably be understood as parodying the popular market for Orientalia. The disjunction between a sophisticated conceptualization of cultural translation like *A + B Painting* on the one hand, and crude Orientalist appropriations on the other, is stark. This disjunction indicates an important register of the exhibit's conceptual play, which dealt with questions of cultural appropriation and translation within global capitalism.

The game of Orientalist parody in Ono's exhibit at AG Gallery linked up with other "capitalist" performances in the space. Maciunas regularly talked up his businesses' capacity for profit, embracing an exaggerated, almost manic discourse about moneymaking.[123] As though haunted by Siemens AG, he even joked that the name of AG Gallery had a meaning "that could be read in many ways: "'A' could stand for Almus and 'G' for George, that's our first names. Or it could mean for Avant Garde. Or it could mean for *Akzien Gesellschaft*, which is in German Stock Company."[124] The gallery's financial fortunes hinged on two import businesses Maciunas had started—one dealing in replica antique instruments from East Germany, and the other in canned gourmet foods from the Soviet Union and France. According to Maciunas's FBI file, these businesses had been in operation at least since September 1955. (The FBI first investigated Maciunas on the basis of an informant who found his business activities suspicious, but no evidence for concern was found.)[125] As Ono remembered, "George had a closet full of very expensive canned goods. . . . That was our meal every day: canned foie gras. It wasn't bad."[126] "I fervently helped him," Leokadija recalled, "spending hours over hundreds of letters [advertising fish from the Soviet Union and pâté de foie gras from France] which distributed all over America."[127] No matter that the businesses failed; they helped to solidify imaginative links to the lands Maciunas fantasized of returning to.

Having incurred insurmountable debts in these joint ventures, Maciunas signed up for work with the US Air Force and prepared to move to Wiesbaden with his mother the subsequent winter. As he put it to La Monte Young, "Too many [creditors] knew where to find me and it was unsafe to stay any longer. Now I get a big kick when I hear these nice looking scrubbed and polished officials getting all smeared while looking for me in various basements and lofts. . . . I consider myself lucky having had a passport and visa ready for such emergency."[128] Playing the refugee and criminal, Maciunas had "rapidly liquidated" most of his things to escape once more to Germany, rehearsing a form of flight and erasure that also remembered.[129]

Remigration as Sabotage in Wiesbaden

Fluxus was born of many disparate stories, just as it brought forth many in turn. As Owen Smith and Hannah Higgins remind us, the flamboyant, event-based ethos we now associate with Fluxus mediated elements from the 1950s downtown New York scene with the experimental performance circles cultivated by Mary Bauermeister in Cologne and intermedial performance art movements in Tokyo and elsewhere.[130] When Maciunas founded Fluxus in Wiesbaden, he brought these local scenes further into communication through publications, correspondence, and festivals. As I have suggested, early Fluxus emerges here not so much as an affirmative story about "liberating experience," but as an extended and troubled working-through of traumas of state violence, which varies in the explicitness of its articulation. In this framing, Wiesbaden figured not only as a vexed site of return for Maciunas, but as a site of newfound power within an "infrastructure of prestige" for US art abroad during the Cold War—a system anchored in the US cultural-diplomatic, economic, and military presence in Germany that Maciunas both depended upon and detested.

In order to make his new organization public, Maciunas wore many hats: concert and festival programmer; corresponding secretary; author of manifestos; graphic designer and printer of flyers, pamphlets, and posters; documentary photographer; composer of works; performer; editor, and printer of group publications and newsletters; financial patron; and archivist. Julia Robinson compares this complex authorial persona to Walter Benjamin's notion of *Umfunktionierung*—the appropriation of elements from a capitalist system of production in order to change their function toward new ends that undermine the system.[131] Robinson's argument finds even greater significance within the specific setting of the Wiesbaden Air Force base, where Maciunas styled himself as a saboteur at the heart of the US military-industrial complex. In Wiesbaden, Maciunas diverted Air Force materials, money, labor, and time toward Fluxus programming while planning an eventual return to Eastern Europe. In doing so, he subverted more than just the "author function" in an abstract field of capitalist cultural production. Rather, he tried to undermine a specific mission of pro-American cultural diplomacy that oriented the entire US mission in Germany as a frontline during one of the "hottest" times of the Cold War: between the August 1961 construction of the Berlin Wall and the October 1962 Cuban missile crisis.

His political motivations can hardly be disentangled from his complicated "homecoming" to Hesse, Germany—the very region he had inhabited as an adolescent in the 1940s—to work for the very US military his father had served. Within this setting, "sabotage" became the primary sign under which his emerging persona took hold. Like a guiding star, it oriented his relationship to materials, technologies, institutions, nations, and empires. It also guided his relation to the past. As the historian Marita Krauss has written with regard to literatures on Jewish remigration to Germany, many returning German Jews fantasized about remigration as "an attempt to reverse the migratory process of one's own life."[132] No comparable scholarly literature documents the cultural remigration of non-Jewish Baltic returnees during the Cold War. Yet it seems reasonable to speculate about a fantasy of return—different from that of Jewish victim returnees—in which sabotage would symbolically reverse a Lithuanian family's past of collaboration.

Wiesbaden was a site where American power worked to replace, reshape, and selectively revivify the institutions of the Third Reich during West Germany's de-Nazification. "Both the new and the old environments *of empire* are vivid, actual, occurring together contrapuntally," we might say in reformulation of Said's familiar words about exile quoted above. At Wiesbaden Air Force Base, Maciunas inhabited a "city in a city," comprising a mixture of former Luftwaffe buildings in the Nazi architectural style and new mid-century modern constructions.[133] This architecture mirrored the uneasy Cold War alliance between US occupiers and former Nazi personnel that defined the base as a first line of defense in the Cold War. During the era of Adenauer's government in West Germany, this alliance famously depended on a partially amnesiac relationship with histories of Nazi violence. As the historian Jeffrey Herf has written, "The establishment of a functioning democracy required less memory and justice for the crimes of the Nazi era and more 'integration' of those who had gone astray."[134] Indeed, 1961 and 1962 represented a startling time in this history of disavowal: while the 1961 Eichmann Trial had finally forced the German courts to bring more Nazi war criminals to justice, filling the news, the resulting trials produced lenient sentences—such as that of Otto Bradfisch, responsible for the killing of more than ten thousand Jews in Eastern Europe by the Einsatzgruppen, who was sentenced to ten years of hard labor.[135] As Arendt writes, "After May 1960, the date of Eichmann's capture, only first-degree murders could be prosecuted. All other offenses were wiped out by the statute of limitations."[136] Many victims of Nazi violence responded to this injustice with feelings of alarm and betrayal—a common theme in scholarship on postwar Jewish remigration to Germany.[137]

As a rule, Maciunas, like many of his generation, tended not to address memories of Nazism directly. Yet it is worth considering what his return to a culture of disavowal might have meant. We have already identified his generalized rebellion against the strategic forgetting of violence within the Lithuanian-American community in New York. Yet the amnesia at the US Air Force base in Wiesbaden was of a different order, forming the basis for a transatlantic alliance that oriented Cold War strategy. Moreover, the demand to forget would have posed particular challenges to workers on US military bases, who, according to the historian Donna Alvah, were charged to serve as personal examples within this setting of denazifying integration and partial amnesia:

> The postwar occupation and opposition to the spread of world communism required both "hard power" and "soft power": military might in the form of overseas bases, soldiers, and weapons, as well as friendly American influence on residents of occupied and host nations. . . . [Model military family members] were expected to help wage the ideological war against communism by conveying the presumed superiority of American ideals and institutions through their deportment, family relations, and homes.[138]

US soft power appealed to German subjects by promising a modern capitalist consumer democracy modeled on the lifestyles of the military base families and personnel.[139]

Not surprisingly, Maciunas recoiled at this "integration" via American soft power and capitalism in Germany. To him in 1962, Germans and Americans blended together as objects of political critique and personal disgust—almost as though the Nazi Reich of the past and the US superpower of the present blended to become the same enemy. By contrast, Eastern Europe and the Soviets—the enemies of his enemies—loomed large in his fantasies of a new life "home" behind the Iron Curtain. "Maybe in a few years I will try to settle in East Europe," Maciunas wrote to his collaborator Dick Higgins. "People here [in Germany are] just like in U.S., like pigs stuffing themselves with all kinds of garbage, food, goods, automobiles, bad art, till they are ready to burst. It makes one sick to look at them."[140] At a time when Maciunas was still debating whether to name his fledgling organization "Fluxus" or "Neo-Dada," his frequent invocation of sickened revulsion may have tipped the balance.[141]

Sabotage provided a means through which Maciunas could articulate to himself and others his antagonistic but dependent relationship with American power. He recognized the new possibilities for patronage afforded American cultural workers by the Cold War. Within his correspondence, he took aim at the nexus of US cultural diplomacy and foundation-based philanthropy in their furtherance of imperial interests. At a time when the Rockefeller Foundation provided an increasingly generous bounty of cultural patronage, he criticized its philanthropy in a long letter to Higgins: "It is totally inconsistent and unrealistic to expect others to be benefitted in philanthropies (voluntary) of creative portions of society, because this does not take into consideration the many, many cases of selfishness among creative portions."[142] Maciunas understood artists' participation in these patronage programs as rewarding a venality that would hardly benefit others outside the United States. According to one source, he and Salcius had already considered satirizing the American exceptionalism of the Rockefeller Foundation in the Lithuanian-American periodical they had planned in 1961.[143] In his 1962 letter to Higgins, Maciunas ruminated on American empire more generally. He argued that "Puerto Rico . . . Okinawa. . . . etc. etc." need "anti-colonial action," while stressing that they should seek unity in regionally defined "supra-national structures" that would allow for a fluid intermingling of ethnic identities to counteract purist ideologies of nationalism and presumably ward off genocidal violence.[144] American democracy and the philanthropies of the Rockefeller Foundation, he implied, had nothing to do with achieving such a future. Rather, they simply fed people's "crav[ing] for leisure to do nothing."[145] He added ominously, "To extract all possible contributions from all requires strong totalitarianism." We will return to this statement at the end of this chapter.[146]

Maciunas's feelings of moral and political disgust authorized his unrelenting sabotage—a subversion he conceived in both material and symbolic terms. In his prolific correspondence, he played up his role as saboteur with a mixture of humor and earnestness. "BIG NEWS," he announced to La Monte Young. "I got a . . . job with U.S. Air Force printing place so I can use APO. . . . I may swipe a small offset press from this Air Force so I will be able to print just about anything. So start collecting bulk [materials] for the big box."[147] Years later, Fluxus cofounder Benjamin Patterson joked that "the first sponsor of Fluxus was the United States [Military]."[148] Patterson worked long hours with Maciunas at the Air Force base, "so late at night, the printer was still grinding on printing this—what airplane is called Fluxus? And stuff like that. So yes, that was [George's] gig."[149] In Wiesbaden, Maciunas's "gig" transformed the arts into a playful realm for experimenting with the very strategies of sabotage that might have been used in the totalitarian settings that had unmoored families like his own. At the same time, sabotage rooted him in a radical art lineage beginning with Dada and the Soviet Left Front of the Arts (LEF) group, as other scholars have emphasized, guiding him with exemplary personae and strategies.[150]

Much could be said about how a related poetics of material destruction, reappropriation, and traumatic memory played out in Fluxus's first performances in Wiesbaden and elsewhere. These performances fixated on media technologies that summon histories of empire across time, which Dumett describes as calling forth "the past's bearing on the present."[151] For our purposes, it is worth focusing on the Fluxus Internationale Festspiele Neuester Musik (Fluxus International Festival for Newest Music) in 1962, the first festival held under the name Fluxus. Its very name— with its reference to "newest music"—parodied other new music festivals like the one at Darmstadt, funded as US-supported projects of cultural diplomacy and reconstruction.[152] In Wiesbaden, Maciunas quickly found that his US citizenship and persona opened doors in the city's art scene, and that local audiences craved American cultural offerings. This situation contrasted with his experience in New York, where the AG Gallery had struggled to attract an audience despite advertisements and publicity.[153] After Maciunas had organized successful preliminary events in Wuppertal and Düsseldorf in spring 1962, the director of the Städtisches Museum in Wiesbaden granted him access to the museum auditorium for four weekends between September 1 and September 23, 1962.[154] The festival proved a watershed: it cemented a "core group" of Fluxus artists in Europe— including Patterson, Williams, Higgins, Allison Knowles, Nam June Paik, Daniel Spoerri, and others—and launched a series of sixteen Fluxus festivals across Western Europe over the next two years.[155]

Maciunas's four-week Festival of Newest Music set off a flurry of international media coverage for Fluxus, set off by a five-minute television segment produced by the Hessian Broadcasting Corporation (HR), which culminated in a sensational depiction of Maciunas and his collaborators destroying a piano with bricks, axes, a hacksaw, hammer, and other instruments (figure 5.2).[156] The event was covered in at least ten major news outlets, from *Bild* to *La Nazione* to the Associated Press.[157] Maciunas

FIGURE 5.2. Philip Corner, *Piano Activities* (1962), performed during Fluxus Internationale Festpiele Neuester Musik, Hörsaal des Städtischen Museums, Wiesbaden, Germany, September 1, 1962. Gelatin silver print, 8³/₁₆ × 6⁵/₁₆ in. (20.8 × 16 cm). Performers: Emmett Williams, George Maciunas, Benjamin Patterson, Dick Higgins, Alison Knowles. Photographed by Deutsche Presse Agentur. Gilbert and Lila Silverman Fluxus Collection Gift, Museum of Modern Art, New York, 2125.2008. Digital image © The Museum of Modern Art / Licensed by SCALA / Art Resource, NY.

savvily designed a scroll with reproductions of the news coverage to be mailed as a press kit.[158] The staged destruction of the piano can be understood in the terms of Daniel Boorstin's notion of "pseudo-event," an important concept in Danielle Fosler-Lussier's analysis of Cold War cultural diplomacy: the shocking and enigmatic action was planned by Maciunas to generate publicity, and its importance corresponded to the loops of media attention it generated.[159] Yet the ends of Maciunas's work clearly differed from standard American cultural diplomacy goals, as reflected in newspaper coverage that equated Fluxus with terrorism.[160]

The wreckage of the piano was ostensibly a realization of Philip Corner's composition *Piano Activities*, though Maciunas had utterly transformed the spirit of the work. Corner, inspired by the work of John Cage and Lucia Dlugoczewski, had originally conceived the composition as embodying qualities of discipline and ecstatic improvisation; Maciunas's version instead made a spectacle of destruction.[161] Over the course of the festival, Maciunas had programmed his version of *Piano Activities* as the "grand finale" to each concert, concluding each gathering with the gradual decimation of the instrument—which, unbeknownst to television viewers, was a *Schrottklavier* (junk piano) he had acquired for free. As Emmett Williams remembered, "The objective was to reduce this thing to nothing."[162] Though Corner was initially "shocked," he eventually reasoned that Maciunas had deliberately chosen a superannuated piano that became "transformed into something else" in a creative act that adhered to certain laws of morality: "It was destroyed for the purpose of taking it away without paying cartage fees, of being easily transportable. . . . So it was done for a viable, useful social purpose which I totally approve of, and I've accepted, and I've developed further, and in a way that can be considered an essential part of the piece."[163]

Although the television program depicted Fluxus as a whimsical youth culture of rebellion, older generations seem to have been scandalized, or even lacerated, by the scene that appeared to be nothing but butchery. In characteristically dramatic language, Maciunas's mother reported that her German friends found it "painful and terrible to watch. . . . People couldn't hold back their tears. . . . These people felt sorry for me, sympathizing and understanding how a mother's heart would ache seeing what her son was doing. At that time he seemed possessed by a dark strength."[164] As Patterson remembered, "In 1962 it was violent, because the piano was the instrument that every German family of standing had. [It was] holy. Banged on crushed, etc. . . . And of course that is the scandal that opened the media's eyes to this as something new. [And] the sounds from this action were not that different from electronic music studio and *musique concrète*. But the fact that it was done on this holy instrument. . . . The symbolism was what struck the nut and opened the eyes."[165] The televised medium itself surely intensified the blow of this symbolism, conveying sound and image with breathtaking vividness while omitting contextual information to root the scene in an a reassuringly understandable reality. As Fosler-

Lussier notes, "In the 1950s and 1960s, when television was still a marvel, many observers had the disconcerting feeling that reality itself was being destabilized by this new medium."[166]

Here it becomes all the more significant that Maciunas's blunt gesture of destruction evokes a key element of the recent European genocides: the fact that the decimation of human life coincided with the decimation of cultural objects and heritage. Later, Maciunas wryly noted that "the German sentiments about this 'instrument of Chopin' were hurt and they made a row about it."[167] Maciunas's reference to Chopin is jarring, given the material and symbolic violence perpetrated against Chopin's legacy— through acts of appropriation and destruction—during the Nazi occupation of Poland.[168] To evoke that violent history may well have been part of the point. When Maciunas staged Corner's *Piano Activities*, he turned a work conceived as embodying ecstatic improvisation into a symbolically charged performance of cultural annihilation.

As Maciunas's quip about Chopin suggests, evocations of genocide generally present as humor in Fluxus activities in the early 1960s. In a 2002 interview, Ben Patterson recalled how one could not avoid thinking of that history amid the *Trümmerlandschaft* of German cities in the early 1960s. Patterson "went to bed" with readings from Adorno, Benjamin, and Heidegger. Yet when asked if "there was a comment [in Fluxus] about the postwar period in Germany," he steered the interview in other directions. Patterson's suggestion that Germany's violent past was relevant, without elaborating how or why, resonates with his words about racism's effects on his work: "Consciously, I really did not understand how deeply racism affected my work. Obviously, subconsciously a lot was happening."[169] In the work of both Patterson and Maciunas, signs of terror pierce the surface in jokes and gags. Like Mekas and Maciunas's quip "Don't we believe in death anymore?" their jokes targeted the production of knowledge.

Fluxus gags tended to make use of media technologies of empire: mundane objects like newspapers, adding machines, and filing systems, that were critical to the US projection of hard and soft power in the world. In his 1962 lecture "Neo-Dada in the United States," Maciunas described a kind of theater in which objects indexed "a world of concrete realities" rather than conjuring illusion.[170] The props at the center of Fluxus gags— especially in the work of Maciunas and Patterson—invite an archaeology of US power in Wiesbaden, grounded in the realities of material artifacts.

Patterson's *Variations for Double Bass*—another iconic performance filmed by the HR in Wiesbaden—used props to hint at formative conditions of racial discrimination and violence that largely went unspoken. A classically trained bassist and composer, Patterson had spent his early career playing in Canadian orchestras because the racially exclusionary practices of US orchestras precluded his employment there. After serving in the US Army, he played in the 7th US Army Orchestra in Stuttgart before heading to Cologne in 1960 to study with Karlheinz Stockhausen. By 1962, he made a living selling encyclopedias door-to-door to US military personnel while devoting himself to Germany's avant-garde art and music scenes. Like many Fluxus works, *Variations for Double Bass* brought the concert hall into collision with vaudeville humor; but its props and actions also intimated themes of war, migration, and genocide (figure 5.3). In his first variation, Patterson "unfolded a map of Europe on the floor, circled Wiesbaden with a pen and situated the endpin of his contrabass on the floor."[171] His handling of the map shows a way of knowing the world in terms of targets, whether conceived in terms of hard or soft power via military action, terrorism, marketing, or cultural diplomacy. In subsequent variations, he coaxed sounds out of the instrument upside down and right-side-up, with his fingernails and with an assortment of objects he brought out of a suitcase, from balloons and clothespins to food, a hammer, a stomach pump, a stamped letter, and a batonlike newspaper holder bearing scraps of newspaper. The theatrical pairing of the stuffed suitcase with the double bass brings to mind Patterson's own circuitous, itinerant career as a traveling salesman and musical vanguardist, which resulted from the reality of structural racism in the United States.

As Patterson said in an interview with Emmett Williams in the European edition of *Stars and Stripes*, his *Variations for Double Bass* involved "a juxtaposition of objects brought together into a metaphysical relationship ... or let's say a poetic relationship. . . . One variation employs plastic butterflies, another requires a long rope constructed of old rags and pieces of wire, and so forth, torn out of the inside of the instrument, dragged through the strings, and stuffed back inside as fast as possible. In another variation I use a stomach pump to rid the instrument of any foreign bodies."[172] While the interview appeared as a feature next to the syndicated comics section of the newspaper, this placement hardly concealed the brutality of Patterson's imagery ("torn," "dragged," and "stuffed"). His words about "rid[ding] the instrument of any foreign bodies" summons racialized ideologies of *Volksgemeinschaft* in the German context, or white supremacist nativism in the United States. Indeed, these words approach the very definition of genocide as the coordinated destruction of a human collectivity—a definition that also applies to US histories of slavery and racial terror, despite their frequent omission from genocide studies.[173] The US military communities in Germany were in fact sites where two specific racisms came into contact, each historically bearing genocidal dis-

FIGURE 5.3. Benjamin Patterson, *Variations for Double Bass* (1961).
Performed by the artist at Kleinen Sommerfest / Après John Cage, Galerie
Parnass, Wuppertal, Germany, on June 9, 1962. Gelatin silver print, possibly by
Rolf Jährling, 9¼ × 7 in. (23.5 × 17.8 cm). Gilbert and Lila Silverman Fluxus
Collection Gift, Museum of Modern Art, New York, 2664.2008. Digital image
© The Museum of Modern Art / Licensed by SCALA / Art Resource, NY.
Courtesy of the Estate of Benjamin Patterson.

positions stoked by fears of miscegenation: American Jim Crow collaborated with German *Rassenfeindlichkeit* in the public shaming of interracial
relationships between Black GIs and white German women.[174] The persistence of such racial violence under a banner of "freedom" marks the US
military presence in Germany as a scene of subjection.[175]

It is significant that Patterson's words appeared in *Stars and Stripes*,
the news outlet that generated Fluxus's earliest publicity in the lead-up to
the Wiesbaden festival. As the newspaper of the US armed forces in Europe, the publication was both a medium and a mirror of American em-

pire that Fluxus artists co-opted for their own purposes. It was at *Stars and Stripes* that Emmett Williams supported himself with a day job as an editor—a position that allowed him to publicize Fluxus in a newspaper that reached approximately 50 percent of households in the US military community in Europe.[176] The simultaneity of brutal and comic imagery in Patterson's language echoed the pattern of Williams's article more generally, which he illustrated with violent images from the group's "Neo-Dada in der Musik" concert in Düsseldorf the previous June. These included a photo of Nam June Paik smashing a violin in *One for Violin Solo* (1962) and a snapshot of Paik's *Bagatelles américaines* (1958–62), involving a female mannequin strung upside down. In this Düsseldorf performance of *Bagatelles américaines*, Paik had vocalized live verbal instructions to Artus Caspari, who was handling the mannequin: "Do like Mussolini. Up down. The way Mussolini executed people." And the audience egged Caspari on further: "Extract the gut!"[177] As though in direct refutation of music's use in cultural diplomacy, Williams began the *Stars and Stripes* interview ironically with an epigraph from Restoration playwright William Congreve: "Music hath charms to soothe the savage breast, / To soften rocks, or bend a knotted oak." In the article's first line, Williams retorted: "Not this music, man."

Williams's interview with Patterson appeared alongside reportage on American casualties in Vietnam, slow progress on racial integration in Dallas and Atlanta, and West Germans "still singing 'Deutschland über Alles'" despite the fact that the anthem's lyrics had changed ten years earlier in an effort to tamp down national-supremacist ideologies.[178] Patterson's words about "rid[ding] the instrument of any foreign bodies," in other words, resonated specifically with headlines in that day's issue. At the Festival of Newest Music, Patterson literally played the double bass with a montage of such headlines attached to a newspaper holder—headlines that simultaneously testified to American power and American weakness. The performance resonates with the critical history of *Stars and Stripes*, which the historian John W. Lemza describes as having been caught "between military elites who sought to use the newspaper as a vehicle to further the soft-power peddling of American ideals" and "the newspaper's staff and its efforts to enforce the tenet of freedom of speech regardless of its palatability."[179] Fluxus was nourished by *Stars and Stripes*, with both entities defined by their ambiguous relationship to imperial power.

Before specifying this ambiguity further, we should turn to Maciunas's *In Memoriam to Adriano Olivetti* (1962), a staple of the early Fluxus repertory that brings us back full circle to histories of empire, collaboration, sabotage, and escape. The composition honors a storied figure in Italian design, industry, and politics—the scion of the Olivetti industrialist family who pioneered modern typewriters and other business machines. An instruction piece, *In Memoriam to Adriano Olivetti* drew its inspiration from the Olivetti adding machines at the Air Force base. Maciunas filched paper adding machine tape from the base, using it to create a score that assigned specific performers, actions, and sounds to digits printed on the paper tape. Depending on the number of performers, the actions could include lifting a bowler hat, pointing at the audience, striking the floor with a cane, squatting, wheezing asthmatically, performing a military salute, and so on. Dressed in formal attire, the performers stood or sat in a row behind a table, facing the audience, and discharged their actions swiftly in strict time, following the tape's printed numbers, in the style of a mechanical apparatus. In the Wiesbaden realization filmed by HR, we hear a disturbing sense of disjunction between Daniel Spoerri's heavy wheezing on the one hand and Ben Patterson's high-pitched duck calls on the other. Sounding in juxtaposition, they evoke a situation of extreme concern, even life-threatening desperation, and of absurdity. The performers' lineup behind a table onstage suggests an official function, perhaps even a tribunal—complete with Nam June Paik's finger pointing (figure 5.4). Of course, variations in performance produced different effects. In a staging of *Olivetti* in Nice, for example, all the performers wore black suits and bowler hats. About this performance, Maciunas quipped that it "looked much better than other versions—like for a funeral—very appropriate."[180]

Olivetti subjects human action to mechanization, perhaps even parodying the absurdities of modern administered life and death, as Robinson observes,[181] or "symbolically appropriating the structure of the multinational corporation" while probing "the nature of work and the routine of everyday life in advanced capitalism," as Dumett writes.[182] Yet Maciunas's dramatic gestures also call out to be understood in relation to the specific histories of military and governance summoned by the Olivetti adding machine—histories that enlisted corporate bureaucracy into the cause of empire. It is not for nothing, I would suggest, that Maciunas repeatedly juxtaposed adding machine tape with finger-pointing, military salutes, and funerals. Recent studies by the historians Lisa Gitelman, Cornelia Vismann, and others stress the invisible but essential role of bureaucratic machines in the modernization of warfare and the control of subjugated populations.[183] The Olivetti adding machine, in particular, links World War II–era military bureaucracy with the Cold War computing boom essential to command centers like Wiesbaden Air Force Base. Maciunas's work shows a critical engagement with precisely such histories of tech-

FIGURE 5.4. George Maciunas's *In Memoriam to Adriano Olivetti*, performed during Concert no. 5, Fluxus Internationale Festspiele Neuester Musik, Städtisches Museum, Wiesbaden, Germany, on September 8, 1962. Left to right: Nam June Paik, Alison Knowles, Emmett Williams (partially hidden), George Maciunas, Benjamin Patterson. Gelatin silver print. Sheet 7¹⁵⁄₁₆ × 9¹⁵⁄₁₆ in. (20.2 × 25.3 cm). Photographer unknown. Gilbert and Lila Silverman Fluxus Collection Gift, Museum of Modern Art, New York, 2631.2008. Digital image © The Museum of Modern Art / Licensed by SCALA / Art Resource, NY. By permission of Billie J. Maciunas.

nology, with which he had an intimate familiarity through his Air Force work and his father's service as electrical engineer to multiple occupying powers. In this context, the significance of the work's memorial tribute to Adriano Olivetti only compounds. More than a designer and industrialist, Olivetti was also a utopian Marxist theorist and saboteur at the heart of Mussolini's industrial elite, who financially aided resisters and fellow Jewish Italians before he himself fled to Switzerland.[184]

Maciunas's persona as Fluxus saboteur ultimately remained inseparable from the dream of escaping to Eastern Europe, a dream he reiterated in dozens of letters to Fluxus compatriots from Wiesbaden between 1962 and 1964. Notably, this dream sometimes extended to include further trips east—to Siberia (the destination of the Lithuanian deportees his family had displaced in their Kaunas villa) or to Japan (a site for wide-ranging Orientalist fantasy). The persistence, playfulness, and imaginative detail with which he elaborated these plans echoes Krauss's observation that some returnees saw their trajectory "as involving a quest for a lost childhood" in reversing "the migratory process of one's own life."[185] In a tellingly fantastical letter, Maciunas tried to entice his old friend Jonas Mekas into returning to Eastern Europe:

> we will have a gang of bandits established. We will print Fluxus, dollar bills, fake postage stamps and write & perform music (nova et antiqua). You should join us with your [film] apparatus. We will cross border [to the East] when our work becomes troublesome to authorities here [in West Germany]. By then we will get wagons for a caravan and move continuously so no one can catch us, while we give Fluxus festivals and generally throw fluxus about.[186]

Here Maciunas provocatively paired the act of music making with the printing of counterfeit currencies and documents. In his vision, Fluxus would subvert systems of power through a surprising combination of itinerant music making and document reproduction technologies.[187] Music making, and cultural production more generally, would resemble the multiplication of forgeries in an economy where the originals lose value in a migratory stream of doubling. Maciunas appears to have vested his hopes in this process for sabotage against structures of American power abroad on which he depended. The realities of soft power, however, would always complicate this dream, because the success of Fluxus abroad almost invariably burnished the image of US power.

Empires in Counterpoint

To place Maciunas's vexed remigration to Germany at the center of Fluxus does more than just alter our understanding of the genre's early history; it transforms our understanding of Fluxus's afterlife beyond Wiesbaden. While a wide-ranging exploration of this afterlife exceeds the scope of this chapter, I would nonetheless outline some specific possibilities oriented by a fuller theorization of empire, both as a general category of governance and as a descriptor for the specific regimes that structured Maciunas's life. Fluxus remains deeply contested in its meanings and legacy, yet Fluxus artists and scholars of the phenomenon broadly agree that it was an organization and an "attitude" that interrogated boundaries between art and life.[188] Through such questioning, Maciunas himself arrived at a radical position that defined Fluxus as an "anti-art"—a movement that would undermine and ultimately destroy the institutions of high art from within, on the path toward a more egalitarian society.

My own account, however, frames Fluxus not so much as "anti-art" but rather as an art of *playing at empire* that also scrutinizes *empire as an object of knowledge*. For Maciunas, "playing at empire" extended the techniques of skeptical mirroring through which he and his family had survived as insider-outsiders in a succession of occupying regimes via his father's technical-bureaucratic position, essential to the regimes' administration and armaments production. In mirroring such imperial structures, Maciunas impersonated power ambiguously. Many of his Fluxus fellow travelers have characterized his leadership as "tyrannical" and "antidemocratic," especially in the forms it assumed during his final months in Wiesbaden in 1963 and during his subsequent return to New York. He enjoyed playing the part of the devil, so to speak. Maciunas accentuated his role as the "central political authority" of Fluxus, styling himself as the "chairman" in obvious reference to the Red regimes that were demonized in the United States. He acted as the head of the presidium of a bureaucratized empire that he sought to consolidate and expand.

During the turbulent period of his departure from Germany and return to New York, Maciunas went beyond mere jest in this play-acting when he "purged" or "excommunicated" Fluxus members, with the effect of alienating friendships and creative alliances over the long term. As Patterson remembered, Maciunas tried "to force [an organization] onto the whole thing [of Fluxus]. You're a member, you're not a member, or you're excommunicated for all sorts of reasons."[189] "As that shift came about it became less interesting to me."[190] Maciunas's purges went hand in hand with changes in Fluxus's institutional policies as he sought exclusive copyright for all affiliated artists. It also reinforced his newly consolidated political platform advocating acts of "sabotage & disruption" in protest of US imperialism, a program that targeted New York City's transportation, communication, and arts infrastructure.[191] He proposed, for example, "prearranged 'breakdowns' of a fleet of Fluxus autos and trucks bearing posters, exhibits etc." in the middle of busy Manhattan intersections, "stuffing postal boxes with thousands of packages (containing bricks) addressed to various newspapers, galleries, artists etc.," and "disrupting concerts at 'sensitive' moments with 'smell bombs,' 'sneeze bombs,' etc."[192] The "purges" of dissenting Fluxus artists continued through 1964 and 1965, intensifying around the time that Maciunas and Henry Flynt picketed the US premiere of Karlheinz Stockhausen's *Originale* in New York in April 1964. As Benjamin Piekut emphasizes, these actions should not be understood simply "on the level of intertribal feuding," but rather as "part of a larger intervention into the public discourse of avant-gardism,

European imperialism, and the structures of power and knowledge supporting these systems."[193]

Maciunas assumed the German label *Kulturbolschewik* in carrying out his protests and purges—the very word used by Nazis against Jews, communists, gay citizens, and Roma to incite genocide in Lithuania and elsewhere. His self-identification as *Kulturbolschewik* shows just how thickly charged the haunting of empires had become for him. The militarized US hegemony of the Vietnam War era contrasted with a Soviet empire that for Maciunas served ambivalently as an inaccessible homeland and as an imagined alternative that had been demonized in Nazi-occupied Lithuania, Germany, and the United States.

Maciunas's attempt to solidify Fluxus as an institution and as a political venture against US imperialism compensated for his irretrievable loss of Eastern Europe as a fetishized place of return. Little heart had he for leaving Europe after the Air Force terminated his contract in 1963 on the grounds of respiratory illnesses; he had intended Wiesbaden to serve as a staging ground for heading eastward. In the United States, his plan to tour in the Soviet Union and its satellites, with the indefinite possibility of settling there, would have begun to seem like a mirage. He appears to have been unwilling to attempt a risky defection to the Soviet Union. And as a Lithuanian-American, he could never have secured a tourist visa. If the "chairman" could never really return "home" behind the Iron Curtain, he could nonetheless rule over Fluxus, complete with bureaucratic institutional processes.

Maciunas launched his first "purge" at a telling moment after the Danish artist Eric Andersen staged a hoax against him while traveling in Eastern Europe in the summer of 1964. Andersen attempted to convince the Fluxus chairman via a series of postcards that he and other Fluxus compatriots had beaten Maciunas to the punch in launching a major tour eastward. He even pretended that they had staged unauthorized performances of *Olivetti* that involved "drinking, eating and pissing" in front of "thousands of happy communists" in Warsaw, Prague, Budapest, and Leningrad.[194] Caught up in the Fluxus spirit of parody, Andersen appears not to have realized that he was rubbing Maciunas's impossible fantasies of remigration in his face. Maciunas responded by purging not only Andersen but also the other unwitting members Andersen had falsely implicated in the hoax. Together with official letters denouncing their "apostasy," Maciunas mailed them "a package of Fluxus goodies" (high-handedly showing his benevolence) alongside copies of a letter he had sent to Nikita Khrushchev denouncing Andersen's unauthorized tour, written in his authority as Fluxus chairman. As Emmett Williams recalled, "Addi Køpcke,

Tomas Schmit, and I were equally surprised when the letters arrived, denouncing us for crimes we were totally unaware of having committed. A cruel joke? It was certainly no laughing matter to George, who regarded it as the Gospel Truth; and it cost me, through no fault of my own, his friendship and trust for many years to come."[195]

This episode in failed friendship shows how acts of parody risk becoming mired in involution—within the ambiguities of irony, in the tangle of power and subversion—to the point where reality and its funhouse mirrors tumble into confusion. It also shows how, in the midst of this disorientation, Fluxus's "intertribal feuding" in fact staged a miniature reenactment of imperial power relationships. Maciunas's purges may have fostered a paranoia among the Fluxus ranks, meant to ensure their loyalty. His correspondence with Khrushchev established his parity with the leader of "another" imperial sovereignty, intimating a formal equivalence between Fluxus and the Soviet Union. Such power moves loosely recall Maciunas's flirtation with a positive valuation of "strong totalitarianism" (which "extracts all possible contributions from all") in his correspondence with Higgins, as mentioned earlier. They also speak to the elaborate vertical filing systems through which he kept tabs on creative associates and their loyalty in the mid-1960s—like a parody of the file-based administration and surveillance techniques that characterize modern state power, and totalitarianism in particular.[196] While Fluxus works like *Olivetti* tended to make a study of imperial violence, the Fluxus community as shepherded by Maciunas also "played" at violence in ways that severed bonds of friendship, especially during the period of the "chairman's" unhappy return from Wiesbaden to New York.

Maciunas's Fluxus therefore represents a double-edged legacy, divided between a partially aestheticized and ironized *reenactment* of violence and a *study* of violence. To recognize how Fluxus was haunted by empire is not just to better understand the "intertribal feuding" of Fluxus that has dominated so much historiography, but also to put Fluxus's critique of imperialism at center stage. Dumett emphasizes Maciunas's penchant to "fold" historical references within one another in his performative practice.[197] The same could be said of his treatment of empire as a topic of historical reference, with particular emphasis on the Nazi and Stalinist regimes that had recently been conceptualized as "totalitarian" within the intellectual landscape of early Cold War New York. It is striking here that the ostensibly pro-Soviet Maciunas chose to use the word "totalitarianism" in his correspondence with Higgins, when American communists would generally have avoided the term as a pejorative. This fact reminds us of the often quicksilver nature of Maciunas's political position-taking. For Arendt, the word "totalitarianism" pointed to similarities between the Nazi and Stalinist regimes, opening up a comparative study of empire from the standpoint of the recent European genocides. Such an open-ended study brings us closer to the substance of Maciunas's political imagination, I believe, than attempting to affiliate him fixedly and exclusively with a specific political program.

In closing, I would draw attention to the specific components that oriented Fluxus's analysis of empire as an object of knowledge. As we have already seen, the key features Arendt identified as paving the way from European high imperialism to totalitarianism also appear as prominent themes in Fluxus: expansionism, racism, bureaucracy, secret agents, terror, and genocide. While it is uncertain whether Maciunas read Arendt, we do know that his experiential basis for dealing with these questions would have been closely related to her own, since both thinkers' understanding derived overwhelmingly from the case of Nazi Germany. Indeed, Arendt derived crucial material for her thought by studying Nazism's aftermath during a six-month stay in Wiesbaden in 1949 and 1950, one year after the Maciunas family's emigration from the same region.[198] Arendt's theory of politics responded to the atomization of individuals caught in totalitarianism's net of terror. In her terms, politics derives not from ties to a nation, but from the common interest that binds people together in speech and action no matter where they happen to be. This common interest and the capacity for action it harbors is what totalitarianism sought to destroy by fanning paranoia to sever the bonds of ordinary human interaction.

Much like the musical quiz show Maciunas organized in the DP camp, Fluxus at its best offered a space for the kinds of spontaneous, unpredictable interaction-in-collectivity that institutions like the Ernst-Ludwig Schule, Siemens AG, and IG Farben had foreclosed during the final years of Nazi terror. Maciunas's distrust of institutional bureaucracies as extensions of state power clearly persisted throughout his life in tandem with his frequent parody of those mechanisms. His later enterprises in cooperative housing in Soho and cooperative farming in the Berkshires—including an attempt to reestablish Black Mountain College—aimed to make homes for artists outside of a bureaucratic-institutional net. As his sister Nijole recalled, "He had an intense dislike for bureaucracy and played hide-and-seek with government agents [in New York] by exiting through secret passages in his [Soho] apartment, disguising himself with masks and wigs to avoid recognition once outside his building."[199] This anecdote works as a vivid metaphor for Maciunas's wider experimentation with diverse personae and positions, and his refusal to be pinned down in this play.

Yet even if his political positions remained ambiguous—caught in nesting involutions of parody and irony—he nonetheless enacted a politics by helping to create a space for human solidarities independent of blood or soil, through which unpredictable paths of action would offer the potential for mobilization.

Coda

Capping off his studies of empire, Maciunas's 1966 flag poster *U.S.A. Surpasses All the Genocide Records!* (figure 5.5) finally emblematizes the problems of memory, forgetting, and obfuscation that thread throughout my narrative. Genocide stands out as an extreme but recurring strategy of empire because it offers a "solution" to the management of internally differentiated peoples that characterize the expansionist state. For this reason, it always remains a possibility on the horizon. I would like to dwell on Maciunas's flag poster, because its provocations and erasures still resound in the present day. Made famous in the peace activism of John Lennon and Yoko Ono, the poster registers a contrapuntal experience informed by the genocides in the specific lands Maciunas inhabited—the genocides he long referenced in performance without naming.

This multiply reproduced lithograph compares the United States with Nazi Germany, Stalinist Russia, Spanish colonialism, and Kublai Khan's Mongol Empire. Fifty skulls-and-crossbones replace the stars of the flag, its stripes formed by bold-print text detailing the percentages of the targeted populations killed in each of the genocides. To my knowledge, this poster represents Maciunas's first explicit public reference to the genocide in which his family had been implicated through his father's work. I therefore see it as a watershed in his practice, which had long referenced practices associated with genocide without naming it explicitly. (This watershed coincides with the period when the term "Holocaust," in reference to the Nazi genocide against Jews, had begun to find general currency.) As though inviting interaction, the bottom strip of the flag shares with viewers an anonymous post office box address for "calculations & references." Maciunas prepared a leaflet to send in response, which detailed the evidence for his claims while asking polemically, "Are we becoming a nation of criminals? or have we lost our capacity to reason under the magic spell of Our Leader? or were the Nazis innocent after all, since they, like the U.S. leaders, did it all in the name of 'anticommunism?'"[200] The flag poster launched an information campaign and invited interaction.

To a limited extent, Maciunas's treatment of genocide resonates with practices of genocide memory and forgetting associated with a subset of

U.S.A. SURPASSES ALL THE GENOCIDE RECORDS!

KUBLAI KHAN MASSACRES 10% IN NEAR EAST

SPAIN MASSACRES 10% OF AMERICAN INDIANS

JOSEPH STALIN MASSACRES 5% OF RUSSIANS

NAZIS MASSACRE 5% OF OCCUPIED EUROPEANS AND 75% OF EUROPEAN JEWS

U.S.A. MASSACRES 6.5% OF SOUTH VIETNAMESE & 75% OF AMERICAN INDIANS

FOR CALCULATIONS & REFERENCES WRITE TO: P.O. BOX 180, NEW YORK, N.Y. 10013

FIGURE 5.5. George Maciunas, *U.S.A. Surpasses All the Genocide Records!* c. 1966. Offset lithograph. Sheet 21⅜ × 34⅝ in. (54.3 × 88 cm). Gilbert and Lila Silverman Fluxus Collection Gift, Museum of Modern Art, New York, 3001.2008.x3. Digital image © The Museum of Modern Art / Licensed by SCALA / Art Resource, NY. By permission of Billie J. Maciunas.

the "'68ers" in Germany—the young adults who protested against the values and institutions of their parents. The older generation's complicity in the Holocaust irredeemably destroyed their moral authority in the eyes of their children (like Alexander Maciunas's moral authority in the eyes of his son) and motivated the call for deep-rooted social and political transformation. Maciunas's poster links up with a certain current of 1960s German protest, because it simultaneously acknowledges the Holocaust while nesting that acknowledgment within a larger critique of US power. Often this approach would equate fascism with capitalism. State capitalism fueled the Holocaust, and the United States emblematized the fullest realization of that system and its ideologies. In its most extreme manifestations, this logic could lead to the trivialization of the Holocaust and a seeming absolution of Nazi guilt. For example, Ulrike Meinhof equated the Holocaust with the US bombings of Dresden in her mid-1960s journalism.[201] This move amplified the sort of evasion common in Germany during the immediate postwar period, the tendency "to draw up a balance between German suffering and the suffering of others, the implication being that one side cancels the other."[202]

Yet Maciunas's poster does something far more provocative than simply reproducing such evasions, even though it also does its share of forgetting. Maciunas frames his flag poster as a comparative statement about empire, rather than about capitalism. This framing is crystal clear because he included expansionist, precapitalist, and anticapitalist power formations in his list, in addition to the capitalist ones he usually targeted for critique. The poster demonstrates knowledge akin to that in recent historiographies of genocide that foreground connections between victim groups across a spectrum of difference. It reminds us of Snyder's insight: "Often what happened to one group is intelligible only in light of what happened to another."[203] It also evokes Weheliye's call to "emphasize the family ties between political violence and suffering."[204] Such an approach distinguishes among the experiences of different victim groups while examining structural connections between their victimizations. It also depends upon understanding linkages between internal subjugation and external exercises of power that define the study of empire.

From this perspective, the central omission in Maciunas's flag becomes all the more glaring. Maciunas's erasure of the Atlantic slave trade and subsequent racial terror from his calculations replicates a blind spot in white scholarship from his own era to the present. It ignores the campaign to recognize the history of systemic Black human rights violations in the United States as a form of genocide, as articulated most forcefully in the Civil Rights Congress petition "We Charge Genocide," submitted to the United Nations in December 1951, led by William Patterson and signed by leading activists (including W. E. B. Du Bois, Paul Robeson, and Claudia Jones) and family members of victims of lynching, of death row executions, and of unfair legal proceedings (including Amy and Doris Mallard, whose family member Robert Childs Mallard had been lynched for voting in 1948).[205] As that petition argued,

It is sometimes incorrectly thought that genocide means the complete and definitive destruction of a race or people. The Genocide Convention, however, adopted by the General Assembly of the United Nations on December 9, 1948, defines genocide as any killings on the basis of race, or, in its specific words, as "killing members of the group." Any intent to destroy, in whole or in part, a national, racial, ethnic or religious group is genocide, according to the Convention. Thus, the Convention states, "causing serious bodily or mental harm to members of the group," is genocide as well as "killing members of the group." We maintain, therefore, that the oppressed Negro citizens of the United States, segregated, discriminated against and long the target of violence, suffer from genocide as the result of the consistent, conscious, unified policies of every branch of government.

Signatories of the petition subsequently experienced persecution, including the revoking of passports, as the State Department sought to minimize any effects on the global public image of the United States. By the late 1960s, the budding academic field of genocide studies tended to follow the State Department's lead in refusing to classify slavery and its aftermath as a genocidal object of study.[206] In accord with this tendency, Maciunas's flag poster represents a way of knowing genocide through the high proportion of a population's eradication—the very terms on which anti-Black violence in the United States tended erroneously to be dismissed from the category of genocide.

This flag poster's omission of US state-sanctioned anti-Black violence reinforces the "color-blind" dynamics within the downtown New York art scene where Maciunas had made his mark—dynamics that removed questions of race from explicit discussion. As Philip Corner notes, Fluxus members (with a few exceptions) may have thought, "It's just, like, avant-garde art is progress enough." Corner further elaborated, with hindsight and a critical spirit of irony on that attitude, "It's enough to have the right idea, and we're not overt racists, and we have Black friends—Ben [Patterson]! . . . I think that there may have been that kind of thing. . . . Working for progress in the arts was enough and we were open-minded, Fluxus accepted people from everywhere, without regard to . . . there may have been something like that."[207] He made these remarks to me after recounting a painful and revelatory encounter with his old friend and colleague Patterson late in that artist's life. Patterson had expressed sorrow that the Fluxus community had not cared more about the civil rights movement. Corner, a white American artist and composer of Jewish heritage, responded to Patterson that he had in fact engaged as an activist. He had traveled to Meridian, Mississippi, in 1964 to participate in the Freedom Summer, and had taught in the Freedom School movement in Brooklyn in the mid-1960s.[208] When Patterson voiced surprise that he had never known those facts after years of working together, the two marveled at the silences about race that had defined their "progressive" community in Fluxus, and the pain—especially for Patterson—that had resulted from those silences. As many scholars have noted, Fluxus was a movement that tended to admit a degree of gender, ethnic, and racial diversity in the 1960s, which seemed greater, for example, than the Eighth Street Artists' Club in the 1940s and 1950s. Yet this diversification of the white avant-garde remained tethered to repressive discursive practices that tended to prevent any deep reckoning with persistent inequalities—especially with regard to race.

It is, then, the extra "stripe" of anti-Black genocidal violence, which

Maciunas's flag poster failed to include, that ultimately would have enhanced its claim to truth about American power. The flag references genocide against American Indians and against Vietnamese, yet these hardly make sense as an "assemblage of relation," as described by Weheliye, without understanding the institution of slavery and its aftermath. In the service of the antiwar effort, the flag poster makes an effort at multidirectional remembrance, yet it remains haunted by its own omissions. Rendering a full array of practices across the wider Fluxus community, as I have attempted to do, helps to make those omissions knowable and palpable, especially when relevant genocidal histories are restored to the story of Fluxus's creation. From the current standpoint, looking back on the recent history of US. empire, music and the sonic arts continue to provoke consideration of that which cannot yet be articulated, that which is too shameful to be said, that which is common knowledge and therefore not necessary to say, and that which lies in the wide interstices of such realms of the unsaid.

✳ 6 ✳

Concluding Thoughts

Haunting, translation, technological mediation, import/export, exploitation, freedom struggles—these terms strongly characterize the scenes of my narrative, flagging its status as a story of the imperial metropolis. The terms signal not only mere processes but inclinations, moods, affects, ways to gesture and transact. They "give physiognomy" to the dates of American empire in the late 1950s and early 1960s, an era that produced long-lasting musical canons and an arts infrastructure that cannot now be taken for granted. What does it mean to set certain dates apart—to insist upon their significance in a setting of critical remembrance—while also refusing to naturalize them within the larger continuities that usually make up "music history"? Benjamin's term "physignomy" may seem overly optical, yet its emphasis on outward qualities and motifs is indispensable, just as music, sound, and the sonic arts should be indispensable to notions of historiography as physiognomy. Specific life narratives have brought shape to my chapters, yet they call attention to *patterns* of music-professional personae, or recognized and replicated ways of knowing, doing, and being in the world through sound: the musician-artist-activist, the composer-improviser, the composer-diplomat, the composer-engineer, the *Macher*, the intercultural creator, the provocateur. These character types leap off the page of this study. They emerged from within the imperial metropolis, from its burgeoning infrastructures and patronage systems, from the push to project soft power abroad, and from the pull to extract resources from the periphery. As my chapters have shown, these physiognomies are racialized, gendered, classed, and conditioned by citizenship status. The protagonists of my narrative inhabited these overlapping personae in varying ways, always responding to contestations over citizenship connected with their backgrounds in uprooting.

Ambiguous external borders, migrating peoples, and internal gradations of citizenship define empires as state power formations. Renewed attention to processes of displacement and hierarchies of citizenship is what makes the imperial character of my Cold War scenes apparent. Far from being irrelevant to empire, music and sound help to create "the habits of heart, mind, and comportment" that Stoler identifies as the very substance of empire. Yet for many years, questions of migration and uprooting remained negligible to historical studies of "art music" in the United States after World War II, just as empire and imperialism lay dormant as underexamined categories. Although historical musicology has witnessed a growing interest in mid-century American politics, questions of displacement and empire in this context have only just begun to gain traction despite their centrality to the study of the Cold War. This gap arises from a haunting: from the aftermath of music history's long-standing investment in national models for understanding cultural heritage, even after decades of research on globalization, migration, and diaspora. This haunting abides with special resilience in the domains of "high art" that often constituted the official culture of the state: domains that traditionally organized themselves along stable lines of *medium, genre,* and *nationality,* or by categories such as "French symbolist poetry" and "American experimentalist music." What would then become lost, or understudied, are the chancy spaces of cultural translation that enable aesthetic innovations, even when themes of migration or globalization enter into the music-historical literature. In the scenes of my study, displaced and geographically mobile individuals fostered such aesthetic transformations by crossing disciplinary and genre boundaries in conjunction with cultural and national ones. For example, Ono's early intermedia practice—which brought calligraphy together with vocal experimentation, the manipulation of sound recordings, dramatic play, and much more—both referenced and scrambled traditional disciplinary and genre categories from her two homelands. Yet relatively little musical research has focused on such multivalent boundary crossings to date, because they evade familiar categories of music history and those of its sister disciplines in the arts and humanities. In contrast, my own project has situated such boundary crossings squarely within a narrative of empire and uprooting, a story about how external geopolitical power plays intersect with internal contestations over citizenship. The smallest details of aesthetic practice open onto and participate in these domains of conflict.

In other words, the expressive forms of music have the potential to assume a physiognomic quality, like a set of gesticular habits of movement or speech that indicate patterns or perplexities of identity within wider structures. Music and the sonic arts carry a visceral quality of percept that connects the perceiver with the perceived, flooding subjects with knowledge and feeling. They also stand out as a salient medium of "third space," "a translational space of negotiation" between idioms, languages, and cultures that opens up across an uneven field of power.[1] They move between various cultural and social formations, adapting, attaching, and detaching themselves in a nomadic fashion.[2] Several of the protagonists in my narrative understood music as a mode of self-revelation that spoke to larger social, cultural, or political realities. Mingus tried "to play the truth of what I am," as he put it, while noting that "it's difficult because I'm changing all the time."[3] Toyama's deeply lyrical poetics and Ono's "opera" pertaining to childhood experiences of war also furthered projects of self-revelation, as did Ussachevsky's autobiographical play with sounding Chinese dinner plates and Morse code, and as did Patterson's performances pertaining to racial trauma and genocide. Yet a physiognomy of musical form also plays out in the poetic worlds of those who eschewed self-revelatory poetics, such as Varèse and Maciunas, as is evident in the sounds of white hipness and the gestures of bureaucratic violence they respectively conjured. In attending to the poetics of these performances and works, I have refrained from a top-down approach that would start from a perspective of applying labels of style or genre. (The poetics of the artifacts themselves resist this.) Rather, I contemplated sensuous details of form and performance through repeated listening and study (including a sort of imagined audition and visualization, as in my engagement with Ono's works that were recorded neither in musical notation nor on tape).

In the ideological study of music and musical worlds, I homed in on multiple registers of analysis: on specific scenes of interaction; on particular institutions; on characteristic personae, discourses, and practices that crossed institutions; and on a global stage of nations and empires acting in competition, conflict, occupation, alliance, negotiation, and genocide. While my chapters have tended to telescope outward from scenes of encounter (chapter 1) to the sweep of global history (chapter 5), all of the registers have remained in play as objects of analysis throughout. It is my conviction that music and the sonic arts help to shape "habits of heart, mind, and comportment"; therefore, it is important to deal with theories of ideology that pertain to each of the scales of analysis detailed above. Hartman's work showcases how notions of consent, humanity, and leisure sanction anti-Black cruelty and dehumanization in everyday *scenes* of interracial encounter such as the Greenwich House improv sessions. Althusser points toward the "teeth-gritting harmony" that unites the cultural and repressive *institutions* of the state in processes of subject formation, such as the ones that transpired at the Columbia-Princeton Electronic Music Center as a product of the military-industrial-educational complex. Klein adumbrates Cold War Orientalism as a *structure of feel-ing, discourse,* and *practice* that camouflages exploitative political and eco-nomic policies within gestures of sentimentality and reciprocity—not unlike musical Orientalisms of the postwar US avant-garde. Arendt iden-tifies genocidal possibilities within the sensorially rich alternative reali-ties curated by *states* on the world stage, possibilities that come to fruition when everyday citizens become perpetrators motivated by paranoia and the perverse logics of alternative reality. Fluxus emerged as a movement that reenacted and studied such a dynamic of totalitarian violence via the sonic arts, and it did so from a perspective that tended to recognize a con-junction of "genocide" and "America" not as oxymoronic. My chapters make the point that all these ways of thinking about ideology have pur-chase on the understanding of music performances, works, scenes, and institutions in mid-century New York as a capital of empire. Music faces *onto* the world, and it is *of* the world. Its revelation of ideology is its phys-iognomy. Yet in this revelation also lies its promise for the future.

To apprehend music as physiognomic is not to pin particular works or performances down to one meaning or disclosure of identity, but rather to attune oneself to its revelation (and possible transformation) of worlds. Musical artifacts are outward-facing things designed for some sort of public engagement. They are at once personal and impersonal. They channel intimate knowledge, discipline, routine, and affect; yet they also assume a form that is destined for life beyond the intimacies of their creation, with the promise to gather together a new set of relations among strangers. Their promise lies in what these variable sets of assemblage may bring, just as music itself works as a goad for the imagination. It is in this manner that musical performances and works resemble the creation of worlds. Arendt compares the world to a table, to that which "relates and separates men at the same time. . . . [It] gathers us together and yet pre-vents us from falling over each other."[4] The form and decor of the table have a bearing on postures and attitudes, on how individuals think, feel, and interact. The table may outlast the creatures who orient themselves around it, even as the funiture itself gradually decays. So it is with music and the sonic arts, which despite their vaunted ephemerality nonetheless contribute to a built environment and its long-term conditions for alter-ation. They pertain to the past, present, and future of an arts infrastruc-ture that currently stands at a moment of juncture.

To give dates their physiognomy through the study of music, migra-tion, and US empire is to confront the recent past in the present with a call to judgment. Much of the music and performance art, which I have considered here in great detail, is not extensively remembered. The stories of uprooting, transnational mediation, unequal citizenship, and institutional gatekeeping that defined the arts boom of the early Cold War period in New York have also tended to remain obscure, despite the canonization of that scene. As I described in my introduction to this book, immersing myself in the archives and oral history of these scenes was an eerie experience because of these materials' simultaneous proximity to and distance from the present. This feeling only intensified in the end stages of the project, when the COVID-19 pandemic brought into high relief the existential stakes of the ongoing fight over racialized hierarchies of citizenship *and* the utter anachronism of any Cold War–era ethos of investment in public goods, infrastructure, diplomacy, and soft power in the United States. Under these conditions, the arts capital blatantly becomes a stranger to itself. At this writing, the performance venues of New York City are closed, and 95 percent of the members of Local 802 of the American Federation of Musicians in New York are unable to work on a regular basis.[5] All this is set against the nation's wider crisis of democracy and an expanding gulf between rich and poor, amid a significant reconfiguration of foreign policy and global power alignments. It is against this backdrop, and with an eye toward the reforms and rebuilding to come, that I have chosen my narratives with the belief that history facilitates judgments about who should be at the table and under what terms, just as music challenges how to be and think in the world.

Acknowledgments

I am grateful for the support of Marta Tonegutti over the last eight years during which this project came to be. She and the other members of my team at the University of Chicago Press—Rae Ganci Hammers, Renaldo Migaldi, Dylan Montanari, and Meredith Nini—shepherded the project with insight and care. Ryan Dohoney, Danielle Fosler-Lussier, and Dörte Schmidt read the manuscript from beginning to end, offering encouragement and constructive criticism. I also owe thanks to colleagues who thoughtfully commented on early versions of chapters: Tamar Barzel, Andrea Bohlman, Martin Brody, Kwami Coleman, and Viktoria Tkazcyk. Lilli Elias aided my research by attending select interviews to facilitate recording, transcription, and lively conversation. Together with Brian Fairley, she also provided bibliographic assistance. Josh Rutner completed an essential round of copyediting for the manuscript before submission to the press, and Derek Gottlieb created the index.

This book developed during residencies at the American Academy in Berlin, the Harvard University Department of Music, the Wellesley College Humanities Center, and the Max Planck Institute for History of Science. Pamela Rosenberg, Suzannah Clark, Carol Dougherty, and Viktoria Tkaczyk generously coordinated my research stays. A National Endowment for the Humanities Fellowship gave me the gift of time to immerse myself in writing. New York University also supported my work through a sabbatical and book subvention.

The organizers of workshops, colloquia, and conferences—where I tested my ideas—deserve special thanks. While the resulting conversations are too numerous to list, I would note the importance of certain words of advice, which lodged themselves in my mind, from Joel Burges, Brenna Wynn Greer, Shana Redmond, and Ken Ueno.

My research would be impossible without archives and libraries. I am grateful to the administrators, curators, and librarians at the Archiv Sohm,

Staatsgalerie, Stuttgart; the Earle Brown Foundation; Fondation Le Corbusier; the Getty Research Center; the Library of Congress; the Museum of Modern Art Archive and Library; the New York Public Library; the New York University Libraries; the Paul Sacher Foundation, Basel; and the Ralph Rinzler Folklife Archives and Collections, Smithsonian Foundation.

My work also depends on the afterlife of oral history, and I am deeply indebted to the generosity of my interlocutors: Styra Avins, Philip Corner, Bill Crow, alcides lanza, Peter Mauzey, Yoko Ono, Alice Shields, and Pril Smiley. I also carry the memory of those interlocutors who have passed away: Mario Davidovsky, Halim El-Dabh, Jonas Mekas, and Chou Wen-chung.

In addition to the friends and mentors named above, I thank Emily Abrams Ansari, Martin Brody, Ryan Dohoney, Glenda Goodman, Sindhumathi Revuluri, Erica Schattle, Bridget K. Smith, Anne Shreffler, and Kay Kaufman Shelemay for cheering me on year after year. And I am grateful to my exemplary students and colleagues at New York University, to whom I owe the blessing of a nurturing and creative workplace. In the earliest stage of this project, I benefited from a writing group with David Samuels and Lauren Ninoshvilli; in the last stage, with Martin Daughtry and Cristina Vatulescu. In addition to those already mentioned, I learned from countless conversations with NYU colleagues: Michael Beckerman, Christopher Campo-Bowen, Suzanne Cusick, Christine Dang, Fanny Gribenski, Elizabeth Hoffman, Lou Karchin, Maureen Mahon, Matthew D. Morrison, Jaime Oliver, Mark Sanders, Yunior Terry, and Alice Teyssier.

Because of the pandemic, intergenerational support became a necessity for completing this book. I am obliged to my mother-in-law, Gwen Steege, and my late father-in-law, Richard Steege, for taking care of my son Julian over many months. And I thank my parents, Mary Burns and Martin Cohen, together with the other members of my family, for fostering a spirit of inquiry about the past and supporting all of my endeavors. Also to Benjamin Steege, my abiding thought companion, I owe a debt of gratitude with joy.

Notes

Introduction

1. Saskia Sassen, *The Global City: New York, London, Tokyo*, revised edition (Princeton, NJ: Princeton University Press, 2001), esp. 259.

2. The commentators who make this point range across a wide political spectrum. W. E. B. Du Bois, "Peace Is Dangerous," pamphlet of speech partially delivered at the National Council of Arts, Sciences and Professions on September 28, 1951, and at Community Church in Boston, W. E. B. Du Bois papers (MS 312), Special Collections and University Archives, University of Massachusetts Amherst Libraries, digitized, https://credo.library.umass.edu/cgi-bin/pdf.cgi?id=scua:mums312-b227-i084, accessed June 25, 2020; Niall Ferguson, *Empire: The Rise and Demise of the British World Order and the Lessons for Global Power* (New York: Basic Books, 2004), 317; Julian Go, *Patterns of Empire: The British and American Empires, 1688 to the Present* (Cambridge: Cambridge University Press, 2011), 2–5; David Harvey, *The New Imperialism* (Oxford: Oxford University Press, 2003), 6.

3. Henry R. Luce, "The American Century," *Life* (February 17, 1941): 61–65.

4. Penny Von Eschen and Danielle Fosler-Lussier make this point powerfully in their studies of jazz and cultural diplomacy. My own work makes similar arguments, bringing together the study of race and immigration within a specifically imperial framework that deals explicitly with non–native-born creators. Penny M. Von Eschen, *Satchmo Blows Up the World: Jazz Ambassadors Play the Cold War* (Cambridge, MA: Harvard University Press, 2006); Danielle Fosler-Lussier, *Music in America's Cold War Diplomacy* (Oakland: University of California Press, 2015).

5. Ana R. Alonso-Minutti, Eduardo Herrera, Alejandro Madrid, eds., *Experimentalisms in Practice: Music Perspectives from Latin America* (New York: Oxford University Press, 2018); Amy Beal, *Carla Bley* (Urbana: University of Illinois Press, 2011); Amy Cimini, *Wild Sound: Maryanne Amacher and the Tense of Audible Life* (New York: Oxford University Press, 2021); Ryan Dohoney, *Saving Abstraction: Morton Feldman, the de Menils, and the Rothko Chapel* (New York: Oxford University Press, 2019); Bernard Gendron, *Between Montmartre and the Mudd Club: Popular Music and the Avant-Garde* (Chicago: University of Chicago Press, 2002); Eduardo Herrera, *Elite Art Worlds: Philanthropy, Latin Americanism, and Avant-Garde Music* (New York: Oxford University Press, 2020); George Lewis, *A Power Stronger Than Itself: The AACM and American Experimental Music* (Chicago: University of Chicago Press, 2009); Alejandro L.

Madrid, *In Search of Julián Carillo and* Sonido 13 (New York: Oxford University Press, 2015); Benjamin Piekut, *Experimentalism Otherwise: The New York Avant-Garde and Its Limits* (Berkeley: University of California Press, 2011); Piekut, *Henry Cow: The World Is a Problem* (Durham, NC: Duke University Press, 2019); Piekut, ed., *Tomorrow Is the Question: New Directions in Experimental Music Studies* (Ann Arbor: University of Michigan Press, 2014). I would also draw attention to the landmark symposium "After American Music," organized by Piekut and Jeremy Strachan at Cornell University in February 2018.

6. Emily Abrams Ansari, *The Sound of a Superpower: Musical Americanism and the Cold War* (New York: Oxford University Press, 2018); Amy Beal, *New Music, New Allies: American Experimental Music in West Germany from the Zero Hour to Reunification* (Berkeley: University of California Press, 2006); Martin Brody, ed., *Music and Musical Composition at the American Academy in Rome* (Rochester, NY: University of Rochester Press, 2014), 222–56; Von Eschen, *Satchmo*; Fosler-Lussier, *Cold War Diplomacy*; Felix Meyer, Carol J. Oja, Wolfgang Rathert, and Anne C. Shreffler, eds., *Crosscurrents: American and European Music in Interaction (1900–2000)* (Woodbridge, UK: Boydell and Brewer, 2014); Simo Mikkonen and Pekka Suutari, eds., *Music, Art and Diplomacy: East-West Cultural Interactions and the Cold War* (Farnham, UK: Ashgate, 2016).

7. My thoughts here loosely adapt related imagery from Convolute N of Benjamin's *Arcades Project*, and from Michel de Certeau. Walter Benjamin, *The Arcades Project*, trans. Howard Eiland and Kevin McLaughlin (Cambridge, MA: Belknap Press of Harvard University Press, 2002), 456–88; Michel de Certeau, *Heterologies: Discourse on the Other*, trans. Brian Massumi (Minneapolis: University of Minnesota Press, 1986), 151.

8. Saidiya Hartman, *Scenes of Subjection: Terror, Slavery, and Self-Making in Nineteenth-Century America* (Oxford: Oxford University Press, 1997); Matthew D. Morrison, "The Sound(s) of Subjection: Constructing American Popular Music and Racial Identity through Blacksound," *Women & Performance* 27, no. 1 (2017): 13–24.

9. Benjamin, *Arcades Project*, 476.

10. Martin Heidegger, *Being and Time* (New York: Harper, 1962). Gayatri Chakravorty Spivak, "Three Women's Texts and a Critique of Imperialism," *Critical Inquiry* 12, no. 1 (1985): 243–61.

11. Hyung-Gu Lynn, "Globalization and the Cold War," *Oxford Handbook of the Cold War*, ed. Richard H. Immerman and Petra Goedde (2013), https://www-oxfordhandbooks-com.proxy.library.nyu.edu/view/10.1093/oxfordhb/9780199236961.001.0001/oxfordhb-9780199236961-e-33, accessed June 4, 2020.

12. *OED Online*, Oxford University Press, s.v. "world, n.," https://www-oed-com.proxy.library.nyu.edu/view/Entry/230262?rskey=O9eU8D&result=1&isAdvanced=false, accessed June 4, 2020.

13. Abram Smythe Palmer, *Folk-Etymology: A Dictionary of Verbal Corruptions or Words Perverted in Form or Meaning, by False Derivation or Mistaken Analogy* (London: George Bell and Sons, 1882), 448.

14. I see related notions of worldhood in Piekut, *Henry Cow*.

15. My thoughts here are informed by Pheng Cheah, *What Is a World? On Postcolonial Literature as World Literature* (Durham, NC: Duke University Press, 2016).

16. For more on related situations, see Yascha Mounk, *Stranger in My Own Country: A Jewish Family in Modern Germany* (New York: Farrar, Straus and Giroux, 2014); Graham Dawson, Jo Dover, and Stephen Hopkins, eds., *The Northern Ireland Troubles*

in Britain: Impacts, Engagements, Legacies and Memories (Manchester, UK: Manchester University Press, 2017).

17. I deliberately refer both to "empire" and to "imperialism" because I make reference to both the comparative empire studies and to the Marxist traditions with which these terms tend to be associated respectively. See Utsa Patnaik and Prabhat Patnaik, *A Theory of Imperialism* (New York: Columbia University Press, 2016), 1–7.

18. Robert J. C. Young, *Postcolonialism: A Historical Introduction* (Oxford: Blackwell, 2001), 25--34.

19. Craig Calhoun, Frederick Cooper, and Kevin W. Moore, introduction to *Lessons of Empire: Imperial Histories and American Power*, ed. Craig Calhoun, Frederick Cooper, and Kevin W. Moore (New York: The New Press, 2006), 3.

20. Go, *Patterns of Empire*, 9.

21. Ann Laura Stoler, "Imperial Formations and the Opacities of Rule," in *Lessons of Empire*, 52.

22. Alejandro L. Madrid, ed., *Transnational Encounters: Music and Performance at the U.S.-Mexico Border* (New York: Oxford University Press, 2011), 2.

23. Young, *Postcolonialism*, 27.

24. Hannah Arendt, *The Origins of Totalitarianism* (New York: Harcourt, Brace, 1979), 143. See also Harvey, *New Imperialism*, 15–16.

25. Fosler-Lussier, *Cold War Diplomacy*, 22. For more discussion of such programs as they developed within music institutions, see Ansari, *Sound of a Superpower*; Beal, *New Music*; Martin Brody, "Class of '54: Friendship and Ideology at the American Academy in Rome," in Brody, ed., *Music and Musical Composition*, 222–56; Von Eschen, *Satchmo*.

26. Du Bois, "Peace Is Dangerous."

27. Go, *Patterns of Empire*, 131–32.

28. For a recent iteration of such arguments, see Ronald Radano and Tejumola Olaniyan, eds., *Audible Empire: Music, Global Politics, Critique* (Durham, NC: Duke University Press, 2016).

29. Edward W. Said, *Musical Elaborations* (New York: Columbia University Press, 1991), 15.

30. Said, *Musical Elaborations*, 70. Bracketed addition mine.

31. They met through their membership in the Arab-American Association of University Graduates, which was founded by Ibrahim Abu-Lughod in 1968. Halim El-Dabh, interview by the author, December 7, 2014, Kent, Ohio; digital recording.

32. UNYAZI Music Festival website, www.sacmmt.com/unyazi-electronic-music-festival-2016, accessed May 22, 2020. "UNYAZI Electronic Music Symposium and Festival 2005," *Art Africa*, artafricamagazine.org/unyazi-electronic-music-symposium-and-festival-2005-2/?v=e4dd286dc7d7, accessed May 22, 2020; George Lewis, "Foreword: After Afrofuturism," *Journal of the Society for American Music* 2, no. 2 (2008): 146.

33. Edward Said, "Reflections on Exile," in *Reflections on Exile and Other Essays* (Cambridge, MA: Harvard University Press, 2000), 174.

34. Radano and Olaniyan, *Audible Empire*, 4.

35. Lawrence D. Bobo, "An American Conundrum: Race, Sociology, and the African American Road to Citizenship," in *The Oxford Handbook of African American Citizenship, 1865–Present*, ed. Henry Louis Gates, Jr., et al. (New York: Oxford University Press, 2012), 22.

36. Aihwa Ong, "Cultural Citizenship as Subject-Making: Immigrants Negotiate Racial and Cultural Boundaries in the United States," *Current Anthropology* 37, no. 5 (1996): 737.

37. Jennifer Lynn Stoever, *The Sonic Color Line: Race and the Cultural Politics of Listening* (New York: New York University Press, 2016).

38. Avishai Margalit, *The Decent Society*, trans. Naomi Goldblum (Cambridge, MA: Harvard University Press, 1996), 150–61.

39. Revuluri writes here specifically of opera. Sindhumathi Revuluri, "A Note from the Guest Editor," *Opera Quarterly* 32, no. 1 (2016): 1.

40. Bobo, "American Conundrum," 22.

41. Nancy Foner, *From Ellis Island to JFK: New York's Two Great Waves of Immigration* (New Haven, CT: Yale University Press, 2000).

42. Alonso-Minutti et al., *Experimentalisms in Practice*; Ignacio Corona and Alejandro L. Madrid, eds., *Postnational Musical Identities: Cultural Production, Distribution, and Consumption in a Globalized Scenario* (Lanham, MD: Lexington Books, 2007); Brent Hayes Edwards, *The Practice of Diaspora: Literature, Translation, and the Rise of Black Internationalism* (Cambridge, MA: Harvard University Press, 2003); Paul Gilroy, *The Black Atlantic: Modernity and Double-Consciousness* (Cambridge, MA: Harvard University Press, 1993); Nancy Yunhwa Rao, *Chinatown Opera Theater in North America* (Urbana: University of Illinois Press, 2017); Shana Redmond, *Everything Man: The Form and Function of Paul Robeson* (Durham, NC: Duke University Press, 2020); Florian Scheding, *Musical Journeys: Performing Migration in Twentieth-Century Music* (Woodbridge, UK: Boydell Press, 2019).

43. Lorraine Daston and H. Otto Sibum, "Introduction: Scientific Personae and their Histories," *Science in Context* 16, no. 1–2 (2003): 2–3, 4.

44. For more on this persona, see Joseph William Pfender, "Oblique Music: American Tape Experimentalism and Peripheral Cultures of Technology, 1887 and 1950" (PhD diss., New York University, 2019). For more on this complex, see Cyrus C. M. Mody and Andrew J. Nelson, "'A Towering Virtue of Necessity': Interdisciplinarity and the Rise of Computer Music at Vietnam-Era Stanford," *Osiris* 28 (2013): 254–77.

45. Suzanne G. Cusick, *Francesca Caccini at the Medici Court: Music and the Circulation of Power* (Chicago: University of Chicago Press, 2009); Madrid, *In Search of Julián Carillo*; Guthrie P. Ramsey, Jr., *The Amazing Bud Powell: Black Genius, Jazz History, and the Challenge of Bebop* (Berkeley: University of California Press, 2013); Shana Redmond, *Everything Man*; Nichole Rustin-Paschal, *The Kind of Man I Am: Jazzmasculinity and the World of Charles Mingus Jr.* (Middletown, CT: Wesleyan University Press, 2017).

46. My thoughts here are indebted to Homi Bhabha's lectures in the seminar "Literary Theory in the Life of Literature," from the spring of 2002.

47. Stoler writes of colonial governance in the Dutch East Indies, but her words apply well to the US settings of my study. Ann Laura Stoler, *Along the Archival Grain: Epistemic Anxieties and Colonial Common Sense* (Princeton, NJ: Princeton University Press, 2010), 38.

48. IStoler, *Along the Archival Grain*, 3.

49. For related discussions see Louis Chude-Sokei, *The Sound of Culture: Diaspora and Black Technopoetics* (Middletown, CT: Wesleyan University Press, 2016); Elizabeth Hinkle-Turner, *Women Composers and Music Technology in the United States* (Aldershot, UK: Ashgate, 2006); Tara Rodgers, *Pink Noises: Women on Electronic Music and Sound* (Durham, NC: Duke University Press, 2010); Alexander G. Weheliye, *Phonog-*

raphies: Grooves in Sonic Afro-Modernity (Durham, NC: Duke University Press, 2005); Michael Veal, *Dub: Soundscapes and Shattered Songs in Jamaican Reggae* (Middletown, CT: Wesleyan University Press, 2007).

50. Homi K. Bhabha, "In the Cave of Making: Thoughts on Third Space," *Communicating in the Third Space*, ed. Karin Ikas and Gerhard Wagner (New York: Routledge, 2009), x.

51. Hartman, *Scenes of Subjection*.

52. Yoko Ono, "The Word of a Fabricator," in *Imagine Yoko* (Lund, Sweden: Bakhall 2005), 113–19. Translated by Yoko Ono. Originally published in Japanese in *SAC Journal* 24 (May 1962).

53. Christina Klein, *Cold War Orientalism: Asia in the Middlebrow Imagination, 1945–1961* (Berkeley: University of California Press, 2003), 13.

54. Said, "Reflections on Exile," 148.

55. Timothy Snyder, *Bloodlands: Europe between Hitler and Stalin* (New York: Basic Books, 2012), xix.

56. Hartman, *Scenes of Subjection*; Alexander G. Weheliye, *Habeas Viscus: Racializing Assemblages, Biopolitics, and Black Feminist Theories of the Human* (Durham, NC: Duke University Press, 2014).

57. I am drawing partly from Stoler, *Archival Grain*, 3.

58. Hartman, "Venus in Two Acts," *Small Axe: A Caribbean Journal of Criticism* 26 (June 2008): 12.

59. The quotation comes from Frank Wittendorfer, head of Siemens Archive, in email correspondence with the author, July 4, 2018.

60. Michael C. Heller, *Loft Jazz: Improvising Music in New York in the 1970s* (Oakland: University of California Press, 2017), 145–78.

61. This dynamic is somewhat similar to one Michael Heller describes in *Loft Jazz*, 145–46.

62. David Blake, "Musical Omnivory in the Neoliberal University," *Journal of Musicology* 34 (2017): 340.

63. Stoler, *Along the Archival Grain*, 1.

64. Alejandra Bronfman, *Isles of Noise: Sonic Media in the Caribbean* (Chapel Hill: University of North Carolina Press, 2016); Hyun Kyong Hannah Chang, "A Vocal Interior: Korean Hymns and Prayers between US and Japanese Empires," unpublished manuscript; Chang, "Musical Encounters in Korean Christianity: A Trans-Pacific Narrative" (PhD diss., University of California, Los Angeles, 2014); Herrera, *Elite Art Worlds*; Thomas Irvine, *Listening to China: Sound and the Sino-Western Encounter, 1770–1839* (Chicago: University of Chicago Press, 2020); Sergio Ospina Romero, "Ghosts in the Machine and Other Tales around a 'Marvelous Invention': Player Pianos in Latin America in the Early Twentieth Century," *Journal of the American Musicological Society* 72, no. 1 (2019): 1–42; Jessica Schwartz and April L. Brown, "Challenging Voices: Relistening to Marshallese Histories of the Present," in *The Oxford Handbook of Voice Studies*, ed. Nina Eidsheim and Katherine Meizel (New York: Oxford University Press, 2019), 191–213; Schwartz, "How the Sea Is Sounded: Remapping Indigenous Soundings in the Marshallese Diaspora," in *Remapping Sound Studies*, ed. Gavin Steingo and Jim Sykes (Durham, NC: Duke University Press, 2019), 77–105.

65. Chang, "Singing and Praying among Korean Christian Converts (1896–1915): A Trans-Pacific Genealogy of the Modern Korean Voice," in *The Oxford Handbook of Voice Studies*, eds. Nina Sun Eisheim and Katherine Meizel (New York: Oxford

University Press, 2019); Zhuqing (Lester) S. Hu, "From *Ut Re Mi* to Fourteen-Tone Temperament: The Global Acoustemologies of an Early Modern Chinese Tuning Reform" (PhD diss., University of Chicago, 2019); Hu, "A Global Phonographic Revolution: Trans-Eurasian Resonances of Writing in Early Modern France and China," in *Acoustemologies in Contact: Sounding Subjects and Modes of Listening in Early Modern Europe*, ed. Emily Wilbourne and Suzanne Cusick (Cambridge, UK: Open Book Publishers, 2021); Yvonne Liao, "'Die gute Unterhaltungsmusik': Landscape, Refugee Cafés, and Sounds of 'Little Vienna' in Wartime Shanghai," *Musical Quarterly* 98, no. 4 (December 2015): 350–94.

Katherine Butler Schofield, "Music under Mughal Patronage: The Place of Pleasure," in *The Oxford Handbook of the Mughal World*, ed. Richard M. Eaton and Ramya Sreenivasan (Oxford: Oxford University Press, forthcoming).

66. Gilroy, *Darker than Blue*; Weheliye, *Habeas Viscus*; Kira Thurman, "Singing the Civilizing Mission in the Land of Bach, Beethoven, and Brahms: The Fisk Jubilee Singers in Nineteenth-Century Germany, *Journal of World History* 27, no. 3 (September 2016): 443–71.

67. Ann Laura Stoler, *Duress: Imperial Durabilities in Our Times* (Durham, NC: Duke University Press, 2016), 36.

Chapter 1

1. John F. Goodman, *Mingus Speaks* (Berkeley: University of California Press, 2013), 227.

2. Charles Mingus, EV CD 20, track 2, digital recording transferred from reel EV TS 53, Edgard Varèse Collection, Paul Sacher Foundation.

3. This chapter is a revision of my article "Enigmas of the Third Space: Mingus and Varèse at Greenwich House," *Journal of the American Musicological Society* (2018) 81, no. 1 (Spring 2018): 155–211. It restores an expanded discussion of Mingus that had become abridged during the peer review process, which called for a more extensive discussion of Varèse and a shortening of the section on Mingus. I note this peer review process, which took place before tenure and involved seven readers and three resubmissions, because it speaks to the manner in which disciplinary patterns reproduce themselves even when scholars, editors, and communities seek to do otherwise.

4. These accounts derive from Olivia Mattis's interviews with Teo Macero and Earle Brown and from my own interview with Bill Crow: Earle Brown and Teo Macero, "From Bebop to Poo-wip: Jazz Influences in Varèse's Poème Électronique," interview by Olivia Mattis, *Edgard Varèse: Composer, Sound Sculptor, Visionary*, ed. Felix Meyer and Heidy Zimmermann (Woodbridge, UK: Boydell and Brewer, 2006), 309–17; Bill Crow, interview by the author, New York City, February 19, 2014. See also Bill Crow, *From Birdland to Broadway: Scenes from a Jazz Life* (New York: Oxford University Press, 1992), 204–5. In a diary entry dated April 4, 1957, Brown also wrote that guitarist Barry Galbraith and bassist Milt Hinton would also participate. Rebecca Y. Kim, ed., *Beyond Notation: The Music of Earle Brown* (Ann Arbor: University of Michigan Press, 2017), 128, 174.

5. Arranger George Handy and critic Robert Reisner also participated, and James Tenney may have been in the audience. For more on the participants, see Mattis, "From Bebop to Poo-wip," 312–13.

6. See, for example, "'Edgar [*sic*] Varèse and the Jazzmen' (MP3s)," *WFMU's Be-*

ware of the Blog: A Radio Station That Bites Back (blog), WFMU website, June 1, 2009, http://blog.wfmu.org/freeform/2009/06/edgar-var%C3%A8se-and-the-jazzmen -mp3s.html; and "Edgard Varèse Conducts a Jazz Workshop (1957)," UbuWeb, http://www.ubu.com/sound/varese.html, accessed June 9, 2016.

7. John Cage, "Edgard Varèse," in *Silence: Lectures and Writings* (Middletown, CT: Wesleyan University Press, 1939), 83–86.

8. Peter Yates, "Fifteen Composers in the American Experimental Tradition," *Bulletin of the New York Public Library* 63 (1959): 509. See also Fernand Ouellette, *Edgard Varèse* (Richmond, UK: Calder & Boyars, 1973), 156.

9. Mattis, "From Bebop to Poo-wip."

10. George E. Lewis, "Improvised Music after 1950: Afrological and Eurological Perspectives," *Black Music Research Journal* 16, no. 1 (Spring 1996): 91–122.

11. Relevant secondary literature includes Tamar Barzel, *New York Noise: Radical Jewish Music and the Downtown Scene* (Bloomington: Indiana University Press, 2015); Rebecca Kim, "In No Uncertain Musical Terms: The Cultural Politics of John Cage's Indeterminacy" (PhD diss., Columbia University, 2008); Lewis, *Power Stronger Than Itself*; Piekut, *Experimentalism Otherwise*; Scott DeVeaux, *The Birth of Bebop: A Social and Musical History* (Berkeley: University of California Press, 1999); Bernard Gendron, *Between Montmartre and the Mudd Club* (Chicago: University of Chicago Press, 2002); Ingrid Monson, *Freedom Sounds: Civil Rights Call Out to Jazz and Africa* (Oxford: Oxford University Press, 2007).

12. It is not clear when or how these bootlegged copies were made. The master recordings had been in Chou Wen-chung's possession before their acquisition by the Paul Sacher Foundation.

13. For more on "after-hours," see Shane Vogel, *The Scene of Harlem Cabaret: Race, Sexuality, Performance* (Chicago: University of Chicago Press, 2009).

14. Don Butterfield and Frank Rehak went on to perform Cage's work in 1958 and 1960. See Paul van Emmerik, ed., "A John Cage Compendium: Chronology 1912–1971," *A John Cage Compendium*, September 18, 2020, https://cagecomp.home.xs4all .nl/chronology_1912–1971.html; and William Fetterman, *John Cage's Theatre Pieces: Notations and Performances* (Abingdon, UK: Routledge, 1996), 108.

15. Earle Brown Lecture at Peabody Conservatory, "Peabody Lecture, Part II," 1969, MD19, Earle Brown Archive, Earle Brown Music Foundation, Rye, New York.

16. Crow, interview.

17. I discuss Varèse's reception below.

18. Bill Crow did not remember having been paid for playing at Greenwich House. Crow, interview. Though Mingus kept careful financial records, the Charles Mingus Collection at the Library of Congress includes no documentation of payment for such a session in 1957. Transcribed public talks by and interviews with Brown (as listed under "Archival Sources" in the "Works Cited" list below) do not touch on the question of remuneration.

19. See, for example, Karin Ikas and Gerhard Wagner, ed., *Communicating in the Third Space* (New York: Routledge, 2009); Edward W. Soja, *Thirdspace: Journeys to Los Angeles and Other Real-and-Imagined Places* (Cambridge, MA: Blackwell Publishers, 1996); and Robert J. C. Young, *Colonial Desire: Hybridity in Theory, Culture, and Race* (London: Routledge, 1994), 21–22.

20. Homi K. Bhabha, "In the Cave of Making: Thoughts on Third Space," *Communicating in the Third Space*, ed. Karin Ikas and Gerhard Wagner (New York: Routledge, 2009), x.

21. Hartman, *Scenes of Subjection,* 6.

22. Hartman, *Scenes of Subjection,* 4, 25–36.

23. Hartman, *Scenes of Subjection,* 5.

24. Hartman, *Scenes of Subjection,* 3–14, 35–36.

25. Lewis, *Power Stronger Than Itself,* xiii.

26. Piekut, *Experimentalism Otherwise,* 3.

27. Bhabha, "On Cultural Choice" in *The Turn to Ethics,* ed. Marjorie Garber, Beatrice Hanssen, and Rebecca L. Walkowitz (New York: Routledge, 2000), 182; Hartman, *Scenes of Subjection: Terror, Slavery, and Self-Making in Nineteenth-Century America* (Oxford: Oxford University Press, 1997), 109–10.

28. Elizabeth F. Cohen, *Semi-Citizenship in Democratic Politics* (Cambridge: Cambridge University Press, 2009); Benjamin N. Lawrance and Jacqueline Stevens, eds., *Citizenship in Question: Evidentiary Birthright and Statelessness* (Durham, NC: Duke University Press, 2017); and Bryan S. Turner, "We Are All Denizens Now: On the Erosion of Citizenship," *Citizenship Studies* 20, no. 6–7 (2016): 679–92.

29. See Lawrence D. Bobo, "An American Conundrum: Race, Sociology, and the African American Road to Citizenship," in *The Oxford Handbook of African American Citizenship, 1865–Present,* ed. Henry Louis Gates Jr. et al. (New York: Oxford University Press, 2012), 22

30. Charles Mingus, *Beneath the Underdog,* ed. Nel King (New York: Alfred A. Knopf, 1971); Mingus, *Mingus Speaks;* Thomas Reichman, *Mingus: Charlie Mingus 1968* (Inlet Films, 1968), 58 mins.

31. See Bobo, "An American Conundrum."

32. See Olivia Mattis, "Edgard Varèse's 'Progressive' Nationalism: Amériques Meets Américanisme" in *Edgard Varèse, die Befreiung des Klangs: Symposium Edgard Varèse Hamburg 1991,* ed. Helga de la Motte-Haber (Hofheim, Germany: Wolke, 1991), 149–80.

33. See Carol J. Oja, *Making Music Modern: New York in the 1920s* (Oxford: Oxford University Press, 2003), 25–44.

34. See Robert George Reisner, ed. *Bird: The Legend of Charlie Parker* (New York: Da Capo, 1962), 65, 229.

35. Michael Leja, *Reframing Abstract Expressionism: Subjectivity and Painting in the 1940s* (New Haven, CT: Yale University Press, 1993), 84; see also Ann Eden Gibson, *Abstract Expressionism: Other Politics* (New Haven, CT: Yale University Press, 1999), 31. To recognize the Eighth Street Artists' Club as a white, masculinist space is not to ignore the work of women and people of color who participated in the community, but simply to acknowledge the majority demographics of club membership alongside the racialized and gendered nature of the discourses through which value was often adjudicated. For more on women at the club, see Mary Gabriel, *Ninth Street Women* (New York: Back Bay Books, 2018).

36. See Rep. George Anthony Dondero, "Modern Art Shackled to Communism, United States House of Representatives, August 16, 1949," reproduced in *Art in Theory 1900–2000: An Anthology of Changing Ideas,* ed. Charles Harrison and Paul Wood, 2nd ed. (London: Blackwell, 2003).

37. See Leja, *Reframing Abstract Expressionism,* 22.

38. Mattis, "From Bebop to Poo-wip," 314. "Edgard Varèse weekly planners," MF 785, Edgard Varèse Collection, Paul Sacher Foundation, Basel, Switzerland.

39. Salim Washington, "All the Things You Could Be By Now: Charles Mingus Presents Charles Mingus and the Limits of Avant-Garde Jazz," in *Uptown Conversation: The New Jazz Studies*, ed. Robert G. O'Meally, Brent Hayes Edwards, and Farah Jasmine Griffin (New York: Columbia University Press, 2004), esp. 35–38.

40. Chou Wen-chung, email correspondence with the author, facilitated by Belinda Quan, May 3, 2017.

41. Charles Mingus, draft preface for *Beneath the Underdog*, Charles Mingus Collection, Library of Congress, box 45, folder 2.

42. Grove Music Online, s.v. "Third Stream," by Gunther Schuller, http://www.oxfordmusiconline.com.proxy.library.nyu.edu/subscriber/article/grove/music/27850, accessed October 30, 2016.

43. Mattis, "From Bebop to Poo-wip," 313.

44. The address book (from the 1950s and 1960s) is found in the Charles Mingus Collection, Library of Congress, boxes 72–73. With the exception of Bill Crow, all reputed participants in the sessions have died. The fact that neither Earle Brown nor Crow recalled Mingus's presence there hardly undermines the authority of Macero's remembrance. Crow was himself a bassist and therefore would have been unlikely to overlap with Mingus at the one session Crow attended. Brown, who had no close personal relation to Mingus, did not remember Mingus being there; but he also recalled only six players—not one a bassist—despite the fact that a bass is heard in almost all of the recordings. Moreover, Crow remembers having played in only one unrecorded session, thus supporting the idea that a different bassist must have been recorded in the Greenwich House sessions.

45. Geoffrey C. Bowker, *Memory Practices in the Sciences* (Cambridge, MA: MIT Press, 2005), 2, 9.

46. Michel Foucault, *The Archaeology of Knowledge and the Discourse on Language* (New York: Vintage, 1982), 129.

47. Hartman, "Venus in Two Acts," *Small Axe: A Caribbean Journal of Criticism* 26 (June 2008): 12.

48. Hartman, "Venus in Two Acts," 11.

49. Michael Gallope, "On Close Reading and Sound Recording," Humanities Futures, Franklin Humanities Institute, published 2016, http://humanitiesfutures.org/papers/close-reading-sound-recording, accessed July 6, 2020.

50. The Sacher Foundation call numbers for the three reels are EV TS 53, EV TS 1009, and EV TS 1038. These reels were transferred onto compact discs with the call numbers EV CD 20, EV CD 24, and EV CD 46. The disc reel diameters are ten, five, and seven inches respectively.

51. "Edgard Varèse weekly planners." These dates include Sunday, March 31, 1957; Sunday, April 14, 1957; Sunday, June 30, 1957; Saturday, July 27, 1957; and Sunday, August 4, 1957. See also Mattis, "From Bebop to Poo-wip."

52. See Aaron Fox, "Repatriation as Reanimation through Reciprocity," in *The Cambridge History of World Music*, ed. Philip V. Bohlman (Cambridge: Cambridge University Press, 2013), 522–54; Noel Lobley, "Taking Xhosa Music Out of the Fridge," *Ethnomusicology Forum* 21, no. 2 (2012): 181–95; and Anthony Seeger, "Who Should Control Which Rights to Music?" in *Current Issues in Music Research: Copyright, Power, and Transnational Music Processes*, ed. Susana Moreno Fernández et al. (Lisbon: Colibri, 2012), 27–49.

53. Edgard Varèse, "Radio interview with Varèse late Nov. 1958" (interview on the New York Philharmonic Network), EV CD 15, track 2, Edgard Varèse Collection, Paul Sacher Foundation.

54. Amy Cimini, *Wild Sound: Maryanne Amacher and the Tense of Audible Life*, (New York: Oxford University Press, 2021).

55. This excerpt, minus the first few seconds, can be heard on Varèse, "Edgard Varèse Conducts a Jazz Workshop (1957)," track 1.

56. In addition to Mingus, Macero, and Charles, five other members of the Greenwich House sessions were JCW regulars: Bert, Butterfield, Farmer, Overton, and Shaughnessy.

57. Brown, "Peabody Lecture, Part II."

58. Crow, interview. For a similar discussion, see Crow, *From Birdland to Broadway*, 204–5.

59. Robert Frost, "Some Obstinacy," in *Robert Frost: Speaking on Campus: Excerpts from His Talks, 1949–1962*, ed. Edward Connery Lathem (New York: W. W. Norton, 2009); "A Poet's Pilgrimage: Robert Frost Goes Back to England," *Life* (September 23, 1957): 109.

60. Ted Gioia, "Jazz and the Primitivist Myth," *Musical Quarterly* 73, no. 1 (1989): 138; Ingrid Monson, "The Problem with White Hipness: Race, Gender, and Cultural Conceptions in Jazz Historical Discourse," *Journal of the American Musicological Society* 48, no. 3 (1995): 396–422.

61. Jennifer Lynn Stoever, *The Sonic Color Line: Race and the Cultural Politics of Listening* (New York: New York University Press, 2016).

62. For more on such stereotypes, see Lewis, "Improvised Music," 147. For more on the ambivalent structure of stereotypes, see Homi Bhabha, *The Location of Culture* (London: Routledge, 1994), 94–120.

63. Quoted in Vivian Perlis and Libby Van Cleve, *Composers' Voices from Ives to Ellington: An Oral History of American Music* (New Haven, CT: Yale University Press, 2005), 115.

64. Russell, interview by Ingrid Monson (1995), quoted in Monson, "Oh Freedom: George Russell, John Coltrane, and Modal Jazz," in *In the Course of Performance: Studies in the World of Musical Improvisation*, ed. Bruno Nettl and Melinda Russell (Chicago: University of Chicago Press, 1998), 157.

65. Jairo Moreno, "Imperial Aurality: Jazz, the Archive, and U.S. Empire," in *Audible Empire: Music, Global Politics, Critique*, ed. Ronald Radano and Tejumola Olaniyan (Durham, NC: Duke University Press Books, 2016), 136.

66. Monson, "Oh Freedom," 158, 161.

67. Moreno, "Imperial Aurality," 139.

68. This excerpt can be heard on Varèse, "Edgard Varèse Conducts a Jazz Workshop (1957)," track 2.

69. Benjamin Steege, "Varèse in Vitro: On Attention, Aurality, and the Laboratory," *Current Musicology* 76 (2003): 35.

70. See Varèse, "Electronic Medium," in *Contemporary Composers on Contemporary Music*, ed. Elliott Schwarz and Barney Childs (New York: Da Capo, 1978), 207.

71. Varèse, "Electronic Medium," 208.

72. See Varèse, "Spatial Music," in *Contemporary Composers on Contemporary Music*, 206.

73. Quoted in Perlis and Van Cleve, *Composers' Voices*, 115.

74. Bill Brown, "Reification, Reanimation, and the American Uncanny," *Critical Inquiry* 32, no. 2 (2006): 179. Louis Chude-Sokei, *The Sound of Culture: Diaspora and Black Technopoetics* (Middletown, CT: Wesleyan University Press, 2016).

75. Brown, "Reification," 180, 183, 185.

76. Hortense J. Spillers, "Mama's Baby, Papa's Maybe: An American Grammar Book," in *Black, White, and in Color: Essays on American Literature and Culture* (Chicago: University of Chicago Press, 2003), 208.

77. Bhabha, "Cave of Making," x.

78. This excerpt can be heard at Varèse, "Edgard Varèse Conducts a Jazz Workshop (1957)," tracks 5 and 6.

79. Mattis, "From Bebop to Poo-wip," 312–13.

80. See, for example, Perlis and Van Cleve, *Composers' Voices*, 111, which shows an image of the first page of the autograph manuscript of *Déserts*.

81. Chou Wen-chung, email correspondence.

82. Phil Ford, *Dig: Sound and Music in Hip Culture* (Oxford: Oxford University Press, 2013), 25.

83. Chou Wen-chung, email correspondence. Chou does recall "helping set up one of the sessions at Greenwich House but then he left because Varese did not ask him to stay."

84. See Brian Priestley, *Mingus: A Critical Biography* (New York: Da Capo Press, 1984), 77.

85. These excerpts can be heard at Varèse, "Edgard Varèse Conducts a Jazz Workshop (1957)," tracks 7 and 8.

86. I am grateful to Jason Cady of the Earle Brown Archive for helping me to identify Brown's voice.

87. Ingrid Monson, *Saying Something: Jazz Improvisation and Interaction* (Chicago: University of Chicago Press, 1996).

88. These recordings are not available online, but are held in the Edgard Varèse Collection of the Paul Sacher Foundation.

89. I am grateful to Michael Heller for our conversations about this music.

90. Von Eschen, *Satchmo*, 4.

91. Ruth Phelps and Henri Morane, "Artistes d'avant-garde en Amériques," quoted in Mattis, "Edgard Varèse's 'Progressive' Nationalism," 167. Mattis raised the question of Varèse's anti-Semitism by reproducing this passage, which had been intentionally buried in the composer's earlier historiography: ibid., 167–70. The interview in *Le Figaro hebdomadaire* had previously been reprinted in Louise Hibour, ed. *Edgar Varèse: Écrits* (Paris: C. Bourgois, 1983), 54–55, but with the anti-Semitic and racist passage elided.

92. Ruth HaCohen, *The Music Libel against the Jews* (New Haven, CT: Yale University Press, 2012), 53.

93. See Varèse, "Electronic Medium," 207.

94. Anti-Semitic tropes persisted in his words even through the 1960s. In a 1965 interview, while criticizing anti-Semitism in the United States, he also explains that "a Jew is not afraid to go and do what he has to do, and to delve into society. And if they don't like them [the Jews], he buys them. You can be bought, you know. Art is a whore." Quoted in Perlis and Van Cleve, *Composers' Voices*, 105–6.

95. See Oja, *Making Music Modern*, 25–44.

96. See Mattis, "Edgard Varèse's 'Progressive' Nationalism," 167–70; Rachel

Mundy, "The 'League of Jewish Composers' and American Music," *Musical Quarterly* 96, no. 1 (2013): 50–99; and Oja, *Making Music Modern*, 217–18.

97. Mattis, "Edgard Varèse's 'Progressive' Nationalism," 167.

98. Mundy, "'League of Jewish Composers.'"

99. Olivia Mattis, "Edgard Varèse and the Visual Arts" (PhD diss., Stanford University, 1992), 21, 41–43, 61, 67, 184–85, 236.

100. John Higham, *Strangers in the Land: Patterns of American Nativism, 1860–1925* (New Brunswick, NJ: Rutgers University Press, 2002), 4.

101. Jane F. Fulcher, "The Preparation for Vichy: Anti-Semitism in French Musical Culture between the Two World Wars," *Musical Quarterly* 79, no. 3 (1995): 462.

102. Walter Benn Michaels, *Our America: Nativism, Modernism, and Pluralism* (Durham, NC: Duke University Press, 1995), 2.

103. T. J. Clark, *Farewell to an Idea: Episodes from a History of Modernism* (New Haven, CT: Yale University Press, 1999), 9; Michaels, *Our America*, 2.

104. Varèse, "Radio interview with Varèse late Nov. 1958." See also Edgard Varèse, "Music as an Art-Science," lecture, University of Southern California, 1939. Cited in Edgard Varèse and Chou Wen-chung, "The Liberation of Sound," *Perspectives of New Music* 5, no. 1 (1966): 11–19.

105. Michaels, *Our America*, 2.

106. For more on these nativist currents and the backlash against them, see Martin Brody, "Founding Sons: Copland, Sessions, and Berger on Genealogy and Hybridity," in *Aaron Copland and His World*, ed. Carol J. Oja and Judith Tick (Princeton, NJ: Princeton University Press, 2005), 15–44.

107. For more on Varèse's intermittent attraction to fascism, see Mattis, "Edgard Varèse's 'Progressive' Nationalism," 169.

108. "Quel pitoyable cabotin et pauvre con / Dans le fond un pauvre Salaud. / FINI d' être là / Bon Samaritain." Microfilm 14.10 Diverses, 0786–0798, Edgard Varèse Collection MF 786, Paul Sacher Foundation. I am grateful to Joel Rust for having alerted me to the existence of this document.

109. Edgard Varèse, letter to Carl Ruggles, November 1944, Carl Ruggles papers in the Irving S. Gilmore Music Library of Yale University. Quoted in Joel Rust, "Edgard Varèse and the Sounds of the Early Twentieth-Century City" (PhD diss., New York University, 2020), 82.

110. For relevant French anti-Italian contexts, see Fulcher, "Preparation for Vichy," 462–63, 468.

111. Mundy, "League of Jewish Composers," 65–66.

112. Henry Cowell, "American Composers," in *Proceedings of the Ohio State Educational Conference, Eleventh Annual Session* (Columbus: Ohio State University, 1932), 378–79. For an illuminating discussion of this essay, see Mundy, "League of Jewish Composers," 66.

113. Matthew D. Morrison, "The Sound(s) of Subjection: Constructing American Popular Music and Racial Identity through Blacksound," *Women & Performance* 27, no. 1 (2017): 13–24; Matthew D. Morrison, "Race, Blacksound, and the (Re)Making of Musicological Discourse," *Journal of the American Musicological Society* 72, no. 3 (2019): 781–823.

114. I use the term "noble savage" to refer to depictions of "primitive" non-Western man as embodying qualities of innocence, vitality, and virtue inaccessible to his "civilized" European counterpart. See, for example, Ter Ellingson, *The Myth of the No-*

ble Savage (Berkeley: University of California Press, 2001); Hoxie Neale Fairchild, "Noble Savage: A Study in Romantic Naturalism," *Journal of American History* 15 (1929): 567–68; and Ted Gioia, "Jazz and the Primitivist Myth," *Musical Quarterly* 73 (1989): 131.

115. Heidy Zimmermann, "Lost Early Works: Facts and Suppositions," in *Edgard Varèse: Composer, Sound Sculptor, Visionary*, ed. Felix Meyer and Heidy Zimmermann (Woodbridge, UK: Boydell and Brewer, 2006), 46.

116. Michaels, *Our America*, 12.

117. Zimmermann, "Lost Early Works"; Ernst Lichtenhahn, " 'New Primitiveness' " in *Edgard Varèse: Composer, Sound Sculptor, Visionary*, ed. Felix Meyer and Heidy Zimmermann (Woodbridge, UK: Boydell and Brewer, 2006), 193–201.

118. Mattis, "Edgard Varèse's 'Progressive' Nationalism," 154–56.

119. See David Trotter, *Literature in the First Media Age: Britain between the Wars* (Cambridge, MA: Harvard University Press, 2013), 110.

120. Chude-Sokei, "Sound of Culture," 16.

121. Chude-Sokei, "Sound of Culture," 31.

122. See, for example, Marc Treib, *Space Calculated in Seconds: The Philips Pavilion, Le Corbusier, Edgard Varèse* (Princeton, NJ: Princeton University Press, 1996).

123. Letter from Varèse to Le Corbusier on January 31, 1957, and letter from Le Corbusier to Varèse on June 22, 1957, file R3 06, pp. 50 and 58, Fondation Le Corbusier. For more on these contexts, see R. D. Lukes, *"Poème électronique* of Edgard Varèse," (PhD diss., Harvard University, 1996), 182–211.

124. For more on relevant community ties, see Mattis, "Edgard Varèse and the Visual Arts," 67, 236.

125. Le Corbusier, *When the Cathedrals Were White*, trans. Francis E. Hyslop Jr. (New York: McGraw Hill, 1964).

126. See Mardges Bacon, *Le Corbusier in America: Travels in the Land of the Timid* (Cambridge, MA: MIT Press, 2001), 256–59; Vikramaditya Prakash, *Chandigarh's Le Corbusier: The Struggle for Modernity in Postcolonial India* (Seattle: University of Washington Press, 2002), 80–82; and Adolf Max Vogt, *Le Corbusier, the Noble Savage: Toward an Archaeology of Modernism*, trans. Radka Donnell (Cambridge, MA: MIT Press, 2000).

127. Le Corbusier, *When the Cathedrals Were White*, 158.

128. Le Corbusier, *When the Cathedrals Were White*, 160. According to artist Abel Warshawsky, Varèse had a similar reaction to jazz upon first arriving in New York. "Varèse found New York, with its skyscrapers and teeming streets, a joy and inspiration for his ultra-modernistic tendencies. He declared that the noise and racket inspired him with leitmotifs for new musical compositions. To produce the desired effects, new instruments would be needed. [. . .] One night at a Negro cabaret, in the company of [Francis] Picabia, the Cubist, and myself, he heard for the first time real Negro jazz and found, to his chagrin, that the instruments he was dreaming of were already in use!" See Abel G Warshawsky, *The Memories of an American Impressionist* (Kent, OH: Kent State University Press, 1980), 177–78. If this anecdote is true, then it might suggest that Varèse arrived in New York with Parisian negrophilic attitudes similar to Le Corbusier's, but acquired a more "American" negrophobic nativism over the course of the 1920s.

129. Le Corbusier, *When the Cathedrals Were White*, 158.

130. Chude-Sokei, "Sound of Culture," 33–34.

131. Chude-Sokei, "Sound of Culture," 35.

132. Chude-Sokei, "Sound of Culture," 161.

133. Quoted in Reisner, *Bird*, 229.

134. Lisa E. Davenport, *Jazz Diplomacy: Promoting America in the Cold War Era* (Jackson: University Press of Mississippi, 2013); Von Eschen, *Satchmo*; Danielle Fosler-Lussier, *Cold War Diplomacy* (Oakland: University of California Press, 2015); and Monson, *Freedom Sounds*.

135. See Treib, *Space Calculated in Seconds*, 9.

136. Treib, *Space Calculated in Seconds*, 9.

137. Letters of November 3, 1956, and January 31, 1957, file R3 06, pp. 91 and 50, Fondation Le Corbusier. These letters include, respectively, the following newspaper clippings: "Soviet Spends Heavily on Fair," *New York Herald Tribune*, October 31, 1956; and "U.S. to Build $5,000,000 Pavilion for '58 World's Fair in Brussels," *New York Times*, January 28, 1957.

138. James Hughes, letter of February 24, 1958, "Exposition universelle et internationale," Correspondence, Vladimir Ussachevsky Collection, Library of Congress. James Hughes was general manager of the Performing Arts Program for the Office of the US Commissioner General.

139. James Hughes, letter of March 11, 1958, "Exposition universelle et internationale," Correspondence, Vladimir Ussachevsky Collection, Library of Congress.

140. Earle Brown, interview by Petr Kotik, January 29, 2000, transcript, Earle Brown Archive, Earle Brown Music Foundation.

141. Brown, interview by Peter Dickinson, Rye, NY, July 1, 1987, in Dickinson, ed. *CageTalk: Dialogues with and about John Cage* (Rochester, NY: University of Rochester Press, 2006), 138.

142. Earle Brown, interview by Bruce Duffie, New York, December 1991, http://www.bruceduffie.com/brown.html, accessed November 3, 2020.

143. I am grateful to Thomas Fichter and Jason Cady of the Earle Brown Music Foundation for our conversations about this piece.

144. Earle Brown, letter to Ray Grismer, August 8, 1957, f. 3–74, Earle Brown Music Foundation. Cited in Kim, *Beyond Notation*, 128.

145. Monson, *Freedom Sounds*, 398.

146. Gibson, *Abstract Expressionism*, 31, 122.

147. Gibson, *Abstract Expressionism*, 122.

148. As he put it in an unpublished interview by Olivia Mattis, "I don't really have any nationalistic feelings or whatever. But I do think there's an American kind of music."

149. Brown, interview by Bruce Duffie.

150. See Brigid Cohen, *Stefan Wolpe and the Avant-Garde Diaspora* (Cambridge: Cambridge University Press, 2012), 254. See also Brigid Cohen, "Diasporic Dialogues in Mid-Century New York: Stefan Wolpe, George Russell, Hannah Arendt, and the Historiography of Displacement," *Journal of the Society for American Music 6*, no. 2 (2012): 143–73.

151. See Sally Banes, *Greenwich Village 1963: Avant-Garde Performance and the Effervescent Body* (Durham, NC: Duke University Press, 1993), 205–6. Mattis identifies Tenney as one of the probable attendees of the Greenwich House Sessions; she also describes his string quartet *Parabolas and Hyperbolas for Edgard Varèse* (1973) as being based on the graphic notation that Varèse used in the sessions. See Mattis, "From Bebop to Poo-wip," 313–30.

152. Yates, "Fifteen Composers," 502.

153. Yates, "Fifteen Composers," 511.

154. Yates, "Fifteen Composers," 504.

155. Yates, "Fifteen Composers," 505.

156. Letter from Yates to John Edmunds, August 17, 1959, quoted in Amy Beal, "'Experimentalists and Independents Are Favored': John Edmunds in Conversation with Peter Yates and John Cage, 1959–61," *Notes* 64, no. 4: 666. For more on relevant contexts, see Beal, *New Music, New Allies: American Experimental Music in West Germany from the Zero Hour to Reunification* (Berkeley: University of California Press, 2006), especially the discussion of Wolfgang Rebner, 62–64.

157. Yates, "Fifteen Composers," 509.

158. See Beal, "Experimentalists and Independents," 662.

159. Beal, "Experimentalists and Independents," 659–87.

160. For more on Varèse's reception during the 1920s, see Oja, *Making Music Modern*, 25–44.

161. Grunfeld, "Adventurers in Sound," 39.

162. This question is the "hook" to the article in the issue's table of contents. See *High Fidelity*, September 1954, 3.

163. *High Fidelity*, September 1954, 46.

164. "Olivia Mattis: Conversation with Earle Brown."

165. Teo Macero, interview by Iara Lee, New York, September 1997, *Perfect Sound Forever* (online magazine), last updated 2008, http://www.furious.com/perfect/teomacero.html.

166. See Macero, "Teo Macero on Producing Jazz and Classical Musicians," You-Tube video, published February 17, 2011, https://www.youtube.com/watch?v=Mqu -NulrKJQ. See also H.C.S., "2 Works Debut at Philharmonic," *New York Times*, January 13, 1958; and John Holmes, "Lion about Music: Noble Undertaking?" *Columbia Spectator*, April 24, 1956. I am grateful to Ryan Maloney for our conversations about this work.

167. Mattis alludes to this document in her essay "The Physical and the Abstract: Varèse and the New York School" in *The New York Schools of Music and the Visual Arts: John Cage, Morton Feldman, Edgard Varèse, Willem de Kooning, Jasper Johns, Robert Rauschenberg*, ed. Steven Johnson (New York: Routledge, 2002), 70–71, which is informed by an interview with Macero. Macero's papers are currently unavailable due to mold contamination at the Library of Congress.

168. Mattis, "From Bebop to Poo-wip," 314. "Jazz spurts" could perhaps instead refer to glissandi. My thanks to Josh Rutner for noting this possibility.

169. In the same bundle as this sketch, there exists a different, hand-notated sketch for *Déserts*, which Varèse appears to have used as inspiration for *Poème électronique*. In this sketch, Varèse labeled as "jazz" a Caribbean-inspired, syncopated percussion texture orchestrated for slapstick, timbales, cencerro, bass drum, guiro, gong, and xylophone, which appears at measures 232–34 of the final score. The sketch is included in the bundle of Varèse's precompositional materials for the *Poème électronique*: film no. 575, p. 805, Edgard Varèse Collection, Paul Sacher Foundation.

170. Film no. 575, p. 731.

171. Regarding the myth of African rhythm, see Kofi Agawu, *Representing African Music* (New York: Routledge, 2003).

172. John F. Goodman, *Mingus Speaks* (Berkeley: University of California Press, 2013), 35–37.

173. Kwami Coleman, "*Free Jazz* and the 'New Thing': Aesthetics, Identity, and Texture ca. 1961," *Journal of Musicology* 38, no. 3 (2021): 261–95.

174. Goodman, *Mingus Speaks*, 38.

175. Goodman, *Mingus Speaks*, 38.

176. Eric Porter, *What Is This Thing Called Jazz?: African American Musicians as Artists, Critics, and Activists* (Berkeley: University of California Press, 2002).

177. See Monson, *Freedom Sounds*, 92; and Priestley, *Mingus*, 57.

178. Goodman, *Mingus Speaks*, 35.

179. The example of Dave Brubeck's 1954 *Time* magazine cover story, which painted its subject as more cerebral, literate, and respectable than his Black counterparts, famously emblematized this disparity See Monson, *Freedom Sounds*, 92–95; and Porter, *What Is This Thing Called Jazz?*, 119–20.

180. Goodman, *Mingus Speaks*, 35. Goodman does not recall having spoken much about Varèse with Mingus outside the discussion included in the published interview. John Goodman, email correspondence with the author, 28 August 2015.

181. Goodman, *Mingus Speaks*, 35

182. See Priestley, *Mingus*, 40–44.

183. Goodman, *Mingus Speaks*, 35–36, here 35.

184. Goodman, *Mingus Speaks*, 36.

185. Daniel Belgrad, *The Culture of Spontaneity: Improvisation and the Arts in Postwar America* (Chicago: University of Chicago Press, 1998), 15–16.

186. Miles Davis made this comparison in a derogatory way in an interview published in *DownBeat* magazine in 1955. See Porter, *What Is This Thing Called Jazz?* 122.

187. See, for example, Charles Mingus, "Open Letter to the Avant-Garde," *Changes*, reproduced and abridged in *Charles Mingus: More Than a Fake Book*, ed. Sue Mingus (New York: Jazz Workshop, 1991), 119; and Goodman, *Mingus Speaks*, 24–31. For more references and context, see Washington, "All the Things," 35–49.

188. Goodman, *Mingus Speaks*, 37.

189. Piekut, 105–8; Lewis, *Power Stronger Than Itself*, 85–114.

190. Porter, *What Is This Thing Called Jazz?* 119–20. The article dismissed bebop, which was largely associated with Black innovators, as a "briefly fashionable" protest music that "quickly palled" in comparison with "more interesting matters, such as tinkering up a little canon a la Bach or some dissonant counterpoint a la Bartok." See "The Man on Cloud No. 7," *Time* 64, no. 19 (November 8, 1954).

191. Monson, *Freedom Sounds*, 92–93.

192. Mingus, "Open Letter to the Avant-Garde," *Changes* (June 1973), reproduced and abridged in Mingus, *More Than a Fake Book*, 119. See Mingus's discussion of the letter and its circumstances in Goodman, 27.

193. Mingus, "Open Letter to the Avant-Garde."

194. See, for example, Monson, *Freedom Sounds*, 71–73; Lewis, *Power Stronger than Itself*, 37. For a discussion of literary Afro-modernism, see Houston Baker Jr., *Modernism and the Harlem Renaissance* (Chicago: University of Chicago Press, 1998).

195. Goodman, *Mingus Speaks*, 37.

196. Porter's account of Mingus suggests this, as do Mingus's own self-narratives. See Porter, *What Is This Thing Called Jazz?* 101–48.

197. Porter, *What Is This Thing Called Jazz?* 117. For the phrase "It's all one music," see Ralph Gleason, "Charles Mingus: A Thinking Musician," *DownBeat* (March 9, 1951): 7.

198. A recording of this panel discussion, titled "Jazz from the Inside Out" (July 17, 1955), is preserved at RGA 0020–0021 in the Voice of America Music Library Collection, Library of Congress.

199. See Jeremy D. Goodwin, "Lenox's Music Inn Was Jazz's Secret Hotspot," *Boston Globe*, July 8, 2012. See also John Gennari, *Blowin' Hot and Cool: Jazz and Its Critics* (Chicago: University of Chicago Press, 2006), 207–49; and Jeremy Yudkin, *The Lenox School of Jazz: A Vital Chapter in the History of American Music and Race Relations* (South Egremont, MA: Farshaw, 2006).

200. Priestley, *Mingus*, 82.

201. See Mingus's letter to Gary A. Soucie on July 2, 1957, box 57, folder 15, Charles Mingus Collection, Library of Congress.

202. Goodman, *Mingus Speaks*, 227.

203. See Porter, *What Is This Thing Called Jazz?* 124.

204. Mingus, *Pithecanthropus Erectus*, liner notes.

205. Mingus, *Pithecanthropus Erectus*, liner notes.

206. Janet Coleman and Al Young, *Mingus/Mingus: Two Memoirs* (Montclair, NJ: Limelight Editions, 2004), 24.

207. See, for example, Priestley, *Mingus*, 71.

208. Mingus, *Pithecanthropus Erectus*, liner notes.

209. Paul Gilroy, *The Black Atlantic: Modernity and Double-Consciousness* (Cambridge, MA: Harvard University Press, 1993), 113.

210. Mingus, *Pithecanthropus Erectus*, liner notes.

211. Leja, *Reframing Abstract Expressionism*, 49–120, here 57.

212. Mingus, *More Than a Fake Book*, 109.

213. Quoted in Nat Hentoff, *The Nat Hentoff Reader* (Cambridge, MA: Da Capo, 2001), 99.

214. See Belgrad, *Culture of Spontaneity*, esp. 196–221; Gibson, *Abstract Expressionism*, esp. xix–xxi; and Leja, *Reframing Abstract Expressionism*, esp. 1–17, 203–74.

215. See Priestley, *Mingus*, 88.

216. Fred Moten, *In the Break: The Aesthetics of the Black Radical Tradition* (Minneapolis: University of Minnesota Press, 2003), 26.

217. Priestley dates the first drafts to 1957, following conversations with Celia Mingus. *Mingus*, 97.

218. Vilde Aaslid, "The Poetic Mingus and the Politics of Genre in String Quartet No. 1," *Journal of the Society for American Music* 9 (2015): 5.

219. Box 45, folders 1–2, Charles Mingus Collection, Library of Congress. All subsequent references to Mingus's autobiography draft make reference to documents in this box.

220. Box 45, folders 1–2, Charles Mingus Collection, Library of Congress.

221. Box 45, folders 1–2, Charles Mingus Collection, Library of Congress.

222. Nichole T. Rustin, "Mingus Fingers: Charles Mingus, Black Masculinity, and Postwar Jazz Culture" (PhD diss., New York University, 1999), 21.

223. Rustin, "Mingus Fingers," 16; Nichole Rustin-Paschal, *The Kind of Man I Am: Jazzmasculinity and the World of Charles Mingus Jr.* (Middletown, CT: Wesleyan University Press, 2017).

224. See Lewis, "Improvised Music," 156.

225. Gilroy, *The Black Atlantic*, 37–38.

226. Von Eschen, *Satchmo*, 4.

227. Monson, "Problem with White Hipness," 396–422.

228. Lewis, *Power Stronger Than Itself*, 360.

229. Shana Redmond, "'And You Know Who I Am': Paul Robeson Sings America," *Massachusetts Review* 57, no. 4 (2016): 617–18.

Chapter 2

1. The first quotation comes from Wilbur C. Munnecke, a social scientist commissioned by David Rockefeller to study community options in the Morningside Heights neighborhood of Columbia University. David Rockefeller, "International House, New York, Second Interim Report and Recommendations," August 30, 1946, 9; and "International House, New York, Final Report of Wilbur C. Munnecke, the University of Chicago," October 30, 1946, in box 121, folder 6, Hutchines. Cited in Samuel Zipp, *Manhattan Projects: The Rise and Fall of Urban Renewal in Cold War New York* (New York: Oxford University Press, 2012), 167. See also Joel Schwartz, *The New York Approach: Robert Moses, Urban Liberals, and the Redevelopment of the Inner City* (Columbus: Ohio State University Press, 1993), 151, for his coining of the phrase "Cold War Acropolis."

2. Robert J. Gluck, "The Columbia-Princeton Electronic Music Studio: Educating International Composers," in *Computer Music Journal* 31, no. 2 (2007): 20–38; Nick Patterson, "The Archives of the Columbia-Princeton Electronic Music Center," *Notes* 67, no. 3 (2011): 483–502.

3. Gluck, "Columbia-Princeton," 20–38.

4. Gluck, "Columbia-Princeton," 22. For more a more detailed discussion of CLAEM in relation to Cold War cultural diplomacy, see Eduardo Herrera, "Electroacoustic Music at CLAEM: A Pioneer Studio in Latin America," *Journal of the Society for American Music* 12, no. 2 (2018): 180; Herrera, *Elite Art Worlds: Philanthropy, Latin Americanism, and Avant-Garde Music* (New York: Oxford University Press, 2020); Herrera, "The Rockefeller Foundation and Latin American Music in the 1960s: The Creation of Indiana University's LAMC and Di Tella Institute's CLAEM," *American Music* 35, no. 1 (2017): 54.

5. Gluck, "Columbia-Princeton," 20–21.

6. François Jacob, *The Statue Within: An Autobiography* (New York: Basic Books, 1988), 9. Cited in Hans-Jörg Rheinberger, "Experimental Systems: Difference, Graphematicity, Conjuncture," in *Intellectual Birdhouse*, ed. Claudia Mareis, Florian Dombois, Michael Schwab, and Ute Meta Bauer (London: Walther Koening, 2012), 89–99.

7. For more on this context, see Paul Erickson et al., *How Reason Almost Lost Its Mind: The Strange Career of Cold War Rationality* (Chicago: University of Chicago Press, 2015); Stuart W. Leslie, *The Cold War and American Science: The Military-Industrial Academic Complex at MIT and Stanford* (New York: Columbia University Press, 1993); Rebecca S. Lowen, *Creating the Cold War University: The Transformation of Stanford* (Berkeley: University of California Press, 1997); Cyrus C. M. Mody and Andrew J. Nelson, "'A Towering Virtue of Necessity': Interdisciplinarity and the Rise of Computer Music at Vietnam-Era Stanford," *Osiris* 28 (2013): 254–77; and Audra J. Wolfe, *Freedom's Laboratory: The Cold War Struggle for the Soul of Science* (Baltimore: Johns Hopkins University Press, 2018). For more on electronic music studios in relation to Cold War configurations of power from a European perspective, see Jennifer Iverson, *Electronic*

Inspirations: Technologies of the Cold War Musical Avant-Garde (New York: Oxford University Press, 2018).

8. Edward W. Said, *Orientalism* (New York: Vintage, 1979), 3.

9. For more on unequal status in these circles, see Ellie M. Hisama, "Getting to Count," *Music Theory Spectrum*, 2021, https://doi.org/10.1093/mts/mtaa033, accessed July 27, 2021.

10. Rockefeller Foundation, "Area Studies," *The Rockefeller Foundation: A Digital History*, accessed July 7, 2020.

11. Rockefeller Foundation, "Area Studies."

12. Vladimir Ussachevsky, "A Draft of a Proposal to the Humanities Division of the Rockefeller Foundation Outlining a Program of Support to Encourage the Development of Electronic Music Throughout the Universities in the United States." Otto Luening papers, box 23, folder 11, New York Public Library.

13. Herrera, *Elite Art Worlds*, 61–81; Carol A. Hess, *Representing the Good Neighbor: Music, Difference, and the Pan American Dream* (New York: Oxford, 2013), 50–80.

14. Inderjeet Parmar, *Foundations of the American Century: The Ford, Carnegie, and Rockefeller Foundations in the Rise of American Power* (New York: Columbia University Press, 2012), esp. 180–220.

15. See Martin Brody, "Music for the Masses: Milton Babbitt's Cold War Music Theory," *Musical Quarterly* 77, no. 2 (1993): 161–92.

16. John Marshall, "Adventuring in the Arts," 1958, folder 36, box 3, series 1 general files, FA053, Rockefeller Foundation records, Rockefeller Archive Center.

17. Milton Babbitt, *Words about Music*, ed. Stephen Dembski and Joseph Straus (Madison: University of Wisconsin Press, 1987), 163.

18. Marshall, "Adventuring," 4.

19. Sindhumathi Revuluri, "A Note from the Guest Editor," *Opera Quarterly* 32, no. 1 (2016): 1.

20. Susan McClary, "Terminal Prestige: The Case of Avant-Garde Music Composition," *Cultural Critique*, no. 12 (Spring 1989): 57–81.

21. Homi K. Bhabha, "In the Cave of Making: Thoughts on Third Space," in *Communicating in the Third Space*, ed. Karin Ikas and Gerhard Wagner (New York: Routledge, 2009), x.

22. Ann Laura Stoler, *Duress: Imperial Durabilities in Our Times* (Durham, NC: Duke University Press, 2016), 179.

23. Dean Rusk, letter to Chester I. Barnard, April 17, 1958, Collection RG, record group 3, series 911, box 5, folder 47, Rockefeller Archive Center.

24. Rachel Vandagriff, "The Pre-History of the Columbia-Princeton Electronic Music Center," lecture delivered at the annual meeting of the American Musicological Society, November 4, 2016, Vancouver.

25. Elizabeth Kray, undated letter fragment to Mario Davidovsky, correspondence, Vladimir Ussachevsky Collection, Library of Congress.

26. Otto Luening, letter to Vladimir Ussachevsky, August 21, 1957, Vladimir Ussachevsky Collection, series IV, box 12, Library of Congress.

27. Joel Schwartz, *The New York Approach: Robert Moses, Urban Liberals, and the Redevelopment of the Inner City* (Columbus: Ohio State University Press, 1993); Samuel Zipp, *Manhattan Projects*, 166–69.

28. Columbia University, Committee on Research in Urban Land Use and Housing, "Memorandum on Redevelopment of Morningside Heights (confidential, Janu-

ary 17, 1947), Morningside Heights, Inc., box M, Russell papers. Cited in Schwartz, *New York Approach*, 155.

29. Steven Gregory, "Making the 'American Acropolis': On Verticality, Social Hierarchy, and the Obduracy of Manhattan Schist," *Annals of the American Association of Geographers* 110, no. 1 (2020): 79. Gregory cites Argyro Loukaki, "Whose Genius Loci? Contrasting Interpretations of the 'Sacred Rock of the Athenian Acropolis,'" *Annals of the Association of American Geographers* 87, no. 2 (1997): 306.

30. Zipp, *Manhattan Projects*, 167–69.

31. Italics mine. "Teachers College Open: President of Three Universities Assist at the Ceremonies," *New York Times*, November 16, 1894, 8. At this dedication, President Gilman of Johns Hopkins University significantly expanded the use of this image into a metaphor for the nation and empire: "The preparation of an imperial domain to be the home of a hundred million people, governed by a Democracy. . . . Dissimilar parts will make a harmonious whole. Our Parthenon will be a university."

32. Meyer Liebowitz, "City's 'Acropolis' Combating Slums," *New York Times*, May 21, 1957, 37. "The hope is to have a continuous diversified but well balanced community of good homes and cultural institutions extending from the Columbia–New York Cathedral–Riverside Church complex to the City College–St. Nicholas Park area."

33. Louis Althusser, *Lenin and Philosophy, and Other Essays*, trans. Ben Brewster (New York: Monthly Review Press, 2001), 142.

34. See Joseph William Pfender, "Oblique Music: American Tape Experimentalism and Peripheral Cultures of Technology, 1887 and 1950" (PhD diss., New York University, 2019), 170–264.

35. Documents and receipts pertaining to these grants are held in JPB 94–7, Otto Luening papers, New York Public Library.

36. John Marshall, inter-office correspondence, July 25, 1957, box 315, folder 2910. series 200 V.S., record group 1.2, Rockefeller Foundation Collection, Rockefeller Archive.

37. Dipesh Chakrabarty, *Provincializing Europe: Postcolonial Thought and Historical Difference* (Princeton, NJ: Princeton University Press, 2000), 3–23.

38. Marshall uses this vocabulary in the following papers. John Marshall, "In returning to officer responsibilities in Europe," undated, box 3, folder 38, series 1 general files, RF, FA053, John Marshall papers, Rockefeller Foundation records (RF), Rockefeller Archive Center; Marshall, "By direction of the trustees, the foundation is giving particular attention to the underdeveloped countries of Asia," undated, box 3, folder 38, series 1 general files, RF, FA053, John Marshall papers, Rockefeller Foundation records (RF), Rockefeller Archive Center.

39. These themes and terms appear prominently in Charles Burton Fahs, "The Program in the Humanities: A Statement by Charles B. Fahs," in "The Rockefeller Foundation Confidential Monthly Report for the Information of the Trustees," ed. George W. Gray, February 1, 1951, box 3, folder 38, series 1 general files, RF, FA053, John Marshall papers, Rockefeller Foundation records (RF), Rockefeller Archive Center. They also appear retrospectively in John Marshall, "In reviewing [the] program in the Humanities toward 1960," 1959, box 3, folder 36, series 1 general files, RF, FA053, John Marshall papers, Rockefeller Foundation records (RF), Rockefeller Archive Center.

40. John Marshall, "Program in the Humanities: Experimental Phase," undated

(early 1950s), box 3, folder 35, series 1 general files, RF, FA053, John Marshall papers, Rockefeller Foundation records (RF), Rockefeller Archive Center.

41. Michael Sy Uy, *Ask the Experts: How Ford, Rockefeller, and the NEA Changed American Music* (New York: Oxford University Press, 2020), 26.

42. Carolyn Birdsall, *Nazi Soundscapes: Sound, Technology and Urban Space in Germany, 1933–1945* (Amsterdam: University of Amsterdam Press, 2012); Roland Wittje, *The Age of Electroacoustics: Transforming Science and Sound* (Cambridge, MA: MIT Press, 2016).

43. Fahs, "The Program in the Humanities: A Statement by Charles B. Fahs."

44. Marshall, "Adventuring in the Arts."

45. Letter to the ambassador, Rome, undated (1955), Otto Luening papers, music division, New York Public Library. Cited in Martin Brody, "The Enabling Instrument: Milton Babbitt and the RCA Synthesizer," *Contemporary Music Review* 39, no. 6 (2020): 776–94.

46. Fahs, "The Program in the Humanities: A Statement by Charles B. Fahs."

47. Raymond B. Fosdick, "The Symbol of History," "Presidential Review of the Work of the Foundation in 1944," John Marshall papers, box 3, folder 38, series 1 general files, FA053, John Marshall papers, Rockefeller Foundation records (RF), Rockefeller Archive Center.

48. Robert K. Faulkner, *The Case for Greatness: Honorable Ambition and its Critics* (New Haven, CT: Yale University Press, 2008), 67–68.

49. Brody, "Enabling Instrument"; Herrera, *Elite Art Worlds*; Herrera, "Rockefeller Foundation"; Patterson, "The Archives"; Pfender, "Oblique Music"; Vandagriff, "The Pre-History."

50. See, for example, Greg Barnhisel, *Cold War Modernists: Art, Literature, and American Cultural Diplomacy* (New York: Columbia University Press, 2015); Serge Guilbaut, *How New York Stole the Idea of Modern Art: Abstract Expressionism, Freedom, and the Cold War*, trans. Arthur Goldhammer (Chicago: University of Chicago Press, 1985); Frances Stonor Saunders, *The Cultural Cold War: The CIA and the World of Arts and Letters* (New York: New Press, 1999).

51. Barnhisel, *Cold War Modernists*, 11.

52. Otto Luening, letter to Vladimir Ussachevsky, August 21, 1957, Vladimir Ussachevsky papers, series IV, box 12, Library of Congress.

53. Otto Luening, *The Odyssey of an American Composer: The Autobiography of Otto Luening* (New York: Charles Scribner's Sons, 1980).

54. Otto Luening, recorded interview by Vivian Perlis, May 5, 1982. Oral History of American Music, Yale University.

55. Luening's and McCormick's relationship is documented in their correspondence. Otto Luening papers, JPB-94-07, box 37, folder 6, New York Public Library.

56. "Friends and Relations: McCormick, Harold F. Jr. (Fowler), 1915–1924," box 89, folders 665–66, Office of the Messrs. Rockefeller Records, Friends and Services, series H, FA317, Rockefeller Archive Center. "Friends and Relations: McCormick, Edith Rockefeller, 1915–1921," box 80, folders 609–12, Office of the Messrs. Rockefeller Records, Friends and Services, series H, FA317, Rockefeller Archive Center.

57. Richard Noll, *The Aryan Christ: The Secret Life of Carl Jung* (New York: Random House, 1997), 200–235.

58. Otto Luening, draft letter to Edith Rockefeller McCormick, January 1924, Otto Luening papers, JPB-94-07, box 37, folder 6, New York Public Library.

59. Underlining in original. Otto Luening, letter to Edgard Varèse, June 9, 1948, Edgard Varèse Collection, Paul Sacher Foundation.

60. "I have worked hard in the last year [in Chicago]. The studio, which I started under your patronage, is now on a paying basis." Luening, draft letter to Edith Rockefeller McCormick, January 1924, Otto Luening papers, JPB-94-07, box 37, folder 6, New York Public Library.

61. Luening, *Odyssey*, 282–90.

62. Mario Davidovsky, interview by the author, March 1, 2019, New York.

63. Luening, "General Correspondence Rockefeller Foundation: 1948–49," Otto Luening papers, JPB94-07, box 32, folder 4.

64. Excerpt from Mr. D'Arms interview of General McClure, September 29, 1948, box 6, folder 42, FA 387a, series 200, RG 1.2, RF Collection, Rockefeller Archive Center.

65. Excerpt from Mr. D'Arms interview of General McClure, September 29, 1948.

66. Elizabeth Kray, undated letter fragment to Mario Davidovsky, Vladimir Ussachevsky papers, Library of Congress.

67. Ussachevsky, "A Draft of a Proposal." The RF provided positive feedback on this draft, and suggested the modifications that they included in an abbreviated final proposal, which refrained from making the large-scale contribution arguments they had already made in the draft document. The RF recommended that the proposal should involve fewer educational institutions that would share a common facility at Columbia University, that Luening and Ussachevsky should secure a financial commitment from Columbia, and that they should secure a loan of major equipment from IBM or RCA. All of these conditions were met, and the final proposal was approved. August 22, 1958, memo to John Marshall from Burton Fahs, RF 1.2, series 200, box 315, folder 2911.

68. "A Proposal to the Humanities Division of the Rockefeller Foundation for Support to Develop a Program of Electronic Music at Columbia and Princeton Universities," Rockefeller Archive Center, Collection RF, record group 1.2, series 200, box 315, folder 294.

69. Ussachevsky, "A Draft of a Proposal."

70. Ussachevsky, "A Draft of a Proposal."

71. Ussachevsky, "A Draft of a Proposal."

72. Marshall, "Adventuring in the Arts."

73. Marshall, "Adventuring in the Arts," page 1.

74. Marshall, "Adventuring in the Arts, 1.

75. Fahs, "The Program in the Humanities: A Statement by Charles B. Fahs."

76. Fahs, "The Program in the Humanities: A Statement by Charles B. Fahs."

77. Fahs concluded his recorded remarks thus during the meeting that positively resolved the CPEMC's funding: "The present proposal by Columbia and Princeton represents a promising development of major proportion which will make it possible for the first time for composers in this country to address themselves to electronic music on a scale comparable to what is taking place in Europe." "Resolved RF 58223" (notes from discussion and resolution following Burton Fahs's presentation of the Columbia-Princeton Electronic Music Center project), 1958, project collection RF, record group 1.2, series 200, box 315, folder 2911, Rockefeller Archive Center.

78. See Belgrad, *Culture of Spontaneity*, 196–221; Gibson, *Abstract Expressionism*, xix–xxi; and Leja, *Reframing Abstract Expressionism*, 1–17, 203–74.

79. Vladimir Ussachevsky, "Time Off to Consolidate," Vladimir Ussachevsky papers, Music Division, Library of Congress. Cited in Carl Rahkonen and Ralph Hartsock, "The Smoking Gun: Evidence That Vladimir Ussachevsky used Chinese Timbres as the Basis for his Electronic Music (Expanded Edition)," paper given at the 2008 annual conference of SEAMUS, Salt Lake City, https://digital.library.unt.edu/ark:/67531/metadc801972/, accessed May 24, 2019, 7.

80. Rahkonen and Hartsock, "The Smoking Gun," 11.

81. Brigid Cohen, *Stefan Wolpe and the Avant-Garde Diaspora* (Cambridge: Cambridge University Press, 2012); Cohen, "Limits of National History: Yoko Ono, Stefan Wolpe, and Dilemmas of History," *Musical Quarterly* 97, no. 2 (2014): 181–237.

82. Scheding, *Musical Journeys*, 1–14.

83. Brian Kane, *Sound Unseen: Acousmatic Sound in Theory and Practice* (New York: Oxford University Press, 2014).

84. Ussachevsky, transcribed interview by Joan Thomson, 201 h-l, 48, Oral History of American Music, Yale University.

85. Ussachevsky, interview by Thomson, 12–13. Maria Ussachevsky, correspondence with American Consulate, Latvia, US Foreign Service, July 26, 1937, Ussachevsky papers, Library of Congress.

86. Gundula Kreuzer, *Curtain, Gong, Steam: Wagnerian Technologies of Nineteenth-Century Opera* (Oakland: University of California Press, 2018), 129, 132, 156–57.

87. Bernhard Siegert, "Mineral Sound or Missing Fundamental: Cultural History as Signal Analysis," *Osiris* 28 (2013): 105–118.

88. Kreutzer, *Curtain, Gong, Steam*, 142.

89. Ussachevsky, transcribed interview by Joan Thomson, 201 m-p, 2.

90. Letter to the ambassador, Rome, undated (1955), Otto Luening papers, music division, New York Public Library. Cited in Martin Brody, "The Enabling Instrument: Milton Babbitt and the RCA Synthesizer," *Contemporary Music Review* 39, no. 6 (2020): 776–94.

91. Vladimir Ussachevsky and Otto Luening, *Electronic Tape Music by Vladimir Ussachevsky and Otto Luening: The First Compositions* (New York: Highgate, 1977), 41.

92. Rheinberger, "Experimental Systems," 89–99.

93. Pfender, "Oblique Music," 184–85.

94. Ussachevsky, interview by Joan Tomson, 35–45. Peter Mauzey, interview by the author, April 18, 2019, New York.

95. Peter Mauzey, interview by the author, April 18, 2019, New York.

96. Pril Smiley, interview by the author, August 7, 2019, New Paltz, NY. For more discussion of such questions in relation to Stockhausen and the WDR studio, see Iverson, *Electronic Inspirations*.

97. Pril Smiley, interview by the author, August 7, 2019, New Paltz, NY.

98. Richard Beaudoin, "Counterpoint and Quotation in Ussachevsky's *Wireless Fantasy*," *Organized Sound* 12, no. 2 (2007): 143. James A. Hijiya, *Lee de Forest and the Fatherhood of Radio* (Bethlehem, PA: Lehigh University Press, 1992).

99. Beaudoin, "Counterpoint and Quotation," 143.

100. Richard Taruskin, email correspondence with the author, September 19, 2020.

101. Beaudoin, "Counterpoint and Quotation," 146; Samuel D. Miller, "Can Selections for Children Be Avant-Garde?" *Music Educators Journal* 68 (October 1981): 32; Eric Salzman, "Music of Vladimir Ussachevsky," liner notes for *Music of Vladimir Ussachevsky* (New York: CRI, 1987), 4–14.

102. Lisa Gitelman, "Media History and Its Objects," lecture delivered at the Max Planck Institute for the History of Science, Berlin, June 19, 2018.

103. Gitelman, "The Phonograph's New Media Publics," in *The Sound Studies Reader*, ed. Jonathan Sterne (New York: Routledge, 2012), 283–84; James Lastra, *Sound Technology and the American Cinema: Perception, Representation, Modernity* (New York: Columbia University Press, 2000), 8.

104. Beaudoin, "Counterpoint and Quotation," 142.

105. See Birdsall, *Nazi Soundscapes*; Wittje, *Age of Electroacoustics*.

106. Pril Smiley, interview by the author.

107. Ussachevsky, interview by Thomson, 3.

108. "Mongolian Prince," undated, Vladimir Ussachevsky Papers, box 11, folder 9, series III, Rare Books and Manuscripts Collection, Columbia University.

109. Tim Jordan, *Cyberpower: The Culture and Politics of Cyberspace and the Internet* (London: Routledge, 1999), 110–14.

110. Vladimir Ussachevsky, interview by Joan Thomson, Columbia-Princeton Electronic Music Center, February 17, 1977, Oral History of American Music, Yale University.

111. Ussachevsky, interview by Thomson; see also Jonathan Michaels, *McCarthyism: The Realities, Delusions and Politics behind the 1950s Red Scare* (New York: Routledge, 2017), 165–66.

112. Paul F. Hooper, "The Institute of Pacific Relations and the Origins of Pacific and Asian Studies," *Pacific Affairs* 61 (1988): 100. Institute of Pacific Relations, "Hearings before the Subcommittee to Investigate the Administration of the Internal Security Act and Other Internal Security Laws of the Committee on the Judiciary, United States Senate, Eighty-Second Congress, Second Session," http://www.archive.org/stream/instituteofpacif11unit/instituteofpacif11unit_djvu.txt, accessed Feburary 28, 2019. Michaels, *McCarthyism*, 165–66.

113. Lawrence T. Woods, "Rockefeller Philanthropy and the Institute of Pacific Relations: A Reappraisal of Long-Term Mutual Dependency," *Voluntas: International Journal of Voluntary and Nonprofit Organizations* 10, no. 2 (1999): 154.

114. Ussachevsky, interview by Thomson.

115. "Your letter seemed to have had a magic effect on the passport division." Ussachevsky, letter to Secretary of the University Richard Herpers, June 8, 1953, correspondence with Columbia University, Ussachevsky papers, Library of Congress.

116. Ussachevsky, interview by Thomson.

117. Internal Security Act of 1950 (McCarran Act), US Statutes at Large, 81st Congress, II sess., chapter 1024, pp. 987–1031, https://loveman.sdsu.edu/docs/1950InternalSecurityAct.pdf, accessed October 22, 2019. See also Michaels, 164.

118. US Naturalization Record Index, 1891–1992, Ksenia Terry [Ksenia Terechovskaya], California District Court, August 7, 1959; indexed in World Archives Project.

119. US Department of Justice Immigration and Naturalization Service, Chief of Special Investigations, letter to FBI Special Agent John J. Hayes, December 18, 1964, FBI file 100–98817.

120. Security obligations, Vladimir Ussachevsky, November 5, 1945.

121. Pril Smiley, interview by the author, August 7, 2019, New Paltz, NY.

122. Confidential memo to Major Parkins from J. W. Hoot, (administrative assistant, Research & Analysis Branch, Office of Strategic Services, July 15, 1944.

123. Confidential OSS requisition, April 5, 1944, by W. L. Langer, for Vladimir Ussachevsky.

124. Charles C. Stelle, letter of recommendation for Vladimir Ussachevsky, June 25, 1946, US State Department correspondence, Ussachevsky papers, Library of Congress.

125. Ross Y. Koen, *The China Lobby in American Politics* (New York: Macmillan, 1960), 63. Cited in Michaels, *McCarthyism*, 155.

126. Michaels, *McCarthyism*, 152.

127. Olive Gilbreath, "Where Yellow Rules White," *Harper's Magazine*, February 1929: 367. Cited in Blaine R. Chiasson, *Administering the Colonizer: Manchuria's Russians under Chinese Rule, 1918–29* (Vancouver: UBC Press, 2011), 1.

128. Chiasson, *Administering the Colonizer*, 4.

129. "Area Studies," *The Rockefeller Foundation: A Digital History*, rockfound .rockarch.org/area-studies.

130. Confidential Security Office investigation report number 20603, September 23, 1944, by J. C. O'Donnell (security officer), to J. W. Hoot. Obtained by FOIA request.

131. Cristina Vatulescu, *Police Aesthetics* (Stanford, CA: Stanford University Press, 2010), 195.

132. Vatulescu, *Police Aesthetics*, 192.

133. Michaels, *McCarthyism*, 158–59.

134. Michaels, *McCarthyism*, 159.

135. Michaels, *McCarthyism*, 167.

136. Letter to director of FBI, April 17, 1950, "Owen Lattimore, espionage," originally filed in FBI file 100–24628–821. Obtained by FOIA request.

137. Letter from Emily Lattimore to Elizabeth Kray, September 17, 1975, correspondence, Ussachevsky papers, Library of Congress.

138. Micki McGee, ed., *Yaddo: Making American Culture* (New York: Columbia University Press, 2008), 11.

139. "In March 1949, Mrs. MARY TOWNSEND, employee of Yaddo, advised that Dr. VLADIMIRE [*sic*] USSACHEVSKY, Columbia University Music Department, New York City, a composer, has been a guest at Yaddo and is a communist. He likewise appeared to be on intimate terms with other Communists." Letter to director of FBI, June 26, 1950, FBI file 100–98817. Obtained by FOIA request.

140. Memorandum for director of FBI, Attn: Mr. S. J. Papich from James Angleton, July 29, 1965, item 65F22AV. Obtained through FOIA request.

141. Richard Taruskin, *On Russian Music* (Berkeley: University of California Press, 2009), 1–5.

142. Emily Abrams Ansari, "Aaron Copland and the Politics of Cultural Diplomacy," *Journal of the Society for American Music* 5, no. 3 (2011): 335–64.

143. Ussachevsky, interview by Thomson.

144. Vladimir Ussachevsky, letter to Charles Burton Fahs, March 12, 1953, Rockefeller Foundation correspondence, Ussachevsky papers, Library of Congress.

145. Ussachevsky, letter to Fahs, March 12, 1953.

146. "The Senate and FBI investigations of the Institute for Pacific Relations and the charges preferred by Representative Cox indicate the belief in at least a few minds that The Rockefeller Foundation is either unwittingly giving support to the enemies

of our country or is itself fuzzy-minded, unrealistic and even pinkishly inclined." "The Rockefeller Foundation vis-a-vis National Security," November 19, 1951, collection RG5, record group 3, series 900, box 25, folder 201, Rockefeller Archive Center. The RF finally withdrew funding from the IPR, although their tapering-off of support had already begun as early as 1946. For more on the RF/IPR funding relationship, see Woods, "Rockefeller Philanthropy," 151–66.

Chapter 3

1. By permission this chapter incorporates revised material from my article "Sounds of the Cold War Acropolis: Halim El-Dabh at the Columbia-Princeton Electronic Music Center," *Contemporary Music Review* 39, no. 6 (2020): 684–707. It is accessible at https://tandfonline.com/.

2. Contradictory information about Toyama's birthdate has been published. WorldCat identifies her birth year as 1912, while WebCat Plus identifies it as 1913. The ship manifest from her 1955 journey on the *Liberté* from Le Havre to New York indicates that she was forty-two years old in July 1955. Hiromi Tsuji identifies her birth year as 1919. "Year 1955; arrival: New York, New York; microfilm serial T715, 1897–1957; microfilm roll *8608*, line 15, page 156." New York Passenger and Crew Lists (including Castle Garden and Ellis Island), 1820–1957, Ancestry.com, accessed May 5, 2020. Hiromi Tsuji, "Erased from History: The First Japanese Composer to Win an International Prize," in *Josei sakkyokuka retsuden* (Portraits of Women Composers), ed. Midori Kobayashi (Tokyo: Keibonsha, 1999), 301–4.

3. El-Dabh, phone interview by Bob Gluck, May 23, 2002, October 9, 2005, and January 21, 2006: "like a sculptor, taking chunks of sound and chiseling them into something beautiful." *eContact!* 15, no. 2, http://econtact.ca/15.2/gluck_el-dabh .html, accessed January 19, 2019. Foundational events in the reclamation of El-Dabh's legacy include the 2005 UNYAZI Electronic Music Festival in Johannesburg, the 2011 celebration at the New York Public Library, and the planned "Here History Began" exhibition at Savvy Contemporary in Berlin in 2020 (postponed due to COVID-19).

4. Ussachevsky, "A Draft of a Proposal."

5. Relatively little scholarship addresses El-Dabh's work in depth. Denise Seachrist's biography is the primary authority, alongside work by Delinda Collier, Michael Khoury, George E. Lewis, Kamila Metwaly, and Nicolas Puig. See Delinda Collier, *Media Primitivism: Technological Art in Africa* (Chicago: University of Chicago Press, 2020), 61–92; Thom Holmes, *Electronic and Experimental Music: Technology, Music, and Culture* (New York: Routledge, 2016), 47–48, 203–4; Michael Khoury, "A Look at Lightning: The Life and Compositions of Halim El-Dabh," in *The Arab Avant-Garde: Music, Politics, Modernity,* ed. Thomas Burkhalter, Kay Dickinson, and Benjamin J. Harbert (Middletown, CT: Wesleyan University Press, 2013), 165–82; George E. Lewis, *Recharging Unyazi 2005, Herri* 4, https://herri.org.za/4/george-lewis; Kamila Metwaly, "A Sonic Letter to Halim El-Dabh," *Herri* 4, https://herri.org.za/4/kamila-metwalyl; Nicolas Puig, "Une figure égyptienne du XXe siècle: Halim El-Dabh, compositeur, collecteur et pionnier des musiques électroniques," *Annales Islamologiques* 53 (2019): 113–36; Denise Seachrist, *The Musical World of Halim El-Dabh* (Kent, OH: Kent State University Press, 2002). Laurel Hurst has also played an invaluable part in publicizing El-Dabh's music and organizing his archive. I am grateful to her for having made possible my interviews with El-Dabh in December 2014.

6. El-Dabh, interview by the author, December 6, 2014, Kent, Ohio; transcribed from digital recording.

7. Discussing his experimentations with tape in 1952, Ussachevsky recalled, "I was quite ignorant, as I think I mentioned before, of anything that was going on in Europe in electronic music, and I also hadn't heard any musique concrète, so I thought that I was inventing it all by myself." Ussachevsky, interview bby Thomson.

8. Their cofounder Milton Babbitt was not an author of this document, nor did he emphasize the cultural diplomatic angle of the studio in writings and correspondence.

9. Ussachevsky, "A Draft of a Proposal."

10. Ussachevsky, "A Draft of a Proposal."

11. Ussachevsky, "A Draft of a Proposal."

12. Ussachevsky, "A Draft of a Proposal."

13. Ussachevsky, "A Draft of a Proposal."

14. Christina Klein, *Cold War Orientalism: Asia in the Middlebrow Imagination, 1945–1961* (Berkeley: University of California Press, 2003), 7, 13.

15. Marshall uses this vocabulary in the following papers: John Marshall, "In returning to officer responsibilities in Europe," undated, box 3, folder 38. series 1 general files, RF, FA053, John Marshall papers, Rockefeller Foundation records (RF), Rockefeller Archive Center; Marshall, "By direction of the trustees, the foundation is giving particular attention to the underdeveloped countries of Asia," undated, box 3, folder 38, series 1 general files, RF, FA053, John Marshall papers, Rockefeller Foundation records (RF), Rockefeller Archive Center.

16. Dipesh Chakrabarty, *Provincializing Europe: Postcolonial Thought and Historical Difference* (Princeton, NJ: Princeton University Press, 2000), 3–23.

17. "Area Studies," *The Rockefeller Foundation: A Digital History*, rockfound.rockarch .org/area-studies, accessed September 10, 2019.

18. Ussachevsky, "A Draft of a Proposal."

19. Brian Kane, "Relays: Audiotape, Material Affordances, and Cultural Practice," *Twentieth-Century Music* 14, no. 1 (2017): 65–75.

20. Benjamin Steege, "Between Race and Culture: Hearing Japanese Music in Berlin," *History of Humanities* 2, no. 2 (2017): 363.

21. Chiasson, *Administering the Colonizer*, 2, 5–7.

22. Alice Shields, email correspondence with the author, August 7, 2021.

23. Alice Shields, digitally recorded interview by the author, June 16, 2016, New York.

24. Kathleen Norris, *The Virgin of Bennington* (New York: Riverhead Books, 2001), 198; Pril Smiley, digitally recorded interview by the author, August 7, 2019, New Paltz, NY.

25. Stoler, *Along the Archival Grain*, 38.

26. Michiko Toyama, *Waka and Other Compositions*, with the Juilliard Orchestra, Folkways Records FW 881, 1960. Accessed via online audio stream. https://search .alexanderstreet.com/view/work/bibliographic_entity%7Crecorded_cd%7C72570.

27. Aaron I. Cohen, *International Encyclopedia of Women Composers* (New York: Books & Music, 1987), 703; Tsuji, "Erased." See also Teruka Nishikawa, Wesley Berg, and Janice Brown, "From 'Good Wife, Wise Mother' to the Otaka Award: Japanese Women Composers 1868 to the Present," *U.S.-Japan Women's Journal: English Supplement* 22 (2002): 95–96, 100, Nishikawa, "Four Recitals and an Essay: Women and Western Music in Japan. 1868 to the Present," DM thesis, University of Alberta, 2000.

28. See Toyama's 1939 portrait in Tsuji, "Erased," 301. Here she wears a modern European-style draped, high-necked dress in a monochrome dark color with a small bow and shoulder pads.

29. I am grateful to Stephanie Su for helping me to identify the print.

30. Toyama, *Waka*.

31. Kenneth Rexroth, *One Hundred Poems from the Japanese* (New York: New Directions, 1955).

32. Rica Narimoto, "Heritage within the Avant-Garde? Traditional and Contemporary Musics in Post-War Japan," in *Music as Heritage: Historical and Ethnographic Perspectives*, ed. Barley Norton and Naomi Matsumoto (London: Routledge, 2018), 244–60; W. Anthony Sheppard, *Extreme Exoticism: Japan in the American Musical Imagination* (New York: Oxford University Press, 2019), 317–71.

33. Tony Olmsted, *Folkways Records: Moses Asch and his Encyclopedia of Sound* (London: Routledge, 2013).

34. For these pieces, the liner notes provide short commentary on literary sources, English-language translations of texts, a koto manuscript, and examples of koto scales transcribed in Western notation.

35. Yayoi Uno Everett, "Intercultural Synthesis in Postwar Western Art Music: Historical Contexts, Perspectives, and Taxonomy," in *Locating East Asia in Western Art Music*, ed. Yayoi Uno Everett and Frederick Lau (Middletown, CT: Wesleyan University Press, 2004), 16.

36. Nancy Yunhwa Rao, "The Role of Language in Music Integration: *Poéme Lyrique II* by Chen Qigang," *Journal of Music in China* 2 (2000): 274.

37. Sindhumathi Revuluri, "Tan Dun's *The First Emperor* and the Expectations of Exoticism," *Opera Quarterly* 32, no. 1 (2016): 89.

38. Homi K. Bhabha, "In the Cave of Making: Thoughts on Third Space," *Communicating in the Third Space*, ed. Karin Ikas and Gerhard Wagner (New York: Routledge, 2009), x; Bhabha, *The Location of Culture* (London: Routledge, 1994), 19, 240, 277, 322.

39. She frequently uses this name in her correspondence in the Ussachevsky Collection at the Library of Congress and the Varèse Collection at the Sacher Foundation.

40. Karen Kelsky, *Women on the Verge: Japanese Women, Western Dreams* (Durham, NC: Duke University Press, 2001); Midori Yoshimoto, *Into Performance: Japanese Women Artists in New York* (New Brunswick, NJ: Rutgers University Press, 2005).

41. Kazuaki Matsumoto, "Shibusawa Eiichi and Local Entrepreneurs in the Meiji Period," *Nagaoka kenkyū ronsō* (Bulletin of Nagaoka University), no. 15 (August 2017): 43–49, https://www.nagaokauniv.ac.jp/wp2014/wp-content/uploads/2011/12/ronso15-matsumoto.pdf, accessed February 11, 2019. See also Lui Fenghua, "Modern Chinese Credit Agencies Vary from Western Models," *Chinese Social Sciences Today* (2019), http://www.csstoday.com/Item/7490.aspx, accessed February 11, 2019.

42. Tsuji, "Erased," 302.

43. Bonnie C. Wade, *Composing Japanese Musical Modernity* (Chicago: University of Chicago Press, 2014), 18, 25–26.

44. Tsuji, "Erased," 304.

45. Jan Bardsley, ed., *The Bluestockings of Japan: New Woman Essays and Fiction from Seitō, 1911–16* (Ann Arbor: University of Michigan Press, 2007), 1–21; Vera Mackie, "Embodied Subjects: Feminism in Imperial Japan," in *Japanese Women: Emerging from Subservience, 1868–1945*, ed. Hiroko Tomida and Gordon Daniels (Folkestone, UK:

Brill, 2005), 95–118; Hiroko Tomida, "Hiratsuka Raichō, the Seitō Society, and the Emergence of the New Woman in Japan," in *Japanese Women: Emerging from Subservience, 1868–1945*, Hiroko Tomida and Gordon Daniels, eds. (Folkestone, UK: Global Oriental, 2005), 192–221.

46. Gail Lee Bernstein, introduction to *Recreating Japanese Women, 1600–1945*, ed. Gail Lee Bernstein (Berkeley: University of California Press, 1991), 8; Sharon H. Nolte and Sally Ann Hastings, "The Meiji State's Policy toward Women, 1890–1910," in *Recreating Japanese Women*, 154–57; Kathleen S. Uno, "Women and Changes in the Household Division of Labor," in *Recreating Japanese Women*, 35–39.

47. The code subordinated women by requiring wives to obtain their husband's consent before entering into legal contracts, by granting custody of children to the husband in cases of divorce, by deeming female adultery as grounds for criminal prosecution, and by requiring women under the age of twenty-five to obtain the household head's permission for marriage. Bernstein, 8.

48. Uno, "Women and Changes," 38.

49. Bardsley, *Bluestockings of Japan*.

50. Nishikawa, Berg, and Brown, "From 'Good Wife,'" 87–88.

51. Takashi Funayama, "*Three Japanese Lyrics* and Japonisme," in *Confronting Stravinsky*, ed. Jann Pasler (Berkeley: University of California Press, 1986): 278; Megumi Shirahama, "Commemorative Exhibition for Donated Collection Related to Jirohachi Satsuma: Baron Satsuma Has Arrived!" https://yab.yomiuri.co.jp/adv/wol/dy/culture/120523.html, accessed March 25, 2020.

52. Shirahama, "Commemorative Exhibition."

53. Lorraine Daston and H. Otto Sibum, "Introduction: Scientific Personae and their Histories," *Science in Context* 16 (2003): 2–3.

54. Daston and Sibum, "Introduction," 4.

55. "Modern Paris Festival," *New York Times*, July 11, 1937. "International Society for Contemporary Music, 1930s," League of Composers/ISCM Records, JPB 11–5, box 9, folder 20, New York Public Library.

56. I examined ISCM programs and news coverage from the 1930s. Other women composers I could identify with a composition performed at the ISCM Festivals were Elizabeth Maconchy, whose *Deuxième Quatour à cordes* premiered at the ISCM Festival in Paris in 1937, and Vítězslava Kaprálová, who conducted her own *Military Sinfonietta* at the ISCM Festival in London in 1938. "Contemporary Music Festival Held in London," *Musical America* (July 1938): 15. "International Society for Contemporary Music, 1930s," League of Composers/ISCM Records, JPB 11–5, box 9, folder 20, New York Public Library.

57. "Modern Paris Festival," *New York Times*, July 11, 1937. Other selection committee members included Albert Roussel (chair), Arthur Hoérée, Arthur Honegger, Darius Milhaud, and Henry Prunières. Nigel Simeone, "Music at the 1937 Paris Exposition: The Science of Enchantment," *Musical Times* 143 (2020): 10.

58. Simeone, "Music at the 1937 Paris Exposition," 9.

59. F. Bonavia, "New Music in London," *New York Times*, July 17, 1938, 122.

60. Said, *Orientalism*, 2.

61. For an extended exploration of how these stereotypes have played out across media, see Jonathan Wisenthal, Sherrill Grace, Melinda Boyd, Brian McIlroy, and Vera Micznik, eds., *A Vision of the Orient: Texts, Intertexts, and Contexts of Madame Butterfly* (Toronto: University of Toronto Press, 2006). Among other texts, see also

Ralph P. Locke, *Musical Exoticism: Images and Reflections* (Cambridge: Cambridge University Press, 2009); W. Anthony Sheppard, *Extreme Exoticism: Japan in the American Musical Imagination* (New York: Oxford University Press, 2019); Mari Yoshihara, "Flight of the Japanese Butterfly: Orientalism, Nationalism, and Performances of Japanese Womanhood," *American Quarterly* 56 (2004): 975–1001.

62. Revuluri, "*Orientalism* and Musical Knowledge: Lessons from Edward Said," *Journal of the Royal Musical Association* 141 (2016): 205.

63. Yoshihara, "Flight of the Japanese Butterfly," 977.

64. Aya Fujiwara, "The Myth of the Emperor and the Yamato Race: The Role of the *Tairiku nippô* in the Promotion of Japanese-Canadian Transnational Ethnic Identity in the 1920s and the 1930s," *Journal of the Canadian Historical Association* 21 (2010): 37–58, esp. 42.

65. Fujiwara, "Myth of the Emperor," 48.

66. Robert Tuck, *Scribbling Rhymers: Poetry, Print, and Community in Nineteenth-Century Japan* (New York: Columbia University Press, 2018), 147–91.

67. Tuck, *Scribbling Rhymers*, 161–62, 173–74.

68. Tomiko Yoda, *Gender and National Literature: Heian Texts and the Constructions of Japanese Modernity* (Durham, NC: Duke University Press, 2004), 52.

69. Tuck, *Scribbling Rhymers*, 163. Tuck here is specifically addressing the writings of Tekkan Yosano and Yoshiyuki Hagino, respectively.

70. Tuck, *Scribbling Rhymers*, 164.

71. Tuck, *Scribbling Rhymers*, 164.

72. Emiko Ohnuki-Tierney, *Kamikaze, Cherry Blossoms, and Nationalisms: The Militarization of Aesthetics in Japanese History* (Chicago: University of Chicago Press, 2002), 77–78.

73. For an exemplary and rich example of the latter, see Hideo Kobayashi, *Literature of the Lost Home: Kobayashi Hideo—Literary Criticism, 1924–1939*, trans. Paul Anderer (Stanford, CA: Stanford University Press, 1995). For an overview, see Donald Keene, "The Barren Years: Japanese War Literature," *Monumenta Nipponica* 33 (1878): 67–112.

74. Alexander Vovin, trans., *Man'Yōshū, Book 15: A New English Translation Containing the Original Text, Kana Transliteration, Romanization, Glossing and Commentary* (Folkestone, UK: Global Oriental, 2009), 136–38. In this edition, the relevant poem is numbered 15.3688.

75. Vovin, trans., *Man'Yōshū, Book 15*, 103, 136–38.

76. Laurel Resplica Rodd and Mary Catherine Henkenius, trans., *Kokinshū: A Collection of Poems Ancient and Modern* (Boston: Cheng & Tsui, 1996), 57, 198. The relevant poems are numbers 28 (in book 1: Spring) and 521 (in book 11: Love Poems).

77. Tsuji, "Erased," 303.

78. I. J. Fisher, "Music Notes," *Japan Advertiser*, August 22, 1937 (Showa 12): 7.

79. Fisher, "Music Notes."

80. The ship manifest lists Toyama's destination as "Berkshire Music Center, Tanglewood, Lenox, MA." Her *Waka* liner notes and an article in the *Berkshire Eagle* also refer to her presence there. "Year: 1955; arrival: New York, New York; microfilm serial: T715, 1897–1957; microfilm roll 8608, line 15, page 156. Ancestry.com, *New York, Passenger and Crew Lists (including Castle Garden and Ellis Island), 1820–1957*, accessed May 5, 2020. Toyama, *Waka*; "Tanglewood Tales," *Berkshire Eagle*, August 5, 1955: 17.

81. I have not yet found confirmation of this hypothesis after having consulted

the Aaron Copland, David Diamond, and Louise Talma collections at the Library of Congress. Copland played an important role in mentoring Halim El-Dabh and Mario Davidovsky on their path toward the CPEMC.

82. Fahs, "Program in the Humanities: A Statement by Charles B. Fahs."

83. Revuluri, "Tan Dun's *The First Emperor* and the Expectations of Exoticism," 89.

84. Toyama, *Waka*.

85. Michael Leja, *Reframing Abstract Expressionism: Subjectivity and Painting in the 1940s* (New Haven, CT: Yale University Press, 1993), 9.

86. Rica Narimoto, "Heritage within the Avant-Garde? Traditional and Contemporary Musics in Post-War Japan," in *Music as Heritage: Historical and Ethnographic Perspectives*, ed. Barley Norton and Naomi Matsumoto (London: Routledge, 2018), 253.

87. Ann Eden Gibson, *Abstract Expressionism: Other Politics* (New Haven, CT: Yale University Press, 1997). To be sure, this interpretive framework would link Toyama's work with Mingus's avant-garde ambivalence (see chapter 1) and Ono's preoccupation with "word of mouth" reputation and appearance (see chapter 4).

88. Ussachevsky, "A Draft of a Proposal."

89. "200R Columbia Univ Electronic music," memo received from Charles Burton Fahs, sent to Otto Luening, February 21, 1958, Collection RF, Record Group 200R, series 1.2, box 315, folder 2910, Rockefeller Archive Center.

90. Toyama's temporary Huntington Hartford Foundation address is included in Toyama, letter to Vladimir Ussachevsky, July 28, 1959, Ussachevsky Collection, Library of Congress.

91. "Je suis allée voire finalement cet harmonium intempéré à Kyoto, et je peuse d'en avoir une avec oscilators à l'université de Kyoto aussitôt que j'avrai une bourse de Rockefeller ce qui me passait assez 'hopeful.'" Michiko Toyama, letter to Edgard Varèse, April 27, 1960, Varèse Collection, Paul Sacher Foundation, Basel.

92. Erwin Hiebert, *The Helmholtz Legacy in Physiological Acoustics* (Cham, Switzerland: Springer, 2014), xxi.

93. Daniel Walden, "Recovering the Instruments of a Musical Esperanto," www .danielwaldenpiano.com/new-page-1, accessed August 23, 2019.

94. Walden, "Recovering the Instruments."

95. Hiebert, *The Helmholtz Legacy*," xii; Walden, "Recovering the Instruments." For more on Helmholtz's liberal milieu and politics, see Benjamin Steege, *Helmholtz and the Modern Listener* (Cambridge: Cambridge University Press, 2012), esp. 17–19.

96. "International Association for Testing Materials," *Engineering and Mining Journal* 94 (1912): 440.

97. Walden, "Emancipate the Quartertone: The Call to Revolution in Ninetheenth-Century Music Theory," *History of Humanities* 2 (2017): 343.

98. Walden, "Emancipate the Quartertone," 343.

99. Many aspects of Toyama's unexplored connection with Tanaka deserve a full examination beyond the scope of this chapter, not least in relation to Toyama's possible compositional applications of his tuning system and other music-theoretical concepts.

100. Joseph Pfender, "Oblique Music: American Tape Experimentalism and Peripheral Cultures of Technology, 1887 and 1950" (PhD diss., New York University, 2019), 195.

101. Eric John Abrahamson, Sam Hurst, and Barbara Shubinski, *Democracy and Philanthropy: The Rockefeller Foundation and the American Experiment* (New York:

Rockefeller Foundation, 2013), 60; Steven C. Wheatley, introduction to Raymond B. Fosdick, *The Story of the Rockefeller Foundation* (London: Routledge, 1989, 1952), esp. xvi–xviii.

102. Marshall uses this vocabulary in the following papers: John Marshall, "In returning to officer responsibilities in Europe," undated, box 3, folder 38, series 1 general files, RF, FA053, John Marshall papers, Rockefeller Foundation records (RF), Rockefeller Archive Center; Marshall, "By direction of the trustees, the foundation is giving particular attention to the underdeveloped countries of Asia," undated, box 3, folder 38, series 1 general files, RF, FA053, John Marshall papers, Rockefeller Foundation records (RF), Rockefeller Archive Center.

103. Charles Burton Fahs, diary entry, April 22, 1960, "Diary Trip to Japan and Korea 8 April–7 May 1960," electronic resource, Rockefeller Archive Center, dimes .rockarch.org, accessed August 29, 2019.

104. W. E. B. du Bois, *The Souls of Black Folk* (New York: Dover, 1903), 2.

105. Saidiya Hartman, *Scenes of Subjection: Terror, Slavery, and Self-Making in Nineteenth-Century America* (Oxford: Oxford University Press, 1997), 109–10.

106. "Luening's Request for RF aid to Françoise Michiko Toyama declined," Collection RF, record group 200R, series 1.2, box 315, folder 2910, Rockefeller Archive Center, Sleepy Hollow, New York.

107. Fahs, diary entry, April 22, 1960.

108. For more on the East-West Music Encounter and Cage's tour, see Sheppard, *Extreme Exoticism*, 324–42, 348–53.

109. Toyama's role in mediating Varèse's proposed visit becomes apparent in his correspondence with him and in Varèse's correspondence with Hiroshi Teshigahara. Varèse Collection, Paul Sacher Foundation, Basel.

110. Fahs, diary entry, April 22, 1960.

111. Walden, "Emancipate the Quartertone," 340–41.

112. For more details on gender barriers to female composers and artists in mid-twentieth-century Japan, see Nishikawa, Berg, and Brown, "From 'Good Wife,'" 87–105; and Yoshimoto, *Into Performance*, 92.

113. "La vie ici est bièn loin de celle de New York. Mais c'est un mélange curieux d'ancien et de modern. Je me réjouis à dêcouvrire tous ce qui est de Japon "pure" mais hélas! personne ne peut partager mes sentiments. Quant à musique, c'est dominée par doudécaphonists ces sont eux qui dirigent NHK Radio, les publications concerts etc. . . ." Toyama, letter to Edgard Varèse, September 30, 1959, Varèse Collection, Paul Sacher Foundation, Basel.

114. Michiko Toyama, undated letter to Vladimir Ussachevsky (1959), correspondence, Vladimir Ussachevsky Collection, Library of Congress.

115. Ussachevsky, letter to Michiko Toyama, January 30, 1960, correspondence, Vladimir Ussachevsky Collection, Library of Congress.

116. Fahs, diary entry, April 27, 1960.

117. Fahs, diary entry, May 3, 1960.

118. Letter from Michiko Toyama to Vladimir Ussachevsky, January 6, 1960, correspondence with Michiko Toyama, Ussachevsky papers, Library of Congress. In addition to Hirasawa, Toyama mentions a Prof. Maeda (a friend of her brother) and the engineer Takeshi Kiyono (her collaborator).

119. Letter from Charles B. Fahs to Michiko Toyama, December 30, 1960, correspondence with Rockefeller Foundation, Ussachevsky Papers, Library of Congress.

120. "As I claim to be one of the founders of the studio I have long wanted to express how much personal time and work got buried in that act of founding. My own part in the founding is this: I sat up all night editing and typing and retyping the final draft to the Rockefeller Foundation, going to work the next morning and putting in 8 hours at the YMHA. Before that I had gone twice with Vladimir to discuss this project with Burton Fahs, then head of the Rockefeller Foundation Humanities Division." Elizabeth Kray, undated letter fragment to Mario Davidovsky, correspondence, Ussachevsky Papers, Library of Congress.

121. Toyama, letter to Louise Talma, February 18, 1960, Louise Talma Collection, Library of Congress.

122. "The Japan Society is going to sponsor me and [Beate Gordon] is now taking care of my visa." Toyama, letter to Talma, February 18, 1960. "I made the reservation for Dec 16th (the President Line) but I may take the next boat and arriving only in January." Toyama, letter to Louise Talma, November 2 [1961], Louise Talma Collection, Library of Congress.

123. Ussachevsky, letter to Moe Asch, December 12, 1956, Vladimir Ussachevsky Collection, Library of Congress.

124. *Sounds of New Music*, Folkways Records FX 5160, 1956.

125. The Folkways Collection at the Smithsonian would provide further insight into the circumstances of Toyama's album project, yet the collection currently remains inaccessible due to ongoing building renovations.

126. Ussachevsky, letter to Michiko Toyama, May 10, 1960, Vladimir Ussachevsky Collection, Library of Congress.

127. Toyama, letter to Vladimir Ussachevsky, May 17, 1960, Ussachevsky Collection, Library of Congress. Toyama, letter to Vladimir Ussachevsky, November 16 [1960?], box 21, folder 2, series IV, correspondence 1958–68, Vladimir Ussachevsky papers MS #1492, Columbia Rare Book and Manuscript Library.

128. Vladimir Ussachevsky, letter to Otto Luening, October 27, 1960, Vladimir Ussachevsky Collection, Library of Congress.

129. Vladimir Ussachevsky, correspondence with Henry Jacobs, January 10, 1961, box 12, folder 3, series IV, Vladimir Ussachevsky papers MS #1492, Columbia Rare Book and Manuscript Library.

130. Ussachevsky, interview by Thomson.

131. Ralph Greenhouse, "Review of '*Waka* and Other Compositions' by Michiko Toyama," *Ethnomusicology* 5 (1961): 141.

132. Greenhouse, "Review of '*Waka* and Other Compositions.'"

133. Malm, cited in Greenhouse, "Review of '*Waka* and Other Compositions,'" 141. Bracketed interjection by Greenhouse.

134. Tsuji, "Erased," 304.

135. Tsuji, "Erased," 304.

136. Tsuji, "Erased," 304.

137. Toyama, letter to Louise Talma, October 16, 1961, Louise Talma Collection, Library of Congress.

138. Toyama, letter to Louise Talma, March 31, 1961, Louise Talma Collection, Library of Congress.

139. Tsuji, "Erased," 303. The books to which Tsuji alludes do not appear on World-Cat.

140. See for example, "A Study of the Transient Sounds of the Shakuhaehi Based

on ARMA Modeling with Residual Excitation," *Journal of the Acoustical Society of America* 84 (1988): S105.

141. These included the CPEMC archive at Columbia University and the Ussachevsky Collection at the Library of Congress.

142. El-Dabh, interview by the author, December 6, 2014, Kent, Ohio, transcribed from digital recording.

143. El-Dabh, interview by the author, December 6, 2014, Kent, Ohio, transcribed from digital recording.

144. El-Dabh, interview by the author, December 6, 2014, Kent, Ohio, written notes.

145. Lucie Ryzova, *The Age of the Efendiyya: Passages to Modernity in National-Colonial Egypt* (New York: Oxford University Press, 2014); Omnia El Shakry, *The Great Social Laboratory: Subjects of Knowledge in Colonial and Postcolonial Egypt* (Palo Alto, CA: Stanford University Press, 2007), 16.

146. Aziz Benyiamin Fam (1882–1971) was naturalized as a US citizen in 1926. National Archives at Chicago; ARC Title: *Naturalization Petitions and Records, 1906–1991*; NAI number 1137682; record group title: Records of District Courts of the United States, 1685–2009; record group number RG 21. *Michigan, Federal Naturalization Records, 1887–1931* (online database) Ancestry.com, accessed May 5, 2020. El-Dabh discussed his uncle in our interviews. See also Seachrist, *The Musical World of Halim El-Dabh*, 19–20, 30.

147. In 1916 he divorced Nannie Fam, and in 1948 he married Lilyon E. Sussman, according to the Michigan Department of Community Health Division for Vital Records and Health Statistics. Ancestry.com, accessed May 5, 2020.

148. El-Dabh, interview by the author, December 6, 2014, Kent, Ohio, transcribed from digital recording.

149. Ryzova, *The Age of the Efendiyya*, 3.

150. As Seachrist recounts, El-Dabh also spent time at a "regular government school" after the family moved in 1932. Seachrist, *The Musical World of Halim El-Dabh*, 8–12. For El-Dabh to receive Western education as the youngest son replicates patterns of family and education described in Ryzova, *The Age of the Efendiyya*, 1–14.

151. El-Dabh, interview by the author, December 7, 2014, Kent, Ohio, transcribed from digital recording.

152. El-Dabh, interview by the author, December 6, 2014, Kent, Ohio, transcribed from digital recording. Laura Robson, "A Civilizing Mission? Music and the Cosmopolitan in Edward Said," *Mashriq & Mahjar* 2 (2014): 107–29.

153. Seachrist, *The Musical World of Halim El-Dabh*, 13–14.

154. Khoury, "A Look at Lightning," 169.

155. El-Dabh, interview by the author, December 6, 2014, Kent, Ohio, transcribed from digital recording. For more on the YMCA in Heliopolis during this period, see Collier, *Media Primitivism*, 67.

156. Khoury, "A Look at Lightning," 172.

157. Collier argues that El-Dabh likely used C. Lorenz wire recorders imported from Germany, which had been bought by Egyptian radio stations. Collier, *Media Primitivism*, 73.

158. El-Dabh, interview by the author, December 6, 2014, Kent, Ohio, written notes.

159. Omnia El Shakry, *The Great Social Laboratory*, 11. For further relevant discussion of the Cairo Congress, see A. J. Racy, "Comparative Musicologists in the Field: Reflections on the Cairo Congress of Arab Music, 1932," in *This Thing Called Music: Essays in Honor of Bruno Nettl*, ed. Victoria Lindsay Levine and Philip V. Bohlman (Lanham, MD: Rowman and Littlefield Publishers, 2015), 123–33; and Racy, "Historical Worldviews of Early Ethnomusicologists: An East-West Encounter in Cairo, 1932," in *Ethnomusicology and Modern Music History*, eds. Stephen Blum, Philip V. Bohlman, and Daniel M. Neuman (Champaign: University of Illinois Press, 1991), 68–91.

160. El Shakry, *Great Social Laboratory*, 6.

161. El Shakry, *Great Social Laboratory*, 5.

162. Puig, "Une figure égyptienne du XXe siècle."

163. El-Dabh, interview by the author, December 6, 2014, Kent, Ohio, written notes.

164. Anonymous, "Hal Hunīqa Musīqa Sharíqīyyah wa Charbiyyah?" (Is There an Oriental and a Western Music?), *Al-Idha 'ah Al-Masriyyah* 937 (1952): 12. Cited in Salwa El-Shawan, "Western Music and its Practitioners in Egypt (ca. 1925–1985): The Integration of a New Musical Tradition in a Changing Environment," *Asian Music* 17 (1985): 146.

165. Composers Forum Concert, January 17, 1959, recording. Archives of the Columbia-Princeton Electronic Music Center, Columbia University.

166. El-Dabh, interview by the author, December 6, 2014, Kent, Ohio, transcribed from digital recording.

167. The recording must have been made before El-Dabh's 1950 departure from the United States, but we have no further confirmation of the 1944 dating other than El-Dabh's memory. His personal archive may provide further confirmation. *Wire Recorder Piece* is "the widely available adaptation of *Ta'abir A-Zaar*," as Delinda Collier describes. Collier, *Media Primitivism*, 63. I use Andrea Bohlman's conception of the term "sound document"; Bohlman writes that sound documents "facilitate the reconstruction of [a] soundscape, are themselves relics of the creative spirit at the scene, and, as narratives, interpret the events of . . . history in the making." Andrea Bohlman, "Solidarity, Song, and the Sound Document," *Journal of Musicology* 33 (2016): 237.

168. Hager El Hadidi, *Zar: Spirit Possession, Music, and Healing Rituals in Egypt* (Cairo: American University in Cairo Press, 2016).

169. El-Dabh, interview by the author, December 6, 2014, Kent, Ohio, transcribed from digital recording.

170. El-Dabh, interview by the author, December 6, 2014, Kent, Ohio, transcribed from digital recording.

171. El-Dabh, interview by the author, December 6, 2014, Kent, Ohio, transcribed from digital recording. El-Dabh's accounts to Michael Khoury and Nicolas Puig emphasized that he entered into the ceremony together with his friend Kamal Iskander. He did not include this element of the story in his interview by me.

172. See Puig, "Une figure égyptienne du XXe siècle."

173. Collier, *Media Primitivism*, 64.

174. Collier, *Media Primitivism*, 64.

175. El-Dabh, interview by the author, December 6, 2014, Kent, Ohio, transcribed from digital recording.

176. Khoury, "A Look at Lightning," 172.

177. Metwaly, "A Sonic Letter to Halim El-Dabh."

178. Amy Cimini, *Wild Sound: Maryanne Amacher and the Tense of Audible Life* (New York: Oxford University Press, 2021), forthcoming.

179. Khoury, "A Look at Lightning," 172.

180. El-Dabh, interview by the author, December 6, 2014, Kent, Ohio, transcribed from digital recording.

181. El-Dabh, interview by the author, December 6, 2014, Kent, Ohio, transcribed from digital recording.

182. El-Dabh's use of sound recording technologies resonates here with Michael Veal's discussion of dub's echo effects. Michael Veal, *Dub: Soundscapes and Shattered Songs in Jamaican Reggae* (Middletown, CT: Wesleyan University Press, 2007), 196–219.

183. Peter L. Hahn, *The United States, Great Britain, and Egypt, 1945–1956: Strategy and Diplomacy in the Early Cold War* (Chapel Hill, NC: University of North Carolina Press, 1991).

184. Hahn, *The United States, Great Britain, and Egypt*, 1.

185. The Swiss critic A. J. Patry published a front-page rave review in *La Bourse Egyptienne* after initially having expressed skepticism about El-Dabh's abilities on the program committee (according to El-Dabh). A. J. Patry, *La Bourse Egyptienne*, February 15, 1949: 1. See also Seachrist, *The Musical World of Halim El-Dabh*, 17.

186. Khouri, "A Look at Lightning," 174.

187. Khouri, "A Look at Lightning."

188. Khouri, "A Look at Lightning."

189. El-Dabh, interview by the author, December 8, 2014, Kent, Ohio, transcribed from digital recording.

190. El-Dabh, interview by the author, December 8, 2014, Kent, Ohio, transcribed from digital recording.

191. El-Dabh, interview by the author, December 8, 2014, Kent, Ohio, transcribed from digital recording.

192. Khoury, "A Look at Lightning," 175.

193. El-Dabh, interview by the author, December 6, 2014, Kent, Ohio, transcribed from digital recording.

194. El-Shawan, "Western Music and its Practitioners in Egypt," 146–47.

195. El-Dabh, interview by the author, December 6, 2014, Kent, Ohio, transcribed from digital recording.

196. El-Dabh, interview by the author, December 8, 2014, Kent, Ohio, transcribed from digital recording.

197. "The Egyptian Diaspora in the United States," Migration Policy Institute report, RAD Diaspora Profile Series, May 2015 revised, https://www.migrationpolicy.org/research/select-diaspora-populations-united-states, accessed May 5, 2020.

198. Hisham S. Foad, "Waves of Immigration from the Middle East to the United States" (December 20, 2013), *Social Science Research Network*, https://ssrn.com/abstract=2383505, accessed January 14, 2020.

199. El-Dabh, interview by the author, December 7, 2014, Kent, Ohio, transcribed from digital recording.

200. El-Dabh, interview by the author, December 8, 2014, Kent, Ohio, transcribed from digital recording. These words referred specifically to a group of musicians El-Dabh met from the Denver Symphony in 1950, but they are echoed in repeated re-

marks about encounters in the United States premised on his exceptionality as an Egyptian. For example, he recalled the following from his first meeting with the pianist and Martha Graham collaborator Eugene Lester, who became a dear friend: "I'm meeting this crazy Egyptian. I don't know where you're coming from!"

201. El-Dabh, interview by the author, December 6, 2014, Kent, Ohio, written notes.

202. Judith A. Hoffberg, "Ben Patterson in Los Angeles: A Flux-Interview," *Umbrella* 24 (2011): 81. See also George Lewis, "Benjamin Patterson's Spiritual Exercises," in *Tomorrow Is the Question: New Directions in Experimental Music Studies*, ed. Benjamin Piekut (Ann Arbor: University of Michigan Press, 2014), 99; Lewis, "In Search of Benjamin Patterson," 984.

203. Marcelle Hitschmann, *Foreign Press News* 77 (April 1958). Cited in Seachrist, *The Musical World of Halim El-Dabh*, 55.

204. Walter Terry, "Graham: Monumental Dance," *New York Herald Tribune*, April 6, 1958, sec. 4, 6. Cited in Seachrist, *The Musical World of Halim El-Dabh*, 56.

205. John Martin, "Dance: Miss Graham's Clytemnestra," *New York Times*, April 2, 1958, 37. Cited in Seachrist, *The Musical World of Halim El-Dabh*, 56.

206. Caroline Joan S. Picart, "A Tango between Copyright and Choreography: Whiteness as Status Property in Balanchine's Ballets, Fuller's Serpentine Dance and Graham's Modern Dances," *Cardozo Journal of Law and Gender* 18 (2012): 715, 723. I am grateful to Daniel Callahan for directing me to this source.

207. "The persona: a cultural identity that simultaneously shapes the individual in body and mind and creates a collective with a shared and recognizable physiognomy. The bases for personae are diverse: a social role (e.g. the mother), a profession (the physician), an anti-profession (the flâneur), a calling (the priest). . . . Personae are creatures of historical circumstance; they emerge and disappear within specific contexts." Lorraine Daston and H. Otto Sibum, "Introduction: Scientific Personae and their Histories," *Science in Context* 16 (2003): 2–3.

208. Ussachevsky, "A Draft of a Proposal."

209. Akin Euba, foreword to Denise A. Seachrist, *The Musical World of Halim El-Dabh*, xiii–xiv.

210. Seachrist, *The Musical World of Halim El-Dabh*, 67–72. The archives of the Rockefeller Foundation provide further details regarding the dates of his travel. "Halim El-Dabh," Collection RF, RG 10.1, series 200E, box 7, folder 182, Rockefeller Archive Center.

211. Seachrist, *The Musical World of Halim El-Dabh*, 16.

212. "Halim El-Dabh," Collection RF, RG 10.1, series 200E, box 7, folder 182, Rockefeller Archive Center.

213. See Mark Dery, "Black to the Future: Interviews with Samuel B. Delany, Greg Tate, and Tricia Rose," in *Flame Wars: The Discourse of Cyberculture*, ed. Mark Dery (Durham, NC: Duke University Press, 1994), 179–222; Kodwo Eshun, "Further Considerations on Afrofuturism," *CR: The New Centennial Review* 3 (2003): 287–302; George Lewis, "Foreword: After Afrofuturism," *Journal of the Society for American Music* 2 (2008): 139–53; Alondra Nelson, "Introduction: Future Texts," *Social Text* 71 (2002): 1–15; Erik Steinskog, *Afrofuturism and Black Sound Studies: Culture, Technology, and Things to Come* (London: Palgrave Macmillan, 2017); Alexander G. Weheliye, "'Feenin': Posthuman Voices in Contemporary Black Popular Music," *Social Text* 71 (2002): 21–47. George Lewis refers to the importance of considering "non-popular

musics" such as El-Dabh's electronic composition work within constellations of Afro-futurism. Lewis, 142–43.

214. Nelson, "Introduction: Future Texts," 4–6.

215. El-Dabh, *Leiyla and the Poet*, Columbia-Princeton Electronic Music Center, Columbia Records MS 6566 (1964).

216. "Poet-final master after revision," tape reel 151 01022, Archives of the Columbia-Princeton Electronic Music Center, Columbia University; El-Dabh, *Leiyla Visitations I–XIV, Crossing into the Electric-Magnetic*, CD Baby B07897Y8CS (2001).

217. El-Dabh, interview by the author, December 6, 2014, Kent, Ohio.

218. El-Dabh, interview by the author, December 8, 2014, Kent, Ohio, transcribed from digital recording.

219. Lalita Sinha, *Unveiling the Garden of Love: Mystical Symbolism in Layla Majnun and Gita Govinda* (Bloomington, IN: World Wisdom, 2008), 171.

220. Annemarie Schimmel, *My Soul Is a Woman: The Feminine in Islam*, trans. Susan H. Ray (New York: Continuum, 1997), 99.

221. Christine Thu Nhi Dang, "Erotics, Poetics, Politics: The Spheres of Action of Senegalese Sufi Voices," *Ethnomusicology Forum* 26 (2017): 359.

222. A. A. Seyed-Gohrab, *Laylī and Manjūn: Love, Madness, and Mystic Longing in Niẓāmī's Epic Romance* (Leiden, Netherlands: Brill, 2003), 244–49.

223. Seyed-Gohrab, *Laylī and Manjūn*.

224. El-Dabh, interview by the author, December 6, 2014, Kent, Ohio, transcribed from digital recording.

225. El-Dabh, interview by the author, December 6, 2014, Kent, Ohio, transcribed from digital recording; Alice Walker, "Coming Apart," in *Take Back the Night: Women on Pornography*, ed. Laura Lederer (New York: Harper, 1980), 100.

226. "Poet-[work materials]" and "Poet-final master after revision," tape reels 151 01019 and 151 01022, Archives of the Columbia-Princeton Electronic Music Center, Columbia University.

227. Seachrist, *The Musical World of Halim El-Dabh*, 60.

228. El-Dabh, interview by the author, December 6, 2014, Kent, Ohio, transcribed from digital recording.

229. El-Dabh, interview by the author, December 6, 2014, Kent, Ohio, transcribed from digital recording.

230. Fred Turner, *The Democratic Surround: Multimedia and American Liberalism from World War II to the Psychedelic Sixties* (Chicago: University of Chicago Press, 2013), 7.

231. El-Dabh, interview by the author, December 6, 2014, Kent, Ohio, transcribed from digital recording.

232. Harold C. Schonberg, "Concert without Performers," *New York Times*, May 10, 1961.

233. El-Dabh, interview by the author, December 6, 2014, Kent, Ohio, transcribed from digital recording.

234. El-Dabh, interview by the author, December 8, 2014, Kent, Ohio, transcribed from digital recording.

235. A. J. Racy, *Making Music in the Arab World: The Culture and Artistry of Ṭarab* (Cambridge: Cambridge University Press, 2003), 5–6.

236. Bruno Latour, "Give Me a Laboratory and I Will Raise the World," in *Science Observed: Perspectives on the Social Study of Science*, ed. Karin D. Knorr-Cetina and Michael Mulkay (London, Sage, 1983), 141–70.

237. Holmes, *Electronic and Experimental Music*, 204.

238. Lewis, "Foreword: After Afrofuturism," 143.

239. *New York Amsterdam News* reported on the use of El-Dabh's music in a program presented by the Association of Black Choreographers at the West Side YWCA in 1967. *New Pittsburgh Courier* mentioned a workshop he held at an Afro-American Festival at St. Augustine's College in Raleigh, North Carolina, in 1968 and on talks he delivered about sub-Saharan musical cultures at the Africa Symposium at Carnegie-Mellon University in 1969. The *Chicago Daily Defender* promoted his 1971 lecture "Arabic and Spanish Music: An Interaction" at the University of Illinois at Chicago. "Carnegie-Mellon U. Slates Africa Symposium Week Nov. 3 to 8," Perdita Duncan, "Music in Review," *New York Amsterdam News*, June 10, 1968: 18. *New Pittsburgh Courier*, 1 November 1969: 24. Toki Johnson, "On Campus," *New Pittsburgh Courier* November 30, 1968: 14. "Calendar of Events," *Chicago Daily Defender*, December 2, 1971, 2.

240. Eric Salzman, "Program Is Sung by Miriam Burton," *New York Times*, February 3, 1962, 11. Seachrist, *The Musical World of Halim El-Dabh*, 76–77.

241. Michael Steinberg, "Impressive Variety in Electronic Music," *Boston Globe*, June 7, 1964, A 79.

242. Alfred V. Frankenstein, "LPs: Electronic Music, Ives Quartets, Old Voices," *San Francisco Chronicle*, December 11, 1964. Included in Rockefeller Archive Center, RG 1.2 series 200, box 315, folder 2913.

243. Seachrist, *The Musical World of Halim El-Dabh*, 77.

244. Laurel Hurst, conversation with the author, Columbus, Ohio, February 24, 2020.

245. El-Dabh, phone interview by Bob Gluck, May 23, 2002, October 9, 2005, and January 21, 2006. ". . . Like a sculptor, taking chunks of sound and chiseling them into something beautiful." *eContact!* 15.2, econtact.ca/a5.2/gluck_el-dabh.html, accessed January 19, 2019.

246. Kay Kaufman Shelemay, "When Ethnomusicology Meets History: Longitudinal Research in Ethnomusicology," unpublished ms. See also Seachrist, *The Musical World of Halim El-Dabh*, 86.

247. This environment might be compared to an ethos of Black study. See Stefano Harney and Fred Moten, *The Undercommons: Fugitive Planning & Black Study* (New York: Autonomedia, 2013).

248. I am grateful to Kwami Coleman, who coined this term in conversation about a related context.

249. El-Dabh, interview by the author, December 7, 2014, Kent, Ohio, written notes. The majority of this monologue unfolded at a moment when the recording device was off, though he referred back to it during our recorded conversation. He provided a similar version of this story to Seachrist, who quotes him as having told Luening, "Hey, if you don't watch it, I know this place is going to fly. . . . The whole building is going to end up in space." She writes, "El-Dabh eventually became aware that, following this incident, Luening left him alone most of the time." Seachrist, *The Musical World of Halim El-Dabh*, 62. See also Collier, *Media Primitivism*, 79–80.

250. Halim El-Dabh, interview by the author, December 7, 2014, Kent, Ohio, transcribed from digital recording.

251. See, for example, Meyer Liebowitz, "City's 'Acropolis' Combating Slums," *New York Times*, May 21, 1957, 37. "The hope is to have a continuous diversified but well balanced community of good homes and cultural institutions extending from

the Columbia-New York Cathedral-Riverside Church complex to the City College-St. Nicholas Park area."

252. Zipp, *Manhattan Projects*, 207–8.

253. Ann Laura Stoler, *Along the Archival Grain: Epistemic Anxieties and Colonial Common Sense* (Princeton, NJ: Princeton University Press, 2009), 237.

254. Eduardo Herrera, "Electroacoustic Music at CLAEM: A Pioneer Studio in Latin America," *Journal of the Society for American Music* 12 (2018): 179–212; Herrera, *Elite Art Worlds: Philanthropy, Latin Americanism, and Avant-Garde Music* (New York: Oxford University Press, 2020); Herrera, "The Rockefeller Foundation and Latin American Music in the 1960s: The Creation of Indiana University's LAMC and Di Tella Institute's CLAEM," *American Music* 35 (2017): 51–74.

255. Alcides lanza, email communication with the author, August 28, 2019. This communication expanded upon a phone interview by the author, July 10, 2019, documented with written notes.

256. Lanza, email communication with the author, August 28, 2019.

257. Lanza, phone interview by the author, July 10, 2019, documented with written notes.

258. Alice Shields, email correspondence with the author, April 6, 2021.

259. Alice Shields, email correspondence with the author, April 6, 2021.

260. According to RF officer John Marshall, the RG Humanities Division should continue "by diminishing concern with the institutional establishment of intercultural studies. . . . We should [instead] be readier than we have been to agree, even in the absence of precise criteria, as we have not infrequently agreed, that someone, or something, is so promising that he or it deserves the foundation's consideration." John Marshall, "In reviewing [the] program in the Humanities toward 1960," 1959, box 3, folder 36, series 1 general files, RF, FA053, John Marshall papers, Rockefeller Foundation records (RF), Rockefeller Archive Center.

261. Milton Babbitt, *Words about Music*, ed. Stephen Dembski and Joseph Straus (Madison: University of Wisconsin Press, 1987), 163.

262. Martin Brody, "Music for the Masses: Milton Babbitt's Cold War Music Theory," *Musical Quarterly* 77 (1993): 161–92.

263. Anne Shreffler, "The Myth of Empirical Historiography: A Response to Joseph N. Straus," *Musical Quarterly* 84 (2000): 30–39; Emily Abrams Ansari, *The Sound of a Superpower: Musical Americanism and the Cold War* (New York: Oxford University Press, 2018), esp. 4–7.

264. Memo from Gerald Freund to Norman Loyd, December 8, 1966, box 315, folder 2913, series 200, record Group 1.2, Rockefeller Foundation archives (RF), Rockefeller Archive Center. A number of memos in the relevant file address Davidovsky's "genius" and "exceptionality."

265. Michael Uy, *Ask the Experts: How Ford, Rockefeller, and the NEA Changed American Music* (New York: Oxford University Press, 2021), 109–10.

Chapter 4

1. Yoko Ono, interview by Miya Masaoka, "Unfinished Music: An Interview with Yoko Ono," *San Francisco Bay Guardian*, August 27, 1997, http://miyamasaoka.com /writings-by-miya-masaoka/1997/unfinished-music/, accessed July 9, 2020.

2. Yoko Ono, "The Word of a Fabricator," in *Imagine Yoko* (Lund, Sweden: Bakhåll,

2015), 113–19. Translated by Yoko Ono. Originally published in Japanese in *SAC Journal* 24 (May 1962). This chapter incorporates revised material from my article "Ono in Opera: A Politics of Art and Action, 1960–1962," *ASAP/Journal* 3, no. 2 (January 2018): 41--66.

3. In this chapter I use the term "indeterminacy" in a dual sense: (1) to designate those qualities and parameters of a notated musical work not determined for performance by the score, and (2) to describe Cage's poetics, which experimented expansively with elements of indeterminacy in compositional practice in the effort to distance that practice from ego and intentionality. Following Cage, "chance operation" refers to one method or technique among several that allows the composer to operate "exterior to his mind" in the generation of musical outcomes, including in the determination of score directions and features. A classic example of a chance operation is the use of coin tosses to help determine score features. John Cage, "Composition as Process," in *Silence: Lectures and Writings* (Middletown, CT: Wesleyan University Press, 1961), 35.

4. Benjamin Piekut, "Chance and Certainty: John Cage's Politics of Nature," *Cultural Critique* 84 (2013): 146; John Cage, "The History of Experimental Music in America," in *Silence: Lectures and Writings* (Middletown, CT: Wesleyan University Press, 1961), 73.

5. Ono, "The Word of a Fabricator," 115.

6. Ono, "The Word of a Fabricator," 117.

7. Ono, "The Word of a Fabricator," 117.

8. Alexandra Munroe, "Spirit of YES: The Art and Life of Yoko Ono," in *Y E S Yoko Ono*, ed. Alexandra Munroe (New York: Harry N. Abrams, 2000), 23.

9. Martin Puchner, *Poetry of the Revolution: Marx, Manifestos, and the Avant-Gardes* (Princeton, NJ: Princeton University Press, 2006), 2.

10. Christina Klein, *Cold War Orientalism: Asia in the Middlebrow Imagination, 1945–1961* (Berkeley: University of California Press, 2003).

11. Klein, *Cold War Orientalism*, 13. Klein borrows this phrase from Mary Louise Pratt, as discussed below.

12. Yoshimoto, *Into Performance*, 81.

13. Moreover, Zen would not have held an unblemished appeal, given its historical association with Japanese nationalist and imperialist ideologies throughout the twentieth century. Robert H. Sharf, "The Zen of Japanese Nationalism," *History of Religions* 33, no. 1 (1993): 1–43; Brian Victoria, *Zen at War* (Lanham, MD: Rowman and Littlefield, 2006).

14. My own interpretations of Ono's early career draw on foundational critical and art historical work by Bruce Altschuler, Edward M. Gomez, Jon Hendricks, Alexandra Munroe, Kristine Stiles, and Midori Yoshimoto.

15. See, for example, Ono's appearance in a classic survey text. "Cage's embrace of indeterminacy and of all types of sounds and actions as possible material for composition inspired others to challenge accepted definitions of music and art. Performance art, in which performing an action is a public place constitutes a work of art, came into its own in the 1960s. . . . *Grapefruit* (1964) by Yoko Ono (b. 1933) is a collection of such pieces, many of them conceptual, aimed as much at the performer as at any observers." Donald J. Grout, James Peter Burkholder, and Claude V. Palisca, *A History of Western Music*, 7th ed. (New York: W. W. Norton, 208), 936.

16. These words were included in a 1964 note to Maciunas accompanying Ono's

manuscript *Grapefruit,* which Maciunas intended to publish. Lila and Gilbert Silverman Fluxus Collection, Museum of Modern Art, series I, folder 927.

17. Thomas E. Crow, *The Rise of the Sixties: American and European Art in the Age of Dissent* (New Haven, CT: Yale University Press, 1996), 8–9, 11.

18. See, for example, Ryan Dohoney, "John Cage, Julius Eastman, and the Homosexual Ego," in *Tomorrow Is the Question: New Directions in Experimental Music Studies,* ed. Benjamin Piekut (Ann Arbor: University of Michigan Press, 2014), 39–62; Piekut, *Experimentalism Otherwise;* Branden W. Joseph, *Experimentations: John Cage in Music, Art, and Architecture* (New York: Bloomsbury, 2016).

19. Cage appears first to have referred to anarchism in 1960 in a suggestive statement that was too cursory and isolated to constitute a political theory of art practice comparable to the work of some of his counterparts, including Ono's "The Word of a Fabricator." John Cage, "Form is a Language" (1960), in *John Cage: An Anthology,* ed. Richard Kostelanetz (New York: Da Capo, 1970), 135. For more on Cage's anarchism, see Rob Haskins, *Anarchic Societies of Sounds: The Number Pieces of John Cage* (Saarbrücken, Germany: VDM Verlag Dr. Müller, 2009); Joseph, *Experimentations,* 173–204.

20. John Cage, "Experimental Music," in *Silence* (Middletown, CT: Wesleyan University Press, 1991), 12.

21. Caroline A. Jones, "Finishing School: John Cage and the Abstract Expressionist Ego," *Critical Inquiry* 19, no. 4 (1993): 656.

22. Yvonne Rainer, "Looking Myself in the Mouth," *October* 17 (1981): 67.

23. For a rich account of such formats, see Natilee Harren, *Fluxus Forms: Scores, Multiples, and the Eternal Network* (Chicago: University of Chicago Press, 2020).

24. See Heather La Bash, "Yoko Ono: Transnational Artist in a World of Stickiness" (MA thesis, University of Kansas, 2008).

25. Michel Foucault, "The Order of Discourse," in *Untying the Text: A Post-Structuralist Reader,* ed. Robert Young (London: Routledge & Kegan Paul, 1981), 53.

26. Amy Beal, *New Music, New Allies: American Experimental Music from the Zero Hour to Reunification* (Berkeley: University of California Press, 2006), 6.

27. Beal, *New Music, New Allies,* 1.

28. Raymond Williams, *Keywords: A Vocabulary of Culture and Society* (New York: Oxford University Press, 1985), 156.

29. Cage, "History of Experimental Music," 69.

30. Cage, "History of Experimental Music," 70, 72.

31. Cage, "History of Experimental Music," 73.

32. Cage, "History of Experimental Music," 73.

33. Cage, "History of Experimental Music," 75.

34. Klein, *Cold War Orientalism,* 5.

35. Klein, *Cold War Orientalism,* 6.

36. Klein, *Cold War Orientalism,* 7.

37. Klein, *Cold War Orientalism,* 7.

38. Klein, *Cold War Orientalism,* 11–13.

39. Raymond Williams, *The Long Revolution* (1961; repr., Peterborough, ON: Broadview Press, 2001), 86.

40. Mary Louise Pratt, *Imperial Eyes: Travel Writing and Transculturation* (New York: Routledge, 1992), 7.

41. Raymond Williams, *Marxism and Literature* (Oxford: Oxford University Press, 1977), 132.

42. Ming Tiampo, *Gutai: Decentering Modernism* (Chicago: University of Chicago Press, 2010), 43.

43. Tiampo, *Gutai*, 16.

44. Tiampo, *Gutai*, 17.

45. Bruce Cumings, *Parallax Visions: Making Sense of American-East Asian Relations* (Durham, NC: Duke University Press, 1999), 24.

46. W. Anthony Sheppard, "Cold War Transnationalism: Musical Encounters from Tokyo to UCLA," UCLA Distinguished Lecture Series, April 6, 2017.

47. Toru Takemitsu, quoted and translated in Mikiko Sakamoto, "Takemitsu and the Influence of 'Cage Shock': Transforming the Japanese Ideology into Music" (DMA diss., University of Nebraska at Lincoln, 2010).

48. Tiampo, *Gutai*, 110.

49. Tiampo, *Gutai*, 111.

50. Tiampo, *Gutai*, 111.

51. Ray Falk, "Japanese Innovators," *New York Times*, December 8, 1957.

52. Tiampo, *Gutai*, 106.

53. Tiampo, *Gutai*, 112.

54. Ralph Greenhouse, "Review of '*Waka* and Other Compositions' by Michiko Toyama," *Ethnomusicology* 5, no. 2 (1961): 141.

55. Ono, "Word of a Fabricator," 119.

56. Ono, "Word of a Fabricator," 119. "I cannot stand the fact that everything is the accumulation of 'distortion' owing to one's slanted view: I want someone or something to let me feel it. I can neither trust the plantlikeness of my body or the manipulation of my consciousness."

57. Ono, "To the Wesleyan People (1966)," in *Imagine Yoko* (Lund, Sweden: Bakhåll, 2005), 103.

58. Munroe, "Spirit of YES," 15. Bruce Altshuler, "Instructions for a World of Stickiness: The Early Conceptual Work of Yoko Ono," in Munroe, ed., *Y E S Yoko Ono*, 68, 71. "Yoko Ono: Celebrating Her 80th Birthday in Berlin," www.artbabble.org/video/louisiana/yoko-ono-celebrating-her-80th-birthday-berlin, accessed May 30, 2017.

59. Ono, "Recollections of Stefan Wolpe," *Wolpe.org: Home of the Stefan Wolpe Society*, 2002, http://www.wolpe.org/page10/page10.html#Yoko%20Ono, accessed July 8, 2020. For more on Wolpe's relationship with Ono, see Brigid Cohen, "Limits of National History: Yoko Ono, Stefan Wolpe, and Dilemmas of Cosmopolitanism," *Musical Quarterly* 97, no. 2 (2014): 181–237.

60. For more on these relationships, see Cohen, "Diasporic Dialogues in Mid-Century New York: Stefan Wolpe, George Russell, Hannah Arendt, and the Historiography of Displacement," *Journal of the Society for American Music* 6, no. 2 (2012): 143–73.

61. Wolpe, diary entry from the early 1950s in "Numbers are . . ." Wolpe Collection, Paul Sacher Foundation. The second quotation comes from Wolpe, "'Any Bunch of Notes': A Lecture (1953)," ed., Austin Clarkson, *Perspectives of New Music* 21, nos. 1–2 (1982–1983): 310.

62. Wolpe, diary entry from 1946 in "Ich bin in einem grenzenlosen Sinn . . ." (1946–50), Wolpe Collection, Paul Sacher Foundation.

63. Hannah Arendt, *The Human Condition* (Chicago: University of Chicago Press, 1958), 184.

64. Arendt, *The Human Condition*, 283.

65. Arendt, *The Human Condition*, 198.

66. Munroe, "Spirit of YES," 13.

67. Julia C. Bullock, "'Female Students Ruining the Nation': The Debate over Co-education in Postwar Japan," *U.S.-Japan Women's Journal* 46 (2014): 34.

68. Yoshimoto, *Into Performance*, 92.

69. Munroe, "Spirit of YES," 15.

70. Quoted in Munroe, "Spirit of YES," 17.

71. See, for example, Bret W. Davis, Brian Schroeder, and Jason M. Wirth, eds. *Japanese and Continental Philosophy: Conversations with the Kyoto School* (Bloomington: Indiana University Press, 2011).

72. Yoshihiro Nitta, Hirotaka Tatematsu, and Eiichi Shimomissē, "Phenomenology and Philosophy in Japan," in *Japanese Phenomenology*, ed. Yoshihiro Nitta and Hirotaka Tatematsu (Dordrecht, Netherlands: D. Reidel, 1979), 3.

73. For a nuanced perspective on Nishida's politics, see Christopher S. Goto-Jones, *Political Philosophy in Japan: Nishida, the Kyoto School, and Co-Prosperity* (London: Routledge, 2005). See also James W. Heisig and John C. Maraldo, eds., *Rude Awakenings: Zen, the Kyoto School, and the Question of Nationalism* (Honolulu: University of Hawai'i Press, 1995); Satofumi Kawamuro, "Introduction to the 'Nishida Problem': Nishida Kitarō's Political Philosophy and Governmentality" (working paper, *Studies on Multicultural Societies*, no. 15, Afrasian Research Centre, Ryukoku University, 2013); Sharf, "Zen of Japanese Nationalism," 20–24.

74. Arendt, *The Human Condition*, 274.

75. "Man is indeed a project that has a subjective existence, rather unlike that of a patch of moss, a spreading fungus, or a cauliflower." Jean-Paul Sartre, *Existentialism Is a Humanism*, tr. Carol Macomber (New Haven, CT: Yale University Press, 2007), 23.

76. Andrew Feenberg, "The Problem of Modernity in the Philosophy of Nishida," in *Rude Awakenings: Zen, the Kyoto School, and the Question of Nationalism*, ed. James W. Heisig and John C. Maraldo (Honolulu: University of Hawai'i Press, 1995), 135.

77. Arendt, *The Human Condition*, 52.

78. Arendt, *The Human Condition*, 184.

79. Arendt, *The Human Condition*, 207.

80. Arendt, *The Human Condition*, 206.

81. These words were included in a 1964 note to Maciunas accompanying Ono's manuscript *Grapefruit*, which Maciunas intended to publish. Lila and Gilbert Silverman Fluxus Collection, Museum of Modern Art, series I, folder 927.

82. A copy of Ono's rental contract exists in the Lila and Gilbert Silverman Fluxus Collection, Museum of Modern Art, series IV B, folder 1. For more on gender dynamics and bias downtown, see Midori Yoshimoto et al., "An Evening with Fluxus Women: A Roundtable Discussion," *Women & Performance: A Journal of Feminist Theory* 19, no. 3 (2009): 369–89. See also Elizabeth Ann Lindau, "'Mother Superior': Maternity and Creativity in the Work of Yoko Ono," *Women & Music* 20 (2016): 57–76.

83. Jonathan Cott, "Yoko Ono and Her Sixteen-Track Voice," *Rolling Stone*, March 18, 1971, https://www.rollingstone.com/music/music-news/yoko-ono-and -her-sixteen-track-voice-237782/, accessed March 16, 2017. See also Edward M. Go-

mez, "Music of the Mind from the Voice of Raw Soul," in Munroe, *Y E S Yoko Ono*, 233, 237.

84. Yoshimoto, *Into Performance*, 86.

85. Ono, "Unfinished Music."

86. Owen Smith, "Proto-Fluxus in the United States, 1959–1961: The Establishment of a Like-Minded Community of Artists," *Visible Language* 26, nos. 1–2 (1992): 49.

87. Smith, "Proto-Fluxus in the United States."

88. Philip Corner, correspondence with the author, August 11, 2016.

89. Yoshimoto, *Into Performance*, 86.

90. See, for example, Japan's first full-length animated film, *Momotaro's Divine Sea Warriors*, shot in 1944 and screened in 1945.

91. Ono, "To the Wesleyan People," 103.

92. Arendt, *The Human Condition*, 198.

93. Munroe, "Spirit of YES," 13.

94. Yoko Ono, *Grapefruit* (1964; repr. New York: Simon & Schuster, 2000).

95. Ono, cited in Barbara Haskell and John D. Hanhardt, *Yoko Ono: Arias and Objects* (Salt Lake City: Peregrine Smith Books, 1991), 15.

96. Rather than focusing on the historical or social resonances of this work, critics appear to focus on questions of conceptual and technical innovation. Bruce Altshuler writes, "Ono's work provides a test of the viewer's willingness to reject traditional ideas about art." See Altshuler, "Instructions," 71.

97. Altshuler, "Instructions," 71.

98. Yoshimoto, *Into Performance*, 87.

99. "I have had a memory all these years of a large loft painted black, top, sides and bottom, and footprints spaced a pace apart painted in white on the floor. They were all the same size, by the way, clearly painted with a stencil. I don't remember ever thinking that the footprints were painted on fabric (which would have to have been painted black). . . . the footprints were already painted on the floor, and we participants lined up one behind the other and rather ceremoniously walked the length of the loft, placing our feet on the spaced out footprints." Styra Avins, written correspondence with the author, August 19, 2016.

100. This image connects with Akira Kanayama's *Footprints*, which consisted of stenciled footprints on a long swath of canvas. Ray Falk described *Footprints* in his 1957 *New York Times* piece on the Gutai group, so it is conceivable that Ono would have been familiar with the work's reception.

101. Styra Avins, written correspondence with the author, August 19, 2016.

102. Ono, "The Word of a Fabricator," 113.

103. Ono, "The Word of a Fabricator," 117.

104. Ono, "The Word of a Fabricator," 115, 117.

105. Ono, "The Word of a Fabricator," 117.

106. Ono, "The Word of a Fabricator," 119.

107. The *New York Times* noted that the 268-seat hall was "packed." A. R., "Far-Out Music Is Played at Carnegie," *New York Times*, November 25, 1961.

108. Ono, "The Word of a Fabricator," 113.

109. Harren, *Fluxus Forms*, 165.

110. A sampling of news stories from mid-November 1961 would include the Algerian war moving into the Sahara, living conditions on the Bowery, NYU students

fasting outside the Maryland governor's mansion to protest segregation in restaurants, defense talks between the Soviet Union and Finland, tank traps at Berlin's border wall, antinuclear protests outside the White House, and the US Navy searching for Governor Rockefeller's lost son Michael.

111. For more on the "starting point," see Sara Ahmed, "Orientations Matter," in *New Materialisms: Ontology, Agency, and Politics*, ed. Diana Coole and Samantha Frost (Durham, NC: Duke University Press, 2010), 236.

112. Robert Harvey, "The Sartrean Viscous: Swamp and Source," *SubStance* 20, no. 1, issue 64 (1991): 49–66.

113. Yoshimoto, *Into Performance*, 90.

114. Joan Rothfuss, *Topless Cellist: The Improbable Life of Charlotte Moorman* (Cambridge, MA: MIT Press, 2014), 48–49. It is worth noting that this earlier version of *AOS* was misattributed to Ono's husband, Toshi Ichiyanagi, on the program—a circumstance that might suggest the gender bias she confronted.

115. Bruce Webber, "Norman Seaman, Filler of Concert Halls' Odd Hours, Dies at 86," *New York Times*, September 12, 2009.

116. Webber, "Norman Seaman."

117. Philip Corner, digital correspondence with the author, August 10, 2016.

118. A. R., "Far-Out Music," 27.

119. Jonas Mekas, interview by the author, May 26, 2016, New York.

120. Haskell and Hanhardt, *Yoko Ono: Arias and Objects*, 30.

121. Ahmed, "Orientations Matter," 236.

122. Paul K. Saint-Amour, *Tense Future: Modernism, Total War, Encyclopedic Form* (New York: Oxford University Press, 2015), 92.

123. Saint-Amour, *Tense Future*, 92.

124. Saint-Amour, *Tense Future*, 92.

125. Chrissie Iles, "Yoko Ono," in *Yoko Ono: Have You Seen the Horizon Lately?* by Yoko Ono, with essay by Chrissie Iles (Oxford: Museum of Modern Art, Oxford, 1997), 40. For more on the theme of maternity, see Lindau, "Mother Superior."

126. Saint-Amour, *Tense Future*, 306–7.

127. Jill Johnston, "Life and Art," *Village Voice* 7, no. 7 (December 7, 1961).

128. Ahmed, "Orientations Matter," 66.

129. Ahmed, "Orientations Matter," 235.

130. Ahmed, "Orientations Matter," 248.

131. Munroe, "Spirit of YES," 23.

132. Yoko Ono, undated (spring 1962) letter to David Tudor, box 57, David Tudor papers, Getty Research Library.

133. Cohen, "Limits of National History," 210–12.

134. These qualities may, however, link Ono's work with an interest in Antonin Artaud expressed by others in her circle, most notably David Tudor. See Eric Smigel, "Recital Hall of Cruelty: David Tudor, Antonin Artaud, and the 1950s Avant-Garde," *Perspectives of New Music* 45, no. 2 (2007): 171–202.

135. Throughout her career, Ono has rarely used key terms without double or triple meanings. Her use of the term "operational" as a synonym with "efficacy" or "agency" in "The Word of a Fabricator" is one clue that leads to this particular interpretation of "opera."

136. Ono, "*AOS, the Opera, 1961*," in Munroe, *Y E S Yoko Ono*, 274.

137. Ono, quoted in Cott, "Yoko Ono."

138. Johnston, "Life and Art."

139. Jonas Mekas, interview by the author, Brooklyn, August 25, 2016.

140. Sianne Ngai, *Ugly Feelings* (Cambridge, MA: Harvard University Press, 2005), 271.

141. Ono, quoted in Cott, "Yoko Ono."

142. Saint-Amour, *Tense Future*, 20, 96.

143. I imagine this scene as dramatizing Virginia Woolf's famous interwar statement and question, "The world has raised its whip; where will it descend?" Cited in Saint-Amour, *Tense Future*, 1.

144. Johnston, "Life and Art."

145. Kristine Stiles, "Being Undyed: The Meeting of Mind and Matter in Yoko Ono's Events," in Munroe, *Y E S Yoko Ono*, 147. See also Ono, "*AOS, the Opera*."

146. Ono, "*AOS, the Opera*, 1961," in Munroe, *Y E S Yoko Ono*, 274.

147. Arendt, *The Human Condition*, 283; Sjöholm, "Bodies in Exile," 283, 293.

148. Yoshimoto, *Into Performance*, 93. Donald Richie, "Tsumazuita saizensen: Ono Yoko no zen'ei shou" (Stumbling front line: Yoko Ono's avant-garde show), *Geijutsu shinchō* 17, no. 7 (1962): 60–61. Translated in Klaus Biesenbach and Christophe Cherix, eds., *Yoko Ono: One Woman Show, 1960–1971* (New York: Museum of Modern Art, 2015), 122–23.

149. Ono, "The Word of a Fabricator," 117.

150. Johnston, "Life and Art."

151. Ono quoted in Mark Kemp, "She Who Laughs Last: Yoko Ono Reconsidered," *Option: Music Alternatives* (July-August 1992): 78.

152. Quoted in Susan Rosenberg, *Trisha Brown: Choreography as Visual Art* (Middletown, CT: Wesleyan University Press, 2017), 26.

153. Miki Kaneda, "A Very Brief History of the Sōgetsu Art Center," *Post: Notes on Contemporary and Modern Art around the Globe*, February 15, 2013, post.at.moma.org, accessed May 22, 2017.

154. Thomas R. H. Havens, *Radicals and Realists in the Japanese Nonverbal Arts: The Avant-Garde Rejection of Modernism* (Honolulu: University of Hawai'i Press, 2006), 108.

155. Yayoi Uno Everett, "'Scream against the Sky': Japanese Avant-Garde Music in the Sixties," in Robert Adlington, ed., *Sound Commitments: Avant-Garde Music in the Sixties* (New York: Oxford University Press, 2009), 192.

156. Nell Baram and Carolyn Boriss-Krimsky, *Yoko Ono: Collector of Skies* (New York: Amulet Books, 2013), 170. Details of their plans appear in a letter from Ono to Tudor in the David Tudor papers. Yoko Ono, undated letter to David Tudor [late spring 1962], box 57, David Tudor papers, Getty Research Institute.

157. Yoshimoto, *Into Performance*, 92.

158. Yoshimoto, *Into Performance*, 92.

159. Yoko Ono, undated letter to David Tudor [late spring 1962], box 57, David Tudor papers, Getty Research Institute.

160. These "thirty luminaries" included Genpei Akasegawa (a Neo-Dadaist who would eventually form the Hi-Red Center with Jiro Takamatsu), Kuniharu Akiyama (composer, musicologist, poet, and member of Tokyo-based Jikken Kobo), Joji Yuasa (composer and member of Jikken Kobo), Takehisa Kosugi (composer and violinist later associated with Fluxus), Tatsumi Hijikata (dancer, choreographer, and founder of butoh dance), Toshiro Mayuzumi (composer later associated with nation-

alist trends), Yuji Takahashi (composer and pianist), Kohei Sugiura (photographer and designer), Théo Lésoualc'h (French pantomimist), and Yoshiaki Tōno (one of the most influential voices in Japanese art criticism). Yoshimoto, *Into Performance*, 93. Yoshimoto, "Fluxus Nexus: Fluxus in New York and Japan," *Post: Notes on Modern and Contemporary Art around the Globe* (July 9, 2013), http://post.at.moma.org/content _items/199-fluxus-nexus-fluxus-in-new-york-and-japan, accessed May 22, 2017.

161. Toshi Ichiyanagi, "Saizen'ei no koe: Donarudo Richī eno hanron" (Voice from the forefront of the avant-garde: Objection to Donald Richie), *Geijutsu shinchō* 13, no. 8 (1962): 138.

162. Yoshimoto, *Into Performance*, 109. "Daitan na kokoromi: Ono Yoko no ibento" (Bold Experiment: Yoko Ono's Event), *Asahi Journal*, June 1962, 45. Translation by You Nakai.

163. "Daitan na kokoromi."

164. Yoshimoto, *Into Performance*, 94.

165. Yoshimoto, *Into Performance*, 93.

166. Yoshimoto, 92. Ono, "Touch Poem #5," in Biesenbach and Cherix, *Yoko Ono*, 54–57.

167. Everett, "Scream against the Sky," 201–2. Richie, "Stumbling Front Line: Yoko Ono's Avant-Garde Show," in Biesenbach and Cherix, *Yoko Ono: One-Woman Show, 1960–1971*, 122–23.

168. Yoshimoto, *Into Performance*, 92.

169. Richie, "Stumbling Front Line."

170. Richie, excerpt from *The Inland Sea* (1971) in *The Donald Richie Reader*, ed. Arturo Silva (Berkeley, CA: Stone Bridge Press, 2005), 34–35.

171. Ichiyanagi, "Saizen'ei no koe."

172. Ichiyanagi, "Saizen'ei no koe."

173. Ichiyanagi, "Saizen'ei no koe."

174. Ichiyanagi, "Saizen'ei no koe."

175. Ono, cited in Ichiyanagi, "Saizen'ei no koe."

176. Ono, cited in Ichiyanagi, "Saizen'ei no koe."

177. Ichiyanagi, "Saizen'ei no koe."

178. Ichiyanagi, "Saizen'ei no koe."

179. Haskins, *Anarchic Societies*; Joseph, *Experimentations*.

Chapter 5

1. Patterson, quoted in Emmett Williams, "Way Way Way Out," *Stars and Stripes* (European Edition), August 30, 1962, 11.

2. *Guns of the Trees*, DVD, directed by Jonas Mekas (1962; Paris: Re:Voir Video, 2012).

3. Emmett Williams and Ann Noël, eds. *Mr. Fluxus: A Collective Portrait of George Maciunas, 1931–1978* (New York: Thames & Hudson, 1997), 16.

4. Timothy Snyder, *Bloodlands: Europe between Hitler and Stalin* (New York: Basic Books, 2012), xi–xix.

5. Julia Robinson, "Maciunas as Producer: Performative Design in Art of the 1960s," *Grey Room* 33 (2008): 57. See also Harren, *Fluxus Forms: Scores, Multiples, and the Eternal Network* (Chicago: University of Chicago Press, 2020), 133–68.

6. An important partial exception here is Thomas Kellein, who addresses Maci-

unas's wartime childhood, yet refrains from linking this history with Fluxus's founding moment in Wiesbaden as a site of remigration. Thomas Kellein, *The Dream of Fluxus: George Maciunas: An Artist's Biography* (London: Edition Hansjörg Mayer, 2007).

7. Edward Said, "Reflections on Exile," in *Reflections on Exile and Other Essays* (Cambridge, MA: Harvard University Press, 2000), 148.

8. Michael Casper, "I Was There," *New York Review of Books*, June 7, 2018; https://www.nybooks.com/articles/2018/06/07/jonas-mekas-i-was-there/, accessed July 11, 2020.

9. Lewis, "In Search of Benjamin Patterson," 979–92; Lewis, "Benjamin Patterson's Spiritual Exercises" in *Tomorrow Is the Question: New Directions in Experimental Music Studies*, ed. Benjamin Piekut (Ann Arbor: University of Michigan Press, 2014), 86–108.

10. Alexander G. Weheliye, *Habeas Viscus: Racializing Assemblages, Biopolitics, and Black Feminist Theories of the Human*, (Durham, NC: Duke University Press, 2014), 13–14.

11. Timothy Snyder, *Bloodlands*, xix.

12. Homi K. Bhabha, "In the Cave of Making: Thoughts on Third Space," *Communicating in the Third Space*, ed. Karin Ikas and Gerhard Wagner (New York: Routledge, 2009), x.

13. Hannah Higgins, *Fluxus Experience* (Berkeley: University of California Press, 2002), 171.

14. Higgins, "Border Crossings: Three Transnationalisms of Fluxus," in *Not the Other Avant-Garde: The Transnational Foundations of Avant-Garde Performance*, eds. James M. Harding and John Rouse (Ann Arbor: University of Michigan Press, 2006), 266.

15. The one exception to Maciunas's residency in New York during early adulthood was his time in Pittsburgh during academic semesters while attending the Carnegie Institute of Technology from 1952 to 1954.

16. Higgins, *Fluxus Experience*, 170.

17. Astrit Schmidt-Burkhardt, *Maciunas' Learning Machines: From Art History to a Chronology of Fluxus* (Vienna: Springer, 2011).

18. Cuauhtémoc Medina, "The 'Kulturbolschewiken' I: Fluxus, the Abolition of Art, the Soviet Union, and 'Pure Amusement,'" *RES: Anthropology and Aesthetics*, no. 48 (2005): 179.

19. Mari Dumett, *Corporate Imaginations: Fluxus Strategies for Living* (Oakland: University of California Press, 2017), 51, 70.

20. Schmidt-Burckhardt, *Maciunas' Learning Machines*, 62.

21. Maciunas's approach here might in limited ways be compared to Ben Patterson's defensive use of humor and resistance to "having the reception of his work overdetermined by race." See Lewis, "In Search of Benjamin Patterson," 985.

22. James Clifford, *Routes: Travel and Translation in the Late Twentieth Century* (Cambridge, MA: Harvard University Press, 1997), 43.

23. Billie Maciunas, *The Eve of Fluxus: A Fluxmemoir* (Orlando, FL: Arbiter Press, 2010).

24. Edward W. Said, *Out of Place: A Memoir* (London: Granta, 1999), 24.

25. Maciunas, "Biographical Data." Jean Brown papers, box 31, folder 57, Getty Research Library.

26. Lorraine Daston and H. Otto Sibum, "Introduction: Scientific Personae and their Histories," *Science in Context* 16, nos. 1–2 (2003): 2–3.

27. Daston and Sibum, "Introduction," 5.

28. Daston and Sibum, "Introduction," 4.

29. Snyder, *Bloodlands*, 190.

30. This information comes from email correspondence with Frank Wittendorfer, director of the Siemens Archive, Berlin, June 19, 2018.

31. "Alexander Maciunas," *Lithuanian Encyclopedia*, vol. 17 (Boston, 1948), 48. Translated by Jonas Mekas. Jean Brown papers, box 31, folder 56, Getty Research Library.

32. Snyder, *Bloodlands*, 190.

33. Kellein, *Dream of Fluxus*, 17. This information comes from Kellein's conversations with Nijole Valaitis, the sister of George Maciunas.

34. This information can be gleaned from family genealogical research that has been shared online. www.geni.com/people/Boleslav-Andreevich-Saikowski /600000005l435406325, accessed August 8, 2018.

35. Leokadija Maciunas, "My Son." Jean Brown papers, Box 31, folder 56, Getty Research Library.

36. Leokadija Maciunas, "My Son."

37. Kellein, *Dream of Fluxus*, 17.

38. Snyder, *Bloodlands*, 191.

39. Snyder, *Bloodlands*, 192.

40. Robert van Voren, *Undigested Past: The Holocaust in Lithuania* (Amsterdam: Editions Rodopi, 2011), 80–81.

41. Van Voren, *Undigested Past*, 82–83.

42. Edna Kantorovitz Southard and Robert Southard, "Lithuanian Nationalism and the Holocaust: Public Expressions of Memory in Museums and Sites of Memory in Vilnius, Lithuania," in *National Responses to the Holocaust: National Identity and Public Memory*, ed. Jennifer Taylor (Newark: University of Delaware Press, 2014), 61.

43. Southard and Southard, "Lithuanian Nationalism and the Holocaust," 59.

44. Giedrė Jankevičiūtė, "Art as a Narrative of Everyday Life in Lithuania during World War II," in *The Art of Identity and Memory: Toward a Cultural History of the Two World Wars in Lithuania*, ed. Giedrė Jankevičiūtė & Rasutė Žukienė (Boston: Academic Studies Press, 2016), 129.

45. Alex Faitelson, *The Truth and Nothing but the Truth*, 26. Cited in van Voren, *Undigested Past*, 80.

46. Van Voren, *Undigested Past*, 130.

47. Leokadija Maciunas, "My Son."

48. Leokadija Maciunas, "My Son."

49. Williams and Noël, *Mr. Fluxus*, 17–18.

50. Kellein, *Dream of Fluxus*, 17.

51. Leokadija Maciunas, "My Son."

52. Adolf Hitler, cited in Geert Platner, ed., *Schule im Dritten Reich: Erziehung zum Tod, eine Dokumentation* (Cologne: Pahl-Rugenstein Verlag, 1988), 18.

53. Klaus Theweleit, *Male Fantasies*, trans. Stephen Conway, vol. 1, *Women Floods Bodies History* (Minneapolis: University of Minnesota Press, 1987).

54. Platner, *Schule im Dritten Reich*, 26–27.

55. Platner, *Schule im Dritten Reich*, 17.

56. Kellein, *Dream of Fluxus*, 17.

57. Frank Wittendorfer, head of Siemens Archive, email correspondence with the author, July 4, 2018.

58. Peter Hayes, *Industry and Ideology: IG Farben in the Nazi Era* (Cambridge: Cambridge University Press, 1987), 390.

59. Stephan H. Lindner, *Inside IG Farben: Hoechst during the Third Reich* (Cambridge: Cambridge University Press, 2008), 309, 333–35.

60. Hayes, *Industry and Ideology*, 375.

61. Affidavit by Georg von Schnitzler, Nürnberg Military Tribunal, vol. 7, 1510–11. Quoted in Hayes, *Industry and Ideology*, 185–86.

62. Hayes, *Industry and Ideology*, 185–86.

63. Hannah Arendt, *The Origins of Totalitarianism* (New York: Schocken Books, 2004), 620–27.

64. Hayes, *Industry and Ideology*, 382.

65. As would be expected, the Bundesarchiv has no record of Alexander Maciunas having joined the Nazi party. Correspondence with I. A. Simone Langner, Bundesarchiv Berlin, July 4, 2018.

66. Kellein, *Dream of Fluxus*, 17.

67. Leokadija Maciunas, "My Son."

68. Leokadija Maciunas, "My Son."

69. Kellein, 18.

70. Leokadija Maciunas, "My Husband," unpublished manuscript, Jean Brown papers, box 31, Getty Research Library.

71. Alexander Squadrilli, a top supervisor for UN and US government refugee relief efforts, recalled, "There was an invitation on my desk every week to a play, a ballet, a show, even banquets." At Hanau, "the Lithuanians took the lead" by changing the town's riding school into a theater seating three thousand spectators, as described by historian Mark Wyman. "Its grand opening in 1946 featured violinists, a ballet, and other performers drawn from the ranks of the Baltic DPs." At the camp, Yurgis Maciunas also perfected his drawing skills, creating an elaborate pair of arabesque monograms for his parents that prefigure similar graphic odes to Fluxus fellow travelers like Yoko Ono. Mark Wyman, *DP: Europe's Displaced Persons, 1945–1951* (Philadelphia: Balch Institute Press, 1989), 120–21; Leokadija Maciunas, "My Son."

72. Leokadija Maciunas, "My Son."

73. "Alexander Maciunas," *Lithuanian Encyclopedia*, vol. 17.

74. "Alexander Maciunas," *Lithuanian Encyclopedia*, vol. 17.

75. Arendt, "Truth and Politics," in *Between Past and Future: Eight Exercises in Political Thought* (Harmondsworth, UK: Penguin, 1968), 258. See also Arendt, "The Aftermath of Nazi Rule: Report from Germany," *Commentary* 10 (October 1950): 342–53.

76. He included it prominently on the resume-like "Biographical Data Sheet" he compiled near the end of his life. Jean Brown papers, box 31, folder 57, Getty Research Library.

77. Schmidt-Burckhardt, *Maciunas' Learning Machines*, 19.

78. For a description of Maciunas's anxious desire to produce the maximally efficient chart, see Schmidt-Burkhardt, 19, 59.

79. Claude Lévi-Strauss, *The Savage Mind* (Chicago: University of Chicago Press, 1966), 23. Cited in Schmidt-Burckhard, 81.

80. Walter Benjamin, *The Arcades Project*, trans. Howard Eiland and Kevin Mc-Laughlin (Cambridge, MA: Belknap Press of Harvard University Press, 2002), 220–21.

81. Lila and Gilbert Silverman Fluxus Collection, Museum of Modern Art Archives, Subseries V.D. For more on Fluxkits, see Harren, *Fluxus Forms*, 133–68.

82. Howard Brick, "Neo-Evolutionist Anthropology, the Cold War, and the Beginnings of the World Turn in U.S. Scholarship," in *Cold War Social Science: Knowledge Production, Liberal Democracy, and Human Nature*, ed. Mark Solovey and Hamilton Cravens (New York: Palgrave Macmillan, 2012), 167.

83. During this period, Mekas markedly abstained from writing the kind of anti-Semitic propaganda pieces that otherwise populated the pages of these publications. Casper, "I Was There."

84. Mekas, email correspondence with the author, September 7, 2018.

85. Quoted in Casper, "I Was There."

86. Williams and Noël, *Mr. Fluxus*, 32–34.

87. Williams and Noël, *Mr. Fluxus*, 32–34.

88. Kellein, *Dream of Fluxus*, 37.

89. Algirdas M. Budreckis, ed., *The Lithuanians in America, 1651–1975: A Chronology and Fact Book* (Dobbs Ferry, NY: Oceana Publications, 1976), 51–52.

90. Leokadija Maciunas, "My Son."

91. Word of the scandal apparently spread quickly within the Lithuanian-American community: a political cartoon in a Lithuanian exile newspaper in Ohio even denounced *Fluxus* as an organ of the KGB. Jonas Mekas, cited in Williams and Noël, *Mr. Fluxus*, 37.

92. George Maciunas, FBI file, reference file number 105-HQ-50761.

93. Memorandum, August 23, 1961, from special agent in charge to director, FBI, reference file number 105-HQ-50761.

94. Leokadija Maciunas, "My Son."

95. See, for example, Maciunas correspondence with Bill Higgins, Jean Brown papers, Getty Research Institute, box 31, folders 4–5.

96. Klaus Theweleit, *Male Fantasies*, trans. Erica Carter and Chris Turner, vol. 2, *Male Bodies: Psychoanalyzing the White Terror* (Minneapolis: University of Minnesota Press, 1989). See also Theweleit, *Male Fantasies*, vol. 1.

97. Ono, cited in Jon Hendricks, ed., *Fluxus Scores and Instructions: The Transformative Years* (Detroit: Gilbert and Lila Silverman Fluxus Collection, 2008), 40.

98. Leokadija Maciunas, "My Son."

99. Casper points to one exception in Mekas's 1957 short story "The Wolf." Casper, "I Was There."

100. Jonas Mekas, *Guns of the Trees*, DVD (1962; Paris: Re:Voir Video, 2012).

101. Paul K. Saint-Amour's "perpetual interwar," as discussed in chapter 4, is highly pertinent to Mekas's treatment of violence here. Saint-Amour, *Tense Future*, 306–7.

102. Jonas Mekas, *I Had Nowhere to Go* (Leipzig: Spector Books, 2017), 21–54.

103. Jonas Mekas, interview by Amy Taubin, "Jonas Mekas: Making Guns of the Trees," https://www.youtube.com/watch?v=I-YFnFAPV7M&t=30s, accessed November 21, 2018.

104. "It was my line in the 'script,' written by me." Jonas Mekas, email correspondence with the author, September 7, 2018.

105. In the late 1950s, Maciunas worked as an architect in the New York office of Skidmore, Owings & Merrill. He subsequently also worked as an interior architect

for Olin Mathieson Chemical Group and for Knoll International. Kellein, *Dream of Fluxus*, 31.

106. Leokadija Maciunas, "Inserts," included in "My Son."

107. Leokadija Maciunas, "Inserts," included in "My Son."

108. Kristine Stiles, "Anomaly, Sky, Sex, and Psi in Fluxus," in *Critical Mass: Happenings, Fluxus, Performance, Intermedia and Rutgers University, 1958–1972*, ed. Geoffrey Hendricks (New Brunswick, NJ: Rutgers University Press, 2003), 74.

109. See, for example, Williams and Noël, *Mr. Fluxus*, 277–94. For a thoughtful discussion of Maciunas's work and sexuality, see Stiles, "Anomaly."

110. This quotation from a June 24, 1952, Selective Service System report was cited in an Internal Security Report, May 29, 1961, reference file number 105-HQ-50761.

111. Kirsten Yri, "Noah Greenberg and the New York Pro Musica: Medievalism and the Cultural Front," *American Music* 24, no. 4 (2006): 427–28.

112. Maciunas, "This is George Maciunas Speaking, Talking about Fluxus History," April 20, 1978, transcript for cassette tape recording, Silverman Fluxus Collection, Museum of Modern Art archives, series I, folder 962.

113. Maciunas, "Neo-Dada in den Vereinigten Staaten" (Neo-Dada in the United States"; 1962), Silverman Fluxus Collection, Museum of Modern Art archives, series IV.B, folder 7.

114. Maciunas, "This is George Maciunas Speaking."

115. Maciunas, "This is George Maciunas Speaking."

116. Michael Warner, *Publics and Counterpublics* (New York: Zone Books, 2005), esp. 31.

117. Yoko Ono, interview by Gustav Metzger, London, June 2009, in *Yoko Ono*, ed. Hans Ulrich Obrist (Cologne: Verlag der Buchhandlung Walter König, 2009), 83.

118. Warner, *Publics and Counterpublics*, 56.

119. Ono, *Grapefruit*.

120. Hendricks, "Yoko Ono and Fluxus," in Munroe, *Y E S Yoko Ono*, 40.

121. For more on the rediscovery of the photos, see Hendricks, ed., *Paintings & Drawings by Yoko Ono* (Budapest: Galeria 56, 1993), 3.

122. Bruce Altschuler, "Instructions for a World of Stickiness: The Early Conceptual Work of Yoko Ono," in Munroe, *Y E S Yoko Ono*, 66.

123. Dumett provides extensive analysis of Maciunas's self-image as businessman and entrepreneur. Dumett, *Corporate Imaginations*.

124. Maciunas, "This is George Maciunas Speaking."

125. FBI report, August 6, 1956, George Maciunas, FBI file, reference file number 105-HQ-50761.

126. Ono, "Summer of 1961," in Jon Hendricks, ed., *Fluxus Scores and Instructions: The Transformative Years*, 40.

127. Leokadija Maciunas, "My Son."

128. George Maciunas, undated letter to La Monte Young, postmarked January 24, 1962, Silverman Fluxus Collection, MoMA, V.A.1.49.

129. Leokadija Maciunas, "My Son."

130. Higgins, *Fluxus Experience*, 19. Owen F. Smith, *Fluxus: The History of an Attitude* (San Diego, CA: San Diego State University Press, 1998), 13–68.

131. Robinson, "Maciunas as Producer," 57.

132. Marita Krauss, "Jewish Remigration: An Overview from an Emerging Discipline," *Leo Baeck Institute Yearbook* 49 (2004): 118.

133. Jutta Schwidessen, "Wie eine Stadt in der Stadt" (Like a city in the city), *Wiesbadener Kurier*, August 24, 2011.

134. Jeffrey Herf, *Divided Memory: The Nazi Past in the Two Germanys* (Cambridge, MA: Harvard University Press, 1999), 267.

135. Hannah Arendt, *Eichmann in Jerusalem: A Report on the Banality of Evil* (London: Penguin, 2006), 127.

136. Arendt, *Eichmann in Jerusalem*, 127.

137. See, for example, Lars Rensmann, "Returning from Forced Exile: Some Observations on Theodor W. Adorno's and Hannah Arendt's Experience of Postwar Germany and Their Political Theories of Totalitarianism," *Leo Baeck Institute Yearbook* 49 (2004): 171–94.

138. Donna Alvah, "American Military Families in West Germany: Social, Cultural, and Foreign Relations, 1946–1965," in *GIs in Germany: The Social, Economic, Cultural, and Political History of the American Military Presence*, ed. Thomas W . Maulucci Jr. and Detlef Junker (Cambridge: Cambridge University Press, 2015), 162.

139. John W. Lemza, *American Military Communities in West Germany: Life in the Cold War Badlands, 1945–1990* (Jefferson, NC: McFarland, 2016), 38–54.

140. George Maciunas, letter to Dick Higgins, postmarked January 18, 1962, box 31, folder 5, Jean Brown Collection, Getty Research Library.

141. For more on this question, see related correspondence with Raoul Hausmann about the label "neodadaism" in Williams and Noël, *Mr. Fluxus*, 40–41.

142. George Maciunas, undated 1962 letter to Dick Higgins, box 31, folder 5, Jean Brown Collection, Getty Research Library.

143. "Salcius . . . started to write an article, 'Lithuania Belongs to the World.' He had read an article entitled 'The United States Belongs to the World,' written by an executive at the Rockefeller Foundation, and considered its polemics useful." Mats B, cited in Williams and Noël, *Mr. Fluxus*, 32–33.

144. George Maciunas, undated 1962 letter to Dick Higgins, box 31, folder 5, Jean Brown Collection, Getty Research Library.

145. Maciunas, undated 1962 letter to Dick Higgins.

146. Maciunas, undated 1962 letter to Dick Higgins.

147. George Maciunas, letter to La Monte Young, undated (early 1961), V.A.1.49, Lila and Gilbert Silverman Collection, The Museum of Modern Art Archives.

148. Benjamin Patterson, interview by Kathy Goncharov, Archives of American Art, May 22, 2009, https://www.aaa.si.edu/collections/interviews/oral-history -interview-benjamin-patterson-15685, accessed November 20, 2017.

149. Patterson, interview by Goncharov.

150. Robinson, "Maciunas as Producer," 57–62; Schmidt-Burckhardt, *Maciunas' Learning Machines*, 60–62.

151. Dumett, *Corporate Imaginations*, 42.

152. Amy C. Beal, *New Music, New Allies: American Experimental Music in West Germany from the Zero Hour to Reunification* (Berkeley: University of California Press, 2006).

153. "I had a very bad experience (at the AG Gallery in 1961) as regards audiences in N.Y.C. Just couldn't get any. Halls always half filled or less." Maciunas, cited in Williams and Noël, *Mr. Fluxus*, 38.

154. For more details on the Festival of Newest Music, see Henar Rivière Ríos, "Fluxus: Internationale Festspiele Neuester Musik Wiesbade, 1–23 September 1962,"

in Petra Stegmann, ed., *"The Lunatics are on the Loose . . .": European Fluxus Festivals, 1962–1977* (Potsdam: Down with Art! 2012), 49–92. For more on the other festivals, see *"The Lunatics are on the Loose . . ."*

155. Maciunas, cited in Williams and Noël, *Mr. Fluxus*, 49.

156. This segment was filmed on September 8 at the fifth concert of the festival. Rivière Ríos, "Fluxus," 59–62.

157. Item 2012/1233, box 279, Archive Sohm, Staatsgalerie Stuttgart.

158. Item 2012/1233, box 279, Archive Sohm, Staatsgallerie Stuttgart.

159. Danielle Fosler-Lussier, *Music in America's Cold War Diplomacy* (Oakland: University of California Press, 2015), 205–6.

160. "Kunst-Terroristen," *Deutsche Zeitung,* October 19, 1962.

161. Philip Corner, recorded interview by the author, August 20, 2018. See also Gunnar Schmidt, *Klavierzerstörungen in Kunst und Popkultur* (Berlin: Reimer 2012); selected chapters translated by Philip Corner, http://piano-activities.de/englindex .html, accessed November 20, 2017.

162. Williams and Noël, *Mr. Fluxus*, 54.

163. Corner, interview, August 20, 2018.

164. Leokadija Maciunas, "My Son."

165. Ben Patterson, "Ben Patterson Tells Fluxus Stories (from 1962 to 2002)," interview by Gerhard Westerrath and Sabine Felker, March 14, 2002 in Wiesbaden Germany, http://ubu.com/sound/patterson, accessed July 5, 2018.

166. Fosler-Lussier, *Cold War Diplomacy*, 210.

167. George Maciunas, letter to La Monte Young, 1962, Lila and Gilbert Silverman Collection, Museum of Modern Art archives, V.A.1.43.

168. Katarzyna Naliwajek-Mazurek, "The Use of Polish Musical Tradition in the Nazi Propaganda," *Musicology Today* 7 (2010), 243–59; Naliwajek-Mazurek, "Music during the Nazi Occupation of Poland and its Emotional Aspects," in *Besatzungsmacht Musik: Zur Musik- und Emotionsgeschichte im Zeitalter der Weltkriege (1914–1949)*, ed. Sarah Zalfen and Sven Oliver Müller (Bielefeld, Germany: Transcript Verlag, 2012), 207–24; Katarzyna Naliwajek, "The Racialization and Ghettoization of Music in the General Government," in *Twentieth-Century Music and Politics: Essays in Memory of Neil Edmunds,* ed. Pauline Fairclough and Neil Edmunds (Burlington, VT: Ashgate, 2013), 191–210.

169. Patterson, quoted in Kristine Stiles, "Between Water and Stone: Fluxus Performance; A Metaphysics of Acts," in *In the Spirit of Fluxus,* ed. Elizabeth Armstrong and Joan Rothfuss (Minneapolis: Walker Art Center, 1993), 79. See also Lewis, "In Search of Benjamin Patterson," 983.

170. Maciunas, "Neo-Dada in den Vereinigten Staaten." Maciunas's focus on material history also foregrounded certain kinds of timbre as pointing to material conditions of sound production rather than obscuring them.

171. Rivière Ríos, "Fluxus," 59.

172. Patterson, quoted in Emmett Williams, "Way Way Way Out," *Stars and Stripes* (European Edition), August 30, 1962, 11.

173. For an overview of definitions of genocide, see William L. Hewitt, ed., *Defining the Horrific: Readings on Genocide and Holocaust in the Twentieth Century* (Upper Saddle River, NJ: Pearson Education, 2004), 11–15. For more on the inclusion of transatlantic slavery and US racial terror in accounts of genocide, see Adam Jones, *Genocide: A Comprehensive Introduction* (New York: Routledge, 2006), 23–24.

174. Lemza, *American Military Communities*, 61. Maria Höhn, *GIs and Fräuleins: The German-American Encounter in 1950s West Germany* (Chapel Hill: University of North Carolina Press, 2002). For more discussion of this context, see also "Radical Roundtable: Benjamin Patterson & George Lewis," at Radical Presence Black Performance in Contemporary Art at the Studio Museum in Harlem and Grey Art Gallery, NYU, November 15, 2013; https://www.youtube.com/watch?v=3xtkSaN4G6Y, accessed December 13, 2020.

175. *Scenes of Subjection: Terror, Slavery, and Self-Making in Nineteenth-Century America* (Oxford: Oxford University Press, 1997).

176. Lemza, *American Military Communities*, 73–74.

177. Rivière Ríos, "Neo-Dada in der Musik: Düsseldorf, 16 June 1962," in Stegmann, *"The Lunatics are on the Loose . . . ,"* 33–35. Other instructions included "Saw a piano into three parts. hang the first part like Mussolini. burn the second part like Hitler. decide the fate of the third part in a people's court with prosecutor without attorney." Stegmann, *"The Lunatics are on the Loose . . . ,"* 38. Originally cited in Nam June Paik, *"Bagatelles américaines* (1958–1962)," in *Happening & Fluxus: Materialien*, ed. Hanns Sohm and Harald Szeeman (Cologne: Kölnischer Kunstverein, 1970).

178. *Stars and Stripes*, August 30, 1962, 4, 7, 23.

179. Lemza, *American Military Communities*, 78.

180. George Maciunas, undated letter to Emmett Williams, "Dear Emmmettt," fall 1963, Archive Sohm, Staatsgalerie Stuttgart.

181. Robinson, "Maciunas as Producer," 66.

182. Mari Dumett, "The Great Executive Dream: George Maciunas, Adriano Olivetti, and Fluxus Incorporated," *RES: Anthropology and Aesthetics*, nos. 53/54 (2008): 319.

183. Lisa Gitelman, *Paper Knowledge: Toward a Media History of Documents* (Durham, NC: Duke University Press, 2014); Cornelia Vismann, *Files: Law and Media Technology*, trans. Geoffrey Winthrop-Young (Stanford, CA: Stanford University Press, 2008).

184. Sergio Luzzalto, *Primo Levi's Resistance: Rebels and Collaborators in Occupied Italy*, trans. Frederika Randall (New York: Henry Holt, 2016), 58–59.

185. Krauss, "Jewish Remigration," 118.

186. George Maciunas, undated letter to Jonas Mekas, spring 1962, Silverman Fluxus Collection, Museum of Modern Art archives, series V.A.1, folder 20.

187. This vision set the stage for Maciunas's Fluxboxes. See Harren, *Fluxus Forms*, 133–68.

188. Smith, *Fluxus*; Higgins, *Fluxus Experience*.

189. "Radical Roundtable: Benjamin Patterson & George Lewis."

190. "Radical Roundtable: Benjamin Patterson & George Lewis."

191. Maciunas first publicly articulated these proposals in the Fluxus News-Policy Letter no. 6 of April 1963. Silverman Fluxus Collection, Museum of Modern Art archives, series V.A.1, folder 20.

192. Fluxus News-Policy Letter no. 6, April 1963.

193. Piekut, *Experimentalism Otherwise*, 68.

194. Together with his brother, Andersen had indeed assembled some performances in these cities, but "the postcards we sent (to make [Maciunas] happy, now that he was stuck in New York) were a bit exaggerated. . . . We told him that Addi Køpcke, Tomas Schmit and Emmett Williams were with us on the tour, and we told

him we were performing in huge spaces before thousands of spectators." Anderson, cited in Williams and Noël, *Mr. Fluxus*, 110–11.

195. Williams, cited in Williams and Noël, *Mr. Fluxus*, 113.

196. Vismann, *Files*. See, for example, the notecards in the Silverman Fluxus Collection, Museum of Modern Art archives, series V.D.4, folder 2. While these cards began as a moving documentation of friendship, referencing conversations, performances, correspondence, and plans among Fluxus collaborators, they also eventually tracked questions of loyalty in the mid-1960s.

197. Dumett, *Corporate Imaginations*, 70.

198. Elizabeth Young-Bruehl, *Hannah Arendt: For Love of the World*, 2nd ed. (New Haven, CT: Yale University Press, 2004), 244.

199. Nijole Valaitis, letter to the editor, *New York Times*, April 12, 1992, https://www.nytimes.com/1992/04/12/realestate/l-father-of-soho-061292.html, accessed April 3, 2018.

200. Maciunas, *U.S. Surpasses All the Genocide Records!* Silverman Fluxus Collection, Museum of Modern Art archives, series V.G., folder 27.

201. Sarah Colvin, *Ulrike Meinhof and West German Terrorism: Language, Violence, and Identity* (Rochester, NY: Camden House, 2009); Yascha Mounk, *A Stranger in My Own Country* (New York: Farrar, Strauss and Giroux, 2014), 120.

202. Hannah Arendt, "The Aftermath of Nazi Rule: Report from Germany," *Commentary* 10 (October 1950): 342–43.

203. Snyder, *Bloodlands*, xix.

204. Weheliye, *Habeas Viscus*, 13–14.

205. For more on the petition, its submission to the United Nations, the State Department response, and the complex negotiations among its signatories, see Carol Anderson, *Eyes Off the Prize: The United Nations and the African American Struggle for Human Rights, 1944–1955* (Cambridge: Cambridge University Press, 2003), 166–210.

206. Jones, *Genocide*, 23–34.

207. Corner mentioned Jackson Mac Low as one possible exception to the embrace of such an attitude among white Fluxus members. Philip Corner, digitally recorded interview by the author, August 20, 2018, Reggio Emilia, Italy.

208. Philip Corner, digitally recorded interview by the author, August 20, 2018, Reggio Emilia, Italy. Corner, email correspondence with the author, December 4, 2020.

Chapter 6

1. Homi K. Bhabha, "In the Cave of Making: Thoughts on Third Space," *Communicating in the Third Space*, ed. Karin Ikas and Gerhard Wagner (New York: Routledge, 2009), x.

2. Edward W. Said, *Musical Elaborations* (New York: Columbia University Press, 1991), 79.

3. Quoted in Nat Hentoff, *The Nat Hentoff Reader* (Cambridge, MA: Da Capo, 2001), 99.

4. Arendt, *The Human Condition*, 52.

5. Patricia Cohen, "A 'Great Cultural Depression' Looms for Legions of Unemployed Performers," *New York Times*, December 26, 2020.

Archival Sources

Archive Sohm, Staatsgalerie Stuttgart
Archives of the Columbia-Princeton Electronic Music Center, Columbia University
Carl Ruggles Papers in the Irving S. Gilmore Music Library of Yale University
Charles Mingus Collection, Library of Congress
David Tudor Papers, Getty Research Library
Earle Brown Archive, Earle Brown Music Foundation, Rye, NY
Edgard Varèse Collection, Paul Sacher Foundation, Basel, Switzerland.
Fondation Le Corbusier
Jean Brown Papers, Getty Research Library
Lila and Gilbert Silverman Fluxus Collection, Museum of Modern Art
Otto Luening Papers, New York Public Library
Moses and Frances Asch Collection, Ralph Rinzler Folklife Archives and Collections, Smithsonian Institution
Rockefeller Foundation records, Rockefeller Archive Center
Vladimir Ussachevsky Collection, Library of Congress
Voice of America Music Library Collection, Library of Congress
W. E. B. Du Bois Papers (MS 312), Special Collections and University Archives, University of Massachusetts Amherst Libraries

Bibliography

Aaslid, Vilde. "The Poetic Mingus and the Politics of Genre in String Quartet No. 1." *Journal of the Society for American Music* 9, no. 1 (2015): 1–25.

Abrahamson, Eric John, Sam Hurst, and Barbara Shubinski. *Democracy and Philanthropy: The Rockefeller Foundation and the American Experiment.* New York: Rockefeller Foundation, 2013.

Agawu, Kofi. *Representing African Music.* New York: Routledge, 2003.

Ahmed, Sara. "Orientation Matters." In *New Materialisms: Ontology, Agency, and Politics,* edited by Diana Coole and Samantha Frost, 234–57. Durham, NC: Duke University Press, 2010.

Alonso-Minutti, Ana R. "The 'Here and Now': Stories of Relevancy from the Borderlands." *Journal of Music History Pedagogy* 7 (2017): 106–11.

Alonso-Minutti, Ana R., Eduardo Herrera, and Alejandro L. Madrid, eds. *Experimentalisms in Practice: Music Perspectives from Latin America.* New York: Oxford University Press, 2018.

Althusser, Louis. *Lenin and Philosophy, and Other Essays.* Translated by Ben Brewster. New York: Monthly Review Press, 2001.

Altschuler, Bruce. "Instructions for a World of Stickiness: The Early Conceptual Work of Yoko Ono." In *YES Yoko Ono,* edited by Alexandra Munroe, 65–71. New York: Harry N. Abrams, 2000.

Alvah, Donna. "American Military Families in West Germany: Social, Cultural, and Foreign Relations, 1946–1965." In *GIs in Germany: The Social, Economic, Cultural, and Political History of the American Military Presence,* edited by Thomas W. Maulucci Jr. and Detlef Junker, 161–85. Cambridge: Cambridge University Press, 2015.

Anderson, Carol. *Eyes Off the Prize: The United Nations and the African American Struggle for Human Rights, 1944–1955.* Cambridge: Cambridge University Press, 2003.

Ansari, Emily Abrams. "Aaron Copland and the Politics of Cultural Diplomacy." *Journal of the Society for American Music* 5, no. 3 (2011): 335–64.

———. *The Sound of a Superpower: Musical Americanism and the Cold War.* New York: Oxford University Press, 2018.

Arendt, Hannah. "The Aftermath of Nazi Rule: Report from Germany." *Commentary,* October 1950.

———. *Eichmann in Jerusalem: A Report on the Banality of Evil.* London: Penguin, 2006.

———. *The Human Condition.* Chicago: University of Chicago Press, 1958.

———. "Lying in Politics: Reflections on the Pentagon Papers." *New York Review of Books*, November 18, 1972. https://www.nybooks.com/articles/1971/11/18/lying -in-politics-reflections-on-the-pentagon-pape/. Accessed January 11, 2017.

———. *The Origins of Totalitarianism*. New York: Schocken, 2004.

———. "Truth and Politics." In *Between Past and Future: Eight Exercises in Political Thought*, 227–64. Harmondsworth, UK: Penguin, 1968.

Babbitt, Milton. *Words about Music*. Edited by Stephen Dembski and Joseph N. Straus. Madison: University of Wisconsin Press, 1987.

Bacon, Mardges. *Le Corbusier in America: Travels in the Land of the Timid*. Cambridge, MA: MIT Press, 2001.

Banes, Sally. *Greenwich Village 1963: Avant-Garde Performance and the Effervescent Body*. Durham, NC: Duke University Press, 1993.

Baram, Nell, and Carolyn Boriss-Krimsky. *Yoko Ono: Collector of Skies*. New York: Amulet Books, 2013.

Bardsley, Jan, ed. *The Bluestockings of Japan: New Woman Essays and Fiction from Seitō, 1911–16*. Ann Arbor: University of Michigan Press, 2007.

Barnhisel, Greg. *Cold War Modernists: Art, Literature, and American Cultural Diplomacy*. New York: Columbia University Press, 2015.

Barzel, Tamar. *New York Noise: Radical Jewish Music and the Downtown Scene*. Bloomington: Indiana University Press, 2015.

Beal, Amy C. *Carla Bley*. Urbana: University of Illinois Press, 2011.

———. "'Experimentalists and Independents Are Favored': John Edmunds in Conversation with Peter Yates and John Cage, 1959–61." *Notes* 64, no. 4 (2008): 659–87.

———. *New Music, New Allies: American Experimental Music in West Germany from the Zero Hour to Reunification*. Berkeley: University of California Press, 2006.

Beaudoin, Richard. "Counterpoint and Quotation in Ussachevsky's *Wireless Fantasy*." *Organized Sound* 12, no. 2 (2007): 143–51.

Belgrad, Daniel. *The Culture of Spontaneity: Improvisation and the Arts in Postwar America*. Chicago: University of Chicago Press, 1998.

Benjamin, Walter. *The Arcades Project*. Translated by Howard Eiland and Kevin McLaughlin. Cambridge, MA: Belknap Press of Harvard University Press, 2002.

Bernstein, Gail Lee. Introduction to *Recreating Japanese Women, 1600–1945*, edited by Gail Lee Bernstein, 1–14. Berkeley: University of California Press, 1991.

Bhabha, Homi K. "In the Cave of Making: Thoughts on Third Space." In *Communicating in the Third Space*, edited by Karin Ikas and Gerhard Wagner, ix–xiv. New York: Routledge, 2009.

———. *The Location of Culture*. London: Routledge, 1994.

———. "On Cultural Choice." In *The Turn to Ethics*, edited by Marjorie Garber, Beatrice Hanssen, and Rebecca L. Walkowitz, 181–200. New York: Routledge, 2000.

Biesenbach, Klaus, and Christophe Cherix, eds. *Yoko Ono: One Woman Show, 1960–1971*. New York: Museum of Modern Art, 2015.

Birdsall, Carolyn. *Nazi Soundscapes: Sound, Technology and Urban Space in Germany, 1933–1945*. Amsterdam: University of Amsterdam Press, 2012.

Blake, David. "Musical Omnivory in the Neoliberal University." *Journal of Musicology* 34, no. 3 (2017): 319–53.

Bobo, Lawrence D. "An American Conundrum: Race, Sociology, and the African American Road to Citizenship." In *The Oxford Handbook of Afrcian American Citi-*

zenship, 1865–Present, edited by Henry Louis Gates Jr., Claude Steele, Lawrence D. Bobo, Michael Dawson, Gerald Jaynes, Lisa Crooms-Robinson, and Linda Darling-Hammond, 19–70. New York: Oxford University Press, 2012.

Bohlman, Andrea. "Solidarity, Song, and the Sound Document." *Journal of Musicology* 33, no. 2 (2016): 232–69.

Bowker, Geoffrey C. *Memory Practices in the Sciences.* Cambridge, MA: MIT Press, 2005.

Brick, Howard. "Neo-Evolutionist Anthropology, the Cold War, and the Beginnings of the World Turn in U.S. Scholarship." In *Cold War Social Science: Knowledge Production, Liberal Democracy, and Human Nature*, edited by Mark Solovey and Hamilton Cravens, 155–72. New York: Palgrave Macmillan, 2012.

Brinkmann, Reinhold, and Christoph Wolff, eds. *Driven into Paradise: The Musical Migration from Nazi Germany to the United States.* Berkeley: University of California Press, 1999.

Brody, Martin. "Class of '54: Friendship and Ideology at the American Academy in Rome." In *Music and Musical Composition at the American Academy in Rome*, edited by Martin Brody, 222–56. Rochester, NY: University of Rochester Press, 2014.

———. "The Enabling Instrument: Milton Babbit and the RCA Synthesizer." *Contemporary Music Review* 39, no. 6 (2020): 776–94.

———. "Founding Sons: Copland, Sessions, and Berger on Genealogy and Hybridity." In *Aaron Copland and His World*, edited by Carol J. Oja and Judith Tick, 15–44. Princeton, NJ: Princeton University Press, 2005.

———. "Music for the Masses: Milton Babbitt's Cold War Music Theory." *Musical Quarterly* 77, no. 2 (1993): 161–92.

Brody, Martin, ed. *Music and Musical Composition at the American Academy in Rome.* Rochester, NY: University of Rochester Press, 2014.

Bronfman, Alejandra. *Isles of Noise: Sonic Media in the Caribbean.* Chapel Hill: University of North Carolina Press, 2016.

Brown, Bill. "Reification, Reanimation, and the American Uncanny." *Critical Inquiry* 32, no. 2 (2006): 175–207.

Brown, Earle. "Composer Earle Brown: A Conversation with Bruce Duffie." http:// www.bruceduffie.com/brown.html. Accessed November 3, 2020.

Brown, Earle, and Teo Macero. "From Bebop to Poo-Wip: Jazz Influences in Varèse's *Poème Électronique.*" In *Edgard Varèse: Composer, Sound Sculptor, Visionary*, edited by Felix Meyer and Heidy Zimmermann, 309–17. Woodbridge, UK: Boydell and Brewer, 2006.

Budreckis, Algirdas Martin, ed. *The Lithuanians in America, 1651–1975: A Chronology and Fact Book.* Dobbs Ferry, NY: Oceana Publications, 1976.

Bullock, Julia C. "'Female Students Ruining the Nation': The Debate over Coeducation in Postwar Japan." *U.S.-Japan Women's Journal* 46 (2014): 3–23.

Cage, John. "Composition as Process." In *Silence: Lectures and Writings*, 18–56. Middletown, CT: Wesleyan University Press, 1961.

———. "Edgard Varèse." In *Silence: Lectures and Writings*, 83–86. Middletown, CT: Wesleyan University Press, 1961.

———. "Experimental Music." In *Silence: Lectures and Writings*, 7–12. Middletown, CT: Wesleyan University Press, 1961.

———. "Form Is a Language." In *John Cage: An Anthology*, edited by Richard Kostelanetz, 135. New York: Da Capo, 1970.

————. "History of Experimental Music in the United States." In *Silence: Lectures and Writings*, 67–75. Middletown, CT: Wesleyan University Press, 1961.

Calhoun, Craig, Frederick Cooper, and Kevin W. Moore. Introduction to *Lessons of Empire: Imperial Histories and American Power*, edited by Craig Calhoun, Frederick Cooper, and Kevin W. Moore, 1–18. New York: New Press, 2006.

Casper, Michael. "I Was There." *New York Review of Books*, June 7, 2018. https://www.nybooks.com/articles/2018/06/07/jonas-mekas-i-was-there/. Accessed July 11, 2020.

Certeau, Michel de. *Heterologies: Discourse on the Other*. Translated by Brian Massumi. Minneapolis: University of Minnesota Press, 1986.

Chakrabarty, Dipesh. *Provincializing Europe: Postcolonial Thought and Historical Difference*. Princeton, NJ: Princeton University Press, 2000.

Chang, Hyun Kyong Hannah. "Musical Encounters in Korean Christianity: A Trans-Pacific Narrative." PhD diss., University of California, Los Angeles, 2014.

————. "Singing and Praying among Korean Christian Converts (1896–1915): A Trans-Pacific Genealogy of the Modern Korean Voice." In *The Oxford Handbook of Voice Studies*, edited by Nina Sun Eidsheim and Katherine Meizel, 457–74. New York: Oxford University Press, 2019.

————. "A Vocal Interior: Korean Hymns and Prayers between US and Japanese Empires." Unpublished manuscript, n.d.

Cheah, Pheng. *What Is a World? On Postcolonial Literature as World Literature*. Durham, NC: Duke University Press, 2016.

Chiasson, Blaine R. *Administering the Colonizer: Manchuria's Russians under Chinese Rule, 1918–29*. Vancouver: UBC Press, 2010.

Chude-Sokei, Louis. *The Sound of Culture: Diaspora and Black Technopoetics*. Middletown, CT: Wesleyan University Press, 2016.

Cimini, Amy. *Wild Sound: Maryanne Amacher and the Tense of Audible Life*. New York: Oxford University Press, 2021.

Clark, T. J. *Farewell to an Idea: Episodes from a History of Modernism*. New Haven, CT: Yale University Press, 1999.

Clifford, James. *Routes: Travel and Translation in the Late Twentieth Century*. Cambridge, MA: Harvard University Press, 1997.

Cohen, Aaron I. *International Encyclopedia of Women Composers*. New York: Books & Music, 1987.

Cohen, Brigid. "Diasporic Dialogues in Mid-Century New York: Stefan Wolpe, George Russell, Hannah Arendt, and the Historiography of Displacement." *Journal of the Society for American Music* 6, no. 2 (2012): 143–73.

————. "Limits of National History: Yoko Ono, Stefan Wolpe, and Dilemmas of History." *Musical Quarterly* 97, no. 2 (2014): 181–237.

————. *Stefan Wolpe and the Avant-Garde Diaspora*. Cambridge: Cambridge University Press, 2012.

Cohen, Elizabeth F. *Semi-Citizenship in Democratic Politics*. Cambridge: Cambridge University Press, 2009.

Coleman, Janet, and Al Young. *Mingus/Mingus: Two Memoirs*. Montclair, NJ: Limelight Editions, 2004.

Coleman, Kwami. "*Free Jazz* and the 'New Thing': Aesthetics, Identity, and Texture ca. 1961." *Journal of Musicology* 38, no. 3 (2021): 261–95.

Collier, Delinda. *Media Primitivism: Technological Art in Africa*. Chicago: University of Chicago Press, 2020.

Colvin, Sarah. *Ulrike Meinhof and West German Terrorism: Language, Violence, and Identity*. Rochester, NY: Camden House, 2009.

"Contemporary Music Festival Held in London." *Musical America*, July 1938.

Corona, Ignacio, and Alejandro L. Madrid, eds. *Postnational Musical Identities: Cultural Production, Distribution, and Consumption in a Globalized Scenario*. Lanham, MD: Lexington Books, 2007.

Cott, Jonathan. "Yoko Ono and Her Sixteen-Track Voice." *Rolling Stone*, March 18, 1971. https://www.rollingstone.com/music/music-news/yoko-ono-and-her-sixteen-track-voice-237782/. Accessed March 16, 2017.

Cowell, Henry. "American Composers." In *Proceedings of the Ohio State Educational Conference, Eleventh Annual Session*, 378–79. Columbus: Ohio State University, 1932.

Crow, Bill. *From Birdland to Broadway: Scenes from a Jazz Life*. New York: Oxford University Press, 1992.

Crow, Thomas E. *The Rise of the Sixties: American and European Art in the Age of Dissent*. New Haven, CT: Yale University Press, 1996.

Cumings, Bruce. *Parallax Visions: Making Sense of American-East Asian Relations*. Durham, NC: Duke University Press, 1999.

Cusick, Suzanne G. *Francesca Caccini at the Medici Court: Music and the Circulation of Power*. Chicago: University of Chicago Press, 2015.

"Daitan na kokoromi: Ono Yoko no ibento." *Asahi Journal*, June 1962.

Dang, Christine Thu Nhi. "Erotics, Poetics, Politics: The Spheres of Action of Senegalese Sufi Voices." *Ethnomusicology Forum* 26, no. 3 (2017): 349–72.

Daston, Lorraine, and H. Otto Sibum. "Introduction: Scientific Personae and Their Histories." *Science in Context* 16, no. 1–2 (2003): 1–8.

Davenport, Lisa E. *Jazz Diplomacy: Promoting America in the Cold War Era*. Jackson: University Press of Mississippi, 2013.

Davis, Bret W., Brian Schroeder, and Jason M. Wirth, eds. *Japanese and Continental Philosophy: Conversations with the Kyoto School*. Bloomington: Indiana University Press, 2011.

Dawson, Graham, Jo Dover, and Stephen Hopkins, eds. *The Northern Ireland Troubles in Britain: Impacts, Engagements, Legacies and Memories*. Manchester, UK: Manchester University Press, 2017.

Dery, Mark. "Black to the Future: Interviews with Samuel B. Delany, Greg Tate, and Tricia Rose." In *Flame Wars: The Discourse of Cyberculture*, edited by Mark Dery, 179–222. Durham, NC: Duke University Press, 1994.

DeVeaux, Scott. *The Birth of Bebop: A Social and Musical History*. Berkeley: University of California Press, 1999.

Dickinson, Peter, ed. *CageTalk: Dialogues with and about John Cage*. Rochester, NY: University of Rochester Press, 2006.

Dohoney, Ryan. "John Cage, Julius Eastman, and the Homosexual Ego." In *Tomorrow Is the Question: New Directions in Experimental Music Studies*, edited by Benjamin Piekut, 39–62. Ann Arbor: University of Michigan Press, 2014.

———. *Saving Abstraction: Morton Feldman, the de Menils, and the Rothko Chapel*. New York: Oxford University Press, 2019.

Dondero, George Anthony. "Modern Art Shackled to Communism, United States House of Representatives, 16 August 1949." In *Art in Theory 1900–2000: An Anthology of Changing Ideas*, edited by Charles Harrison and Paul Wood, 2nd ed., 665–68. London: Blackwell Publishers, 2003.

Du Bois, W. E. B. *The Souls of Black Folk*. 1903. Reprint, New York: Dover, 1994.

Dumett, Mari. *Corporate Imaginations: Fluxus Strategies for Living*. Oakland: University of California Press, 2017.

———. "The Great Executive Dream: George Maciunas, Adriano Olivetti, and Fluxus Incorporated." *RES: Anthropology and Aesthetics*, no. 53/54 (2008): 314–20.

Dunkel, Mario, and Sina A. Nitzsche. *Popular Music and Public Diplomacy: Transnational and Transdisciplinary Perspectives*. Bielefeld, Germany: Transcript Verlag, 2018.

"Edgard Varèse Conducts a Jazz Workshop (1957)." https://ubu.com/sound/varese.html. Accessed June 9, 2016.

Edwards, Brent Hayes. *The Practice of Diaspora: Literature, Translation, and the Rise of Black Internationalism*. Cambridge, MA: Harvard University Press, 2003.

Eisenberg, Andrew J. "Hip-Hop and Cultural Citizenship on Kenya's 'Swahili Coast.'" *Africa* 82, no. 4 (2012): 556–78.

El-Dabh, Halim. "Leiyla and the Poet." Track 2 on *Columbia-Princeton Electronic Music Center*. Columbia Records MS 6566, 1964.

———. "Leiyla Visitations I-XIV." Tracks 10–23 on *Halim El-Dabh: Crossing into the Electric Magnetic*. Without Fear WFR003, CD 2000.

El Hadidi, Hager. *Zar: Spirit Possession, Music, and Healing Rituals in Egypt*. Cairo: American University in Cairo Press, 2016.

Ellingson, Ter. *The Myth of the Noble Savage*. Berkeley: University of California Press, 2001.

El Shakry, Omnia. *The Great Social Laboratory: Subjects of Knowledge in Colonial and Postcolonial Egypt*. Stanford, CA: Stanford University Press, 2007.

El-Shawan, Salwa Aziz. "Western Music and Its Practitioners in Egypt (ca. 1925–1985): The Integration of a New Musical Tradition in a Changing Environment." *Asian Music* 17, no. 1 (1985): 143–53.

Emmerik, Paul van. "A John Cage Compendium: Chronology 1912–1971." *A John Cage Compendium*, September 18, 2020. https://cagecomp.home.xs4all.nl/chronology_1912–1971.html.

Erickson, Paul, Lorraine Daston, Rebecca Lemov, Thomas Sturm, and Michael D. Gordin. *How Reason Almost Lost Its Mind: The Strange Career of Cold War Rationality*. Chicago: University of Chicago Press, 2015.

Eshun, Kodwo. "Further Considerations on Afrofuturism." *CR: The New Centennial Review* 3, no. 2 (2003): 287–302.

Euba, Akin. Foreword to *The Musical World of Halim El-Dabh*, by Denise Seachrist, ix–xv. Kent, OH: Kent State University Press, 2003.

Everett, Yayoi Uno. "Intercultural Synthesis in Postwar Western Art Music: Historical Contexts, Perspectives, and Taxonomy." In *Locating East Asia in Western Art Music*, edited by Yayoi Uno Everett and Frederick Lau, 1–21. Middletown, CT: Wesleyan University Press, 2004.

———. "'Scream against the Sky': Japanese Avant-Garde Music in the Sixties." In *Sound Commitments: Avant-Garde Music in the Sixties*, edited by Robert Adlington, 187–208. New York: Oxford University Press, 2009.

Faulkner, Robert K. *The Case for Greatness: Honorable Ambition and Its Critics*. New Haven, CT: Yale University Press, 2008.

Feenberg, Andrew. "The Problem of Modernity in the Philosophy of Nishida." In *Rude Awakenings: Zen, the Kyoto School, and the Question of Nationalism*, edited by James W. Heisig and John C. Maraldo, 151–73. Honolulu: University of Hawai'i Press, 1995.

Fenghua, Lui. "Modern Chinese Credit Agencies Vary from Western Models." *Chinese Social Sciences Today*, 2019. http://www.csstoday.com/Item/7490.aspx. Accessed February 11, 2019.

Ferguson, Niall. *Empire: The Rise and Demise of the British World Order and the Lessons for Global Power*. New York: Basic Books, 2004.

Fetterman, William. *John Cage's Theatre Pieces: Notations and Performances*. Abingdon, UK: Routledge, 1996.

Foad, Hisham S. "Waves of Immigration from the Middle East to the United States." *Social Science Research Network*, January 24, 2014. https://ssrn.com/abstract=2383505. Accessed January 14, 2020.

Foner, Nancy. *From Ellis Island to JFK: New York's Two Great Waves of Immigration*. New Haven, CT: Yale University Press, 2000.

Ford, Phil. *Dig: Sound and Music in Hip Culture*. Oxford: Oxford University Press, 2013.

Fosler-Lussier, Danielle. *Music in America's Cold War Diplomacy*. Oakland: University of California Press, 2015.

Foucault, Michel. *The Archaeology of Knowledge and the Discourse on Language*. New York: Vintage, 1982.

———. "The Order of Discourse." In *Untying the Text: A Post-Structuralist Reader*, edited by Robert Young, 48–78. London: Routledge & Kegan Paul, 1981.

Fox, Aaron A. "Repatriation as Reanimation through Reciprocity." In *The Cambridge History of World Music*, edited by Philip V. Bohlman, 522–54. Cambridge: Cambridge University Press, 2013.

Frost, Robert. "Some Obstinacy." In *Robert Frost: Speaking on Campus: Excerpts from His Talks, 1949–1962*, edited by Edward Connery Lathem. New York: W. W. Norton, 2009.

Fujiwara, Aya. "The Myth of the Emperor and the Yamato Race: The Role of the *Tairiku Nippô* in the Promotion of Japanese-Canadian Transnational Ethnic Identity in the 1920s and the 1930s." *Journal of the Canadian Historical Association* 21, no. 1 (2010): 37–58.

Fulcher, Jane F. "The Preparation for Vichy: Anti-Semitism in French Musical Culture between the Two World Wars." *Musical Quarterly* 79, no. 3 (1995): 458–75.

Funayama, Takashi. "*Three Japanese Lyrics* and Japonisme." In *Confronting Stravinsky: Man, Musician, and Modernist*, edited by Jann Pasler, 273–82. Berkeley: University of California Press, 1986.

Gallope, Michael. "On Close Reading and Sound Recording." *Humanities Futures*, 2016. https://humanitiesfutures.org/papers/close-reading-sound-recording/.

Gendron, Bernard. *Between Montmartre and the Mudd Club: Popular Music and the Avant-Garde*. Chicago: University of Chicago Press, 2002.

Gennari, John. *Blowin' Hot and Cool: Jazz and Its Critics*. Chicago: University of Chicago Press, 2006.

Gibson, Ann Eden. *Abstract Expressionism: Other Politics*. New Haven, CT: Yale University Press, 1999.

Gilroy, Paul. *The Black Atlantic: Modernity and Double Consciousness*. Cambridge, MA: Harvard University Press, 1993.

———. *Darker Than Blue: On the Moral Economies of Black Atlantic Culture*. Cambridge, MA: Belknap Press of Harvard University Press, 2010.

Gioia, Ted. "Jazz and the Primitivist Myth." *Musical Quarterly* 73, no. 1 (1989): 130–43.

Gitelman, Lisa. "Media History and Its Objects." Lecture delivered at the Max Planck Institute for the History of Science, Berlin, 2018.

———. *Paper Knowledge: Toward a Media History of Documents*. Durham, NC: Duke University Press, 2014.

———. "The Phonograph's New Media Publics." In *The Sound Studies Reader*, edited by Jonathan Sterne, 282–303. New York: Routledge, 2012.

Gleason, Ralph. "Charles Mingus: A Thinking Musician." *DownBeat*, March 9, 1951.

Gluck, Robert J. "The Columbia-Princeton Electronic Music Studio: Educating International Composers." *Computer Music Journal* 31, no. 2 (2007): 20–38.

———. "Interview with Halim El Dabh, Egyptian Composer: '. . . Like a Sculptor, Taking Chunks of Sound and Chiselling Them into Something Beautiful.'" *EContact!* no. 15.2. Accessed January 19, 2019. http://econtact.ca/15_2/gluck_el-dabh.html.

Go, Julian. *Patterns of Empire: The British and American Empires, 1688 to the Present*. Cambridge: Cambridge University Press, 2011.

Gomez, Edward M. "Music of the Mind from the Voice of Raw Soul." In *YES Yoko Ono*, edited by Alexandra Munroe, 230–37. New York: Harry N. Abrams, 2000.

Goodman John F. *Mingus Speaks*. Berkeley: University of California Press, 2013.

Goto-Jones, Christopher S. *Political Philosophy in Japan: Nishida, the Kyoto School, and Co-Prosperity*. London: Routledge, 2005.

Greenhouse, Ralph. "Review of *Waka and Other Compositions* by Michiko Toyama," *Ethnomusicology* 5, no. 2 (1961): 139–41.

Gregory, Steven. "Making the 'American Acropolis': On Verticality, Social Hierarchy, and the Obduracy of Manhattan Schist." *Annals of the American Association of Geographers* 110, no. 1 (2020): 78–97.

Grout, Donald J., Peter James Burkholder, and Claude V. Palisca. *A History of Western Music*. 8th ed. New York: W. W. Norton, 2010.

Grunfeld, Frederic. "Adventurers in Sound: The Well-Tempered Ionizer." *High Fidelity*, September 1954.

Guilbault, Serge. *How New York Stole the Idea of Modern Art: Abstract Expressionism, Freedom, and the Cold War*. Translated by Arthur Goldhammer. Chicago: University of Chicago Press, 1985.

HaCohen, Ruth. *The Music Libel against the Jews*. New Haven, CT: Yale University Press, 2012.

Hahn, Peter L. *The United States, Great Britain, and Egypt, 1945–1956: Strategy and Diplomacy in the Early Cold War*. Chapel Hill: University of North Carolina Press, 1991.

Harney, Stefano and Fred Moten. *The Undercommons: Fugitive Planning and Black Study*. New York: Autonomedia, 2013.

Hartman, Saidiya. *Scenes of Subjection: Terror, Slavery, and Self-Making in Nineteenth-Century America*. Oxford: Oxford University Press, 1997.

———. "Venus in Two Acts." *Small Axe: A Caribbean Journal of Criticism* 26 (June 2008): 1–14.

Harvey, David. *The New Imperialism*. Oxford: Oxford University Press, 2003.

Harvey, Robert. "The Sartrean Viscous: Swamp and Source." *SubStance* 20, no. 1 (64) (1991): 49–66.

Haskell, Barbara, and John D. Hanhardt. *Yoko Ono: Arias and Objects*. Salt Lake City: Peregrine Smith Books, 1991.

Haskins, Rob. *Anarchic Societies of Sounds: The Number Pieces of John Cage*. Saarbrücken, Germany: VDM Verlag Dr. Müller, 2009.

Havens, Thomas R. H. *Radicals and Realists in the Japanese Nonverbal Arts: The Avant-Garde Rejection of Modernism*. Honolulu: University of Hawai'i Press, 2006.

Hayes, Peter. *Industry and Ideology: IG Farben in the Nazi Era*. Cambridge: Cambridge University Press, 1987.

Heidegger, Martin. *Being and Time*. New York: Harper, 1962.

Heisig, James W., and John C. Maraldo, eds. *Rude Awakenings: Zen, the Kyoto School, and the Question of Nationalism*. Honolulu: University of Hawai'i Press, 1995.

Heller, Michael C. *Loft Jazz: Improvising Music in New York in the 1970s*. Oakland: University of California Press, 2017.

Hendricks, Jon. "Yoko Ono and Fluxus." In *YES Yoko Ono*, edited by Alexandra Munroe, 38–50. New York: Harry N. Abrams, 2000.

Hendricks, Jon, ed. *Fluxus Scores and Instructions: The Transformative Years*. Detroit: Gilbert and Lila Silverman Fluxus Collection, 2008.

———. *Paintings & Drawings by Yoko Ono*. Budapest: Galeria 56, 1993.

Hentoff, Nat. *The Nat Hentoff Reader*. Cambridge, MA: Da Capo, 2001.

Herf, Jeffrey. *Divided Memory: The Nazi Past in the Two Germanys*. Cambridge, MA: Harvard University Press, 1997.

Herrera, Eduardo. "Electroacoustic Music at CLAEM: A Pioneer Studio in Latin America." *Journal of the Society for American Music* 12, no. 2 (2018): 179–212.

———. *Elite Art Worlds: Philanthropy, Latin Americanism, and Avant-Garde Music*. New York: Oxford University Press, 2020.

———. "The Rockefeller Foundation and Latin American Music in the 1960s: The Creation of Indiana University's LAMC and Di Tella Institute's CLAEM." *American Music* 35, no. 1 (2017): 51–74.

Hess, Carol A. *Representing the Good Neighbor: Music, Difference, and the Pan American Dream*. New York: Oxford University Press, 2013.

Hewitt, William L., ed. *Defining the Horrific: Readings on Genocide and Holocaust in the Twentieth Century*. Upper Saddle River, NJ: Pearson Education, 2004.

Hiebert, Erwin. *The Helmholtz Legacy in Physiological Acoustics*. Cham, Switzerland: Springer, 2014.

Higgins, Hannah. "Border Crossings: Three Transnationalisms of Fluxus." In *Not the Other Avant-Garde: The Transnational Foundations of Avant-Garde Performance*, edited by James M. Harding and John Rouse, 265–85. Ann Arbor: University of Michigan Press, 2006.

———. *Fluxus Experience*. Berkeley: University of California Press, 2002.

Higham, John. *Strangers in the Land: Patterns of American Nativism, 1860–1925*. New Brunswick, NJ: Rutgers University Press, 2002.

Hijiya, James A. *Lee de Forest and the Fatherhood of Radio*. Bethlehem, PA: Lehigh University Press, 1992.

Hinkle-Turner, Elizabeth. *Women Composers and Music Technology in the United States*. Aldershot, UK: Ashgate, 2006.

Hoffberg, Judith A. "Ben Patterson in Los Angeles: A Flux-Interview." *Umbrella* 24, no. 3–4 (2001): 79–81.

Höhn, Maria. *GIs and Fräuleins: The German-American Encounter in 1950s West Germany*. Chapel Hill: University of North Carolina Press, 2002.

Holmes, Thom. *Electronic and Experimental Music: Technology, Music, and Culture*. 5th ed. New York: Routledge, 2016.

Hu, Zhuqing (Lester) S. "From Ut Re Mi to Fourteen-Tone Temperament: The Global Accoustemologies of an Early Modern Chinese Tuning Reform." PhD diss., University of Chicago, 2019.

———. "A Global Phonographic Revolution: Trans-Eurasian Resonances of Writing in Early Modern France and China. In *Accoustemologies in Contact: Sounding Subjects and Modes of Listenng in Early Modern Europe*, edited by Emily Wilbourne and Suzanne Cusick. Cambridge, UK: Open Book Publishers, 2021.

———. "The Phonographic Revolution: Writing, Song, and the Advent of Global Modernity." Unpublished manuscript, n.d.

Ichiyanagi Toshi. "Saizen'ei no koe: Donarudo Richī eno hanron." *Geijutsu shinchō* 13, no. 8 (1962): 138.

Ikas, Karin, and Gerhard Wagner, eds. *Communicating in the Third Space*. New York: Routledge, 2009.

Iles, Chrissie. "Yoko Ono." In *Yoko Ono: Have You Seen the Horizon Lately?* by Yoko Ono. Oxford: Museum of Modern Art Oxford, 1997.

"International Association for Testing Materials." *Engineering and Mining Journal* 94, no. 10 (1912): 440.

Irvine, Thomas. *Listening to China: Sound and the Sino-Western Encounter, 1770–1839*. Chicago: University of Chicago Press, 2020.

Iverson, Jennifer. *Electronic Inspirations: Technologies of the Cold War Musical Avant-Garde*. New York: Oxford University Press, 2018.

Jacob, François. *The Statue Within: An Autobiography*. New York: Basic Books, 1988.

Jankevičūtė, Giedrė. "Art as a Narrative of Everyday Life in Lithuania during World War II." In *The Art of Identity and Memory: Toward a Cultural History of the Two World Wars in Lithuania*, edited by Giedrė Jankevičūtė and Rasutė Žukienė, 85–138. Boston: Academic Studies Press, 2016.

Johnston, Jill. "Life and Art." *Village Voice*, December 7, 1961.

Jones, Adam. *Genocide: A Comprehensive Introduction*. New York: Routledge, 2006.

Jones, Caroline A. "Finishing School: John Cage and the Abstract Expressionist Ego." *Critical Inquiry* 19, no. 4 (1993): 628–65.

Jordan, Tim. *Cyberpower: The Culture and Politics of Cyberspace and the Internet*. London: Routledge, 1999.

Joseph, Branden W. *Experimentations: John Cage in Music, Art, and Architecture*. New York: Bloomsbury, 2016.

Juilliard Orchestra, and Juilliard Student Orchestra. *Waka and Other Compositions*. Streaming audio. Folkways Records FW 881, 1960. https://search.alexanderstreet .com/view/work/bibliographic_entity%7Crecorded_cd%7C72570.

Kane, Brian. "Relays: Audiotape, Material Affordances, and Cultural Practice." *Twentieth-Century Music* 14, no. 1 (2017): 65–75.

———. *Sound Unseen: Acousmatic Sound in Theory and Practice*. New York: Oxford University Press, 2014.

Kaneda, Miki. "Acoustics of the Everyday: Between Growth and Conflict in 1960s Japan." *Twentieth-Century Music* 12, no. 1 (2015): 71–96.

———. "A Very Brief History of the Sōgetsu Art Center." *Post: Notes on Modern & Contemporary Art Around the Globe*, February 15, 2013. http://post.at.moma.org /content_items/154-a-very-brief-history-of-the-sogetsu-art-center. Accessed May 22, 2017.

Kawamura, Satofumi. "Introduction to the 'Nishida Problem': Nishida Kitarō's Political Philosophy and Governmentality." Working paper, Afrasian Research Centre, Ryukoku University, 2013.

Keene, Donald. "The Barren Years: Japanese War Literature." *Monumenta Nipponica* 33, no. 1 (1978): 67–112.

Kellein, Thomas. *The Dream of Fluxus: George Maciunas: An Artist's Biography*. London: Edition Hansjörg Mayer, 2007.

Kelsky, Karen. *Women on the Verge: Japanese Women, Western Dreams*. Durham, NC: Duke University Press, 2001.

Kemp, Mark. "She Who Laughs Last: Yoko Ono Reconsidered." *Option: Music Alternatives*, August 1992.

Khoury, Michael. "A Look at Lightning: The Life and Compositions of Halim El-Dabh." In *The Arab Avant-Garde: Music, Politics, Modernity*, edited by Thomas Burkhalter, Kay Dickinson, and Benjamin J. Harbert, 165–82. Middletown, CT: Wesleyan University Press, 2013.

Kim, Rebecca. "In No Uncertain Musical Terms: The Cultural Politics of John Cage's Indeterminacy." PhD diss., Columbia University, 2008.

Klein, Christina. *Cold War Orientalism: Asia in the Middlebrow Imagination, 1945–1961*. Berkeley: University of California Press, 2003.

Kobayashi, Hideo. *Literature of the Lost Home: Kobayashi Hideo–Literary Criticism, 1924–1939*. Translated by Paul Anderer. Stanford, CA: Stanford University Press, 1995.

Krauss, Marita. "Jewish Remigration: An Overview from an Emerging Discipline." *Leo Baeck Institute Yearbook* 49 (2004): 107–19.

Kreuzer, Gundula. *Curtain, Gong, Steam: Wagnerian Technologies of Nineteenth-Century Opera*. Oakland: University of California Press, 2018.

La Bash, Heather. "Yoko Ono: Transnational Artist in a World of Stickiness." MA thesis, University of Kansas, 2008.

Lastra, James. *Sound Technology and the American Cinema: Perception, Representation, Modernity*. New York: Columbia University Press, 2000.

Latour, Bruno. "Give Me a Laboratory and I Will Raise the World." In *Science Observed: Perspectives on the Social Study of Science*, edited by Karin Knorr-Cetina and Michael Joseph Mulkay, 141–70. London: Sage, 1983.

Lawrance, Benjamin N., and Jacqueline Stevens, eds. *Citizenship in Question: Evidentiary Birthright and Statelessness*. Durham, NC: Duke University Press, 2017.

Le Corbusier. *When the Cathedrals Were White*. Translated by Francis E. Hyslop. New York: McGraw-Hill, 1964.

Leja, Michael. *Reframing Abstract Expressionism: Subjectivity and Painting in the 1940s*. New Haven, CT: Yale University Press, 1993.

Lemza, John W. *American Military Communities in West Germany: Life in the Cold War Badlands, 1945–1990*. Jefferson, NC: McFarland, 2016.

Leslie, Stuart W. *The Cold War and American Science: The Military-Industrial Academic Complex at MIT and Stanford.* New York: Columbia University Press, 1993.

Lewis, George E. "Benjamin Patterson's Spiritual Exercises." In *Tomorrow Is the Question: New Directions in Experimental Music Studies,* edited by Benjamin Piekut, 86–108. Ann Arbor: University of Michigan Press, 2014.

———. "Foreword: After Afrofuturism." *Journal of the Society for American Music* 2, no. 2 (2008): 139–53.

———. "Improvised Music after 1950: Afrological and Eurological Perspectives." *Black Music Research Journal* 16, no. 1 (Spring 1996): 91–122.

———. "In Search of Benjamin Patterson: An Improvised Journey." *Callaloo* 35, no. 4 (2012): 979–92.

———. *A Power Stronger Than Itself: The AACM and American Experimental Music.* Chicago: University of Chicago Press, 2009.

Liao, Yvonne. "'Die gute Unterhaltungsmusik': Landscape, Refugee Cafés, and Sounds of 'Little Vienna' in Wartime Shanghai." *Musical Quarterly* 98, no. 4 (2015): 350–394.

Lichtenhann, Ernst, Felix Meyer, and Heidy Zimmermann. "New Primitiveness." In *Edgard Varèse: Composer, Sound Sculptor, Visionary,* 193–201. Woodbridge: Boydell and Brewer, 2006.

Lindau, Elizabeth Ann. "'Mother Superior': Maternity and Creativity in the Work of Yoko Ono." *Women & Music* 20 (2016): 57–76.

Lindner, Stephan H. *Inside IG Farben: Hoechst during the Third Reich.* Cambridge: Cambridge University Press, 2008.

Lobley, Noel. "Taking Xhosa Music out of the Fridge." *Ethnomusicology Forum* 21, no. 2 (2012): 181–95.

Locke, Ralph P. *Musical Exoticism: Images and Reflections.* Cambridge: Cambridge University Press, 2009.

Loukaki, Argyro. "Whose Genius Loci? Contrasting Interpretations of the 'Sacred Rock of the Athenian Acropolis.'" *Annals of the Association of American Geographers* 87, no. 2 (1997): 306–29.

Lowen, Rebecca S. *Creating the Cold War University: The Transformation of Stanford.* Berkeley: University of California Press, 1997.

Luce, Henry R. "The American Century." *Life,* February 17, 1941.

Luening, Otto. *The Odyssey of an American Composer: The Autobiography of Otto Luening.* New York: Charles Scribner's Sons, 1980.

Lukas [pseud.]. "'Edgar Varèse and the Jazzmen' (MP3s)." *WFMU's Beware of the Blog: A Radio Station That Bites Back,* June 1, 2009. https://blog.wfmu.org/freeform/2009/06/edgar-var%C3%A8se-and-the-jazzmen-mp3s.html.

Luzzalto, Sergio. *Primo Levi's Resistance: Rebels and Collaborators in Occupied Italy.* Translated by Frederika Randall. New York: Henry Holt, 2016.

Lynn, Hyung-Gu, and Richard H. Immerman. "Globalization and the Cold War." In *Oxford Handbook of the Cold War.* Oxford: Oxford University Press, 2013. https://www-oxfordhandbooks-com.proxy.library.nyu.edu/view/10.1093/oxfordhb/9780199236961.001.0001/oxfordhb-9780199236961-e-33. Accessed June 4, 2020.

Macero, Teo. "Interview by Iara Lee." *Perfect Sound Forever,* last updated 2008. http://www.furious.com/perfect/teomacero.html. Accessed November 3, 2020.

———. "Teo Macero on Producing Jazz and Classical Musicians." YouTube, February 17, 2011. https://www.youtube.com/watch?v=Mqu-NulrKJQ.

Maciunas, Billie. *The Eve of Fluxus: A Fluxmemoir*. Orlando, FL: Arbiter Press, 2010.

Mackie, Vera. "Embodied Subjects: Feminism in Imperial Japan." In *Japanese Women: Emerging from Subservience, 1868–1945*, edited by Hiroko Tomida and Gordon Daniels, 192–221. Folkestone, UK: Global Oriental, 2005.

Madrid, Alejandro L. *Danzón: Circum-Caribbean Dialogues in Music and Dance*. New York: Oxford University Press, 2013.

———. *In Search of Julián Carillo and Sonido 13*. New York: Oxford University Press, 2015.

Madrid, Alejandro L., ed. *Transnational Encounters: Music and Performance at the U.S.-Mexico Border*. New York: Oxford University Press, 2011.

Margalit, Avishai. *The Decent Society*. Translated by Naomi Goldblum. Cambridge, MA: Harvard University Press, 1996.

Masaoka, Miya. "Unfinished Music: An Interview with Yoko Ono." *San Francisco Bay Guardian*, August 27, 1997. http://miyamasaoka.com/writings-by-miya-masaoka/1997/unfinished-music/.

Matsumoto, Kazuaki. "Shibusawa Eiichi and Local Entrepreneurs in the Meiji Period." *Nagaoka kenkyū ronsō* [Bulletin of Nagaoka University], no. 15 (August 2017): 43–49. https://www.nagaokauniv.ac.jp/wp2014/wp-content/uploads/2011/12/ronso15-matsumoto.pdf. Accessed February 11, 2019.

Mattis, Olivia. "Edgard Varèse and the Visual Arts." PhD diss., Stanford University, 1992.

———. "Edgard Varèse's 'Progressive' Nationalism: *Amériques* Meets Américanisme." In *Edgard Varèse, die Befreiung des Klangs: Symposium Edgard Varèse Hamburg 1991*, edited by Helga de la Motte-Haber. Hofheim, Germany: Wolke, 1991.

———. "The Physical and the Abstract: Varèse and the New York School." In *The New York Schools of Music and the Visual Arts: John Cage, Morton Feldman, Edgard Varèse, Willem de Kooning, Jasper Johns, Robert Rauschenberg*, edited by Steven Johnson, 57–74. New York: Routledge, 2002.

McClary, Susan. "Terminal Prestige: The Case of Avant-Garde Music Composition." *Cultural Critique*, no. 12 (Spring 1989): 57–81.

McDaniel, Cadra Peterson. *American-Soviet Cultural Diplomacy: The Bolshoi Ballet's American Premiere*. Lanham, MD: Lexington Books, 2014.

McGee, Micki, ed. *Yaddo: Making American Culture*. New York: Columbia University Press, 2008.

Medina, Cuauhtémoc. "The 'Kulturbolschewiken' I: Fluxus, the Abolition of Art, the Soviet Union, and 'Pure Amusement.'" *RES: Anthropology and Aesthetics*, no. 48 (2005): 179–92.

Mekas, Jonas. *Guns of the Trees*. DVD. 1962; Paris: Re:Voir Video, 2012.

———. *I Had Nowhere to Go*. Leipzig: Spector Books, 2017.

Metwaly, Kamila. "A Sonic Letter to Halim El-Dabh." *Herri* 4. https://herri.org.za/4/kamila-metwaly.

Meyer, Felix, Carol J. Oja, Wolfgang Rathert, and Anne C. Shreffler, eds. *Crosscurrents: American and European Music in Interaction (1900–2000)*. Woodbridge, UK: Boydell and Brewer, 2014.

Michaels, Jonathan. *McCarthyism: The Realities, Delusions and Politics behind the 1950s Red Scare*. London: Routledge, 2017.

Michaels, Walter Benn. *Our America: Nativism, Modernism, and Pluralism*. Durham, NC: Duke University Press, 1995.

Mikkonen, Simo, and Pekka Suutari, eds. *Music, Art and Diplomacy: East-West Cultural Interactions and the Cold War*. Farnham, UK: Ashgate, 2015.

Miller, Samuel D. "Can Selections for Children Be Avant-Garde?" *Music Educators Journal* 68 (October 1981): 29–33.

Mingus, Charles. *Beneath the Underdog*. Edited by Nel King. New York: Alfred A. Knopf, 1971.

———. *More Than a Fake Book*. Edited by Sue Mingus. New York: Jazz Workshop, 1991.

———. "Open Letter to the Avant-Garde." In *More Than a Fake Book*, edited by Sue Mingus, 119. New York: Jazz Workshop, 1991.

Mody, Cyrus C. M., and Andrew J. Nelson. "A Towering Virtue of Necessity': Inter-disciplinarity and the Rise of Computer Music at Vietnam-Era Stanford." *Osiris* 28 (2013): 254–77.

Monson, Ingrid. *Freedom Sounds: Civil Rights Call Out to Jazz and Africa*. Oxford: Oxford University Press, 2007.

———. "Oh Freedom: George Russell, John Coltrane, and Modal Jazz." In *In the Course of Performance: Studies in the World of Musical Improvisation*, edited by Bruno Nettl and Melinda Russell, 149–68. Chicago: University of Chicago Press, 1998.

———. "The Problem with White Hipness: Race, Gender, and Cultural Conceptions in Jazz Historical Discourse." *Journal of the American Musicological Society* 48, no. 3 (1995): 396–422.

———. *Saying Something: Jazz Improvisation and Interaction*. Chicago: University of Chicago Press, 1996.

Moreno, Jairo. "Imperial Aurality: Jazz, the Archive, and U.S. Empire." In *Audible Empire: Music, Global Politics, Critique*, edited by Ronald Radano and Tejumola Olaniyan, 135–60. Durham, NC: Duke University Press, 2016.

Morrison, Matthew D. "Race, Blacksound, and the (Re)Making of Musicological Discourse." *Journal of the American Musicological Society* 72, no. 3 (2019): 781–823.

———. "The Sound(s) of Subjection: Constructing American Popular Music and Racial Identity through Blacksound." *Women & Performance: A Journal of Feminist Theory* 27, no. 1 (2017): 13–24.

Moten, Fred. *In the Break: The Aesthetics of the Black Radical Tradition*. Minneapolis: University of Minnesota Press, 2003.

Mounk, Yascha. *Stranger in My Own Country: A Jewish Family in Modern Germany*. New York: Farrar, Straus and Giroux, 2014.

Mundy, Rachel. "The 'League of Jewish Composers' and American Music." *Musical Quarterly* 96, no. 1 (n.d.): 50–99.

Munroe, Alexandra. "Spirit of YES: The Art and Life of Yoko Ono." In *YES Yoko Ono*, edited by Alexandra Munroe, 10–37. New York: Harry N. Abrams, 2000.

Munroe, Alexandra, ed. *YES Yoko Ono*. New York: Harry N. Abrams, 2000.

Naliwajek, Katarzyna. "The Racialization and Ghettoization of Music in the General Government." In *Twentieth-Century Music and Politics: Essays in Memory of Neil Edmunds*, edited by Pauline Fairclough and Neil Edmunds, 191–219. Burlington, VT: Ashgate, 2013.

Naliwajek-Mazurek, Katarzyna. "Music during the Nazi Occupation of Poland and Its Emotional Aspects." In *Besatzungsmacht Musik: Zur Musik- und Emotionsgeschichte im Zeitalter der Weltkriege (1914–1949)*, edited by Sarah Zalfen and Sven Oliver Müller, 207–24. Bielefeld, Germany: Transcript Verlag, 2012.

————. "The Use of Polish Musical Tradition in the Nazi Propaganda." *Musicology Today* 7 (2010): 243–59.

Narimoto, Rica. "Heritage within the Avant-Garde? Traditional and Contempoary Musics in Post-War Japan." In *Music as Heritage: Historical and Ethnographic Perspectives*, edited by Barley Norton and Naomi Matsumoto, 244–60. London: Routledge, 2018.

Nelson, Alondra. "Introduction: Future Texts." *Social Text* 20, no. 2 (2002): 1–15.

Ngai, Sianne. *Ugly Feelings*. Cambridge, MA: Harvard University Press, 2005.

Nishikawa, Teruka. "Four Recitals and an Essay: Women and Western Music in Japan: 1868 to the Present." DM thesis, University of Alberta, 2000.

Nishikawa, Teruka, Wesley Berg, and Janice Brown. "From 'Good Wife, Wise Mother' to the Otaka Award: Japanese Women Composers 1868 to the Present." *U.S.-Japan Women's Journal. English Supplement* 22 (2002): 87–105.

Nitta, Yoshihiro, Hirotaka Tatematsu, and Eiichi Shimomissē. "Phenomenology and Philosophy in Japan." In *Japanese Phenomenology*, edited by Yoshihiro Nitta and Hirotaka Tatematsu, 3–17. Analecta Husserliana 8. Dordrecht, Netherlands: D. Reidel, 1979.

Noll, Richard. *The Aryan Christ: The Secret Life of Carl Jung*. New York: Random House, 1997.

Nolte, Sharon H., and Sally Ann Hastings. "The Meiji State's Policy toward Women, 1890–1910." In *Recreating Japanese Women, 1600–1945*, edited by Gail Lee Bernstein, 151–74. Berkeley: University of California Press, 1991.

Norris, Kathleen. *The Virgin of Bennington*. New York: Riverhead Books, 2001.

Obrist, Hans Ulrich, ed. *Yoko Ono*. Cologne: Verlag der Buchhandlung Walter König, 2009.

Ohnuki-Tierney, Emiko. *Kamikaze, Cherry Blossoms, and Nationalisms: The Militarization of Aesthetics in Japanese History*. Chicago: University of Chicago Press, 2002.

Oja, Carol J. *Making Music Modern: New York in the 1920s*. Oxford: Oxford University Press, 2003.

Olmsted, Tony. *Folkways Records: Moses Asch and His Encyclopedia of Sound*. London: Routledge, 2013.

Ong, Aihwa. "Cultural Citizenship as Subject-Making: Immigrants Negotiate Racial and Cultural Boundaries in the United States." *Current Anthropology* 37, no. 5 (1996): 737–62.

Ono, Yoko. "*AOS, the Opera*, 1961." In *YES Yoko Ono*, edited by Alexandra Munroe, 274. New York: Harry N. Abrams, 2000.

————. *Grapefruit: A Book of Instructions and Drawings*. 1964. Reprint, New York: Simon & Schuster, 2000.

————. "Recollections of Stefan Wolpe." *Wolpe.org*, 2002. http://www.wolpe.org/page10/page10.html#Yoko%20Ono. Accessed August 11, 2021.

————. "Summer of 1961." In *Fluxus Scores and Instructions: The Transformative Years*, edited by Jon Hendricks, 40. Detroit: Gilbert and Lila Silverman Fluxus Collection, 2008.

————. "To the Wesleyan People (1966)." In *Imagine Yoko*, 103. Lund, Sweden: Bakhåll, 2005.

————. "Touch Poem #5." In *Yoko Ono: One Woman Show, 1960–1971*, edited by Klaus Biesenbach and Christophe Cherix, 54–57. New York: Museum of Modern Art, 2015.

―――. "The Word of a Fabricator." In *Imagine Yoko*, translated by Yoko Ono, 113–19. Lund, Sweden: Bakhåll, 2005.

Ouellette, Fernand. *Edgard Varèse*. London: Calder & Boyars, 1973.

Paik, Nam June. "*Bagatelles américaines* (1958–1962)." In *Happening & Fluxus: Materialen*, edited by Hanns Sohm and Harald Szeeman. Cologne: Kölnischer Kunstverein, 1970.

Palmer, Abram Smythe. *Folk-Etymology: A Dictionary of Verbal Corruptions or Words Perverted in Form or Meaning, by False Derivation or Mistaken Analogy*. London: George Bell and Sons, 1882.

Parmar, Inderjeeet. *Foundations of the American Century: The Ford, Carnegie, and Rockefeller Foundations in the Rise of American Power*. New York: Columbia University Press, 2012.

Patnaik, Utsa, and Prabhat Patnaik. *A Theory of Imperialism*. New York: Columbia University Press, 2016.

Patterson, Nick. "The Archives of the Columbia-Princeton Electronic Music Center." *Notes* 67, no. 3 (2011): 483–502.

Perlis, Vivian. Otto Luening, recorded interview, May 5, 1982. Oral History of American Music, Yale University.

Perlis, Vivian, and Libby Van Cleve. *Composers' Voices from Ives to Ellington: An Oral History of American Music*. New Haven, CT: Yale University Press, 2005.

Peterson, Marina. "Sonic Cosmopolitanisms: Experimental Improvised Music and a Lebanese-American Cultural Exchange." edited by Thomas Burkhalter, Kay Dickinson, and Benjamin J. Harbert, 185–208. Middletown, CT: Wesleyan University Press, 2011.

Pfender, Joseph William. "Oblique Music: American Tape Experimentalism and Peripheral Cultures of Technology, 1887 and 1950." PhD diss., New York University, 2019.

Picart, Caroline Joan S. "A Tango between Copyright and Choreography: Whiteness as Status Property in Balanchine's Balles, Fuller's Serpentine Dance and Graham's Modern Dances." *Cardozo Journal of Law and Gender* 18, no. 3 (2012): 685–725.

Piekut, Benjamin. "Chance and Certainty: John Cage's Politics of Nature." *Cultural Critique* 84 (2013): 134–63.

―――. *Experimentalism Otherwise: The New York Avant-Garde and Its Limits*. Berkeley: University of California Press, 2011.

―――. *Henry Cow: The World Is a Problem*. Durham, NC: Duke University Press, 2019.

Piekut, Benjamin, ed. *Tomorrow Is the Question: New Directions in Experimental Music Studies*. Ann Arbor: University of Michigan Press, 2014.

Platner, Geert, ed. *Schule im Dritten Reich: Erziehung zum Tod, eine Dokumentation*. Cologne: Pahl-Rugenstein Verlag, 1988.

"A Poet's Pilgrimage: Robert Frost Goes Back to England." *Life*, September 23, 1957.

Porter, Eric. *What Is This Thing Called Jazz? African American Musicians as Artists, Critics, and Activists*. Berkeley: University of California Press, 2002.

Prakash, Vikramaditya. *Chandigarh's Le Corbusier: The Struggle for Modernity in Postcolonial India*. Seattle: University of Washington Press, 2002.

Pratt, Mary Louise. *Imperial Eyes: Travel Writing and Transculturation*. New York: Routledge, 1992.

Priestley, Brian. *Mingus: A Critical Biography*. New York: Da Capo, 1984.

Puchner, Martin. *Poetry of the Revolution: Marx, Manifestos, and the Avant-Gardes.* Princeton, NJ: Princeton University Press, 2006.

Puig, Nicolas. "Une figure égyptienne du XXe siècle: Halim El-Dabh, compositeur, collecteur et pionnier des musiques électroniques." *Annales Islamologiques* 53 (2019): 113–36.

Quintero, Michael Birenbaum. *Rites, Rights & Rhythms: A Genealogy of Musical Meaning in Colombia's Black Pacific.* New York: Oxford University Press, 2019.

Racy, Ali Jihad. "Comparative Musicologists in the Field: Reflections on the Cairo Congress of Arab Music, 1932." In *This Thing Called Music: Essays in Honor of Bruno Nettl*, edited by Victoria Lindsay Levine and Philip V. Bohlman, 137–50. Lanham, MD: Rowman & Littlefield, 2015.

―――. "Historical Worldviews of Early Ethnomusicologists: An East-West Encounter in Cairo, 1932." In *Ethnomusicology and Modern Music History*, edited by Stephen Blum, Philip V. Bohlman, and Daniel M. Neuman, 68–91. Urbana: University of Illinois Press, 1991.

―――. *Making Music in the Arab World: The Culture and Artistry of Ṭarab.* Cambridge: Cambridge University Press, 2003.

Radano, Ronald, and Tejumola Olaniyan, eds. *Audible Empire: Music, Global Politics, Critique.* Durham, NC: Duke University Press, 2016.

"Radical Roundtable: Benjamin Patterson & George Lewis." https://www.youtube.com/watch?v=3xtkSaN4G6Y. Accessed December 13, 2020.

Rahkonen, Carl, and Ralph Hartsock. "The Smoking Gun: Evidence That Vladimir Ussachevsky Used Chinese Timbres as the Basis for His Electronic Music (Expanded Edition)." Paper presented at the 2008 annual conference of SEAMUS, Salt Lake City. Accessed May 24, 2019. https://digital.library.unt.edu/ark:/67531/metadc801972/.

Rainer, Yvonne. "Looking Myself in the Mouth." *October* 17 (1981): 65–76.

Ramsey, Guthrie P., Jr. *The Amazing Bud Powell: Black Genius, Jazz History, and the Challenge of Bebop.* Berkeley: University of California Press, 2013.

Rao, Nancy Yunhwa. *Chinatown Opera Theater in North America.* Urbana: University of Illinois Press, 2017.

―――. "The Role of Language in Music Integration: *Poéme Lyrique II* by Chen Qigang." *Journal of Music in China* 2, no. 2 (2000): 273–96.

Redmond, Shana. "'And You Know Who I Am': Paul Robeson Sings America." *Massachusetts Review* 57, no. 4: 615–19.

―――. *Anthem: Social Movements and the Sound of Solidarity in the African Diaspora.* New York: New York University Press, 2014.

―――. *Everything Man: The Form and Function of Paul Robeson.* Durham, NC: Duke University Press, 2020.

Reichman, Thomas. *Mingus: Charlie Mingus 1968.* Inlet Films, 1968.

Reisner, Robert George, ed. *Bird: The Legend of Charlie Parker.* New York: Da Capo, 1962.

Rensmann, Lars. "Returning from Forced Exile: Some Observations on Theodor W. Adorno's and Hannah Arendt's Experience of Postwar Germany and Their Political Theories of Totalitarianism." *Leo Baeck Institute Yearbook* 49 (2004): 171–94.

Revuluri, Sindhumathi. "A Note from the Guest Editor." *Opera Quarterly* 32, no. 1 (2016): 1–4.

———. "*Orientalism* and Musical Knowledge: Lessons from Edward Said." *Journal of the Royal Musical Association* 141, no. 1 (2016): 205–9.

———. "Tan Dun's *The First Emperor* and the Expectations of Exoticism." *Opera Quarterly* 32, no. 1 (2016): 77–93.

Rexroth, Kenneth. *One Hundred Poems from the Japanese*. New York: New Directions, 1955.

Rheinberger, Hans-Jörg. "Experimental Systems: Difference, Graphematicity, Conjuncture." In *Intellectual Birdhouse*, edited by Claudia Mareis, Florian Dombois, Michael Schwab, and Ute Meta Bauer, 89–99. London: Walther Koening, 2012.

Richie, Donald. *The Donald Richie Reader: 50 Years of Writing on Japan*. Edited by Arturo Silva. Berkeley, CA: Stone Bridge Press, 2001.

———. "Stumbling Front Line: Yoko Ono's Avant-Garde Show." In *Yoko Ono: One Woman Show, 1960–1971*, edited by Klaus Biesenbach and Christophe Cherix, 122–23. New York: Museum of Modern Art, 2015.

———. "Tsumazuita saizensen: Ono Yoko no zen'ei shou." *Geijutsu shinchō* 17, no. 7 (1962): 60–61.

Rivière Ríos, Henar. "Fluxus: Internationale Festspiele Neuester Musik Wiesbade, 1–23 September 1962." In *"The Lunatics Are on the Loose . . .": European Fluxus Festivals, 1962–1977*, edited by Petra Stegmann, 49–92. Potsdam, Germany: Down with Art! 2012.

———. "Neo-Dada in der Musik: Düsseldorf, 16 June 1962." In *"The Lunatics Are on the Loose . . .": European Fluxus Festivals, 1962–1977*, edited by Petra Stegmann, 33–35. Potsdam, Germany: Down with Art! 2012.

Robinson, Julia. "Maciunas as Producer: Performative Design in Art of the 1960s." *Grey Room* 33 (2008): 56–83.

Robson, Laura. "A Civilizing Mission?: Music and the Cosmopolitan in Edward Said." *Mashriq & Mahjar* 2, no. 1 (2014): 107–29.

Rockefeller Foundation. "Area Studies." *The Rockefeller Foundation: a Digital History*, n.d. Accessed July 7, 2020.

Rodd, Laurel Respica, and Mary Catherine Henkenius, trans. *Kokinshū: A Collection of Poems Ancient and Modern*. Boston: Cheng & Tsui Company, 1996.

Rodgers, Tara. *Pink Noises: Women on Electronic Music and Sound*. Durham, NC: Duke University Press, 2010.

Romero, Sergio Ospina. "Ghosts in the Machine and Other Tales around a 'Marvelous Invention': Player Pianos in Latin America in the Early Twentieth Century." *Journal of the American Musicological Society* 72, no. 1 (2019): 1–42.

Rosenberg, Susan. *Trisha Brown: Choreography as Visual Art*. Middletown, CT: Wesleyan University Press, 2017.

Rothfuss, Joan. *Topless Cellist: The Improbable Life of Charlotte Moorman*. Cambridge, MA: MIT Press, 2014.

Rust, Joel. "Edgard Varèse and the Sounds of the Early Twentieth-Century City." PhD diss., New York University, 2020.

Rustin, Nichole T. "Mingus Fingers: Charles Mingus, Black Masculinity, and Postwar Jazz Culture." PhD diss., New York University, 1999.

Rustin-Paschal, Nichole. *The Kind of Man I Am: Jazzmasculinity and the World of Charles Mingus Jr.* Middletown, CT: Wesleyan University Press, 2017.

Ryzova, Lucie. *The Age of the Effendiyya: Passages to Modernity in National-Colonial Egypt*. New York: Oxford University Press, 2014.

Said, Edward W. *Musical Elaborations*. New York: Columbia University Press, 1991.
———. *Orientalism*. New York: Vintage, 1979.
———. *Out of Place: A Memoir*. London: Granta, 1999.
———. "Reflections on Exile." In *Reflections on Exile and Other Essays*, 173–86. Cambridge, MA: Harvard University Press, 2000.
Saint-Amour, Paul K. *Tense Future: Modernism, Total War, Encyclopedic Form*. New York: Oxford University Press, 2015.
Saitō, Yoshiomi. *The Cultural Politics of Jazz in the Twentieth Century*. London: Routledge, 2020.
Sakamoto, Mikiko. "Takemitsu and the Influence of 'Cage Shock': Transforming the Japanese Ideology into Music." DMA diss., University of Nebraska at Lincoln, 2010.
Salzman, Eric. Liner notes to *Music of Vladimir Ussachevsky*. New York: CRI, 1987.
Sartre, Jean-Paul. *Existentialism Is a Humanism*. Translated by Carol Macomber. New Haven, CT: Yale University Press, 2007.
Sassen, Saskia. *The Global City: New York, Tokyo, London*. 2nd ed. Princeton, NJ: Princeton University Press, 2001.
Saunders, Frances Stonor. *The Cultural Cold War: The CIA and the World of Arts and Letters*. New York: New Press, 1999.
Scheding, Florian. *Musical Journeys: Performing Migration in Twentieth-Century Music*. Woodbridge, UK: Boydell Press, 2019.
Schimmel, Annemarie. *My Soul Is a Woman: The Feminine in Islam*. Translated by Susan H. Ray. New York: Continuum, 1997.
Schmidt, Gunnar. *Klavierzerstörungen in Kunst und Popkultur*. Berlin: Reimer, 2012.
Schmidt-Burkhardt, Astrit. *Maciunas' Learning Machines: From Art History to a Chronology of Fluxus*. Vienna: Springer, 2011.
Schofield, Katherine Butler. "Music under Mughal Patronage: The Place of Pleasure." In *The Oxford Handbook of the Mughal World*. Oxford: Oxford University Press, forthcoming.
Schwartz, Jessica. "How the Sea Is Sounded: Remapping Indigenous Soundings in the Marshallese Diaspora." In *Remapping Sound Studies*, edited by Gavin Steingo and Jim Sykes, 77–105. Durham, NC: Duke University Press, n.d.
Schwartz, Jessica, and April L. Brown. "Challenging Voices: Relistening to Marshallese Histories of the Present." In *The Oxford Handbook of Voice Studies*, edited by Nina Sun Eidsheim and Katherine Meizel, 191–213. New York: Oxford University Press, 2019.
Schwartz, Joel. *The New York Approach: Robert Moses, Urban Liberals, and the Redevelopment of the Inner City*. Columbus: Ohio State University Press, 1993.
Seachrist, Denise. *The Musical World of Halim El-Dabh*. Kent, OH: Kent State University Press, 2002.
Seeger, Anthony. "Who Should Control Which Rights to Music?" In *Current Issues in Music Research: Copyright, Power, and Transnational Music Processes*, edited by Susana Moreno Fernández, Salwa El-Shawan Castelo-Branco, Pedro Roxo, and Iván Iglesias, 27–49. Lisbon: Colibri, 2012.
Seyed-Gohrab, Ali Asghar. *Laylī and Majnūn: Love, Madness, and Mystic Longing in Niẓāmī's Epic Romance*. Leiden, Netherlands: Brill, 2003.
Sharf, Robert H. "The Zen of Japanese Nationalism." *History of Religions* 33, no. 1 (1993): 1–43.

Shelemay, Kay Kaufman. "When Ethnomusicology Meets History: Longitudinal Research in Ethnomusicology." Unpublished manuscript, n.d.

Sheppard, W. Anthony. "Cold War Transnationalism: Musical Encounters from Tokyo to UCLA," UCLA Distinguished Lecture Series, Los Angeles, April 6, 2017.

———. *Extreme Exoticism: Japan in the American Musical Imagination.* New York: Oxford University Press, 2019.

Shirahama, Megumi. "Commemorative Exhibition for Donated Collection Related to Jirohachi Satsuma: Baron Satsuma Has Arrived!" *Waseda OnLine* (blog). https:// yab.yomiuri.co.jp/adv/wol/dy/culture/120523.html. Accessed March 25, 2020.

Shreffler, Anne C. "The Myth of Empirical Historiography: A Response to Joseph N. Straus." *Musical Quarterly* 84, no. 1 (2000): 30–39.

Siegert, Bernhard. "Mineral Sound or Missing Fundamental: Cultural History as Signal Analysis." *Osiris* 28 (2013): 105–18.

Simeone, Nigel. "The Science of Enchantment: Music at the 1937 Paris Exposition." *Musical Times,* Spring 2002.

Sinha, Lalita. *Unveiling the Garden of Love: Mystical Symbolism in Layla Majnun and Gita Govinda.* Bloomington, IN: World Wisdom, 2008.

Smigel, Eric. "Recital Hall of Cruelty: David Tudor, Antonin Artaud, and the 1950s Avant-Garde." *Perspectives of New Music* 45, no. 2 (2007): 171–202.

Smith, Owen F. *Fluxus: The History of an Attitude.* San Diego, CA: San Diego State University Press, 1998.

———. "Proto-Fluxus in the United States, 1959–1961: The Establishment of a Like-Minded Community of Artists." *Visible Language* 26, no. 1–2 (1992): 45–57.

Snyder, Timothy. *Bloodlands: Europe between Hitler and Stalin.* New York: Basic Books, 2012.

Soja, Edward W. *Thirdspace: Journeys to Los Angeles and Other Real-and-Imagined Places.* Cambridge, MA: Blackwell Publishers, 1996.

Sounds of New Music. Folkways Records FX 5160, 1956.

Southard, Edna Kantorovitz, and Robert Southard. "Lithuanian Nationalist and the Holocaust: Public Expressions of Memory in Museums and Sites of Memory in Vilnius, Lithuania." In *National Responses to the Holocaust: National Identity and Public Memory,* edited by Jennifer Taylor, 59–82. Newark: University of Delaware Press, 2014.

Spillers, Hortense J. "Mama's Baby, Papa's Maybe: An American Grammar Book." In *Black, White, and in Color: Essays on American Literature and Culture,* 203–29. Chicago: University of Chicago Press, 2003.

Spivak, Gayatri Chakravorty. "Three Women's Texts and a Critique of Imperialism." *Critical Inquiry* 12, no. 1 (1985): 243–61.

Steege, Benjamin. "Between Race and Culture: Hearing Japanese Music in Berlin." *History of Humanities* 2, no. 2 (2017): 361–74.

———. *Helmholtz and the Modern Listener.* Cambridge: Cambridge University Press, 2012.

———. "Varèse in Vitro: On Attention, Aurality, and the Laboratory." *Current Musicology* 76 (2003).

Steinskog, Erik. *Afrofuturism and Black Sound Studies: Culture, Technology, and Things to Come.* London: Palgrave Macmillan, 2017.

Stiles, Kristine. "Anomaly, Sky, Sex, and Psi in Fluxus." In *Critical Mass: Happenings,*

Fluxus, Performance, Intermedia and Rutgers University, 1958–1972, edited by Geoffrey Hendricks, 60–88. New Brunswick, NJ: Rutgers University Press, 2003.

———. "Being Undyed: The Meeting of Mind and Matter in Yoko Ono's Events." In *YES Yoko Ono*, edited by Alexandra Munroe, 144–49. New York: Harry N. Abrams, 2000.

———. "Between Water and Stone: Fluxus Performance; A Metaphysics of Acts." In *In the Spirit of Fluxus*, edited by Elizabeth Armstrong and Joan Rothfuss, 62–99. Minneapolis: Walker Art Center, 1993.

Stoever, Jennifer Lynn. *The Sonic Color Line: Race and the Cultural Politics of Listening.* New York: New York University Press, 2016.

Stoler, Ann Laura. *Along the Archival Grain: Epistemic Anxieties and Colonial Common Sense*. Princeton, NJ: Princeton University Press, 2010.

———. *Duress: Imperial Durabilities in Our Times*. Durham, NC: Duke University Press, 2016.

———. "Imperial Formations and the Opacities of Rule." In *Lessons of Empire: Imperial Histories and American Power*, edited by Craig Calhoun, Frederick Cooper, and Kevin W. Moore, 48–62. New York: New Press, 2006.

Strachan, Jeremy. "'Listening Out' to Experimental Musics in Canada: Publics, Subjects, Places." *Intersections* 36, no. 2 (2016): 67–76.

Taruskin, Richard. *On Russian Music*. Berkeley: University of California Press, 2009.

Theweleit, Klaus. *Male Fantasies*. Translated by Stephen Conway. Vol. 1, *Women Floods Bodies History*. Minneapolis: University of Minnesota Press, 1987.

———. *Male Fantasies*. Translated by Erica Carter and Chris Turner. Vol. 2, *Male Bodies: Psychoanalyzing the White Terror*. Minneapolis: University of Minnesota Press, 1989.

Thurman, Kira. "Singing the Civilizing Mission in the Land of Bach, Beethoven, and Brahms: The Fisk Jubilee Singers in Ninteenth-Century Germany." *Journal of World History* 27, no. 3 (2016): 443–71.

Tiampo, Ming. *Gutai: Decentering Modernism*. Chicago: University of Chicago Press, 2010.

Toyama, Michiko. "A Study of the Transient Sounds of the Shakuhachi Based on ARMA Modeling with Residual Excitation." *Journal of the Acoustical Society of America* 84, no. S1 (1988): S105–6.

Treib, Marc. *Space Calculated in Seconds: The Philips Pavilion, Le Corbusier, Edgard Varèse*. Princeton, NJ: Princeton University Press, 1996.

Trotter, David. *Literature in the First Media Age: Britain between the Wars*. Cambridge, MA: Harvard University Press, 2013.

Tsuji, Hiromi. "Erased from History: The First Japanese Composer to Win an International Prize." In *Josei sakkyokuka retsuden* (Portraits of women composers), edited by Midori Kobayashi, 301–4. Tokyo: Keibonsha, 1999.

Tuck, Robert. *Scribbling Rhymers: Poetry, Print, and Community in Nineteenth-Century Japan*. New York: Columbia University Press, 2018.

Turner, Bryan S. "We Are All Denizens Now: On the Erosion of Citizenship." *Citizenship Studies* 26, no. 6–7 (2016): 679–92.

Turner, Fred. *The Democratic Surround: Multimedia and American Liberalism from World War II to the Psychedelic Sixties*. Chicago: University of Chicago Press, 2013.

Uno, Kathleen S. "Women and Changes in the Household Division of Labor." In *Re-*

creating Japanese Women, 1600–1945, edited by Gail Lee Bernstein, 17–41. Berkeley: University of California Press, 1991.

"UNYAZI Electronic Music Symposium and Festival 2005." *Art Africa*. artafrica magazine.org/unyazi-electronic-music-symposium-and-festival-2005-2/?v= e4dd286dc7d7. Accessed May 22, 2020.

Ussachevsky, Vladimir, and Otto Luening. *Electronic Tape Music by Vladimir Ussachevsky and Otto Luening: The First Compositions*. New York: Highgate, 1977.

Uy, Michael Sy. *Ask the Experts: How Ford, Rockefeller, and the NEA Changed American Music*. New York: Oxford University Press, 2020.

Vandagriff, Rachel. "The Pre-History of the Columbia-Princeton Electronic Music Center." Paper presented at the annual meeting of the American Musicological Society, Vancouver, November 4, 2016.

Varèse, Edgard. *Écrits*. Edited by Louise Hirbour; translated by Christiane Léaud. Paris: C. Bourgois, 1983.

———. "Electronic Medium." In *Contemporary Composers on Contemporary Music*, edited by Elliott Schwarz and Barney Childs, 207–8. New York: Da Capo, 1978.

———. "Spatial Music." In *Contemporary Composers on Contemporary Music*, edited by Elliott Schwarz and Barney Childs, 204–7. New York: Da Capo, 1978.

Varèse, Edgard, and Chou Wen-chung. "The Liberation of Sound." *Perspectives of New Music* 5, no. 1 (1966): 11–19.

Vatulescu, Cristina. *Police Aesthetics: Literature, Film, and the Secret Police in Soviet Times*. Stanford, CA: Stanford University Press, 2010.

Veal, Michael. *Dub: Soundscapes and Shattered Songs in Jamaican Reggae*. Middletown, CT: Wesleyan University Press, 2007.

Victoria, Brian. *Zen at War*. Lanham, MD: Rowman and Littlefield, 2006.

Vismann, Cornelia. *Files: Law and Media Technology*. Translated by Geoffrey Winthrop-Young. Stanford, CA: Stanford University Press, 2008.

Vogel, Shane. *The Scene of Harlem Cabaret: Race, Sexuality, Performance*. Chicago: University of Chicago Press, 2009.

Vogt, Adolf Max. *Le Corbusier, the Noble Savage: Toward an Archaeology of Modernism*. Translated by Radka Donnell. Cambridge, MA: MIT Press, 2000.

Von Eschen, Penny M. *Satchmo Blows Up the World: Jazz Ambassadors Play the Cold War*. Cambridge, MA: Harvard University Press, 2004.

Voren, Robert van. *Undigested Past: The Holocaust in Lithuania*. Amsterdam: Editions Rodopi, 2011.

Vovin, Alexander, trans. *Man'yōshū, Book 15: A New English Translation Containing the Original Text, Kana Transliteration, Romanization, Glossing and Commentary*. Folkestone, UK: Global Oriental, 2009.

Wade, Bonnie C. *Composing Japanese Musical Modernity*. Chicago: University of Chicago Press, 2014.

Walden, Daniel K. S. "Emancipate the Quartertone: The Call to Revolution in Nineteenth-Century Music Theory." *History of Humanities* 2, no. 2 (2017): 327–44.

———. "Recovering the Instruments of a Musical Esperanto." www.danielwaldenpiano .com/new-page-1. Accessed August 23, 2019.

Walker, Alice. "Coming Apart." In *Take Back the Night: Women on Pornography*, edited by Lederer Laura, 95–104. New York: William Morrow, 1980.

Warner, Michael. *Publics and Counterpublics*. New York: Zone Books, 2005.

Warshawsky, Abel G. *Memories of an American Impressionist*. Kent, OH: Kent State University Press, 1980.

Washington, Salim. "All the Things You Could Be by Now: Charles Mingus Presents Charles Mingus and the Limits of Avant-Garde Jazz." In *Uptown Conversation: The New Jazz Studies*, edited by Robert G. O'Meally, Brent Hayes Edwards, and Farah Jasmine Griffin, 27–49. New York: Columbia University Press, 2004.

Weheliye, Alexander G. "'Feenin': Posthuman Voices in Contemporary Black Popular Music." *Social Text 20*, no. 2 (71) (2002): 21–47.

———. *Habeas Viscus: Racializing Assemblages, Biopolitics, and Black Feminist Theories of the Human*. Durham, NC: Duke University Press, 2014.

———. *Phonographies: Grooves in Sonic Afro-Modernity*. Durham, NC: Duke University Press, 2005.

Wheatley, Steven C. Introduction to *The Story of the Rockefeller Foundation*, by Raymond B. Fosdick, vii–xviii. London: Routledge, 1989.

Williams, Emmett, and Ann Noël, eds. *Mr. Fluxus: A Collective Portrait of George Maciunas, 1931–1978*. New York: Thames & Hudson, 1997.

Williams, Raymond. *Keywords: A Vocabulary of Culture and Society*. New York: Oxford University Press, 1985.

———. *The Long Revolution*. 1961. Reprint, Peterborough, ON: Broadview Press, 2001.

———. *Marxism and Literature*. Oxford: Oxford University Press, 1977.

Wisenthal, Jonathan, Sherrill Grace, Melinda Boyd, Brian McIlroy, and Vera Micznik, eds. *A Vision of the Orient: Texts, Intertexts, and Contexts of Madame Butterfly*. Toronto: University of Toronto Press, 2006.

Wittje, Roland. *The Age of Electroacoustics: Transforming Science and Sound*. Cambridge, MA: MIT Press, 2016.

Wolfe, Audra J. *Freedom's Laboratory: The Cold War Struggle for the Soul of Science*. Baltimore: Johns Hopkins University Press, 2018.

Wolpe, Stefan. "'Any Bunch of Notes': A Lecture (1953)." Edited by Austin Clarkson. *Perspectives of New Music 21*, no. 1–2 (1983–82): 295–311.

Woods, Lawrence T. "Rockefeller Philanthropy and the Institute of Pacific Relations: A Reappraisal of Long-Term Mutual Dependency." *Voluntas: International Journal of Voluntary and Nonprofit Organizations 10*, no. 2 (1999): 151–66.

Wyman, Mark. *DP: Europe's Displaced Persons, 1945–1951*. Philadelphia: Balch Institute Press, 1989.

Yates, Peter. "Fifteen Composers in the American Experimental Tradition." *Bulletin of the New York Public Library 63* (1959): 502–14.

Yoda, Tomiko. *Gender and National Literature: Heian Texts and the Constructions of Japanese Modernity*. Durham, NC: Duke University Press, 2004.

Yoshihara, Mari. "Flight of the Japanese Butterfly: Orientalism, Nationalism, and Performances of Japanese Womanhood." *American Quarterly 56*, no. 4 (2004): 975–1001.

Yoshimoto, Midori. "Fluxus Nexus: Fluxus in New York and Japan." *Post: Notes on Modern & Contemporary Art Around the Globe*. http://post.at.moma.org/content_items/199-fluxus-nexus-fluxus-in-new-york-and-japan. Accessed May 22, 2017.

———. *Into Performance: Japanese Women Artists in New York*. New Brunswick, NJ: Rutgers University Press, 2005.

Yoshimoto, Midori, Alison Knowles, Carolee Schneemann, Sara Seagull, and Barbara

Moore. "An Evening with Fluxus Women: A Roundtable Discussion." *Women & Performance: A Journal of Feminist Theory* 19, no. 3 (2009): 369–89.

Young, Robert. *Colonial Desire: Hybridity in Theory, Culture and Race.* 1st ed. London: Routledge, 1994.

———. *Postcolonialism: A Historical Introduction.* Oxford: Blackwell, 2001.

Young-Bruehl, Elizabeth. *Hannah Arendt: For Love of the World.* 2nd ed. New Haven, CT: Yale University Press, 2004.

Yri, Kirsten. "Noah Greenberg and the New York Pro Musica: Medievalism and the Cultural Front." *American Music* 24, no. 4 (2006): 421–44.

Yudkin, Jeremy. *The Lenox School of Jazz: A Vital Chapter in the History of American Music and Race Relations.* South Egremont, MA: Farshaw, 2006.

Zimmermann, Heidy. "Lost Early Works: Facts and Suppositions." In *Edgard Varèse: Composer, Sound Sculptor, Visionary,* edited by Felix Meyer and Heidy Zimmermann, 44–53. Woodbridge: Boydell and Brewer, 2006.

Zipp, Samuel. *Manhattan Projects: The Rise and Fall of Urban Renewal in Cold War New York.* New York: Oxford University Press, 2012.

Index